A Heart at Leisure from Itself

A truly remarkable person, Caroline Macdonald (1874-1931) was a Canadian who spent almost her entire working life in Japan, performing a significant role there both in the establishment of the YWCA and in prison reform. A native of Wingham, Ontario, Macdonald graduated from the University of Toronto in 1901 in mathematics and physics and later moved to Tokyo to work for the YWCA. Her subsequent career in social work made her the best-known foreign woman in Tokyo during the 1920s.

In *A Heart at Leisure from Itself*, Margaret Prang follows Caroline Macdonald's life and career, focusing primarily on her work in Japan on behalf of incarcerated criminals. Working with the prisoners and their families, she became an international interpreter of the movement for prison reform, an achievement for which she is still warmly remembered in that country. She also established a social settlement, Shinrinkan – the Home of the Friendless Stranger – and was a mentor of labour union leaders and social democratic politicians. To a degree unusual among foreigners, Macdonald identified with the lives and aspirations of her Japanese friends and their country. Her story becomes partly their story. Using a deft turn of phrase, Caroline Macdonald once described what she needed in an adult life that engaged all her abilities and energies – 'a heart at leisure from itself.' In the eyes of many individuals, she had achieved this quality by the end of her life.

Margaret Prang is professor emerita of the Department of History at the University of British Columbia. She is a former president of the Canadian Historical Association, founding co-editor of the journal *BC Studies*, and the author of a biography of N.W. Rowell.

MARGARET PRANG

A Heart
at Leisure
from Itself

Caroline Macdonald
of Japan

UBC PRESS / VANCOUVER

Printed in Canada on acid-free paper ∞

ISBN 0-7748-0522-6

Canadian Cataloguing in Publication Data

Prang, Margaret, 1921-
    A heart at leisure from itself

    Includes bibliographical references and index.
    ISBN 0-7748-0522-6

    1. Macdonald, Caroline, 1874-1931. 2 Young Women's Christian associations – Japan – Biography. 3. Missionaries – Japan – Biography. I. Title.

This book has been published with the help of a grant from the Social Science Federation of Canada, using funds provided by the Social Sciences and Humanities Research Council of Canada.

UBC Press gratefully acknowledges the ongoing support to its publishing program from the Canada Council, the Province of British Columbia Cultural Services Branch, and the Department of Communications of the Government of Canada.

This book has also been published with the help of a grant from the Japan Foundation.

UBC Press
University of British Columbia
6344 Memorial Road
Vancouver, BC V6T 1Z2
(604) 822-3259
Fax: (604) 822-6083

Contents

Illustrations

Preface

LIKE MANY BOOKS, this one began with the author's curiosity about an apparently small question: Why do we know next to nothing about a person whose contemporaries thought her so outstanding? I had seen a few passing references to Caroline Macdonald before I came across a more extended comment in the memoirs of the Canadian diplomat and public servant, the late Hugh Keenleyside. While serving as first secretary in the newly established Canadian legation in Tokyo in the late 1920s, he observed Caroline Macdonald's social work and came to know her well. Many years later he described her as one of the dozen or so 'most remarkable men and women' he had ever known, in a roster including Dag Hammarskjöld, Lester B. Pearson, Wilder Penfield, Franklin D. Roosevelt, Barbara Ward, J.S. Woodsworth, and Shigeru Yoshida.[1]

Thinking that Macdonald must be worth an article, I began to search for information and soon found a substantial collection of her letters and papers in the archives of the United Church of Canada at Victoria

University in Toronto. Here was evidence of a life that had to be written!

Perhaps it is not just curiosity, aroused by my reading of the Keenleyside memoirs, that explains my interest in Caroline Macdonald. As a girl, growing up in congregations of the United Church of Canada in the 1930s, I was well aware of the missionary movement, although by then it had passed its zenith. In common with many North Americans of their times, much of what my Methodist grandparents and parents (later of the United Church) knew about the world beyond this continent came from missionary literature and reports. Until the Second World War, missionaries were by far the largest Canadian presence in several Asian countries. I knew that hundreds of Canadian men and women, like others from a host of countries in the western world, had established churches, schools, and hospitals, from Angola to India, from Trinidad to Japan. In particular, the remarkable group of Canadians who were part of the largest missionary enterprise in China, centred in Chengdu in Sichuan, were high on my list of 'achievers.' The West China Union University, with its medical school and dental college, and the schools and churches established by the missionaries, helped to shape my vision of Asia. In common with many Canadians of similar background, I was a 'China buff' from an early age.

Later in life, through a happy circumstance, my education concerning Japan began when I was privileged to share my house for eighteen months with Tsurumi Kazuko, who was teaching at the University of British Columbia while completing his Princeton doctoral thesis, which later became the book *Social Change in Post War Japan* (1970). Through our many stimulating discussions, some of my ignorance, and all of my earlier lack of interest in Japan, was dissipated. This process continued when I visited Tokyo in 1967 and again in 1984 when Dr. Tsurumi was professor of sociology and international relations at Sophia University. Through her contribution to my general education she helped to make this book possible, but she bears no responsibility for it. Later, my education in things Japanese continued thanks to Toriumi Yuriko, who proved to be much more than a research assistant and greatly expanded my understanding of her country.

After I was well launched on writing the book, I suddenly remembered an occasion I had not recalled for many years. In 1963, on the request of a friend, I invited a group of people to my home in Vancouver to meet Emma Kaufman, then in her eighties, who was returning to Toronto after a visit to Japan. Although I had never met her, I knew that Emma Kaufman had devoted her life and wealth to the YWCA in Japan and had sponsored many young Japanese women to study in Canada and the United States. During the evening Kaufman told me that she was looking for a biographer for a missionary who had been her friend. Would I be interested? Nothing interested me less. My energies were directed toward establishing an academic career, and I was already contemplating the biography of a male political figure who fell within the range of acceptable academic subjects. Instinctively, I knew that a biography of an unknown female missionary was not a profitable pursuit and I dismissed the idea without a thought. This was not a story, to quote Carolyn G. Heilbrun, that one was 'permitted to tell,'² at least not in academe. If I heard the name of Caroline Macdonald I did not remember it. Now, it suddenly struck me that this *was* the biography I had so easily rejected more than twenty-five years earlier. I note this not to suggest that I was 'fated' or 'predestined' to be the biographer of Caroline Macdonald but simply as an arresting coincidence, perhaps an example of serendipity, that may cast a little light on how much has changed in the past three decades.

Thanks largely to the work begun by John King Fairbank and his students at Harvard in the 1960s, missionaries have become a subject of serious study not only in their roles as disseminators of the Christian gospel but as agents of 'cross culturalization,' and 'modernization.' There is now a body of scholarly work that places the activities of missionaries in a larger context than the often hagiographical literature published earlier by missionary societies. At the same time, the development of interest in women's history has made *women* missionaries legitimate subjects of intellectual investigation. We are now 'permitted to tell' their stories, although this author, now retired, is no longer concerned about that permission.

Our understanding of groups of women missionaries is well served by a handful of recent books, notably Jane Hunter's *The Gospel of Gentility: American Women Missionaries in Turn-of-the-Century China* (1984), and studies by two Canadian scholars, Ruth Compton Brouwer, *New Women for God: Canadian Presbyterian Women and India Missions, 1876-1914* (1990) and Rosemary R. Gagan, *A Sensitive Independence: Canadian Methodist Women Missionaries in Canada and the Orient, 1881-1925* (1992). Apart from some articles, there are few recent studies of individual women missionaries. Patricia R. Hill in *The World Their Household: The American Woman's Foreign Mission Movement and Cultural Transformation 1870-1920* (1985) discusses the organization and ideas of the women who supported foreign missions; the pattern among Canadian women's missionary societies was similar and they often used the same literature and educational methods.

This book attempts to portray the day-to-day life of one woman missionary, although she can scarcely be considered representative or typical, since few of her activities were within the mainstream of the missionary movement. For Caroline Macdonald, the daughter of a founding mother of the Woman's Foreign Missionary Society in the Presbyterian church in Wingham, Ontario, it did not seem extraordinary to find a career in Japan, especially in service to women.

The expansion of the Young Women's Christian Association (YWCA) to non-western countries was the springboard that launched Macdonald on a lifelong service in Japan, first among educated women, and later with communities of working women. Eventually she was best known for her work with incarcerated criminals, almost entirely male, and their families, and became an international interpreter of the movement for prison reform and of the labour movement. Although she was never in the employ of any mission board, Caroline Macdonald always identified herself as a missionary, even after she came to be highly critical of much missionary endeavour.

Macdonald's letters, mainly to her family, and other documents in her collected papers are the primary source for this account of her life. The limited information I have been able to discover about my subject's childhood and adolescence has saved me from having to speculate extensively about early influences on her development. The title of the book is a phrase Caroline Macdonald used to describe what she needed in an adult life that engaged all her abilities and energies – 'a heart at leisure from itself.'

Although information about her early years is limited, there is rich evidence of Macdonald's theological views in her mature life. She grew up in a family where religious questions were discussed seriously, and it did not seem odd to her to spend her first furlough from Japan in 1910 in the formal study of theology, although it was decidedly odd in the eyes of her fellow students in Aberdeen, who had never seen a woman within their sacred halls. In a secular age many readers find it difficult to understand the compelling force of religious faith. In a time when cultural and religious pluralism is almost universally accepted, it is especially hard to grasp the motivation of missionaries who journeyed to the far corners of the earth out of conviction that they were the bearers of the only true and universal gospel. In the face of these difficulties, religious faith is often seen only as a 'front' for psychological or sociological forces, an example of 'false consciousness.' Such simple reductionism would not do justice to the complexity of Caroline Macdonald's life. Her Christian faith, and her articulation of that faith, that is, her theology, must be treated seriously if her motivation and actions are to be understood. That is not to say that theological statements must always be taken at face value or that they are beyond probing by the social scientist, but only that this author assumes them to possess as much validity as any other assertion of belief.

Regrettably, there are large gaps in the sources available for this book, since Macdonald was away from Japan for extended periods of time, often living with her family, when her correspondence with them ceased. Unfortunately, her side of an extended correspondence with David S. Cairns of Aberdeen has not been preserved. Records that might have added to the picture of perceptions of Macdonald among her Japanese associates were lost in the great Kantō earthquake of 1923 or in the fire bombing of Tokyo during the Second World War. Some of the Japanese with whom Macdonald worked in the YWCA, the church, education, social service, government, and the labour movement have left memoirs or autobiographies. A very few of them mention her in passing, but none, with the notable exception of YWCA histories or memoirs by her closest YWCA colleagues, make any significant comment. This is in accord with a general absence of reference to foreigners in such works, a fact that apparently reflects a persistent Japanese chauvinism.

It has been remarked that there are two histories of Christianity in Japan. One is written by Japanese and pays little attention to missionaries; the other is written by missionaries or their 'fans' from an inadequate understanding of the context in which Japanese Christians were creating their church. Caroline Macdonald's intense identification with her adopted country allows the telling of her life story to open a window through which these two pictures may be expanded and integrated. Although the window may be a small one, its revelation of the interplay between one Canadian woman missionary and her Japanese friends enlarges our appreciation of the possibilities of understanding, friendship, and mutual advantage across cultural boundaries.

Caroline Macdonald was involved with feminists and feminist causes of her time and played a part in the slowly changing position of Japanese women, always with a moderation that did not necessarily reflect her own strongly held opinions. Initially, Macdonald might be described as a 'social feminist,' to use a term common in recent writing on women's history. While it is true that she shared the objectives of 'social feminists,' to embody in the social order domestic values relating to the welfare of women and children, the label is inadequate. As with many other men and women deeply influenced by the ideas of 'the Progressive era' in North America, her concerns expanded to include a broader range of social and political issues.[3]

It will be obvious that this book is not based on any coherent 'feminist theory' or methodology. To make the telling of a life story subservient to a theory is surely to obscure the particularity of the life, although the story may contribute to the creation of theory. My debt to Carolyn G. Heilbrun's provocative and eloquent *Writing a Woman's Life* (1988) will be evident. If this book enables readers to share my interest in a woman whose life I have found endlessly absorbing, I will be rewarded.

Note on Japanese Names

Japanese custom is followed in the use of Japanese names, the family name preceding the personal name, except for the names of Japanese authors of English-language works. Macrons have been omitted in well-known place names such as Tōkyō and Kyōto.

Acknowledgments

It is a pleasure to record the numerous debts I have incurred in the writing of this book. In Japan, many people were generous in searching for information: Shimada Reiko, then general secretary, and Uoki Asa, former general secretary, of the YWCA of Japan and other staff members of the national and Tokyo YWCA; Angata Shizuo, formerly of the Research Institute of the Ministry of Justice, Tokyo; Sasaki Shigenori of the Archives of Prison Reform, Tokyo; Yoshida Masao, former librarian of the Diet Library, Tokyo; Iino Masako of the faculty of Tsuda College; and Hirata Yasuko, archivist of the Tsuda Ume Papers, Tsuda College. Yagi Akiko, Miyazawa Reiko, Kawato Machiko, Kobayashi Setsuko, and Yuasa Yana were vigorous in pursuing information or sharing their memories. Isshiki Yoshiko of Keisen Girls' School, Tokyo; Ikeda Akira, formerly minister of Shinanomachi Church, Tokyo; and the late Morita Sakiko of Kamakura, were generous in granting interviews. I also wish to thank Yamamoto Kazuyo, director of the Women's Education Research Centre at Japan

Women's University, who arranged for me to meet with her and a group of colleagues in November 1984 at the very beginning of my work on this book. Despite the justifiable misgivings members of the group must have had about the wanderings of an audacious foreigner in unfamiliar territory, they welcomed me with tea and stimulating discussion of their research interests and mine.

Ohara Yuko, then with the Centre for American Studies, Tokyo University, played a crucial role through her response to my appeal for help in finding a research assistant. By introducing me to Toriumi Yuriko, she contributed to the solution of a problem in this endeavour – my ignorance of the Japanese language. Although there were few primary documents in Japanese relevant to this book, secondary sources were essential. Toriumi Yuriko found and translated documents, articles, and books in both Tokyo and Vancouver, and located individuals who were able to provide information. Her determined pursuit of answers to the myriad questions I put to her over several years rarely drew a blank, while her careful reading of the manuscript has eliminated many errors of fact and spelling. A bonus from our association is a cherished friendship. Happily, my friend's habitual patience ensured the survival of that friendship in the face of the frustration created by my slow progress.

It is agreeable to record my gratitude to Cyril Powles of Toronto. Without his early and continuing assurance that this enterprise was worthwhile, there would have been no book. Dr. Powles's roots and upbringing in Japan, his later career as a missionary and teacher, and his study and teaching of Japanese history in Canada, made him the ideal mentor. Far beyond the call of friendship or duty to a subject, he has read the entire manuscript in two versions and has made suggestions, both general and detailed, for its improvement. Of course, I alone remain responsible for the final text.

A grant from the Social Sciences and Humanities Research Council of Canada made it possible for me to begin my research. The staff of the Archives of the United Church of Canada at Victoria University, Toronto, and of the National Archives of Canada, extended their customary helpful services. So too did the librarians of the Vancouver School of Theology and of the University of British Columbia, especially Gonnami Tsuneharu of the Asian Studies Library and Dorothy Martin of the Humanities and Social Sciences Division. Members of the staff of the archives of the American YWCA in New York and of the World's YWCA in Geneva provided helpful information. I am grateful to Shirley Donaldson of Wingham, Ontario, for her persistent if often frustrated efforts to secure information about the Macdonald family.

My friends Marlis Dücker, Maria Fürstenwald, June Lythgoe, Jay Macpherson, Dianne Newell, Marjorie Powles, Alison Prentice, and Beryl Young read all or part of the manuscript and made many helpful suggestions. Thanks to my daughter, Carmen Prang, who persuaded me that advancing years need not prevent the acquisition of a modicum of computer literacy and who rescued me regularly from crises with 'the machine.' In a different kind of crisis, when I was suddenly hospitalized a few days before completing the manuscript, Carmen, Maria, Beryl, and Helen Hardern pulled everything together and delivered the manuscript to the Press. For their 'macron bee' and much more, I am deeply grateful.

Working with members of the staff of UBC Press has been a rewarding experience. Warm thanks go to the senior editor, Jean L. Wilson, a steady source of intelligent comment, advice, and good humour. Other debts are noted in the footnotes.

My greatest debt is to Maria, who lived with this book for far too long and remained encouraging always, and patient mostly.

*A Heart
at Leisure
from Itself*

Chapter 1

Pioneering Canadian Roots

*Being a pioneer myself I am more interested in getting on with new
things than bringing up the already done. I like to get ahead ...
and start a new fire burning.*

— Caroline Macdonald, 1925

PIONEERING AND MOVING ON to cultivate new fields was in
the tradition of the descendants of James and Margaret Macdonald. After
migrating from Inverness, Scotland, to Pictou County, Nova Scotia, where
they spent some fifteen years, they sought a brighter future for their family in
Canada West. In the spring of 1846 with their five children, the youngest
being ten-year-old Peter, they set out in a small sailing ship for Fall River,
Massachusetts, then by steamer to New York, up the Hudson River by barge,
and through the Erie Canal to Buffalo. A lake steamer landed them in Port
Stanley on the shores of Lake Erie where they took a stagecoach to London.
That route to the cheap, unsettled lands of Canada West had been traversed
by thousands of immigrants from the Maritime colonies, and many more
were still to follow. Northwest of London, near a crossroads designated as
Clinton in Huron County, James Macdonald took up farming on land purchased from the Canada Company, holders of the vast wilderness domain
known as 'the Huron Tract.' Young Peter Macdonald always remembered

those backbreaking days of felling trees and getting rid of stumps to prepare the land for cultivation. At the age of fifteen he went to work for a harness maker in London, then took up carpentry, and later worked on building bridges in Huron County. In London he shared in the excitement attending the arrival of the first train of the Great Western Railway on the newly completed line from Hamilton.

At a time when little formal training was required, Peter Macdonald became a teacher in a succession of rural schools for ten years, the last four as principal in the village of Exeter. By this time he had saved enough money to expand his interest in science at Trinity College in Toronto where he took a degree in chemistry, and then enrolled in medicine. At the beginning of his medical studies, he had married his second cousin, Margaret Ross of Clinton, whose family were also Pictou County Scots.[1] When the new doctor and his wife returned to Huron County, where he had decided to practise medicine in the village of Wingham, they had two children, James and Leila, and a second daughter, Margaret ('Peg'), arrived shortly. Two years later, in 1874, Annie Caroline was born, to be followed by another daughter, Nellie. The five children, born in less than a decade, were close in feeling as well as age, and gave their parents a lively time with their games and pranks. Occasionally when other means failed, their mother administered discipline with a black leather strap. In retrospect Caroline, usually known as 'Carrie,' considered herself the most 'tomboyish' of the four girls and probably quite deserving of stern treatment now and again. As the noisiest and most garrulous of the young Macdonalds, she acquired the nickname 'Old Crow' within the family circle and she continued to use it into her mature years.

Wingham was one of the many small towns in western Ontario that aspired to greatness in the years following Canadian Confederation in 1867.[2] Located near the junction of the north and south branches of the Maitland River in the midst of a gently rolling agricultural area, increasingly prosperous and famous for its production of excellent pork, Wingham's future seemed bright. With newly opened railway connections to London and Toronto, and the growing towns and villages between, its population of 700 at incorporation as a village in 1874 grew in less than five years to more than 2,000 and merited incorporation as a town. The new settlers in Wingham, like their predecessors, were almost entirely of English, Scottish, or Irish origins. The basis of Wingham's expansion was small industry and the servicing of the local farming community.

Peter Macdonald was involved in local politics from the time of his arrival in Wingham, serving as reeve, municipal councillor, chairman of the school board, and later as mayor. In provincial and federal elections he was a vigorous organizer and campaigner throughout Huron County for the Liberal party. In 1887, when Carrie was thirteen, her father was elected to the Parliament of Canada for East Huron and thus joined Her Majesty's loyal opposition in Ottawa under the leadership of Edward Blake, soon to be succeeded by Wilfrid Laurier. Around the Macdonald dinner table the conversation often concerned the politics of 'Laurier Liberalism.'

Life in Wingham, as in other growing towns of southern Ontario, was more than business, railways, and politics. In succession Baptists, Wesleyan Methodists, Presbyterians, Congregationalists, and Anglicans had established churches that grew with the town, and by the 1890s the Salvation Army and the Plymouth Brethren were on the scene. There was also the Roman Catholic Church of the Sacred Heart, whose parishioners were mainly Irish, but Wingham was overwhelmingly Protestant in its ethos and, within that, strongly evangelical in emphasis.[3] Nearly everyone had at least a nominal church affiliation, but for most families religion was more than a perfunctory commitment and regular church attendance was common. Rare was the child who did not attend Sunday school, and much of the social life of the community, especially of the young, was conducted in the Christmas concerts, picnics, and other entertainments of the Sunday schools and young peoples' societies of the various denominations.

In Wingham the Presbyterians were the most numerous, followed closely by the Methodists. Peter and Margaret Macdonald were active in the Presbyterian congregation from the beginning, especially in the Sunday school where their children were naturally faithful scholars. Peter Macdonald had an extensive knowledge of the Bible, was often the leader of the quarterly meetings for Sunday school teachers of the area to review and prepare the lessons for the coming weeks, and led a large and enthusiastic adult Bible class in his own congregation. Margaret Macdonald, whose biblical knowledge was also impressive, was a Sunday school teacher for many years, and her daughters followed in her steps as they became old enough.

Until Carrie was eighteen, the minister of the Wingham Presbyterian church was the Reverend Hector McQuarrie, who shared the Pictou County origins of many members of his congregation. In common with most Free Church of Scotland ministers in Ontario, he had studied theology at Knox College in Toronto. McQuarrie was called to the Wingham church in 1876, a year after Canadian Presbyterians had united to form the Presbyterian Church in Canada. By far the largest and most dynamic element among the uniting churches, Free Church influences came to dominate central Canadian Presbyterianism, ensuring that the liberal evangelicalism of contemporary Free Church scholars in Scotland would shape the Canadian church. This blend of idealist philosophy, historical criticism of the Bible, and a revivalism oriented toward urban industrial populations provided many Protestants with an intellectually and emotionally satisfying basis for Christian faith. A respected pastor and a good preacher, McQuarrie's views on the Bible's authority reflected the new 'higher criticism,' which he explained in a clear and scholarly manner to illustrate that the Bible was not a textbook on either science or mundane history. Science had its own domain, although the Bible *was* history, but history of a unique kind, for the biblical story was the revelation of God's intentions for humanity. In the best Presbyterian tradition, Hector McQuarrie spoke often of the sovereignty of God, but he was not a believer in predestination and thus spoke just as often of free will. A liberal evangelicalism rooted in the Free Church Presbyterianism of western Ontario remained the bedrock of Caroline Macdonald's religious faith throughout her life. This faith was fundamentally individualistic, being grounded in a sense of personal sin and the need for Christ's saving grace, but it provided the basis for commitment to social transformation and the creation of Christian societies both at home and abroad.[4]

Carrie never had to reject a literalist approach to the Bible nor did she have to be persuaded that theological discussion was a fit occupation for a good mind. Peter Macdonald had a lively interest in current theological thought, especially in the debate over the relationship between science and religion. As in households throughout the Anglo-Saxon Protestant world, the works of the Scottish preacher and writer Henry Drummond were read and discussed in the Macdonald home. In his effort to reconcile Darwin's evolutionary theory, idealist philosophy, and experiential Christianity, Drummond was the preeminent popularizer of the new liberal theology. In *Natural Law in the Spiritual World* (1883), he argued that both natural and spiritual law reveal the governance of a loving God. Drummond's later work, *The Ascent of Man* (1894), gave a new twist to the evolutionary doctrine of the survival of the fittest by asserting that the law of altruism or love, the expression of the struggle for the survival of others, was the highest manifestation of evolution.[5] Peter Macdonald was at ease in this universe of discourse, and so was Carrie as she advanced in years and understanding.

Like other Canadian Protestants, Wingham Presbyterians were caught up in the great missionary movement of the last quarter of the nineteenth century. Peter Macdonald often presided at meetings when missionaries on furlough told of the work supported by Canadian Presbyterians in the New Hebrides, Trinidad, India, and China, and in Canada from Newfoundland through the Northwest Territories to British Columbia. Margaret Macdonald was a founder in 1887 of the Woman's Foreign Missionary Society of the Wingham Presbyterian church and several times represented it at provincial gatherings in Toronto. At the same time she organized the Happy Gleaners Mission Band to encourage interest in missions and the small contributions to the 'mite boxes' through which children, including her own, learned to support the church's emissaries overseas.

Although denominational loyalties were strong, Ontario Protestantism also had a broadly interdenominational and ecumenical character. In Wingham, as elsewhere, there were exchanges of preachers and participation in important events in other congregations. Members of all denominations turned out to hear missionaries tell dramatic stories of the spreading of the Gospel from 'Greenland's icy mountains to India's coral strand,' as the words of a well-loved missionary hymn declared.

Young people of the five Protestant churches in Wingham belonged to the Christian Endeavour Society and together planned major social activities. Protestant women joined together in the Women's Christian Temperance Union to fight for the prohibition of alcoholic beverages as well as for other social reforms. Members of the same congregations promoted the objectives of the Upper Canada Bible Society or the Gospel Temperance Society. In a practical example of interdenominational cooperation, clergy and members of all denominations joined together in the 1890s to found the Wingham Children's Aid Society. On the strength of his reputation as an eloquent, humorous, and effective speaker, Dr. Peter Macdonald was invited to address all these organizations at regular intervals. Both religious conviction and political prudence informed his willingness to accept as many such invitations as possible.

Apart from the churches and interdenominational associations, Wingham boasted an agricultural society, a Chamber of Commerce, a Mechanics Institute with a lecture hall and a small library, plus several fraternal lodges including the Masons, the Independent Order of Foresters, the Loyal Orange Lodge, and its women's auxiliary, the Lady True Blues. As an astute politician Peter Macdonald spoke to Orange Lodge meetings occasionally, but as a good Liberal he neither belonged to the lodge, which was generally allied with the Conservatives, nor did he appear on the platform at celebrations of the Battle of the Boyne on 'the Glorious Twelfth' of July.

Despite his aloofness from the Orange Lodge, Peter Macdonald held to Protestant principles that sometimes modified his loyalty to the Liberal party. The young Macdonalds were always aware that on occasion his Protestantism took precedence over party politics. Thus their father was one of five Liberals and eight Conservatives ('the Black Thirteen') who voted for the disallowance of the Jesuits' Estates Act, which they believed recognized the power of the Pope to intervene in the affairs of the Canadian state.

In the election of 1891, Macdonald was re-elected with a comfortable majority, although he carried the town of Wingham by a slim margin and thus owed his victory mainly to the farming community, which supported the Liberal platform of unrestricted reciprocity in trade with the United States. However, the Conservatives again won a majority in the country, and Peter Macdonald remained on the opposition benches in the House of Commons.

Growing up in a family that was actively involved in the social and religious activities of a prospering town, and with a father who enjoyed theological and political discussion and was immersed in the major issues of Canadian national life, gave Carrie Macdonald an informal education of some breadth. Her formal education began in the local public school. Then, since there was no high school in Wingham, she attended the Stratford Collegiate Institute for a year and boarded with her uncle, John Macdonald, owner of a small manufacturing firm, and his family. The marriage of her oldest sister, Leila, to Dr. E.H. Horsey the following summer had an immediate effect on Carrie's education. Dr. Horsey had just opened a medical practice in Owen Sound, and it was agreed that Carrie would live with her sister and brother-in-law and continue her high school work at the Owen Sound Collegiate. Neither Stratford nor Owen Sound was more than one hundred kilometres from home and both were socially very similar to Wingham, although somewhat larger. During Carrie's three years in Owen Sound, the principal of the collegiate institute was F.W. Merchant, who was also her science teacher. Merchant was making a name for himself as one of the province's ablest teachers and administrators, and in his classes Carrie's interest in science, always encouraged by her father, received further stimulation.

Carrie lost her boarding place in Owen Sound when her brother-in-law, Dr. Horsey, became a medical officer for the Sun Life Assurance Company and with Leila embarked on a round-the-world trip to inspect the company's overseas branches. Sun Life, one of the first Canadian financial institutions to develop a substantial business overseas, settled the couple in Yokohama for a time, where Horsey gave up medicine to become manager of the insurance company's branch in the Japanese port. In less than a year, Leila came home with malaria and waited for her husband while he conducted business in Java. The overseas adventures of the Horseys gave the whole Macdonald family new opportunities to learn about the pleasures and challenges of foreign travel and added to the missionary perspective that largely shaped their views on Asia.

After practising medicine for twenty years, Dr. Macdonald had acquired enough capital to branch out into real estate. He moved his substantial white frame residence from the main thoroughfare, Josephine Street, to a lot on the next street, and on the former site erected 'the Macdonald Block,' the 'handsomest commercial establishment in town' according to the local newspaper. Soon the property was bringing in a substantial revenue. Now, instead of occasional domestic help, the Macdonald household employed a full-time servant girl and a boy to attend to the horse and do general chores in the house and office. In the autumn of 1893, Peter and Margaret Macdonald took a trip to Chicago, as did many citizens of Wingham, to see the World's Fair, and in the following summer they travelled by Great Lakes steamer from Owen Sound to Fort William and back. Carrie's only brother, Jim, had recently graduated from medical school and was assisting with his father's practice and looking after it entirely when Parliament was in session. The family was more affluent than it had ever been, as Carrie, now nineteen years of age, completed her junior matriculation from high school.

Carrie's hopes for her future are unknown. Choices were expanding for the growing number of girls who completed high school at the end of the nineteenth century, but they were still limited. A very few young women went on to take senior matriculation at a collegiate institute and then entered a university. A commonly chosen option was to stay at home until an eligible bachelor proposed marriage. Another was to become an elementary school teacher, which at most required only brief training, while awaiting the appearance of the acceptable suitor. There was a growing demand for nurses and, in the business world, for clerical workers and telephone operators, although daughters of professionals were unlikely to seek employment in the relatively unprestigious world of commerce. Some intelligent and educated women, feeling that social convention, often strongly reinforced by their parents, denied them meaningful work, retreated into a 'nervous breakdown' or some more specifically designated form of ill health.

There is no evidence that Carrie was ill, or that her parents stood in the way of her pursuit of any objective dear to her heart, and it is unlikely that there were monetary barriers to the continuation of her formal education. For whatever reasons, her education was rather spasmodic, a pattern not uncommon at the time. She spent most of the winter of 1893-4 at home, perhaps helping the family settle into the relocated and renovated house, but during two months of the upheaval she and Peg were visiting their Stratford relatives. In the autumn of 1894, Carrie enrolled in the county's Model School in Clinton, a few miles from Wingham, returning home by train on the weekends. The emphasis in the three-month course was on the mastery of pedagogical principles and on practice teaching in the school. The third-class teacher's certificate awarded on successful completion was good anywhere in Ontario.[6] Possibly Carrie taught school in the spring term of 1895, but this is unclear.

In the autumn of 1895, when she was nearly twenty-one, Carrie resumed her education by enrolling for her senior matriculation at the London Collegiate Institute and once again lived with an uncle, James Macdonald, and his wife in their comfortable home on Dufferin Avenue. The London Collegiate in western Ontario's largest city boasted the highest academic standing of any in the province. F.W. Merchant had moved from Owen Sound and now presided as principal over a staff of twenty men and two women in the London school, and himself taught the senior matriculation class in physics.

Carrie's year at the London Collegiate ended in time for her to be home to celebrate her father's re-election to Parliament for a third term. At last the Liberal party was victorious and formed a new government under Prime Minister Wilfrid Laurier. From the government benches Peter Macdonald enhanced his reputation as an eloquent exponent of the traditions of the Liberal party and of Laurier's handling of current issues, and once again showed his independence by abandoning party allegiance to support an unsuccessful bill to give women the vote in federal elections, which was introduced in Parliament by Nicholas Flood Davin, the fiery Conservative member for Assiniboia in the Northwest Territories.

Carrie returned to the London Collegiate for another year to prepare for the writing of the honour senior matriculation examinations. At the same time, in the spring of 1897, she wrote the University of Toronto entrance examinations, emerging with first-class honours in English, mathematics, and physics, second-class honours in chemistry, history, and geography, and an Edward Blake Scholarship to the university.[7]

Like most Presbyterian students who studied in the faculty of arts at the University of Toronto, Carrie enrolled in the nondenominational University College. Thirteen years after they were first admitted, women were still a small minority. Unlike many women students of the time who abandoned their interest in science when they reached the university in favour of the more 'feminine' modern languages or English literature,[8] Carrie chose a major in mathematics and physics with a minor in English and some excursions into other subjects. Economics was not one of them, but in her second year, much to the astonishment of her friends, she entered an annual essay contest conducted by the department of political economy. She hesitated when the topic was announced as 'Banking,' of which she knew nothing, but her vigorous research and clear writing produced the prize-winning essay. It had never occurred to the other contestants, all men, that a woman could successfully invade a domain they assumed was their own.[9]

At the university Carrie soon became active in the student work of the Young Women's Christian Association (YWCA), an organization that was a definitive influence in her life. There had been branches of the YWCA in Canada ever since 1870, but there was no national organization until 1893. As an interdenominational movement, the Student YWCA was a unifying force on the campus, claiming the interest of a majority of female students in many universities.[10] The Student YWCA in University College, organized in 1887, was the first in any Canadian university and was now an active group to which Carrie readily gravitated. In her third year she was president of the University of Toronto YWCA and later was one of the student representatives on the executive committee of the national YWCA.

In Toronto, increasingly the centre of Canadian Presbyterianism, Carrie enjoyed a fresh but not entirely unfamiliar exposure to the lively theological debates going on in her own church on subjects that were also popular in

YWCA discussions. Presbyterian scholars and preachers in Toronto's lecture halls and pulpits conducted their discourse in a liberal spirit, but they were not inclined to abandon traditional evangelical Christian beliefs. Through their understanding of the doctrines of 'The Person of Christ' and 'The Kingdom of God,' they were endeavouring to construct an intellectually satisfying theology that united revelation, personal religious experience, and acceptance of secular knowledge. That theology, they believed, compelled them to assume a prophetic role that called on Christians to create harmonious and moral communities. One such leader was Carrie's distant relative, the Reverend J.A. Macdonald, who had recently amalgamated several Presbyterian publications into two periodicals, the *Presbyterian* and the *Westminster*, through which he hoped to enhance the Christian conscience of the nation.[11] Carrie was at home in the academic and religious world in Toronto and found it all enormously stimulating.

When Caroline Macdonald graduated with honours in the spring of 1901, the second woman in the history of the university to specialize in mathematics and physics, one of her professors, Dr. J.C. McLennan of the department of physics, warned her she might be making a terrible mistake in declining the fellowship offered her for graduate study in physics. Whether Carrie declined the fellowship because she realized how difficult it would be for a woman to have a career in science is unclear.[12] It seems more likely that both her head and her heart were already set in a different direction.

The YWCA actively promoted the higher education of women and attached great importance to its student work, although that was numerically a small part of the organization's total endeavour. Its leaders believed that the entry of educated Christian women into the professions and into the life of church and state in growing numbers would save many women from the uselessness of conventional middle-class domesticity and would contribute profoundly to the regeneration of society. Thus the YWCA consistently held before its college members the call to seek careers of 'service' both at home and on the mission field.[13]

The YWCA itself offered increasing opportunities for service. In the United States where the YWCA had grown earlier and more rapidly, 'YWCA secretary' had become a new occupation for college-educated women.[14] So far there were few such positions in Canada, but some associations were looking for full-time secretaries to promote their work.

Immediately after her graduation, Carrie, now preferring to be known as Caroline, worked for three months with the London YWCA, where her main task was to organize activities among female factory workers. During that summer she came under the eye of Sara Libby Carson, a Wellesley College graduate with experience in the American YWCA who was serving as national 'city secretary' with the Canadian association and had responsibility for recruiting YWCA staff. The Ottawa 'Y' was among the associations looking for a secretary and Carson was sure she knew the ideal candidate: Caroline Macdonald was 'one of, if not *the* brightest young women in her graduating class,' and certainly the brightest she had met in the YWCA. Carson was delighted to recommend for the job in Canada's capital a young woman who was 'so rounded': she wrote and spoke well, was 'splendid socially, and best of all knows how to put other people at work,' while displaying 'originality and adaptability' in her approach to people and problems. Further, this 'leader amongst young women' was an 'honest, consecrated Christian ... who knows God and His word'; moreover, 'through her father who is a member of parliament she knows ... a number of people in Ottawa and will be able to get hold of the young women of leisure as well as the young women of business,' Carson reported with satisfaction.[15] Indeed, Peter Macdonald was no longer simply a member of Parliament: a few months earlier he had been appointed deputy speaker of the House of Commons.

As she contemplated her future, Caroline had reason to feel confident about her academic achievements and her background in the church and the YWCA. Yet there was one area in which she lacked self-confidence: she was not always comfortable with her physical appearance, although this was a relatively minor anxiety that never seriously inhibited her. Five feet, four inches in height and 'well rounded,' she considered herself 'dumpy,' and a head of thin hair was a lifelong trial. Her friends and colleagues paid little attention to these aspects of her person. They were far more aware of the lively, intense blue eyes, fixed on each individual Caroline encountered as if that person were the only one in the world for the time being. Her capacity for attention to others gave Caroline a presence that outshone everything else about her.

At the beginning of September 1901, Caroline Macdonald took up her duties as the first university-educated general secretary of the Ottawa YWCA at a salary of $25 a month, plus room and board and laundry at the YWCA.

She was to have one afternoon and one evening a week free at a time of her choice and a month's vacation during the summer.[16] The 'Y's work in Ottawa was typical of its program in other Canadian cities. Housed in one of the first buildings constructed specifically for a YWCA, and in appearance similar to the substantial private residences nearby, the red brick structure on the corner of Metcalfe and Laurier streets provided accommodation for twenty-seven permanent boarders and a number of transients, and a variety of religious, educational, and recreational activities for young single females, especially those away from home.[17] Caroline's employer and the ultimate authority in planning the association's work was a volunteer board of directors composed of women affiliated with the Protestant churches, especially Presbyterian and Methodist.

When Macdonald accepted the position in Ottawa, the YWCA board had just elected a new president, Mary Ann Blackburn, widow of Robert Blackburn, a wealthy Ottawa merchant and entrepreneur, and onetime Liberal member of Parliament. Mrs. Blackburn, as Caroline always called her, was a staunch Presbyterian, and although women could not vote she was keenly interested in Liberal politics. The attractive and substantial Blackburn home on Sussex Drive, with its board-and-batten construction and gingerbread trim, was soon very familiar to Caroline, and Mrs. Blackburn became a good friend. Almost immediately on Caroline's arrival Mrs. Blackburn agreed to provide special funds for office assistance so that the new general secretary could spend less time on the administration of the association's business and more on working directly with young women.[18]

As the board defined her responsibilities, Caroline was to emphasize evangelistic work by assisting with the Sunday afternoon Bible class, which had more than one hundred members, and leading 'the gospel meeting' on Sunday evenings. During the week she was to give much of her time to developing a program for working girls.[19] This combination of personal evangelism and social service was typical of the YWCA. It was also in tune with the growing emphasis in the Presbyterian church on a 'social Christianity' that began with the individual and would lead, 'Presbyterian progressives' believed, to reform of the social environment and the creation of a Christian civilization in Canada.[20] Caroline had heard many sermons on social Christianity. Now she had an opportunity to turn preaching into practice.

Caroline wasted no time in tackling her new responsibilities. She persuaded the members of the board that more spiritual awareness was needed, and thus they met together to pray for an hour every Tuesday morning. At the same time she was gathering statistics about working women and was soon able to announce that there were more than 5,200 women in employment in Ottawa. They included workers in the city's small textile mills, telephone operators, office workers, and domestics. Caroline saw this as a tremendous opportunity for the 'Y' because 'women can reach women,' as the church itself could not.[21]

Caroline proposed that a girls' club should be organized to meet in the central part of the city daily from twelve to two o'clock. Working women could bring their lunches and the club would provide soup, tea, and coffee for a small sum. By early January 1902, 'the noon rest' program was operating in a room on Bank Street and was meeting with a good response. For many of the young women this was their first contact with the YWCA and, as was hoped, some later became participants in evening activities that included gymnastics, singing, Bible study, and classes in English, French, sewing, cooking, shorthand, and hygiene.[22]

Before Caroline's arrival in Ottawa the 'Y,' as in other centres, was attempting to solve 'the domestic problem' through its employment bureau. Despite the steady influx of young women from rural areas as well as immigrant women, mainly from Britain, there was a chronic shortage of domestic help in the prosperous middle-class homes of Canada's growing urban centres. The turnover among domestic servants, who were often poorly treated by their employers, was high. Many women left domestic jobs to work in factories where they had regular hours and more independence. In 1901 the Ottawa 'Y's employment bureau received 668 applications for domestic help but registered only 394 women seeking employment. Caroline had some clues about the origins of 'this most vexed question,' some of them acquired through leading the meetings of the 'Mutual Improvement Club,' attended weekly at the YWCA by about fifteen girls who were working as domestic servants. Remedies were not so clear, but she was sure they must be based on 'a new appreciation of the dignity of all work' and on a recognition of 'interdependence.' In her first annual report to the board of the YWCA, Caroline argued that the YWCA was in a unique position to study the problem from 'its two sides, for there are two sides.' In her view only the employers could improve the situation. 'The economics of the household,' she contended, 'will have to include ... settled hours for housework' and that might require 'a simpler style of living' in many homes. It was high time 'the mistress and the maid should come together on a common meeting ground and quietly and sanely discuss the matter ... to reach the needed compromise.' Her presentation of the issue left no doubt that most of the compromising would have to come from women employers rather than from their servants.[23]

Apparently neither Caroline nor the Ottawa YWCA as a whole made any progress toward a solution to 'this most vexed problem' of domestic service. In any case, she did not work on it for long, or on any of the other problems facing the Ottawa 'Y,' mainly arising from a slow increase in membership and financial support.[24] Caroline may have concluded that she could contribute little to the solution of these problems in the foreseeable future. It was not in her nature to linger in a situation that held small promise of concrete results.

Early in the autumn of 1902, the Student Volunteer Movement for Foreign Missions (SVM) asked Caroline to work for three months on its behalf in Canadian colleges and universities. She decided 'after prayerful consideration ... that she could not refuse this work.' The board of the Ottawa 'Y' was reluctant to accept her resignation and only after much discussion agreed that it should not try to keep her from undertaking 'a larger work for God.' Registering its dismay and annoyance at losing Macdonald after less than sixteen months of service, the board requested the national office of the 'Y' to recommend as her successor someone who had clearly 'taken up the Young Women's Christian secretaryship as a profession.'[25]

Caroline's acceptance of the assignment with the SVM was a natural development from her undergraduate involvement with the movement. The primary recruiting agency of the Protestant missionary movement, the SVM, with which both the YWCA and the YMCA were affiliated, was active on most Canadian campuses, and foreign missions were a major undergraduate interest.[26] After graduation, Caroline had served on the executive committee of the SVM for North America and had helped to plan the 'quadrennial' meeting at the University of Toronto at the end of February 1902. Held every four years to confront each generation of students with the call to missionary service, this was the fourth such gathering and the first to meet in Canada, bringing some 3,000 delegates to the city from nearly 500 North American colleges and universities.

Caroline was profoundly moved by the whole event, especially by the opening and closing addresses of Robert E. Speer, the American Presbyterian missionary statesman who, while a student at Princeton twenty years earlier, had been one of the founders of the SVM. Much in evidence as well was John R. Mott, popularizer of the missionary movement's provocative and controversial slogan: 'The evangelization of the world in this generation.' The slogan was proclaimed during the quadrennial on a large banner that hung above the platform in Convocation Hall. Mott had recently visited China in the aftermath of the Boxer rebellion, and some delegates to the convention, by volunteering for service in China, took up his challenge to 'fill up the gap' left by the missionaries killed in that revolt against imperialism and Christianity.[27] In the days following the quadrennial, 'the grandeur and the glory of that convention' grew upon Caroline. As she told the registrar of the university, James Brebner, a fellow Presbyterian and family friend, she thought often about 'what it is going to mean for the dear old alma mater.'[28] The call to evangelize the world, she believed, represented a 'comprehensive idea of love and sympathy' that demanded a response from 'educated men and women who have sufficiently caught the world-wide concept of the Master's kingdom to be willing to be used in God's plan for the redemption of the world.'[29]

Now, a year after the Toronto quadrennial, it was Caroline's task to follow up the impact of that gathering in visits to universities and normal schools in central Canada and the Maritimes, and then in Manitoba, where like every other visitor she became enthusiastic about the future of the booming city of Winnipeg and its hinterland, the vast Northwest Territories, where the process of creating the new provinces of Alberta and Saskatchewan was beginning. Her long train journeys showed her more of her own country, most of it under a blanket of snow, than she had ever seen before. At the same time, her presentations to Canadian students of the call to missionary service in lands far from home reinforced the power of that call in her own heart and mind.

The SVM assignment completed, Caroline accepted an appointment as the 'city secretary' of the national YWCA, succeeding Sara Libby Carson who had first recruited her to the YWCA staff. Carson's earlier experience as founder of a settlement house in New York inspired her to take the lead in establishing Evangelia House to serve women factory workers and children in Toronto's east end, a development Caroline applauded without any inkling that she would one day follow a similar path. The city's first settlement house, which reflected the rapid growth of this form of social work in the United States, drew on women university graduates as well as current members of the Student YWCA for resident staff and volunteers.[30]

In her new position Caroline continued to visit urban centres to assist local associations in the expansion of their work. It was agreed that she would give a good part of her time to the Ottawa association, since her successor there was unable to assume her duties until some months later. Thus Caroline was in Ottawa in the spring of 1903 for the visit of Annie M. Reynolds, the first general secretary of the World's Committee of the YWCA in London, England.[31] One of the first students to attend Wellesley College for Women, Reynolds was a formidable personality. She had studied several European languages and had experience as a 'Y' secretary in the United States before 1894, when she put her considerable administrative skills at the service of the World's Committee to bring the several national associations into an international organization.[32]

At a 'drawing room meeting' at the home of Elizabeth Sifton, wife of Clifford Sifton, minister of the interior in the Laurier government, a large group of Ottawa YWCA activists and prospective supporters was assembled to hear Reynolds's message on the international dimension of the YWCA and its mission to the women of the non-western world, notably in China, India, and Japan, where she had recently made extended visits and had been deeply impressed by the opportunities for work among young women.[33] Subsequently, the World's Committee adopted a policy of direct sponsorship of the development of the association in foreign mission fields and of encouragement to national associations to recruit and support secretaries there, rather than working through church mission boards that did not always share the 'Y's priorities for women.[34]

Overseas work was not entirely new in the Canadian YWCA. As early as 1899, the association had sent Englishwoman Ruth Rouse, a lively and effective Oxford graduate with extensive experience in both the British and American YWCAs, to India for a year. Later, it had helped the American YWCA support a doctor in Korea and the British association to pay a student worker in India. The Canadian association was thus open to an appeal from Annie Reynolds and the World's Committee to send a secretary who would help an interdenominational group of women missionaries establish a YWCA in Japan. Further, the Foreign Committee of the Canadian 'Y' agreed with Reynolds that the right person for the job was Caroline Macdonald, and it pledged to pay her salary and meet certain other expenses in Tokyo.[35]

While approval from committees in London, Tokyo, and Toronto was being secured, Caroline had time to think about her decision before the proposal to go to Japan was formally made to her and especially to consult her family. Although reluctant to see her off to a distant land, her parents and Peg, the sister to whom she was closest, understood the strength of the call to evangelize the world and were proud of Caroline's willingness to answer it. Since she had grown up in a family, a church, and a student milieu where interest in foreign missions was strong, and had herself been presenting the claims of the mission field to Canadian students, Caroline appears to have accepted the invitation to go to Japan with some ease; at least there is no record of conflict or hesitation surrounding her decision. In the autumn of 1903, the national convention of the YWCA of Canada gave its formal blessing to the enterprise. For the next year Caroline continued her work as city secretary, taking two months off to attend a course for staff members given by the American YWCA in Chicago, and preparing herself for her encounter with the Empire of the Mikado.

Chapter 2

Christ and the Empire of the Mikado

WHEN CAROLINE MACDONALD went to Japan on behalf of the YWCA, the Protestant missionary movement there was just four decades old. But Christianity had a much longer history in the island kingdom, going back to the mid-sixteenth century when Francis Xavier began a Jesuit mission on the southern island of Kyushu, centred in Nagasaki, from which the work spread to other regions of Japan. Toward the end of the century, Franciscan friars and smaller corps of Augustinians and Dominicans joined the missionary endeavour. As many as 500,000 Japanese were converted to Christianity.

Owing partly to rivalry between the Jesuits and the Franciscans and between their respective supporters among Portuguese and Spanish traders, but primarily to the conviction of leading clan chieftains that the foreign religion was subversive of their power, Christians in the early seventeenth century were repressed, tortured, and put to death with a brutality as great as any in human history. Although the Christians responded with incredible fortitude, their faith disappeared from view and by the mid-seventeenth century Japan was virtually closed to foreign religions and foreign traders.[1]

In 1853, when the American Commodore Matthew Perry 'opened the door' with a show of military force to which the shogunate capitulated, Japan's 200 years of isolation was ended. The ensuing treaty of navigation and commerce between the United States and Japan, negotiated by Townsend Harris, an active Episcopalian and supporter of foreign missions, allowed foreigners to settle in certain ports and to practise their faith, with no specific prohibition of proselytizing among the Japanese.[2]

No treaty could diminish the significance of Japan's first encounter with Christianity for the renewal of Catholic missions or for the new Protestant work. Both had to meet the deeply rooted hostility of the vast majority of Japanese who had been taught that Christians were subversives allied with foreign powers bent on the conquest of Japan. These perceptions were not without some basis, but missionaries were also presented as practitioners of infanticide and cannibalism. Thus, when their country was officially opened to the rest of the world, the anti-Christian and anti-foreign bias of most Japanese was profound.[3]

Since none of the earlier proscriptions against Christianity were formally lifted, the first American missionaries from several denominations proceeded with caution in the 1860s, giving most of their attention to learning the language, translating parts of the Bible into Japanese, and establishing small schools for boys and girls as well as dispensaries for the sick. Although most early missionaries were men of mature years, well educated, with experience as missionaries in China, and usually assisted by wives of ability and dedication, they had baptized only ten converts by 1871 after more than a decade of labour.

As was so often to be the case, attitudes toward Christianity fluctuated with the changing policies of government leaders toward the West. During the 1870s, growing interest in western thought and institutions within Japan brought about some relaxation of the hostility to Christianity. Thus in 1872 the missionaries in Yokohama and other English-speaking residents of all denominations, plus some Japanese students from the mission school, formed the first Protestant congregation, The Church of Christ in Japan, a name symbolizing the intention to establish a national church that would not be identified with any of the denominations represented by the missionaries.[4]

In 1868, with the collapse of the centralized feudalism built up by the

Tokugawa shoguns, the way was opened for a small group of feudal lords from the outer clans to establish their power. In this far from radical revolution, known as 'the Restoration,' the new oligarchy restored formal authority to the emperor who had been no more than a spiritual symbol for centuries. The fifteen-year-old Emperor Mutsuhito was moved from the old capital, Kyoto, to Edo, renamed Tokyo, in a great procession. This procession became a model for subsequent grand tours when, in contrast with earlier practice, the people were allowed to see and feel the imperial presence.[5]

In this new era, designated as the Meiji period, with the emperor as the symbol of national unity and aspiration, the leaders of the new government acted on their conviction that Japan's survival could be assured only by extensive reforms to make their country a modern industrial and military power. One early initiative toward this end took place in 1871, when a large group of the new oligarchs was sent abroad to seek revision of the foreign treaties that restricted Japan's capacity to compete in foreign trade.

The soon famous 'Iwakura Mission,' headed by the president of the Council of State, Count Iwakura Tomomi, failed to secure treaty revision but during its extended observation of social, industrial, and political conditions in the United States and Europe it reached significant conclusions about the means of securing the good will of western nations and promoting change in Japanese society. In several countries the mission was forced to realize that the persecution of Christians and restrictions on missionary work were major stumbling blocks in relations between Japan and the West. Early in 1872, Iwakura cabled his government that his mission would fail unless the persecution ceased. In a matter of days the anti-Christian edicts were taken down from public notice boards throughout Japan.[6]

The next fifteen years saw rapid growth in missionary activity on a variety of fronts, although the number of converts grew slowly. Since the government was actively encouraging westernization, especially among the young, many of whom attended the growing number of Christian schools, there was increasing interest in the religion of the West. Now, in the new atmosphere of relative freedom of enquiry, it was possible to hold public lectures on Christianity and organize mass meetings, such as a gathering in 1880 that drew some 4,000 people to Tokyo's Ueno Park to hear the gospel preached.[7] Interest among intellectuals was dramatically illustrated in 1884 when the leading educator and journalist Fukuzawa Yukichi, who had always opposed Christianity, advocated its adoption because of 'its superiority in wealth, intelligence, virtue and ability to attract persons of wealth.' In common with many Japanese intellectuals then and later who were attracted to the Christian faith, he did not go so far as to be baptized.[8]

The largest single group of converts were members of the feudal warrior class, the samurai, most of whom had backed the Tokugawa shogunate during the waning of its power. Their penalty for being on the losing side in the Restoration battle was exclusion from government and, in large measure initially, from its supporting bureaucracy, as well as from the expanding world of finance and industry. In the long run their education, discipline, and public spirit made them essential to the successful functioning of the Meiji state.[9]

The dilemma of the dispossessed samurai was more than a material one, although many of them became poor when their stipends were commuted into small cash payments or government bonds. With the destruction of traditional institutions they had lost status and the objects of obedience. It became increasingly difficult to see the relevance of *bushidō* (the Way of the Warrior), the code of conduct that traditionally governed samurai behaviour. The samurai were men in search of an identity, a compelling allegiance, and social status.[10] The missionaries and their message filled the deeply felt needs of many samurai and their sons who attended mission schools. In their eyes, their missionary teachers combined the virtues of the Confucian scholar and the samurai warrior. Further, the missionaries' social concerns and their interest in Japan's future as a nation were attractive to the patriotic samurai, as was their devotion to the ideal of a self-supporting, independent national church.

Many former samurai also realized that the western education offered by the missionaries opened the way for their personal survival and advancement in the new society. At the same time, Protestant Christianity's emphasis on the salvation of the individual and on personal responsibility for ethical behaviour provided justification for the initial resistance of most of the samurai to the Restoration and for their later participation in dissenting political parties.

Reflecting the background of their class, young samurai often made their profession of Christian faith as a group or band in response to the leadership of a strong teacher, usually a missionary but sometimes one of the foreign experts (*yatoi*) employed by the Meiji leaders to teach western science and technology in their modernizing society. The most famous, the

'Kumamoto band,' developed under the influence of Captain L.L. Janes, a West Point graduate and former officer in the American army. Janes started a school in the city of Kumamoto in Kyushu at the request of local authorities who wanted the students to learn English and science. Later, school officials gave Janes permission to use the New Testament as a vehicle for teaching English, believing that the understanding the students would thus acquire would help them to refute Christianity. That was not the effect on forty students who climbed up the mountain outside the city early in 1876 to declare their loyalty to Jesus Christ and to dedicate their lives to the salvation of their nation. When Janes's contract was not renewed and the school was closed, most of the new Christians moved to Kyoto, where Niijima Jō, recently returned from years of theological study in the United States, had just opened the Christian college that was to become Dōshisha University. From this group came many of the leaders of the Protestant church, and they were joined by equally able and committed members of the 'Yokohama Band,' the 'Sapporo Band,' as well as other smaller and less famous bands. This first generation of leaders, most of them the sons of former samurai, were at the peak of their influence around the turn of the century.[11] They were shaping the Protestant church that Caroline Macdonald was to serve, and some of them, with their wives, were to be significant in her life and work.

While former samurai constituted a large majority of the ministers and lay leaders of the churches, they also accounted for as much as 40 per cent of the total membership (75 per cent in Tokyo), although they were less than 6 per cent of the population.[12] Thus Protestantism in Japan early assumed the dominantly urban, educated, middle-class character it retained throughout the twentieth century. As the graduates of Dōshisha began to take up pastorates across the country, they preached a gospel that placed great emphasis on the power of the Christian faith to create free and independent individuals who would be inspired to love their fellow men and thus strengthen the community of the nation. It was a message that paid less attention to the understanding of Christian doctrine than to the social utility of Christianity, and this gave a highly moralistic tone to much of Japanese Protestantism.[13]

When a constitution was 'given' to the Japanese people by the emperor in 1889, it guaranteed freedom of religious belief as long as its exercise did not interfere with the duties of a Japanese subject, a provision open to a broad range of interpretation, especially as it was clear that the emperor was the centre of national life and the final authority on the welfare of the nation. The new ruling oligarchs had no intention of establishing a democracy. Their model was the constitutional monarchy of Bismarck's Prussia, and the Diet was elected on a property franchise granted to only 1.1 per cent of the male population. Reinforcing aspects of tradition most serviceable to their economic and military objectives, they developed an ideological system with strongly religious overtones that presented the state as a large family presided over by a father-emperor descended from the Sun goddess Amaterasu.[14] Two agencies were of prime utility in the promotion of official ideology, the army and the educational system.

With the abolition of a class basis for military service and the establishment in 1873 of an army and navy recruited by universal conscription, the government had a powerful vehicle for indoctrinating the male population in the supreme virtue of loyalty to the emperor. The Rescript to Soldiers and Sailors of 1882 made abstention from political opinion or activity an important definition of this loyalty. Similarly, it was made increasingly clear during the 1890s that upper-level career bureaucrats were the emperor's officials and must have no role in politics. Further, teachers were forbidden to 'meddle in politics,' and educational organizations of all kinds were instructed to abjure political debate. Through such measures the oligarchs in effect declared that the nation's finest patriots were above politics, a stance that more than implied that Japan's true interests could not be served through political activity.[15]

By far the most effective instrument for the inculcation of official ideology was the system of universal compulsory education begun in 1872 and implemented over the next three decades. Although the purposes of education were initially defined in strictly utilitarian terms as being for the development of skills needed to strengthen the nation, there soon developed a heated debate over 'ethics instruction' or 'moral education' in the nation's schools, especially at the elementary level where children were expected to attend school for four years, and after 1907 for six years. Long before that, especially with the promulgation of the Imperial Rescript on Education of 1890, 'moral education' had moved to the top of the elementary school agenda and was emphasized at every level of instruction. The education of a 'good Japanese' left no doubt that service and obedience to family, the state, and the emperor were primary and interrelated obligations.[16]

How closely they were related was evident after 1890 in the Ministry of

Education's promotion of the 'good wife, wise mother' ideal. Although often presented in traditional rhetoric, this slogan represented a new determination by the state to enlist women in building the nation. While their role in the home was paramount, many women also contributed directly to the growth of the economy. Well before the turn of the century, young women workers outnumbered males in light industry, most notably in textiles. It was assumed that virtually all women would marry and that most of their lives would then be spent in the home. Accordingly, lower-class women must have an education that would enable them to be productive members of the industrial work force when they were required, and all women must be educated for the rearing of their children.[17] Compulsory education was instituted for girls on the same basis as for boys, although for some years far fewer of them were actually in school. While the core curriculum in elementary school was the same for both sexes, girls took special courses in 'household matters,' including cooking, sewing, handicrafts, the care of the old, and above all the rearing of children according to the latest scientific knowledge. The high school curriculum for girls was less academic than for boys and was not intended to prepare girls for entrance to university but rather for the fulfilling of duties in the middle-class home. Moral education for girls was similar to that for boys, except for the addition of instruction in deportment and manners, and of stories depicting the virtuous deeds of women.[18]

As Japan moved into the twentieth century, the ideal woman as defined by the Meiji rulers was literate, with an education appropriate to her position in society. Whatever her class, she would be modest, courageous, frugal, and hard working, qualities 'so appropriate for economic growth' as to constitute a 'cult of productivity.'[19] Meiji educational authorities and Christians who pioneered expanding educational opportunities for Japanese women believed that western education could help develop these qualities. Japan's ideal woman often sounded rather like the western ideal of the woman, whose main contribution to society was also through the nurture of her family. In fact, there was a considerable difference. Economic productivity was not a domestic requirement for North American women, and when they moved into the outside world they endeavoured to carry domestic and nurturing capacities into 'feminine' professions such as teaching, nursing, and social work, and into movements for social reform that aimed to express the domestic virtues in public life. In contrast, 'the Meiji leaders, recognizing the value of women's economic and educational contributions, claimed the home as a public place.'[20] In 1887 the Ministry of Education stated bluntly that 'the home is a public place where private feelings should be forgotten.'[21] In the home, 'good wives, wise mothers,' sufficiently educated for their task, would bring up scientifically minded and patriotic children who would advance the industrial and military power of the nation.

A corollary of the importance assigned to the home in building the nation was women's exclusion from political life. If women were allowed to vote or take an interest in politics, it would detract from their work as managers and educators in the home. As with military men, teachers, and senior bureaucrats, women's noble service to the state must be above partisan politics. In 1900 the Public Peace Law barred women of all classes from joining political organizations or attending political meetings.[22] Like the vast majority of their sisters in the western world at the time, Japanese women were denied the franchise and active participation in public life. In contrast with the western world, in Japan the rationale for this denial, as with other groups who were similarly excluded, fed an ideology that portrayed politics as detrimental to the nation and public life as an arena unworthy of the good citizen.[23]

Male Christians participated in political life from the beginning, and in 1890 thirteen were elected to the first Diet, where one of their number was chosen as Speaker of the Lower House.[24] They were more influenced by western ideas about the value of public service than others among the elite group eligible to vote and stand for public office and consequently they continued to be disproportionately represented in the Diet.

The many Christians who believed that the new constitution had resolved earlier difficulties about their loyalty to the state were soon disappointed. In 1890 the government promulgated the Imperial Rescript on Education, a declaration on the purpose of the moral and patriotic education of Japanese students. Filial piety and respect for the emperor, who was 'coeval with heaven and earth,' were the core of loyalty and patriotism.[25] Increasingly, official interpretations of the rescript defined the civil morality that Japan's leaders believed would sustain national unity. Christians felt no antagonism toward the document itself, but when asked to bow before a copy signed by the emperor and displayed on a pedestal during a ceremony at the First Higher School in Tokyo in January 1901, one of the teachers, Uchimura Kanzō, founder of the Mukyōkai (non-church Christianity), refused to do so. Although Uchimura later decided that to bow was not an act of worship and agreed to conform, the incident became a cause célèbre

and Uchimura was forced to resign from his position. The affair provided
fuel for conservative nationalists and Buddhist leaders who now renewed
their argument that it was impossible for Christians to be loyal subjects.
There followed another period of hostility to Christianity, and for a time
there was a marked decline in baptisms and attendance at Christian schools.
The ceremony of bowing before the Imperial Rescript became standard
practice in the nation's schools, there was fresh emphasis on the teaching of
'national ethics,' and attempts were made to limit Christian worship and
teaching in mission schools, although these efforts were abandoned from
fear of western opinion.[26]

Just after the turn of the century, when the total population of Japan was
about 44 million, there were some 45,000 baptized Protestant adults and
50,000 children in Sunday schools. Foreign missionaries numbered more
than 800, most of them Americans. They had organized more than 500
churches in eighty-five cities and towns throughout Japan. If wives of missionaries, many of whom were unpaid workers, were added to the large con-
tingent of single women, then women constituted a majority of the
missionaries in Japan. Despite their small numbers, Christians were making
an impact on Japanese society, not only through their schools but in their
work to improve conditions in prisons, in the establishment of orphanages,
schools for the blind, and asylums for lepers, and in the organization of temperance and anti-brothel movements. Some of the early missionaries were
doctors and contributed to the development of medical care in Japan.
However, in contrast with other mission fields, medicine was not a major
missionary frontier, since the technological change encouraged by the government included the introduction of western medicine. Christians had
founded and edited for a decade *Rikugō Zasshi* (Cosmos), one of the most
influential journals of social criticism in the country and widely read by non-
Christian intellectuals as well as by Christian leaders. From 1887 discussion
of Christianity had also been promoted among intellectuals in *Kokumin No
Tomo* (The Nation's Friend), edited by Tokutomi Soho. Christians had been
active in organizing the first labour unions, notably among railway workers,
and in 1901 they played a dominant role in establishing Japan's first socialist
party, although it was immediately closed down by the government.[27]

In 1900 a conference of 435 missionaries representing forty-two mission
boards and agencies, the largest of its kind ever held in Japan, celebrated the
beginning of the new century, took stock of their position, and made plans

for the future. Astonishingly, despite three decades of church life and the formation of an impressive group of Japanese clergy and lay people, the conference made no provision for the participation of Japanese Christians nor was there any fundamental discussion of the religious and cultural milieu in which the missionaries were working. Little wonder that Japanese church leaders were becoming restless about the relationship between their churches and the missions.[28]

This tension did not prevent the churches from embarking on 'The Forward Evangelistic Campaign,' an ambitious four-year program modelled on similar interdenominational endeavours in North America. Some 300,000 people were reported to have attended gatherings ranging from mass rallies in the larger cities to small groups in local congregations, and while 15,000 signed 'inquirers' cards, only 1,000 were baptized as Christians. Although its promoters persuaded themselves that their efforts were worthwhile, the experience confirmed the view of many that Japan was probably the most difficult mission field in the world.[29]

■ ■ ■

As CAROLINE MACDONALD PREPARED for her new life in Japan, she had no difficulty finding information and opinions about the scene of her future work. The western world's fascination with Japan over half a century had produced an enormous literature accessible to an English reader, presenting an array of views and interpretations from a host of travellers, missionaries, diplomats, scholars, journalists, teachers, and traders who had recorded their experiences.[30] At the core of their interest was the impact of the West on Japanese society and the debate about the desirability of 'modernization.' These observers ranged from the long-term resident of Japan, Lafcadio Hearn, the most influential purveyor of a romantic image of the island kingdom's traditional society and arts, to short-term visitors such as Rudyard Kipling, who also deplored westernization and was especially hard on American missionaries he believed were destroying a beautiful status quo by filling Japanese minds with 'wicked ideas of "Progress."'[31]

Other commentators marvelled at the speed of Japan's advance toward the objective of *fukoku-kyōhei* ('rich country-strong army'). How far the modernizers had come was demonstrated by Japan's victory in her war against China (1894-5), which in turn gave renewed impetus to industrialization. While some interpreters saw the growth of Japanese economic and military power as 'the yellow peril,' a coming threat to European leadership of the world, many more viewed the new Japan as a beneficial influence throughout Asia. With the signing of the Anglo-Japanese Alliance in 1902, Japan was often hailed as 'the Britain of Asia.' One of the most balanced pictures of changing Japan was drawn by the Englishman Basil Hall Chamberlain, whose mastery of the Japanese language and its literature was unique among foreigners. Soon after the turn of the century, his encyclopaedic two-volume work *Things Japanese*, originally published in 1876, was in its fourth edition. Chamberlain's compendium of essays on a wide variety of topics was both popular and influential throughout the English-speaking world.[32]

Another interpreter of Japan, William Elliot Griffis, was one of the earliest foreign advisors employed by the Meiji government. After four years (1870-4) spent in preparing a curriculum in the natural sciences for the Japanese Ministry of Education, Griffis returned to the United States and published *The Mikado's Empire* (1876). By 1903, when this work was in its tenth edition,[33] Griffis had published numerous articles and books on Japan. He did not return until the 1920s, but his work remained an excellent guide to nineteenth-century Japan.

Although not officially a missionary, Griffis was a vigorous Christian, as were others among the foreign experts – men such as his mentor, the educator Guido Verbeck; the agriculturalist William S. Clark, the father of the Sapporo Band; and Captain L.L. Janes, the inspirer of the Kumamoto Band. In 1904, as Caroline Macdonald was preparing to go to Japan, women's missionary societies in the United States and Canada were using Griffis's book *Dux Christus* (1904) as their study for the year.[34] Following an historical survey and a discussion of traditional religions, Griffis described the development of Christian missions in Japan. Not surprisingly, given the major audience for his book, he had much to say about the position of Japanese women. Nearly three decades after his first book, Griffis found little reason to alter his view that 'the biography of a good [Japanese] woman is written in one word – obedience.'[35] In obedience the Japanese woman accepted the marriage arranged for her and the rule of her mother-in-law thereafter, and waited on her husband's every need. Poor girls were often sold into prostitution or went into it to support their parents and siblings. In accord with one of the major themes of the Protestant missionary movement everywhere, Griffis was enthusiastic about 'women's work for women' in elevating the status of the whole population.[36]

With few exceptions, western observers, whether male or female, Christian or secular in their viewpoint, were united in the opinion that women occupied a much lower position in Japan than in their home countries, although there was also agreement that they were held in greater respect in Japan than in other parts of Asia. The most widely read account of the female lot in Japan was Alice Mabel Bacon's *Japanese Girls and Women* (1891; 1902). Her book was inspired by the realization that despite the abundant literature on Japan, the female half of the population had been 'left entirely unnoticed.'[37] Bacon, the daughter of an eminent Congregationalist minister in New England, was associated with Japanese women from the age of twelve when her father became the guardian of one of the five young girls sent abroad with the Iwakura mission by the Japanese government, the first to be educated outside Japan.

Yamakawa Sutematsu and Alice Bacon lived together like sisters for ten years. Through this association and her friendship with another of the Japanese girls, Tsuda Ume, Bacon went to Japan in 1888 to teach English at the recently established Peeress's School in Tokyo. Although the women best known to Bacon were the daughters of the noble and upper-class families who sent their daughters to the nation's most exclusive school for young women, she was also a sharp observer of peasant women and domestic servants, nor did she ignore young women who were a substantial majority of the workers in the expanding factories of cities such as Osaka and Tokyo. While Bacon deplored the limited opportunities for girls to acquire a high school education, she noted with approval that all Japanese women, except for the very lowest classes, received instruction in the written language; many wrote poetry and were familiar with the Chinese classics.[38]

Bacon's criticism of traditional Japanese religions was severe, primarily because they ranked loyalty and obedience above all other virtues and were thus the basis of women's lowly position. Although the traditional religions appeared to give women a significant role by placing upon them the primary responsibility for tending the god-shelf in the home and making temple offerings and pilgrimages, this was actually a burden for poor women who were usually the most devout.[39] The higher ideals of Christianity were already having an effect in raising the moral standards of Japanese society as a whole, Bacon believed, and she hoped they would spread rapidly, not least for the welfare of women.[40]

Bacon gave full credit to the pioneering work of mission schools in the education of Japanese girls and believed that their continuing work was essential for the improvement of the status of women. At the same time she was sympathetic to the severe criticism that was almost universal among Japanese to whom 'the manners of the girls in these schools seem brusque and awkward.' Bacon hoped that the 'charm of manner which is the distinguishing feature of the Japanese woman will not be lost by contact with our western shortness and roughness.'[41] Clearly Caroline Macdonald's role in establishing the work of a Christian organization for Japanese women would be a complex one, demanding sensitivity to the need for continuity as well as for change.

■ ■ ■

THE VOLUMINOUS LITERATURE published by the missionary movement was unanimous in the opinion that Japan was not a mission field like others. In contrast with India, China, and Africa, it was not a civilization in apparent decline and disunity, subject to control and exploitation by European powers. Rather it was a sophisticated and self-confident society with a high rate of literacy and education and a profoundly paradoxical relationship to the western world. Despite their eagerness to adopt the science and technology of the West, the fierce determination of Japan's leaders to preserve their distinctive culture was seen by the missionaries as a formidable barrier to their work.

Few missionaries were as pessimistic about their impact as R.B. Peery, an American Lutheran who saw little to enjoy or admire in Japan. He found in the Japanese character 'a lack of seriousness and stability,' an intense nationalism, and a materialism that was almost impenetrable. For these reasons the attitude of most Japanese toward Christianity was 'one of absolute indifference.'[42] Although most missionaries stopped short of such despair, there was general agreement that the Japanese lacked a sense of sin, and thus it was difficult for them to believe that they needed a Redeemer to save them. Moreover, the consequences of conversion in separation from family, neighbourhood, and the wider community were so enormous that many Japanese who felt attracted to Christianity drew back from taking the definitive step of being baptized.[43] Most missionaries correctly perceived that a marked characteristic of the Japanese intellectual tradition was a 'tolerance' that made it possible for an individual to entertain a wide variety of ideas and theories at the same time, even if some were contradictory. This attitude made it impossible for most Japanese to accept Christianity's claim to be a universally valid explanation of human experience, as later most were to reject Marxism.[44]

Pessimism was not the dominant tone of missionary literature, despite general acknowledgment of the enormous difficulties in converting Japanese to the Christian faith. Sidney L. Gulick, a leading American Congregationalist missionary, was representative of the majority of missionaries who, while recognizing obstacles, saw great opportunity for spreading the gospel in Japan. Gulick rejected the view that the Japanese were essentially irreligious or lacking in moral sense. He believed that educated people, who formed an increasing proportion of Japanese society, had outgrown the religious conceptions of a superstitious Shintoism and of a Buddhism in decline from an earlier purity. What Christianity had to offer the 'new Japan' was 'a religion satisfying the intellect as to its world view ... providing sanctions for the social life and sanctions for the individual.'[45]

In common with missionaries everywhere, those in Japan had a natural bias toward positive and enthusiastic reporting, dictated by the demands of fundraising at home and their own need for affirmation of their labours. Apart from that, it was possible to find more objective reasons for believing that in the past five decades Christianity had been firmly established in Japan and would continue to advance.

Typical of the most optimistic missionaries was John H. De Forest, an American Presbyterian who believed that despite the relatively small number of converts, 'no other nation has ever been so rapidly permeated with Christian knowledge as has Japan. There has never been in all the history of missions so great a victory for Christ in so short a time as we see to-day in that beautiful island Empire. There never was a non-Christian nation so open-minded and receptive as Japan.'[46]

William Elliot Griffis reflected accurately the tone of most presentations of the Christian cause when he addressed women in North America in 1904 through *Dux Christus*. While Griffis was entirely negative about the baneful effects of ancestor worship on the growth of a Japanese sense of individual responsibility, lamented a 'fortified ignorance' about the rest of the world based on a narrow and insular nationalism, and deplored a 'national love of untruthfulness,' he was certain that the Christian message would be heard by an intelligent, resourceful, and increasingly educated populace among whom the superstitious and inferior ethics of the old religions had waning appeal.[47] The 'five great gates of opportunity in Japan' were in the evangelistic, educational, medical, charitable, and literary fields.[48] Given adequate resources, Griffis believed, missionaries and their Japanese colleagues would occupy all of them and Japan would be led into 'the light and liberty of the children of God.'[49]

That light and liberty already graced the Christian homes of Japan, according to Griffis. No longer ruled by despotic fathers, they were centres where spiritual equality and mutual helpfulness created comradeship between husbands and wives and an atmosphere where children acquired a sense of individual worth and social responsibility.[50] In the multiplication of Christian homes and the making of a Christian nation, nothing would pay greater dividends than the education of girls in Christian schools. Although many had not become Christians formally, the thousands of girls who had been educated in Christian schools already had elevated ideals of home life and were helping to shape public opinion on social problems and issues. 'Let us reenforce all the agencies that lift up one-half of Japan!' Griffis urged his readers.[51] Paying tribute to the YMCA, whose work among young men, especially students, had made it highly respected in Japan, Griffis asked why there was no similar work among women and appealed to 'the Christian women of America to cease no prayer or effort in behalf of their sisters in the island empire, for Japan is woman's land of hope in Asia.'[52] The Canadian YWCA, through its emissary Caroline Macdonald, was answering a compelling appeal. In the late autumn of 1904, as she bade farewell to her family, made her way across Canada by train to Vancouver, and boarded the *Empress of Japan* for the ten-day voyage across the Pacific, Caroline was full of anticipation, curiosity, some anxiety, and much faith in the importance of her venture for the Kingdom of God.

C h a p t e r 3

'Women's Work for Women'

W HEN THE *Empress of Japan* docked in Yokohama on 12 December 1904, Caroline was met by three Japanese women in elegant kimono, and by Theresa Morrison, whom the American YWCA had sent to Tokyo a year earlier as an advisor on the establishment of the YWCA in Japan. After the short train journey from Yokohama to Shinbashi, Tokyo's main railway station, the five women made their way by *jinrikisha* (rickshaw) to the house Caroline was to share with Morrison and another American, a stenographer at the YMCA.

The house in Kōjimachi, about a ten-minute walk from the Imperial Palace, had been built for an American YMCA secretary currently in Manchuria working among Japanese soldiers, and whose wife had gone home to the United States for the duration of the war against Russia. Caroline found the sparsely furnished 'semi-Japanese' house attractive and comfortable and the service provided by a cook and his wife more than adequate. For the first ten days she took life easily, learning the things any newcomer to Japan needed to know: a few common phrases in Japanese, how to mail letters home, how to hail a *jinrikisha* (also known as a *kuruma*), how to find her way through narrow streets that appeared disconcertingly the same and where sidewalks were still largely unknown, to take off her shoes before entering the house, to sit on the floor for three hours at a dinner party without complaint, to eat raw fish and to handle chopsticks, and to listen appreciatively to an after-dinner performance on the *koto*, where the artist was more likely to be a grandmother than the aspiring teenage piano student familiar at home. Caroline entered into these new experiences with enormous zest and much laughter over her ineptness in mastering the unfamiliar.[1]

Life in her new home could have been trying, or worse, had she not felt blessed with 'a cheerful disposition.' She needed it, 'not for the Japanese, bless them. They seem to have cheerful dispositions too, but the dear people with whom I live are not well & it gives them a gloomy outlook on things.' Since she had some experience in nurturing the spirit of community, she hoped she would be able 'to continue along the line of [her] genius.' For the time being she could be amused by episodes she recounted to her family:

> The day opens warm and beautiful. So down I come to breakfast. 'Isn't it a lovely day!!' 'Yes it's very cold!' ... 'I do like riding in a kuruma,' I say in the exuberance of youthful feeling. 'Doesn't it hurt your back?' 'Not a bit!' 'It will if you ride in them much.' If I mention ... that I passed a good medical examination I am reminded that some who have had the best records have been the first to break down.

In spite of her pessimistic housemates she was 'having a glorious rest' and was 'in fighting form.'[2]

At the beginning of the new year Caroline began to attend a language school conducted by Mr. Matsuda, a teacher at the prestigious Peers' School, and said to be the best teacher of Japanese in the country. For three hours every afternoon, five days a week for the next six months, she wrestled with writing, reading, grammar, and conversation, with three hours of study at home every morning.[3]

Since the YWCA was not yet formally constituted, Caroline had no official position, but she began to work with two groups of girls, one a Bible class for English-speaking Christian students at the Higher Normal School, and the other with girls from the central telephone office with whom discussion was conducted through an interpreter. On her second Sunday in

Tokyo, in the absence of the regular teacher, she was invited to lead the weekly Bible class for young men, mostly students, in Ichibanchō Presbyterian Church. The lesson for the day concerned St. Paul's sermon on Mars' Hill: 'Ye men of Athens, I perceive that in all things ye are too superstitious ... Whom therefore ye ignorantly worship, him declare I unto you.' Caroline 'could easily imagine the speech to be made at the present time in Tokyo, the great intellectual centre of Japan as Athens was of Greece. The young men were exceedingly attentive and it was a great pleasure to teach them.'[4] As it turned out, she continued to teach this group of young men for the next two years.

From the beginning of her association with the Japanese, especially the young people, Caroline was aware of the widespread support for the war against Russia, which had begun ten months before she arrived. One day, as she and Theresa Morrison were chatting at home with a group of girls from a government high school, there was a cry outside in the street: 'Gōgai, gōgai' ('extra, extra'). One of the girls rushed out to buy a newspaper, read it quickly, and made an announcement that obviously delighted the others. Thanks to a dictionary and Morrison's limited knowledge of Japanese, Caroline understood that the students were rejoicing over the navy's sinking of yet another Russian warship, the Sebastopol, an event that confirmed the already proven superiority of Japanese military power in Asia. As the war was drawing to a victorious conclusion, even schoolgirls sensed that the first defeat of a western nation by an Asian power was a landmark in world history. As a respectful newcomer Caroline made no comment on the girls' enthusiasm.[5]

However, for readers at home she recorded with approval the exploits of the YMCA with the Japanese army in Manchuria and North China.[6] Macdonald found it impressive that the YMCA was the only religious organization, Christian or otherwise, that had been allowed to provide 'comfort' to soldiers and that the doors of hospitals across the country were open to YMCA visitors.[7] The government viewed the war service of the YMCA as moral undergirding for the troops and good public relations in a war sometimes viewed in the West as an attempt of 'barbaric orientals' to subdue a Christian Russia. To the YMCA and the churches it was an opportunity to relieve suffering and to spread the gospel among soldiers, most of whom came from peasant families, a class thus far largely untouched by Christian evangelism. Moreover, this apparent identification of the YMCA with

Japanese national objectives enhanced the image of the 'Y' in the minds of politicians and the general public, especially after the emperor contributed 10,000 yen for its war work in one of the first examples of imperial recognition of Christian social service.[8]

The support of the war that was implicit in the YMCA's services at the front was endorsed by the missionaries almost without exception. Most Japanese Christians took the same position, save for a handful of dissidents such as the Bible teacher Uchimura Kanzō, who abandoned his initial support, the novelist Kinoshita Naoe, and a small group of Christian socialists like Abe Isoo, professor of economics at Waseda University. A few Christian socialists left the church in disillusionment over its failure to resist the war. In some small rural churches there was an anti-war movement, but in the larger urban congregations support for the war was firm. Some denominations, including the Presbyterian-Reformed group, issued public statements declaring their approval.[9]

Japan had achieved her spectacular military victories at tremendous financial cost, some of which the Japanese government hoped to recover in the form of a large indemnity. On Japan's invitation, President Theodore Roosevelt agreed to mediate the peace settlement, embodied in the Treaty of Portsmouth of 1905. While recognizing Japanese control over Korea and South Manchuria and the acquisition from Russia of the southern half of Sakhalin Island, Roosevelt opposed Japanese demands for an indemnity. Patriotic journalists and intellectuals led the outcry against the government for accepting a treaty unworthy of victories achieved in the name of the emperor. The day the treaty was signed a large protest rally assembled in Hibiya Park in Kōjimachi ward, where most government buildings were located and where Caroline lived. For the next two days rioting was widespread in several parts of the city, and casualties mounted to more than 1,000 as police and firemen tried to restore order. Their almost universal and often enthusiastic support of the war did not save the Christians from unwanted attention during these days. Ten churches in Tokyo were burned by mobs who apparently connected local Christians with the 'Christian enemy,' Russia. The 'Portsmouth riots' alarmed authorities reluctant to acknowledge the growing force of public opinion, and reminded Christians of their continuing vulnerability to fluctuations in popular attitudes toward Christianity.[10]

Japan's war with Russia brought social changes of significance for an organization proposing to work with women, such as the YWCA. In calling on all the emperor's subjects to support the war effort, the state gave legitimacy to certain activities outside the home for middle- and upper-class women, following the example set by the empress herself and other women in the imperial family and the peerage. In seeing soldiers off to war and welcoming them home, and in visiting the sick and wounded, women became familiar with railway stations, hospitals, and meeting places where they had never been before. They made bandages and clothing for men at the front, and cared for the wounded and the families of the bereaved. In their work to support a conscript army that included men of all classes, elite women were in some measure taken out of their home- and class-bound lives and introduced to aspects of Japanese society previously unknown to them.[11]

The Japan Red Cross had begun to train nurses before the turn of the century, and a few had served in the Sino-Japanese war of 1894-5. Before the end of the Russo-Japanese war in 1905, more than 2,000 female nurses were serving with the army. In the press much was made of the patriotism and self-sacrifice of some upper-class women and widows of army officers who served through the Ladies' Volunteer Nursing Association, but most of the nurses were women who had to support themselves, albeit at very low wages.[12] Thus, Caroline Macdonald began her work in Tokyo at a time when women's participation in the war effort was altering, however slightly, some conventions about their roles in Japanese society.

At the end of her six months' study of Japanese, Caroline took a series of examinations set by the American Methodist Episcopal Mission Board and passed with A and B grades. Henceforth she would study with Mr. Matsuda only three times a week and devote most of her energies to the work of the YWCA. Although she had met with the 'Promoting Committee' on several occasions, it was not until the autumn of 1905 that this group became the National Committee of the Young Women's Christian Association of Japan, which subsequently appointed Caroline Macdonald as national secretary and adopted a draft constitution. The husbands of several of these women had been active in the YMCA over the past two decades. They, and the YMCA staff, did everything possible to assist Caroline and her committee. In particular, the American Galen Fisher, who had been with the YMCA in Japan for several years, and his wife Ella were 'helpfulness itself.'[13] Caroline's feeling that Fisher could be counted on to give perceptive advice never left her; in turn he remained her staunch admirer and supporter throughout her life.

Initially, all the national officers of the YWCA were missionaries or wives of missionaries, with Miss M.A. Whitman, an American Baptist, in the chair. Everyone recognized that this was far from ideal and must be remedied as soon as possible, but foreigners remained in the majority at the national level for several years. The difficulty was that apart from the handful of women who had studied abroad, few Japanese women had experience leading any organization; they lacked self confidence and were often uncertain about the propriety of tackling anything untraditional. How often in the next few years Caroline was to hear: '*Kokujō wa chigaimasu*' ('It is against the customs of Japan'). Most Japanese women seemed to be 'scared of themselves ... scared of conventions, wouldn't do anything that hadn't always been done, and thought they were different from all people under heaven.' Had she taken this attitude at face value she would have 'given up the ghost' then and there.[14]

The National Committee promoted the formation and growth of local associations, but did not carry on local work directly. It took immediate steps to organize a Tokyo association, determined that it must be led primarily by Japanese. Thus a majority of the fifteen members of the first board of the Tokyo Association were Japanese women, most of them teachers. They included Honda Sadako of Aoyama Jogakuin, the Methodist Episcopal school for girls, and wife of Tokyo's leading Methodist minister; Yajima Kaji, one of the first women public-school teachers in Japan and now principal of Joshi Gakuin, the Presbyterian girls' school, as well as leader of the Woman's Christian Temperance Union (WCTU); Ibuka Hana, a graduate of Mount Holyoke College and a teacher of science in Joshi Gakuin; Okada Mitsuko of the Higher Normal School and a recent graduate of Wellesley College; and Kawai Michi, just graduated from Bryn Mawr, whom Caroline had met three years earlier at a YWCA conference in Silver Bay, New York. Caroline thought Kawai 'one of the finest young women' she had ever met anywhere and she was already planning a great future for her. The biggest coup of all was persuading Tsuda Ume to chair the Tokyo board, for there was no one who enjoyed the confidence of both the foreign and Japanese communities more than Japan's foremost woman educator.[15] From this beginning Tsuda became a good friend and a major figure in Caroline's life.

Tsuda Ume's life (1864-1928) epitomized the impact of western education on a small group of upper-class Japanese women, almost always the daughters of politicians or bureaucrats imbued with ideas about the education of women from their reading of John Stuart Mill or of Japan's 'Great Enlightener,' Fukuzawa Yukichi. In 1872, when the first group of girls went abroad to study in the United States, the youngest of the five was seven-year-old Tsuda Ume. Following eleven years in the best American schools she returned to Japan well educated, a Christian, and an independent woman who was almost a stranger in her homeland. After several years teaching English in girls' schools she went back to the United States to study biology at Bryn Mawr College. Subsequently eschewing graduate work in science, Tsuda decided to devote her life to the education of Japanese women. For a time she taught elementary English to girls of noble birth at the Peeress's School until, wearying of 'the red tape and conservatism' inevitable in a court institution, she concluded that she was 'powerless against the current' and must resign to pursue a more independent course.[16] In 1900, with the financial support of her American friends, especially alumnae and faculty of Bryn Mawr organized by her lifelong friend Anna C. Hartshorne, Tsuda opened Joshi Eigaku Juku (Academy of English Studies for Women), the first private women's college in Japan, soon known as Tsuda Juku Daigaku (Tsuda College). Specializing in English, Tsuda was determined that the curriculum of her school would be the most demanding in Japan and that its graduates would be able to earn their own living freed from economic dependence on men and well prepared to be active contributors to society.[17]

In the autumn of 1905, Caroline Macdonald began a long association with Tsuda College when she accepted Tsuda's invitation to teach the history of English literature for two hours a week to the small graduating class. Believing that as a teacher she could influence a key group of students, Caroline also hoped that in this role she could nurture Tsuda's interest in the YWCA. Between them, Tsuda College and the YWCA might go far to change the lives of girls and women in Japan.[18]

■ ■ ■

THE TOKYO YWCA made its formal debut on a sunny afternoon in the autumn of 1905. Guests and organizers were gathered among a profusion of chrysanthemums in the garden of one of Japan's most senior politicians, Count Ōkuma Shigenobu, a former prime minister, founder of Waseda University, and a liberal somewhat sympathetic to Christianity. When Caroline, Tsuda Ume, and Kawai Michi had called on Ōkuma, he was very willing to host the garden party and agreed to welcome the guests himself.

Unfortunately illness forced him to send a message instead, and so Tsuda Ume welcomed the more than 800 guests. Galen Fisher of the YMCA and Yajima Kaji gave brief endorsements, and the main address was delivered by Dr. Motoda Sakunoshin, a leading Episcopal clergyman and educator. Caroline was well pleased with the occasion, especially that 'everything was managed by the Japanese, and there was nothing in English except a few words I spoke under protest.' At the end about one hundred girls and women enrolled as members of the YWCA, while many more departed to consider the draft constitution at home.[19]

The only significant absence from this auspicious beginning was that of Dr. Joseph Naruse, president of Nihon Joshi Daigakkō (Japan Women's University), founded in 1901. Although he had been converted to Christianity while studying in the United States, Naruse's educational philosophy precluded the advocacy of any religion, and the YWCA had thus far been unable to establish contact with his students. Nevertheless, Naruse had agreed to attend the garden party if possible, and although he had not come the appearance of his name on the program as an endorser was 'a distinct triumph' in Caroline's view.[20]

Elsewhere the work that could be undertaken by the YWCA seemed boundless, limited only by a shortage of money and personnel. On the invitation of several leading citizens, including the mayor, Caroline spent a week in Sendai, the largest city in northern Honshu. There she spoke not only to students in three mission schools but also to students at the government normal and high schools and the four public girls' schools. Although none of the principals and only three of the teachers in the non-mission schools were Christians, there was a widespread belief among them that Sendai needed the services of an organization like the YWCA. In schools throughout the country, doors were open to the YWCA but only a few could be entered for the time being.[21]

There was also increasing interest among employers and working women in commercial establishments such as was shown in the invitation to the YWCA to teach English and 'morals' to the young clerks in the large Mitsui silk store. Although the 'Y' accepted this request, it decided before long that work among working women was not its first priority. Rather, its best strategy was to concentrate on middle-class women in schools and colleges, who it was hoped would eventually provide Christian leadership for their sisters in factories, commercial enterprises, and hospitals.[22]

One of the responsibilities Caroline inherited was the editing of a magazine, *Meiji no Joshi* (Women of Meiji), established by the YWCA committee only a year earlier. She thought it a venture undertaken prematurely, but since everyone agreed that the only Christian magazine for Japanese girls could not be abandoned, she struggled on with it. Happily, before long the Pittsburgh YWCA undertook to subsidize the magazine until the YWCA in Japan could support it.[23]

Caroline believed local support would develop soon. After a little more than a year in Japan, she concluded that interest in Christianity was growing rapidly, especially among educated Japanese because 'they realize their own religions have no power.' Shintoism especially was in decline except in some rural areas, and while various forms of Buddhism flourished in certain quarters, 'it is atheism that is growing in Japan.' At the same time 'the woman problem' claimed the attention of serious people as never before. 'The new freedom is finding many victims,' Caroline observed, and the power of Christianity to 'regenerate & make strong' was 'the only ultimate solution.' Clearly the YWCA could play an important role in educating young women in the ways of 'constructive freedom.'[24]

In the eyes of its Christian supporters and other well-wishers, the most immediate contribution of the YWCA to 'the woman problem,' as in North America, was through the establishment of safe boarding homes or hostels for women students. The rationale for student hostels in Japan was explained by Gladys Phillips, a missionary of the Anglican Church Missionary Society who had recently opened St. Hilda's Hostel for twenty-five women students of the Japan Women's University. A former lecturer in biology at Newnham College, Cambridge, Phillips now taught science and English. Caroline approved of Phillips's report on hostels and used it in her own efforts to promote them.[25]

Hostels, it was argued, created a favourable environment for evangelism while providing young women with physical and moral protection that allowed them to study with maximum efficiency. Experience had shown that in a hostel under Christian auspices a majority of the students would be non-Christians but most would voluntarily join a Bible class. Personal contact with the director of the hostel, ideally a missionary working with a Japanese assistant, and the 'Christian atmosphere' of community life provided the setting for training in Christian character. Many parents would send their daughters to hostels run by foreigners 'for the sake of the English teaching or to have them under the best influence,' often thought to be Christian, although few parents wanted their children to become Christians.[26]

So great was the need for housing for women students that in the autumn of 1905 Caroline had eight students living with her. This was only possible because she had recently rented a large house at 15 Dote Sanbanchō in Kōjimachi ward. In addition to her own living quarters, the old western-style house provided offices and meeting rooms for the YWCA and a large hall for a student dormitory. In the next three years some thirty women students stayed with her for varying periods of time, an arrangement that contributed much to her understanding of the lives of young women.[27] Meanwhile the Tokyo Association established a dormitory committee chaired by Mrs. Carlisle T. Hibbard, wife of one of the American YMCA secretaries. With her Caroline 'walked the town' asking Japanese business-men for donations to guarantee the rent of a temporary hostel until a more permanent structure could be built. The two women were pushed into this role because Japanese women in the association were convinced it was impossible for them to raise money. Fortunately, the men, most of whom were already supporters of the YMCA, needed little persuasion and responded so generously that by the spring of 1906 a temporary hostel hous-ing twenty-four young women was open.[28]

Another 'Y' tradition in other countries, the summer conference, also seemed adaptable to Japanese conditions. In 1905 some thirty-five girls had attended the summer conference of the YMCA, and the success of the experiment had heightened feeling among some of the missionaries that the time was ripe for a girls' conference. To Caroline it seemed a great leap of faith to launch the venture so soon, but shortly she and Kawai Michi were planning a program very like the conferences they had attended in North America. Thus in the summer of 1906, 160 girls from twenty-six mission and government schools, most of them Christians, attended the five-day confer-ence held at the Methodist girls' school, Aoyama Jogakuin, in Tokyo.

The content of the program revealed the priorities of the planners for the education of young women in Japan. Every day there was Bible study led by Dr. Motoda of the Episcopal Church and Rev. Hata Shōkichi, a recent graduate of Princeton Theological Seminary. 'Internationalism' was strongly represented by Dr. Ibuka Kajinosuke, a Presbyterian and vice-presi-dent of the World's Student Christian Federation, who spoke on student work elsewhere. Tomeoka Kōsuke gave an account of his pioneering prison work, while writer and educator Ebara Soroku, a Methodist and one of the first Christians elected to the Diet (where he still sat), spoke on Korea. Shimada Saburō, liberal politician and editor and also an original member of the Diet, rejoiced in the expansion of educational opportunities for Japanese women and exhorted his audience to recognize their mission to their sisters in China, Korea, and Siam, beginning with those who were coming in increasing numbers to study in Japan. Kozaki Chiyo, wife of a leading Congregational minister in Tokyo, had just returned from the United States and gave a talk on 'Ideals of Home Life in America,' while Dr. Inoue Tomo, one of the few women doctors in Japan, directed recreation and led discussions on student health. Music, under the direction of a young Japanese woman who had studied at the New England Conservatory of Music in Boston, was devoted mainly to the singing of American camping and college songs. Of course there was 'stunt night' when the Japanese students demonstrated at least as much imagination and sense of the ridiculous as their counterparts in North America. More seriously, under the leadership of Tsuda Ume and Kawai Michi, practical student problems and the role of the YWCA in meeting them were discussed. All concerned agreed that the conference had been a decided success and that it must become an annual event.[29]

■ ■ ■

DESPITE HER LARGE ROLE in planning that first summer conference, Caroline was not present but was 'gadding around England,' as she said. That had not been her first choice, and it was only after much soul-searching that she accepted the invitation of the World's Committee of the YWCA to attend its Third World Conference in Paris. Her decision owed much to an agreement that following the conference she would spend some time in Britain and North America raising money for student hostels in Tokyo. Moreover, it was fortunate that someone was available to take over Caroline's work with the national committee, especially the organization of the summer conference. Stella Fisher, the daughter of Caroline's friends Galen and Ella Fisher, had just graduated from the University of Chicago and was in Japan visiting her parents. She had YWCA experience and was willing to help out for six months.[30]

Thus in late April 1906, eighteen months after her arrival in Japan, Caroline sailed for Europe via the Suez Canal on a North German Lloyd line ship, arriving in Paris for the conference in the third week of May. It was stimulating to be among YWCA secretaries and members from many countries. Although the meetings reflected the strength of the 'Y' in the English-speaking world, there were good delegations from several European countries, and with representatives from India, China, and Japan, Asia was more fully involved than ever before. Caroline reported to the World's Committee that there were now eight associations in the Japanese YWCA, five of them organized in the past year, with a total membership of about 500. Four of them, in mission schools for girls in Osaka, Yokohama, Tokyo, and Sendai, were specifically student associations. The others in Tokyo, Yokohama, Tokushima, and Hakodate were in principle city-wide associations but were working almost entirely with students. Before the meetings ended, the Japanese YWCA was formally welcomed into affiliation with the World's Committee.[31]

At the age of thirty-one Caroline was in Europe for the first time, but there was little opportunity for sightseeing. Immediately after the conference she travelled to London with staff and members of the British YWCA and spent several weeks learning about the activities of the 'Y' there, and becoming more familiar with the staff and work of the London headquarters of the World's Committee. This was 'a liberal education in many ways,' Caroline wrote, 'and in nothing more than in the fact that I learned to appreciate the British way of looking at things.' Later she felt that this facilitated her relations with English missionaries in Japan, some of whom she already assessed highly as 'trumps.'[32]

The most immediate and tangible result of her visit to Britain was financial. As promised, the World's Committee introduced Caroline to prospective contributors to the hostel fund. Especially important was the beginning of her association with Lady Overtoun, the wife of John Campbell White, Baron Overtoun of Glasgow. Lord Overtoun was one of Scotland's wealthiest industrialists, a leading layman of the United Free Church, and famed as a philanthropist and revivalist speaker. He was also one of the most bitterly hated employers in Britain, thanks to his Draconian treatment of the workers in his vast chemical industry.[33] Persuaded of the need for a student hostel in Tokyo, Lord and Lady Overtoun made a substantial contribution, a sum later augmented by a smaller sum from the Association of Women Teachers of Britain. Now Caroline had enough for one hostel.[34]

In the summer of 1906, Caroline sailed from Liverpool to Montreal and was soon promoting hostels, with most notable success among her friends in

Ottawa. After several weeks visiting her family in Wingham, she set out in early autumn on a speaking tour of New England women's colleges. Financially, her visit to Vassar was the most productive, for the faculty and students there undertook to raise $600. She also had the promise of a generous contribution from a recent Vassar graduate, Mary Borden, whom Caroline had met in New York before she went to Japan, and who was now about to go to India with her missionary husband. More important in the long run was Caroline's renewal of her acquaintance with Mary's well-to-do mother, Mrs. William Borden, in whose Poughkeepsie, New York, home Caroline was a guest for several days.[35]

Early in November 1906 Caroline was back in Tokyo after an absence of seven months. The Tokyo committee was exhilarated by the news that she had raised enough money to build and equip two hostels. As she had often explained to foreigners, it cost only $15 to furnish a room for three girls, since Japanese living required almost no furniture, and contributions would therefore be used mainly for the basic building of the hostels. Within two weeks of her return she had brought together several men well known in Christian and educational circles to act as an advisory committee in the search for land for the hostels. In the meantime it was gratifying to learn that the temporary hostel was working well and that all the girls, of whom only four were Christians, were attending a Bible class.

Moreover, the hostel was receiving favourable comment in the secular Tokyo press, including public commendation from the chief of police in one of the congested student sections of the city, who deplored the dangers to which young women students, without friends or relatives in the city, were exposed. For him the solution lay in 'dormitories under responsible management,' and he welcomed the one recently established in Dote Sanbanchō 'by certain eminent Christian ladies' who 'are doing their utmost to care for the moral welfare of the girls ... without controlling them simply by arbitrary rules.'[36]

Caroline continued to make her own personal dint in the housing problem, and five women students lived with her this year. Given the continuing difficulty in making contacts in Japan Women's University, she was pleased that one was a student in that institution, especially as one of her teachers assured Macdonald that she was not only 'the strongest Christian in the school ... but was also the leading girl in other things as well.'[37]

■ ■ ■

SCARCELY HAD CAROLINE RETURNED from abroad than she was plunged into planning for the first international conference of any kind ever held in Japan. She shared the belief of other Christians that the gathering of the World's Student Christian Federation (WSCF), which would bring student leaders and speakers from many countries to Tokyo in the spring of 1907, would have an important evangelistic and ecumenical impact on students and on the whole Japanese church. The delegates were to speak both before and after the conference in centres throughout the country. In chairing the committee charged with arranging the itineraries of the close to a hundred women delegates, Caroline 'nearly lived in a jinrikisha for months going to see ... all sorts and conditions of people ... in all parts of the city from the Minister of Education up & down' about matters relating to the conference. In addition there was a large volume of correspondence about these arrangements. All this, as well as the regular activities of the association, was handled by Macdonald and Stella Fisher, now a full-time staff member, and a secretary, Wakuyama Komako. Kawai Michi, despite her full-time teaching at Tsuda College, volunteered endless hours of work to ensure the success of the conference.[38]

A pre-conference visitor, although not a participant in the WSCF gathering, was General William Booth, head of the worldwide Salvation Army, which had begun work in Japan a decade earlier. Thanks to the remarkable organizing and oratorical skills of its leader, Yamamuro Gunpei, the Salvation Army had grown rapidly and was well known. That, and popular interest in prominent figures from the western world, explained why Booth moved about Japan in something close to a royal procession, speaking at events that both astonished and amused Caroline. At Tokyo's Waseda University, for instance, Booth addressed 10,000 students at an open air meeting presided over by Count Ōkuma, founder and chancellor of the university. A Waseda faculty member reported to Caroline that Booth 'gave them the pure unadulterated gospel.' While she applauded the Salvation Army's good works, especially its war against prostitution, Caroline, like many Protestants everywhere, had reservations about its evangelistic methods. Nevertheless, she approved of the presence of five prominent ministers from as many denominations on Booth's platform at a large meeting sponsored by the YMCA: 'It illustrates the united front which is more & more being shown here,' as 'we are all working for the same end.'[39]

The breadth of the united front was evident at a meeting for students in a Tokyo theatre when General Booth and Dr. Nitobe Inazō spoke from the same platform. In the year the Meiji constitution was promulgated, Nitobe had returned from studies in the United States with a Philadelphia Quaker wife and a Ph.D. from Johns Hopkins. Now, at the age of 45, he was one of Japan's best-known writers and educators, currently the principal of the First Higher School in Tokyo, from which a large proportion of the students of Tokyo Imperial University were selected. Caroline's meeting with the Nitobes soon after her arrival in Tokyo was the beginning of a lifelong friendship. She already admired Nitobe and knew him well enough to realize that the mere thought of his sharing a platform with General Booth would 'make your hair stand on end. He's a Quaker & a Samurai of the Samurai. It illustrates ... that ... Christian men believe in uniting in all that makes for the highest things, & it was extremely interesting to see such extremes meet at an *evangelistic* meeting & a Salvation Army one at that.' She was sure that Nitobe was 'a fine antidote' to Booth's emotional appeal, for he had told the students 'that religion was neither a matter of feeling or intellect, but a matter of will.' The next day she joked with Nitobe that she had heard 'he was going to join the *army*! He screamed with delight.'⁴⁰

Soon there were overseas visitors with whom Caroline felt more affinity than with General Booth. They included Ruth Rouse, the able Oxford graduate and former secretary of the British Student Christian Movement who had recently become the first secretary of the WSCF to have special responsibility for work among women students around the world; and Clarissa Spencer, secretary of the World's Committee of the YWCA. Spencer, a graduate of Goucher College in Baltimore, had earlier spent five years in Japan as a Methodist missionary and had a fair command of the Japanese language. Rouse visited a number of girls' schools prior to the conference to encourage interest in the YWCA, as did Spencer, Una Saunders of the British YWCA, and other women delegates from many countries.⁴¹

Her association with Rouse and Saunders and other delegates from England enhanced Caroline's recently acquired regard for the skills and outlook of British leaders: 'The English women are simply scrumptuous [*sic*]. The American women haven't been in it in this conference. I haven't Anglo-phobia either,' she reported when it was all over. When 'she set these English people on the [American] Episcopalians,' they were so effective that she predicted that schools sponsored by the American Episcopal church would soon have more branches of the YWCA than any others. For

Caroline, this was a most satisfying example of the international cooperation and influence she hoped the WSCF conference would foster.[42]

The decision to bring together in Tokyo more than 600 delegates from twenty-five countries, most of them Asian Christians, including some 300 Japanese, was a piece of missionary strategy that owed much to American Methodist layman John R. Mott, general secretary of the WSCF and the leading figure in the Protestant missionary movement. Mott had a strong conviction that Japan was the key to Christianizing Asia. Although China was a larger mission field, Japan's rapid industrialization and increasing political power made it an unequalled centre of influence in Asia. In two visits to Japan during the past decade, Mott had spoken to thousands of Japanese students, had observed the forces of modernization at work in the country, and had recognized that, in contrast to the situation in China, Christianity was having a considerable impact on intellectuals. By the time the WSCF conference in Tokyo was being organized, Japan's strategic position had been magnified by the presence of some 10,000 Chinese students in Japan, encouraged to study abroad by the abolition of China's traditional examination system. 'The key to China is in Tokyo,' Mott declared, for many future leaders of China would come from this group of overseas students.[43]

Caroline Macdonald and the other planners of the Tokyo conference hoped that while furthering the ecumenical interests of the WSCF the gathering would also make a strong impact on an educated Japanese public curious about Christianity's impact on the progress of the West. The achievement of this objective was not left to chance but was carefully organized by the planning committee. Thus widespread publicity was accorded the welcome given the conference by leading Japanese officials, none of them Christians. The governor of Tokyo prefecture, Viscount Hayashi Tadasu, received the delegates on a conference platform overhung by a large white silk banner upon which a rising sun radiated rays of light and a red cross stood over the motto *Unum in Christo*. Welcoming addresses were given by the mayor of Tokyo, Ozaki Yukio, by Baron Gotō Shimpei, president of the South Manchurian Railway, and by Count Ōkuma, who declared that if Christianity were to prevail in the Orient it must do so 'by the might of the Japanese people.'[44] Although this came close to what Mott and others thought, the Swedish chairman of the WSCF, Karl Fries, in his reply to Ōkuma felt impelled to point out that the student federation only recognized the leadership of a Divine Master and sought 'to extend his

gracious dominion over the hearts of students of all nations and races.'
Nevertheless, throughout the conference there was direct and indirect
acknowledgment of Japan as the dominant power in the Orient.[45]

After the Tokyo meetings some twenty teams composed of foreign and
Japanese participants in the conference visited student centres throughout
the country for a round of welcoming ceremonies from government officials
and evangelistic meetings attended by thousands of students whom Mott
judged 'the most open-minded in the world.' Altogether, Mott concluded
that the WSCF visit to Japan had been 'the most significant and potential
event' in his twenty years of work with students and concurred in the judgment of a missionary that the conference and the evangelistic campaign
constituted 'the heaviest single blow ever struck by united Christianity in the
non-Christian world.'[46]

A Japanese assessment of the conference and its aftermath was more
restrained but entirely positive. Honda Yōichi, just elected first bishop of the
new united Methodist church of Japan, believed that the conference had
gone a long way in breaking down prejudice against Christianity among
Japanese educators and government leaders, in opening Japanese Christians
to the reality of their ties with Christians in other lands, and to 'a sense of
their prestige in the Far East somewhat corresponding to the political prestige the nation enjoys,' a prestige Honda saw as reason both for gratification
and for sober reflection.[47]

For Caroline and her YWCA associates an important feature of the
WSCF conference was its recognition, albeit more verbal than practical, of
the growing importance of work among women students. In no country
were women attending universities or colleges in numbers even approach-
ing male enrolments, but clearly the steady increase warranted giving more
attention to women students. Caroline would have rejoiced to have at her
disposal even a tenth of the resources commanded by the YMCA in Japan,
for it now had fifteen Japanese and six foreign secretaries and a new building
to house the Tokyo association, including the biggest auditorium in the city,
seating 1,000. Another building was under construction in Kyoto. Further,
Mott had just announced a gift of $50,000 for the building of hostels for
men at Waseda and Tokyo Imperial universities, a sum that was shortly doubled to provide hostels at other universities. With his highly developed
fundraising abilities, John R. Mott enjoyed over many years the generous
backing of wealthy Americans such as John D. Rockefeller, Jr., John A.

Wanamaker, and Cyrus McCormick, Jr. and his mother; few projects on which Mott set his heart went unfunded.[48] The YMCA was much closer to his heart than the YWCA, for he perceived men as the creators of the future, a bias that explains Caroline's limited appreciation of Mott and his work.[49]

While the WSCF conference did nothing to augment the YWCA's financial resources, it greatly increased interest in the association. After the conference more than a hundred girls from Tokyo schools joined Bible study classes, giving the Tokyo association a far wider contact with students than before. In Tsuda College the students now requested the formation of a branch of the YWCA there, a student initiative that Tsuda, Macdonald, and others had been awaiting for some time. This expansion underlined the need for a secretary who would work exclusively with the Tokyo association and for a centre for its activities. Macdonald now increased her campaign with the World's Committee and the Foreign Department of the American 'Y' for the early appointment of a Tokyo secretary and for a building in the near future.[50]

The appointment of a staff person to work in Tokyo was essential not only for the advancement of the work: Caroline feared that without rein-forcements 'somebody will be dead before you know it.' She was studying Japanese in class for nine hours a week and was teaching at Tsuda College for another nine hours, including the leadership of the YWCA Bible class there. This last assignment put her in touch with most of the students in the school, now numbering about 150. Caroline knew that in teaching at Tsuda College she was contributing to a pioneer work of unique importance in the education of Japanese women; she hoped she was also helping to build the future leadership of the YWCA.[51]

Then there were all the hours needed 'to build dormitories, hold com-mittee meetings, make investigations, write reports, do one's duty socially as ... one must do here, among the Japanese especially, study for the classes one has, run a monthly magazine, develop leaders, keep house which con-sists of six students as well as my honoured self, entertain people, and gener-ally be a person of affairs.' Admittedly she did not do everything alone, and there were servants in the house, but she felt under constant pressure about what went undone. The situation would become easier when more women were familiar with the principles and methods of the YWCA, but so far there were only two or three members of the national committee who had any background in 'Y' work. At this experimental stage, with 'a constituency which is for the most part made up of school girls,' it was impossible to act on the urging of the Foreign Department of the American Association to hold a national convention and adopt a definite constitution.[52]

For the time being Caroline's most pressing task was finding additional funds for the two student hostels. The money raised in Britain and North America had been contributed only for the buildings and their furnishings, on condition that money for the land be found in Japan. The prospects were poor. Not only did the economic slump at the end of the war with Russia put many potential donors in a less-than-generous mood but the number of women students coming to Tokyo to study was declining, so that some of the few existing hostels were not full to capacity. Macdonald and her dormitory committee insisted that this circumstance would change very shortly and therefore they pushed ahead with their plans. The Tokyo Association managed to borrow 5,000 yen to buy the Andōzaka site of the temporary dormitory for one hostel, but the second would have been delayed indefinitely had not Macdonald's American friend, Mrs. Borden, come to Japan on a round-the-world trip and given 5,000 yen for the purchase of land at Nandochō.[53]

The second summer conference of the YWCA was held in July 1907, with a substantial increase in attendance and a strong international emphasis that reflected the continuing influence of the recent WSCF gathering. Afterwards Caroline spent five weeks as a guest of the Fishers in Karuizawa, the mountain resort 160 kilometres north of Tokyo where foreign diplomats and missionaries escaped from the summer heat of Tokyo.[54] In her first taste of the delights of this retreat, Caroline was more attracted by the physical beauty of the place than by the pleasures of social life. Feeling that she 'lived at a frightfully high tension ... when at work,' she rejoiced in the relaxation afforded by hikes to scenic attractions in the area. One highlight was an expedition with a small group that set out on horseback after midnight to ride thirteen kilometres to the foot of Mt. Asama. After a four-hour, lantern-lit climb up a steep path, the group arrived at the top of the mountain in time to see the sunrise and gaze into an active volcano. From the summit, more than 2,400 metres above sea level and 1,500 metres above Karuizawa, 'it seemed as the mist cleared ... we saw everything on earth. And towering above all ... 75 miles distant the faint outline of Fuji, outlined in a faintly deeper blue against the sky.'[55]

From the beginning Caroline's view of the social scene in Karuizawa was ambivalent. While she enjoyed staying with the Fishers, next summer she hoped for a shorter stay in a house to herself where social duties could be kept to a minimum. 'There's too big a crowd,' mainly 'shoals of missionaries,' she complained. However, she had to be there for a while as 'we have to cultivate the missionaries to some extent' to secure their support for the YWCA. There were few Japanese in Karuizawa, except in a hostel for the staff of the Japan Women's University, among whom she hoped to make some strategic connections. In her view 'a sprinkling would ... be a decided advantage.' Whatever the limitations of Karuizawa, the cool weather was a boon and she returned to Tokyo well rested and 'eager to be back in the fray,' determined above all to study Japanese in the coming year with 'might and main,' for unless she mastered the language she was certainly 'doomed.'[56]

Caroline's dedication to achieving proficiency in Japanese reflected her growing identification with Japan and her belief that her life's work was to be there. One source of this feeling was her increasing involvement in the Japanese church. Through her leadership of the young men's Bible class in Ichibanchō Presbyterian church, she was associated from the beginning with a Japanese congregation whose minister, the Reverend Uemura Masahisa, was Japan's leading Presbyterian clergyman and theologian and a major force in Japanese Protestantism. In 1906 Uemura and his congregation built a new church in Fujimichō district, and shortly Caroline joined that congregation where she was one of the few foreigners among its nearly one thousand members. Her association with Uemura and a congregation that included many government bureaucrats as well as professional and business men and their families, typical of the growing urban middle class to whom Christianity continued to make its greatest appeal in Japan, was a definitive step in her life.

Uemura Masahisa (1858-1925) grew up in a poor samurai family and later became one of the ablest and most zealous members of 'the Yokohama band.'[57] A voracious reader, well versed in Japanese history and classical literature, Uemura declined scholarships to Princeton and Columbia universities, preferring to satisfy his curiosity about other societies by taking a trip around the world in 1888. Increasingly he came to see Japanese traditions as the 'Old Testament' for Japanese, a preparation for the unique revelation of the Christian gospel.

When Caroline first knew Uemura he was not yet fifty years old and at the height of his powers. Always a believer in a church that would speak to the nation of its true destiny, Uemura had attracted considerable public attention, notably over his support of Uchimura Kanzō in the 'disloyalty incident' of 1891. He had used the continuing controversy to argue that 'moral education,' as advocated by the minister of education and other supporters of the famous Rescript on Education, would destroy the nation. Uemura exhorted Christians to show their country that life lived under the grace of the God revealed in Christ was the true basis of morality and patriotism.

Two years later Uemura was prominent in another controversy related to the loyalty of Christians. It centred around Tamura Naomi, the pastor of a Tokyo church who had studied in the United States for four years in the 1880s and had published a book in Japanese on American women. His discussion of the differences in the expectations of Japanese and American brides and in their later status as wives and mothers, his advocacy of equality between the sexes in 'the new home,' and of the same standards of chastity and faithfulness for both men and women, as well as his contention that Christianity was the only force that could raise the status of women, were well received by many Japanese who accepted such changes as part of the westernization of their society. Attitudes shifted dramatically when *The Japanese Bride* was published in English in New York. There was an outcry in the press throughout the country and the government moved to stop distribution of the English edition in Japan. Uemura Masahisa was the first and most vociferous among the many Christians who denounced the book on the grounds that it was based on false information, and was unfair, unpatriotic, and anti-Christian. Uemura went so far as to say that even if everything in the book were true, it was wrong for Tamura to put his country to shame in the eyes of foreigners and to jeopardize the future of the church. For his refusal to 'repent' despite threats to his life, Tamura was ejected from his pastorate by the General Assembly of the Japanese Presbyterian church over the protests of its missionary members. The core of the problem for Uemura and other Christians was not so much Tamura's views, with which they were in general agreement, but rather their own need to demonstrate their loyalty to emperor and nation in a time of rampant nationalism. That need was reinforced by an emotional commitment to traditional family customs and ethics, although many Christians, including Uemura, had ceased to live according to tradition.[58]

Uemura's national pride was also at least partly responsible for the vigorous leadership he gave to the movement to secure the autonomy of the

Japanese church from the jurisdiction of foreign mission boards and missionaries. Not long before Caroline's arrival in Tokyo, Uemura had shown his independence by resigning from his position as a teacher of theology at the Presbyterian college, Meiji Gakuin, when a missionary there objected that the text Uemura used in systematic theology was too liberal.[59] Uemura proceeded to establish his own theological seminary, Tokyo Shingakusha, which flourished without financial support or faculty from overseas.

The conservatism of those who thought his ideas too liberal may be judged by Uemura's record as a consistent defender of classical Protestant orthodoxy. When Caroline arrived in Japan memories were still fresh of the most famous debate in the history of Japanese Christianity, one which had contributed much to the education of Japanese Christians and aroused considerable interest among a wider public. In this encounter, which began in 1901 and continued for two years, Uemura set forth his position against that of Ebina Danjō, a scholarly and more liberal Congregationalist who, like Uemura, ministered to a large congregation in the student quarter of the city. Unlike the unconventional, brusque, square-jawed, and rather rough-looking Uemura who exuded a sense of masculine power, Ebina was slim, elegantly dressed, eloquent, and charming. Ebina emphasized Jesus as teacher and moral example, while Uemura stressed the absolute deity of Christ and humanity's need for a redeemer and saviour. Caroline's membership in Uemura's congregation kept her within the liberal evangelical tradition in which she had been reared.

Although Uemura was theologically orthodox and in some respects became more conservative politically with the passage of time, his deeply held conviction about the essential worth of every person led him to a genuine acceptance of anyone he encountered, regardless of social status, wealth, or education. Nowhere did this egalitarianism cut through the rigidities and conventions of tradition more than in his attitudes toward women, beginning with his wife. Yamanouchi Sueyno, a graduate of the missionary-sponsored Ferris Girls' School in Yokohama, had received an excellent education worthy of her natural abilities. The couple began their life together with a marriage contract, unusual at the time. Uemura, refusing to use the customary *gusai* (foolish wife), always addressed his wife as *kensai* (wise wife). His letters to her were 'rare specimens for the time ... sensitive, poetic,' with extended discussions of a range of ideas.[60] The Uemuras had no sons, but their three daughters enjoyed an education appropriate for the independent women both parents wanted them to be. While Caroline had reservations that she would soon express about some aspects of the feminist movement, whether in Japan or elsewhere, she found Uemura admirable on this as on so many other counts.

■ ■ ■

MACDONALD'S GROWING INVOLVEMENT with the community of Japanese Christians made her increasingly appreciative of the problems facing Japanese society and its leaders. One aspect of this was her acceptance of Japanese objectives in Korea, an attitude shared by the vast majority of missionaries in Japan and by Japanese Christians. Since the end of the Russo-Japanese war, Japan had gradually extended its control in Korea until 1907, when it declared Korea a protectorate, a move that precipitated a good deal of objection in the West. One source of vigorous criticism was the Presbyterian Church in Canada, which had done substantial missionary work in Korea but none in Japan.

Macdonald's wrath was aroused by two comments in the pages of the *Presbyterian*, the official weekly publication of the Presbyterian Church in Canada. One was by its editor, the Reverend Malcolm Macgregor, the other a letter from the Reverend Dr. R.P. Mackay, secretary of the church's Foreign Mission Committee.[61] Professing to believe that her 'fierce invectives' were not suitable for publication in the church magazine or might cause personal offence to its editor, Caroline chose to address her observations to her friend the Reverend J.A. Macdonald, former editor of the *Presbyterian* and now editor of the Toronto *Globe*. Or was she guided by a different reasoning? Perhaps it was more useful to try to influence the editor of a major daily newspaper who still had impeccable Presbyterian connections than to deal with the church paper itself?

Macdonald objected strenuously to the editorial in the *Presbyterian*, which had asserted that 'any unbiased person would admit that the rule of Japan in Korea had been a failure.' Equally objectionable was Mackay's description of Japan as a nation of 'barbarians' and his declaration that 'Britishers' ought to be ashamed of the Anglo-Japanese alliance. In reply, Caroline observed that 'one lives very comfortably and safely in this "barbarian" land' and suggested that 'some of us Britishers ... may feel that the Japanese have almost as much right to blush for their connection with the British.' Referring to recent anti-Oriental riots in her homeland, in

Vancouver, she noted that it was 'Britishers' who had created that 'horrifying spectacle,' while in Japan 'we have never heard that any mob of Japanese have [*sic*] ever pitched helpless foreigners into the sea.'[62]

Launching into an appeal for sympathy for Japan, Macdonald told the Toronto editor: "There isn't a nation on earth ... that has so many problems, moral, intellectual, religious, international ... and there is not another nation that ... has ever struggled more bravely to work them out to some solution.' Japan's rapid emergence as an industrial nation was creating profound moral and religious problems: 'The swing away from the old restraints, the groping for the new ... the necessity for a moral education ... and what that is to be: the Imperial Rescript, the philosophy of Buddhism, loyalty to the Imperial House, sheer plain Stoicism, or the religion of Jesus Christ.'[63]

To those who condemned Japan for its role in Korea, Macdonald pointed out that 'Korea has already embroiled Japan in two wars, and ... cannot govern herself.' After only two years it was 'ridiculous' to say whether Japanese rule in Korea was a success or a failure.[64]

Macdonald had a strong suspicion that the views of many critics of Japan were rooted in a feeling of racial superiority: 'It is hard to inculcate into the Anglo-Saxon consciousness the fact that any other shade of complexion than the white is capable of high ideals and lofty thoughts.' It was 'too late to talk about white man's countries, comparisons between Japanese and negroes, and exclusions and restrictions, etc. These imaginary millions of Orientals, which in the brains of some are already streaming into the prairies of the great west, make a very fine appeal to the sense of the ridiculous.' She believed most Orientals would stay in Asia![65]

Macdonald rejected any suggestion that she thought Japan 'perfect or superior': neither was it 'potentially inferior.' She was simply arguing 'that the gospel of sympathy needs to be preached in our own lands if the people of the East are to see in Christ ... the Desire of all Nations.' Her heart ached when she heard foreigners in Japan making 'unkind, unsympathetic remarks about our "Eastern friends,"' all of which might be true but 'they are unkind, and for the most part, unnecessary.' After five solid typewritten pages of 'unbottling,' Caroline assured the editor of the *Globe*, perhaps with mock modesty, that she would not want him to think that she pretended to know anything about politics; she was only 'trying to see the few things I do see from the standpoint of the land in which I live, and ... of the religion I profess to believe.'[66]

How much effect did Macdonald have on either of the editors she hoped to influence? For whatever reason, the *Presbyterian* had nothing to say about Korea for many weeks, while the scant attention given the subject by the *Globe* was moderate in tone. However uncertain the impact of her effort to educate Canadian Presbyterians about Japan, it is clear that in less than three years she had come to share substantially in the aspirations of her adopted country.

Chapter 4

From Tokyo to Aberdeen: 'The Lady Student'

'I've DREAMED & SLEPT & travelled dormitories for the last ten years, and now please God, we are going to see them no longer castles in the air. I could dance a jig whenever I think that we are really in a position to build.'[1] Caroline's elation was tempered by the realization that continuing inflation since the end of the war with Russia had increased the cost of the dormitories by 25 per cent over the original estimate. The effort to raise funds in Japan for the purchase of land had been disappointing and it was necessary to borrow 7,000 yen ($3,500 Cdn.), but Caroline was confident this could be repaid before long. She was 'counting on the return of Baroness Gotō to do wonders for us.' Baron Gotō Shimpei, president of the South Manchurian Railway, was 'very wealthy & one of the really *great* men in Japan.' On her current trip abroad the baroness, a Baptist, was being 'wined and dined by various YWCA people in both the States and England ... We hope she'll adopt the YW as her pet ... and if she does we'll get money, not only from the Baron, but he will interest others. So we're laying [*sic*] low, & hoping and praying,'[2] a strategy that apparently failed.

At the beginning of September 1908, the first hostel, built for twenty but actually now housing thirty-two young women, was opened with speeches from Count Ōkuma, Dr. Nitobe, and Miss Tsuda. A few days earlier, another of Caroline's hopes was realized when the new secretary of the Tokyo YWCA arrived. Margaret Matthew, a graduate of the University of California, who had experience in student work, would not officially assume her position until she had completed a year of language study, but for Caroline her arrival was assurance of fresh resources and an immediate addition to her circle of friends.

Within nine months the second hostel, sometimes known as 'the Ottawa' because of the source of most of its funding, was ready for occupancy. At the opening ceremony, a letter from the minister of education was read, urging the YWCA to continue placing these 'paradises' in the student sections of Tokyo. In praising the hostels as centres for 'the inculcation of virtue and education,'[3] the minister demonstrated how the concern of Japanese leaders for 'moral education' opened doors for Christian schools and agencies such as the YWCA and the YMCA. Caroline lived in the new hostel with forty students for the first three weeks, an enjoyable and useful experience, until a suitable Japanese matron was found.[4]

Once established, the hostels would be self-supporting, drawing their revenue from rental fees paid by the residents. It was soon evident that hostels could be operated efficiently on terms consistent with YWCA objectives. There were more applicants than could be accommodated, and both Bible classes and English classes were well attended, the former the more popular. The two were separate, in keeping with the 'Y' principle that participation in Bible study should always be voluntary and not a condition of learning English. Within two years the Christians among the residents had begun to conduct Sunday schools in the neighbourhoods of the hostels, thus providing the 'Y' with another form of outreach in the community.[5] This early experience confirmed Caroline's belief that hostels were an effective means of reaching students and that it was vital to have a mixture of Christian and non-Christian students in the residences. Otherwise, 'there is a tendency to imagine that the hostel is a closed community for Christian self-culture. They must have a stimulus of having non-Christians to work for, or the hostel will cease to be Christian because selfish.'[6]

With two hostels established in Tokyo, the national committee responded, within its limited resources, to requests from numerous other centres for help in organizing associations and programs. Caroline accepted a long-standing invitation to visit Hiroshima, an important military and economic centre in southern Japan and site of the largest mission school for girls in the country. The Hiroshima Girls School, sponsored by American Methodists, was largely the creation of its able and determined principal, Nannie B. Gaines, who was eager to have the YWCA in the school. Caroline also visited two 'excellent' government schools for girls. Naturally she had no entry to the three girls' schools recently established by a vigorous Buddhist sect. As elsewhere, Buddhists in Hiroshima had established schools, including the equivalent of Sunday schools, modelled largely on Christian institutions and intended to compete with them.[7]

Caroline's later visits to Kyoto and Osaka confirmed interest in the YWCA there, as did her second visit to Sendai, the growing military and educational centre in northern Honshu. Caroline would have liked to station a trained 'Y' secretary in each of these cities and several other 'open fields,' but none was available. All she could do was help to form local groups, explain the process of affiliation with the national committee, and urge the attendance of student leaders at the annual summer conference.[8]

A promise of fresh resources came when Caroline acquired a new friend in Emma Kaufman, a twenty-eight-year-old Canadian from Berlin (later Kitchener), Ontario. Kaufman came to Japan early in 1909 on a tour of the Orient and remained for six months to teach English at Tsuda College. The daughter of E.R. Kaufman, president of the large rubber manufacturing firm bearing his name, and of Mary Kaufman, first president of the recently organized YWCA in Berlin, Emma Kaufman had studied in the newly established Faculty of Household Science in the University of Toronto, then at the Methodist Training School for deaconesses, and for another year at Teachers College, New York. There was no pressure on Kaufman from her wealthy family to be gainfully employed, but a strong exposure to evangelical ideals of Christian service precluded a life of idleness. Although Kaufman knew that the Canadian YWCA supported Caroline, the two women had never met. Caroline's youngest sister, Nellie, married to a young banker, C.L. Laing, lived in Berlin and was a member of the board of the YWCA, and that was another, more personal connection.

Kaufman soon came to appreciate Caroline's work and was increasingly caught up in her new friend's aspirations for the women of Japan. Not long before her departure, Kaufman asked a question Caroline had waited many weeks to hear: If Kaufman were to return to Japan, would there be a position for her as a volunteer member of the YWCA staff?

Caroline's answer was immediate and enthusiastic, and Kaufman agreed to come soon.[9] Emma Kaufman had found her vocation, and Caroline and the Japanese YWCA a lifelong benefactor.

In the autumn of 1909, when the fiftieth anniversary of the beginning of Protestant missions in Japan was being celebrated with a week-long conference, Caroline chaired a committee charged with planning a special day devoted to recognition of work by women and for women. She took on this task with alacrity as an opportunity to learn more about 'Christian women throughout the Empire' and to correct a grave fault in most missionary reports where 'women's work as a rule does not bulk large,' giving the false impression that 'the world was being evangelized by men!' In Japan, as in most other mission fields, women missionaries outnumbered men by a substantial margin. 'Women's Day' fulfilled Caroline's hopes, and one Japanese newspaper judged it the most interesting feature of the celebration.[10]

After five years of service overseas, YWCA secretaries were eligible to go home on furlough; at the end of 1909 Caroline was beginning to anticipate her leave. Looking back, she concluded that 'very little had been accomplished during the last five years,' although fourteen student associations and four more general groups now existed with a total membership of 1,200. That figure would have been larger had she made rapid expansion the primary objective. She still felt that in a new country it was prudent to act with restraint: 'The danger is that we do too much and learn too little ... concerning the great issues of life ... among other peoples.' The major achievement of these first years was the establishment of 'the confidence and trust of a growing band of Japanese men and women and many missionaries,' a solid foundation for the future.[11] What Caroline had learned had come mainly from friends, including young men and women in her Bible classes, a few select missionaries, especially Galen Fisher of the YMCA, and older Japanese mentors, notably Tsuda Ume, Uemura Masahisa, and Nitobe Inazō.

Before leaving Tokyo, Caroline was challenged to put into writing her views on the education of women in Japan when she was asked to prepare a paper on the subject for the World Missionary Conference in Edinburgh the following summer. Since the WSCF conference in Tokyo in 1907, John R. Mott had been travelling the world laying the groundwork for a conference of leaders of foreign missionary forces that would develop a strategy for the evangelization of the non-Christian world. Reports were being prepared for consideration by eight study commissions on various aspects of the missionary movement. Caroline's submission, in answer to a series of questions, was a document for the use of the Commission on 'Education in Relation to the Christianization of National Life.'[12]

In effect this was an exposition of Caroline's philosophy of missions after five years in a non-Christian society. For her, education was the essential foundation for the building of the Christian community in any country. The long-term missionary objective – the Christianization of a whole society – involved more than the conversion of individuals to a new set of religious beliefs: 'It means the gradual substitution of a new background, a new outlook, a deeper conception of ... reality.' Without sound educational foundations, evangelism would 'produce superficial Christian character and with it the propagation of superstition rather than truth.' The belief that 'religion is a sphere by itself apart from the material facts of life and morality' was 'one of the curses of a non-Christian society.' In Japan, Caroline noted, the denominations that had placed the greatest emphasis on education were the strongest.[13]

Christian education at its best presented an integrated view of the world and, apart from any converts it might win, had a 'leavening influence among the non-Christian community.' Caroline saw this influence working in several ways. While the old religions of Japan 'lose force by the march of modern science ... and education,' Christian schools could demonstrate that 'the facts of life are most intelligible upon the Christian conception of God and the Universe.' Moreover, 'the type of character ... produced in Christian schools' illustrated 'the power of Christianity as a practical force in the moral life.' Yet 'no so-called Christian education' that was used as 'bait to bring students within the sphere of Christian influence' simply to convert them could be tolerated. If 'to know the truth is the end of life, the so-called secular education must be thorough and true ... and an end in itself.'[14]

Given the same technical training, Caroline argued, 'the Christian school ought to be able to demonstrate its ability to turn out men and women of higher character, finer culture, and more efficient in many ways.' In Japan, 'practical demonstrations are of the utmost value. The superiority of Christianity must be demonstrated. It cannot be assumed.' Nor, since the government education system was an excellent one, could it be assumed that education under Christian auspices was superior. Although Christian schools may earlier have offered competition to the government schools, this was no longer true, for the state schools were usually better equipped.[15]

While emphasizing the pioneering role of mission schools in the education of girls in Japan and noting that many prominent women, although not Christians, had been educated in those schools, Caroline pointed out that in the future, thanks to the expansion of the government system, a smaller proportion of leading women would come from Christian schools. Thus the importance of Christian work in government schools could scarcely be overstated, but the difficulties of carrying it on were increasing. Under a recent regulation, only graduates of government-recognized schools could take the qualifying examinations for teachers. Caroline was entirely sympathetic to the intent of this ruling, to force a large number of private schools of very inferior quality to meet government standards. Four mission schools for girls had been recognized in the past year, but graduates of other Christian schools were now prevented from becoming teachers in government schools. Thus, 'if ever the government schools are to be vitalized by Christian thought,' a majority of Christian schools must secure official recognition.[16]

Caroline was convinced that the education of girls must be directed by Japanese women. Although foreigners had done much in the past and would continue to have a role, she looked forward to the growth of a band of Christian Japanese women educators, most of whom would receive graduate education abroad. Thus Christian education would be 'Japonicized,' answering 'the standing criticism of mission schools that their graduates do not know their own language' and 'in many cases ... lose their Japanese manners.'[17]

While acknowledging the validity of such criticism, Caroline had no sympathy for more general charges that education was 'spoiling' women. The answer to 'this superficial view' was not less education but 'more of the deepest and truest kind.' True education would recognize that in the present transition period 'great care must be taken ... not to promulgate radical views concerning the position of women. Careful education which makes for stability of character will gradually change undesirable conditions of which there are many but young women must not be taught to strive for positions of recognition which their innate worth cannot maintain. It is a spiritual process by which women must attain their rightful place in society.'[18]

Finally, Caroline urged the early establishment of a full, degree-granting Christian university for women. Tsuda College was accepted by the government as the highest school in the country for the study of English and most of its graduates became teachers, but it could admit only one-third of the applicants, some of whom did not graduate, thanks to the school's high standards. The Japan Women's University offered college courses recognized by the government in some subjects but was not yet a real university, and the same could be said of two mission schools. Two government Higher Normal Schools trained women as high school teachers, but they graduated only 180 teachers a year. Altogether the demand for higher education for women far exceeded the facilities available.[19]

To Caroline it was obvious that Tsuda College should be the nucleus of the Christian university for women: it was the only one of the higher schools that was both avowedly Christian and had the desired educational standards. Further, Tsuda Ume, the best-known woman educator in Japan, had already shown her ability to gather together a superior group of teachers, both Japanese and foreign. As long as it was specifically Christian, the institution could not be supported solely in Japan, but Caroline stressed that resources from abroad must be controlled by Japanese women who alone understood the environment of their work.[20]

Before leaving Japan for her furlough, Caroline had a long talk about these and other matters with Uemura Masahisa, who, she observed with satisfaction, 'has become a great chum of mine.' Uemura emphatically affirmed her own belief about the importance of women's education and about the role of the YWCA in developing educated volunteer lay workers who would understand that '*every* Christian must be a Christian worker.' Some of the more conservative churches in Japan placed little emphasis on education; they sent women, usually of limited education, to Bible schools for minimal training as evangelists with the result, as Uemura thought, that 'the professional Bible woman is a horror!!'[21]

All this confirmed Caroline's conviction that for the foreseeable future the YWCA must work with Christian students and other educated women to prepare them as leaders of a larger work among other classes of society: 'What seems to some a longer and more round-about method of touching the commercial and industrial classes, may in the end ... be the most effective way.'[22]

■ ■ ■

IN EARLY FEBRUARY 1910, Caroline arrived in San Francisco and immediately began the four-day train journey home to Ontario. Since her last visit, her father, now in his seventies, had been rewarded for his long service to the

Liberal party with appointment as postmaster of London. There her parents received her in a substantial house on Richmond Street in the centre of the city. After ten days' relaxation she was ready to go to Toronto to see friends and supporters, including J.K. Macdonald, president of the Confederation Life Association and leading Presbyterian layman; her former classmate Frank Burton, now a University of Toronto physicist; Clara Benson, professor in the Faculty of Household Science in the university who chaired the Foreign Committee of the YWCA; and J.A. Macdonald of the *Globe*. The Foreign Committee quickly realized that Caroline was very tired and should have no engagements for some months, other than those already scheduled. After a month's rest in London she set out for California by train to a study conference on overseas work organized by the American YWCA.[23] Afterwards, in talks to groups of Japanese immigrants and to university students in several centres, Caroline stressed Japan's importance as a nation 'called to a place among what we call the great Xn [Christian] nations of the world' and the special obligations of Christian people on the Pacific coast to further Japan's desire 'to be an equal' and to learn 'the true foundation of our civilization.'[24]

Then she was back across the continent again to New York for two weeks of meetings and consultations at the national headquarters of the American YWCA. Again she visited Vassar College to sustain the interest of faculty and students in 'the Vassar hostel' in Tokyo. After three weeks' rest at home, she was off to Montreal to embark for Europe and the meeting of the World's Committee of the YWCA in Berlin.[25] The fourth meeting of the Committee displayed the confidence appropriate for a now firmly established international organization, and the gathering was hailed by participants as a turning point in the history of their movement. There were currently fifty-two overseas workers sent out by national committees, with Britain and the United States by far the largest contributors of personnel and funds. A substantial majority of the overseas secretaries were working in India, Burma, and Ceylon, the rest distributed among South and West Africa, Egypt, China, Japan, and Argentina.[26] Prepared reports and papers provided the background for discussions of the evangelistic and missionary emphasis of the YWCA, and Caroline and Kawai Michi both spoke about that area of the work in Japan. What was new at the Berlin meeting was the formal commitment of the World's Committee to deeper study of the social teachings of the Old Testament prophets and of Jesus, and of their application to the problems of women in industrial societies. This social emphasis was promoted largely by YWCA leaders from Great Britain and the United States, and to a lesser degree from the Orient.[27] It was a message Caroline was entirely willing to hear, for it accorded well with her own understanding of the gospel and of the needs of Japanese society.

After the Berlin conference, Caroline was joined by her best-loved sister, Peg, for a month of leisurely travel in Germany, Switzerland, and France. Apart from her attendance at the World's Committee of the YWCA in Paris four years earlier, Caroline had seen nothing of Europe, and Peg had never been on the continent before. A highlight of their trip was the famed passion play at Oberammergau, which left Caroline feeling that she could 'never expect to see anything so wonderful again.'[28]

In Britain, Caroline attended a summer conference of the SCM at Swanwick in Derbyshire, and then the sisters continued their sightseeing through the north of England and into Scotland, arriving in Edinburgh for the World Missionary Conference in mid-June, where Caroline was an observer for the YWCA.

To be present at the most representative gathering in the history of Protestant Christianity was an exhilarating experience, not least because of the presence of delegates from eighteen of the 'younger churches' in Africa and Asia, and for the resolve of the conference to persevere in organized cooperation with the task of evangelizing the world. Some of those present, including John R. Mott, the mastermind of the conference, realized that they were making history in a meeting that would prove to be the beginning of the modern ecumenical movement. All 1,200 delegates who filled the Assembly Hall of the United Free Church of Scotland and additional space in New College were appointed by missionary societies, including fifteen from Japan, only five of whom were Japanese nationals (four clergymen and a banker), while the rest were missionaries, two of them women.[29] Neither the Japanese representation nor the composition of the conference as a whole came close to reflecting the importance of women in the missionary movement or in the churches, a fact that did not escape Caroline's notice.

After more sightseeing en route from Edinburgh to London, Caroline and Peg, between 'rushing about to picture galleries and churches,' spent time with their sister Leila and her family, now resident in Henley-on-Thames. Two days in Oxford made them 'drunk with its beauty' and led Caroline to comment that 'England is a beautiful country, but I breathe freer in my native air and in Japan, where things are *doing* more palpably.' One thing that was 'doing' in England won her hearty disapproval: 'The suffragists make me sick here. Maybe women have as much right to vote as men – surely they couldn't do any worse with the ballot than men have done, but ... women have so much *more* to do than vote. Above all they have the dignity of womanhood to *uphold.*' It was not being upheld by 'a procession of suffragists 20,000 strong marching along the streets ... It seems to be a favorite way here of expressing your opinion. However, it's only a certain set, not at all the best, who belong to them, but people who do not know, think they stand for English women in general.'[30]

* * *

SINCE THE BEGINNING of her furlough, Caroline had given much thought to the organization and future direction of the YWCA in Japan and her own role in it, thought that was stimulated by her discussions with the women at the headquarters of the World's YWCA in London, and with 'dear old Ruth Rouse' of the WSCF. As a result, she was confirmed in her view that it was impossible for her, as national secretary, to continue to be responsible to at least six different committees – the Japan National YWCA, the Canadian and World's YWCAs, the WSCF, the National Board of the USA, and the British Foreign Committee. 'Each one has different ideas about salaries, allowances, ideals of work, etc.,' and she was no longer willing to exert the strenuous effort needed to coordinate them. She was convinced that it would be more efficient if the national committee in Japan were responsible directly to the World's Committee, which in turn would set standards and channel funds from the various supporting agencies. To convince all concerned that the World's Committee must assume its proper role, she prepared 'an *ultimatum* to the various and promiscuous kind committees who with more or less wobbling have been standing behind us.' The time for 'wobbling' and lack of focus was over: The YWCA must 'do effective work or *none at all.* We have no business being in Japan or any other mission country ... unless we are there for some *specific* purpose and are supported so that we can accomplish our mission.'[31]

With an ecumenical sense heightened by her experience at the Edinburgh conference, Caroline described one dimension of the YWCA's task in Japan as 'to do what they haven't been able to do here [England] yet, namely to unite in our work High Church, Low Church, no Church ...

shake them all together ... mix in American and Canadian ingredients of Presbyterian, Baptist, Methodist and what not ... and just before baking add a spice of Japanese flavouring.' She feared that this concoction might 'insist on curdling or effervescing or something ... but we *will* do it!'[32]

What part would she play in this process? As she reflected on her five years in Japan, the conviction had grown that she was 'an awful *amateur*,' for she could do 'a lot of things in a sort of way and nothing well.' By doing 'Jack of all trades things' she had gained 'much promiscuous experience in life and men and events – to say nothing of women,' but she would not continue such 'pottering work' indefinitely. Rather, she vowed 'to find time for the things that count for most – language study, other study and real investigation of true conditions.'[33]

For some months Caroline had been determined that part of her furlough would be spent in systematic study, and now she knew that she wanted to study in Britain, an objective for which her Canadian committee initially felt little sympathy. Nevertheless, after considerable correspondence, the committee agreed to allow her to remain in Britain, mainly because of her health, for it would be easier to rest and study there than in Canada, where more demands would be placed on her time and energies.[34]

Caroline had no difficulty in deciding where or what to study. At the Edinburgh conference she had heard and met David S. Cairns, who had primary responsibility for the writing and presentation of a major report widely regarded as one of the best of the conference. Both the content and the style of 'The Missionary Message in Relation to Non-Christian Religions' appealed to her greatly. A professor at the Aberdeen United Free Church College, Cairns encouraged her to study there, assuring her that although no woman had ever done so, she would be welcomed. Caroline agreed enthusiastically, for she liked everything she had seen of Cairns's mind and spirit, and family tradition would enable her to feel at home in Scotland and in a theological college of the United Free Church.

Since classes in Aberdeen did not start until the second week of October, Caroline had more time to spend in London, and then stayed for a week with the YWCA benefactress, Lady Overtoun, who had become a widow since their last meeting. The Overtoun country estate near Glasgow was a fine place for rest, reading, walking, and good conversation with a lively hostess. Then it was time to go to Aberdeen where she had been invited to stay with David Cairns's family while she looked for lodgings for the term. She was soon comfortably settled in a private home with a bedroom and sitting room. In accord with Scottish boarding house custom, her meals would be served in her sitting room and eaten in 'solitary confinement,' in marked contrast with the sociability of her meals in Japan.[35]

Aberdeen, a town of about 50,000 on the northeast coast of Scotland, constructed almost entirely of light grey granite, was 'the whitest looking city' she had ever seen, inspiring the hope that it would not prove to be a biblical 'whited sepulchre.'[36] On the contrary, her experience in Aberdeen soon confirmed what she had always been told: 'the Scotch *are* the salt of the earth;' was that partly because they were 'nearly all Liberals'?[37]

She looked forward to almost three months in Aberdeen as 'the unrolling of a great load ... To live quietly & regularly, to give consecutive thought to certain well defined duties, to be careful for nothing in a certain sense, will give me a new grip on life again.' Her day was well organized: three hours of lectures in the morning, then dinner, three hours devoted to sleeping and walking until tea, followed by five hours of study and then to bed.[38]

On her arrival in Aberdeen, Caroline discovered that everyone, including the local press, seemed to have heard about 'the lady student' who proposed to study theology. Although she thought herself 'silly,' the commotion made her quite nervous on registration day, she admitted to Peg. She recovered her nerve before lectures began the next morning when the professor of church history, Dr. James Stalker, addressed the class as 'Miss Macdonald and gentlemen,' and proceeded to give the first of the excellent lectures she was to hear from him.[39] Church history was not her primary interest, but 'by way of discipline' she decided to take the course and found it '*very* edifying.'[40]

Since her main objective was to study with David Cairns, she enrolled in his first-year course in apologetics, primarily comparative religion, and in his fourth year dogmatics, 'an awful name,' she thought, preferring the term 'systematic theology.' Cairns's declarations to both classes that he was sure the students would welcome 'the lady student' were greeted with loud applause from 'the young sprouts' who in their early twenties were about fifteen years her juniors.[41] 'They all seem to be very proud of themselves,' Caroline observed, 'as if *they* had achieved something. Au contraire!'[42] Accommodating the presence of a female on the premises, the college administration gave her 'a cloak & waiting room & all *appliances* ... that no one else uses.' Surely, she asserted, 'they are ... treating me like a noble Roman.'[43]

In keeping with the missionary tradition of the United Free Church, the college had an active missionary society to which all the students belonged. Its members had never been addressed by a woman, despite the fact that their church had sent many women overseas as missionaries. Now that they had one in their midst, they 'did themselves grand,' and shortly after Caroline's arrival they asked her to address their next meeting. It was not an easy assignment: 'It does scare me to think of getting up before all those youths with no *females* whatever to keep me in countenance, but it's a great chance to let a lot of theologues ... know how much out of the world they are.'[44] The preparation of an address for an audience 'entirely made up of the male sect' put her into 'throes of agony' for the preceding week: 'I simply couldn't see ... a line of thought & made myself generally *miserable*,' until 'I drove through it at last & the eventful day came.' After a warm introduction by the president, Caroline rose to 'uproarious applause. They really were decent [and] listened for 45 minutes while I told them some things they couldn't read in books.'[45]

Although they could accept her in their classes and their missionary society, the twenty-five theological students were less than eager to have Caroline in the college dining hall where they took dinner together every day at 1 p.m., a different professor presiding each week. Initially, when the principal asked her to dine in the hall she put off giving an answer, deciding that she would not go until the men themselves invited her, for she determined 'they'd see I had no ambition of intruding.' Then she carefully avoided the principal, not wishing to confess that she was waiting for a more 'democratic' bid for her company.[46]

Two weeks later, as she was putting on her coat to go home at noon as usual, a student approached her and said that he had been sent by the others to invite her to dinner with them. Caroline accepted, and 'appeared with the presiding professor [Cairns] & was clapped vociferously. You may laugh at my being nervous' she told her family, 'but I was, but I was *very much* pleased.' Noting that the young man had invited her to take dinner 'to-day,' she thought she 'wouldn't make any mistake by going too far.' The next day when she started to get ready to go home, the same youth appeared and enquired: 'Have you got tired of us already!?' Henceforth she dined with her 'beloved theologicals' every day, always seated next to the presiding professor. Now she learned that some of the students had been absolutely determined that she would never set foot in the dining hall, but eventually they had relented. 'They were a little slow in getting there, but no uncertain sound in the arrival'; she would 'never forget their clapping' as long as she lived.[47] Would 'any one but Old Crow ...,' she asked her father, 'have concocted the scheme of a female retiring from life by entering not a nunnery but a *monastery*, and then to further retire by dining with the Brethren?'[48] The whole affair gave Caroline some hearty chuckles and when the news got about the town there were many more.[49]

News of the presence of 'the lady student' spread to the University of Aberdeen, including the Divinity School, where future ministers of the established Church of Scotland were educated. When Prime Minister Herbert Asquith spoke at the university, one of the divinity students dressed up as a girl and sat among the women students of the university. As Asquith began to speak, the student stood up waving a banner inscribed 'Votes for Women' and there were cries of 'Put Her Out.' When an attempt was made to remove 'her,' 'she' was tied to a chair, 'in proper suffragist fashion,' Caroline learned. Eventually peace was restored and Asquith proceeded with his address, still unconverted to the cause of women's suffrage. Apparently 'the Church of Scotland Divinities are bound to have a woman in their midst somehow,' Caroline observed to her mother, but she was not sure that David Cairns was right to see her as the true originator of the episode. If he was, it was most surprising to one who had 'innocently come up here to have a quiet & dull time,' not to foment demonstrations.[50]

From the beginning Caroline 'fairly revelled' in Cairns's lectures, finding the fourth-year course demanding but 'not entirely beyond [her] comprehension.' As she explained to Peg, 'I have the advantage over the young gents, that I have been experimenting very practically in the realm of applied dogmatics (not always systematic) for some years & I have a working knowledge which is not entirely theoretical. However, I'll have to hump!! It's not a sinecure being a lady student.'[51] After the 'sheer exhilaration' of three hours of lectures every morning and a good deal of reading, she was sure she looked ten years younger.[52]

Initially Caroline fought her inclination to raise questions in class, especially in the senior course where she felt that the students thought her 'a bit cheeky to be going in for anything quite so deep as their lordly brains tackle. It is rather cheeky, I confess myself.'[53] In a class devoted entirely to discussion she struggled to keep quiet: 'The men talked a good deal & I *did want* to make some remarks ... but I desisted as I did not want them to think I was butting in & besides I tho't as I didn't know as much philosophy as they think they know, my remarks might seem very foolish to them.' Later, when she put her question to Cairns outside of the class, he assured her that it was a good point that he would not discuss then because he wanted her to raise it at the next lecture. Thus Caroline gained confidence and after three weeks, the lectures 'getting more exciting all the time,' she forgot restraint and 'flung some questions into their midst.' She had the feeling that 'the youths think I may not know Theology,' but she was sure she knew something of 'problems that can be illuminated by Theology. It is interesting to square Dr. Cairns' theories of life & religion with some of my touches with real life in Japan ... He squares with life, as I have seen it anyway.'[54]

Caroline paid close attention not only to the words of Dr. Cairns but also to his person. Her accounts of 'how such a dull sounding subject as Systematic Theology ... could be so fascinating' were closely interwoven with her impressions of the professor who taught it. The most striking feature of his appearance was his long hair, which was 'never combed – hangs over one eye in a sinister sort of way.' Otherwise he had 'a clear cut face! He's somewhat of the mystic order & when he begins lecturing ... his hands go through his hair & he draws down his brow & rubs his eyes (he sits when he lectures) & then ... you are off into the realms of space where he has gone, peering in to see if you can get even a faint vision of what he sees so *clearly*.'[55]

The view of the universe that David Cairns saw so clearly had not been reached easily. A son of a Scottish manse, Cairns had received a good education in a literate home and at local schools before proceeding to the University of Edinburgh to study classics and English literature. His subsequent theological studies at the United Presbyterian Hall, Edinburgh, were enhanced by a term in Germany at the University of Marburg. Cairns had been through more than one period of doubt, not only about the truth of the Calvinism in which he had grown up but about the validity of any form of religious belief. The intellectual and spiritual quest that gradually made him a persuasive Christian apologist for many twentieth-century men and women, especially university students, was long and strenuous.[56]

When Caroline first met Cairns in 1910 he had been teaching theology in Aberdeen for three years, following twelve years as a country minister among fishermen and farmers in Berwickshire near the Scottish border. Most of his first book, *Christianity in the Modern World: Studies in the Theology of the Kingdom of God* (1906), had originally been published as articles in the *Contemporary Review*, and he was being recognized as a fresh theological voice in the English-speaking world.

Cairns's faith had been rejuvenated by biblical criticism and the redis-covery of 'the Jesus of history,' and he was currently preoccupied with Jesus' teaching about 'the Kingdom of God' and its bearing on the meaning of his-tory. Cairns believed that the scholarship of the last sixty years, far from destroying faith as so many contended, had enabled scholars to confront the modern world with the 'historic Personality of Jesus ... with the force almost of a new revelation.' At the same time he was wrestling with the relationship between Christian belief in the providence of God and a modern scientific view that emphasized the impersonal reign of law. On social issues Cairns was a close and admiring student of the Christian socialism of the Anglican F.D. Maurice.[57] Cairns's teaching and writing on these themes placed him among the 'broad evangelicals' who were the dominant stream in contem-porary Scottish theology.[58] Neither the themes nor Cairns's scholarly and searching approach were foreign to Caroline, and she was more than ready to hear what her new mentor had to say about them. For his part, Cairns was delighted with 'the lady student' and remembered her twenty years later as the best student ever to set foot in the college during all that time.[59]

From the outset, all four professors in the small college were academ-ically and personally hospitable to Caroline. Thinking that she must be lonely in such a male setting, they invited her to their homes for meals, to share their pews in church, or accompany them on family walks. As Caroline soon reported to her mother, three of the four were widowers, their domestic life presided over by a sister or a daughter. None was more wel-coming than the Cairns family, where Jessie Cairns, David's slightly older sister, was helping him to bring up his children, Alison, aged eight, and David, six. Caroline was in the Cairns's home frequently, especially for Sunday dinner following the morning church service, and was sometimes invited to stay for the rest of the day until after tea. Although Cairns was always happy to discuss theology, he was a voracious reader in many fields and kept Caroline supplied with 'light literature,' lest she take her studies too seriously.[60] The two lively conversationalists had many literary interests in common, including the novels of Sir Walter Scott, and Robert Browning's poetry, which had helped to sustain Cairns's religious faith when he most needed it. He could quote from Browning and other Victorian poets at length, as well as from his large collection of nonsense rhymes.[61]

When Caroline was studying with him, the forty-seven-year-old Cairns, twelve years her senior, had been a widower for about a year. His wife's long and painful illness and her death after only eight years of a happy marriage was a greater stretching of his faith than any he had ever encountered. As Caroline knew, a highly personal dimension lay behind his lectures on how pain and death could be part of the Kingdom of God. She must also have known of his strong conviction that his beloved Helen still lived and was close to him, and that he would be reunited with her in 'the world of Light and Life.'[62] That did not prevent Caroline from remarking more than once to her family on his status as a widower.

Although she regretted that she could not remain for the second term, there was some compensation in being able to go home with copies of Cairns's notes for the second half of his course in systematic theology. The 'theologicals' gave her a splendid farewell party, replete with presentation of a book and hearty singing of 'For she's a jolly good fellow,' which Caroline considered preferable to the more pious and sentimental 'God be with you till we meet again,' generally used on such occasions. The only way that she could finish the term and still get home for Christmas was to sail on the new Cunard liner, the *Lusitania*, the fastest ship afloat. Luxuriating in an expensive single cabin, she studied Cairns's notes and reflected on how she would use her experience in Aberdeen in her future work.[63] Five days out of Liverpool she was in New York and on the way home.

C h a p t e r 5

'Grubbing at the Lingo'

AFTER A CHERISHED CHRISTMAS with her family, Caroline was in New York in early January 1911 for a three weeks' training course for YWCA secretaries at the headquarters of the American Association. On her return to Canada, she requested her Toronto committee to change her program for the next few months, notably by cancelling a proposed tour of colleges in the Maritime provinces of Canada and in New England, but this was refused on the grounds that the financial support provided in those regions must not be jeopardized. For similar reasons she attended a student conference of the American YWCA in Indianapolis, believing that the resources of the American association made it a more likely source of support and of recruits for the staff of the 'Y' in Japan than Canada could offer.[1]

The completion of these assignments left Caroline exhausted, and her committee decided to cancel all engagements for the remainder of her sojourn in Canada. That meant that the local associations of the Canadian YWCA would derive only limited benefit from her furlough, nor would she attend the annual national summer conference in Muskoka. Fortunately, Kawai Michi was in Canada visiting the 'Y' in a number of centres and proved to be the star of the conference, so that Japan was well represented to members of the Canadian 'Y.'[2] Thus Caroline spent four months with her family, accepting no assignments of any kind. This period of reading, knitting, walking, and sleeping brought her to midsummer feeling renewed and invigorated and ready to return to work.

At the dock in Yokohama on a hot August day, Caroline found Tsuda Ume, Kawai Michi, and Margaret Matthew, and on her arrival at home her 'beloved parson,' Uemura Masahisa, was waiting to welcome her. Over the next three days she received a host of other Japanese friends, until her departure for Karuizawa, there to be greeted by foreign colleagues and acquaintances.[3] After a week in the mountain resort she was back in Tokyo settling into her work again.

Members of the Fujimichō church held a 'welcome meeting' to mark Macdonald's return to Japan after eighteen months' absence. With an army colonel presiding, several members of the congregation expressed their pleasure that she was among them again. As so often happened, Caroline regretted that she still had to reply in English. Then everyone sat down to a supper featuring one of her favourite dishes – boiled eels on rice, with pickles. The significance of the fact that she was the only non-Japanese present was not lost on her: she had made a place for herself in the congregation, and she was deeply gratified.[4]

Dr. Uemura was about to depart on a trip to North America and she immediately began to arrange for him to visit her family in London, as Kawai Michi had done only weeks earlier, to the great enjoyment of all concerned. Caroline predicted that her family would find Uemura 'inclined to be shy' and 'not much to look at' but 'very interesting.'[5] Since her father was currently active in organizing the Laymen's Missionary Movement in London, he was especially pleased to meet a leading Japanese Christian. For similar reasons she sent Uemura to meet another Presbyterian active in the movement, J.A. Macdonald of the Toronto *Globe*, perhaps hoping as well that Uemura would add to the editor's appreciation of Japan and its aspirations.[6]

While Caroline was away, the 'Great Treason Incident' had somewhat altered the relationship of Christians to the state, or at least had affected the perceptions of some Japanese. In the spring of 1910, the Home Ministry, believing that 'dangerous thought,' especially socialist ideas, threatened the nation, arrested several hundred anarchists and socialists and subsequently brought twenty-six of them to trial on charges of plotting to assassinate the emperor. Although there had been talk of such action among men associated with Kōtoku Shūsui, a leading anarchist intellectual who had earlier been under Christian influences, there was no evidence that any attempt on the life of the emperor had actually been made. Nevertheless, twelve of the alleged plotters were convicted and executed early in 1911. One of them, Ōishi Seinosuke, was a Christian. At the request of Ōishi's relatives, Uemura Masahisa conducted a memorial service for him in Fujimichō church, an act of courage that cast doubt on Uemura's patriotism in some eyes and created considerable dissension among Christians. Uemura's generally conservative and sometimes nationalistic attitudes did not extend to excluding from the community of the church a man whom the state judged to be beyond the pale.[7]

In the aftermath of these events, the government intensified its concern for the 'moral education' of the people. Hoping to mobilize the forces of religion in support of the *kokutai* (national polity), the Home Ministry organized a 'Conference of the Three Religions.' Significantly, the three religions were Shintoism, Buddhism, and Christianity (not Confucianism), an apparent recognition of Christianity as a legitimate part of Japanese society. Not without some misgiving, most Japanese Christians were gratified by this development, and prominent Christian leaders participated in the conference. However, Uemura Masahisa and Uchimura Kanzō refused to have anything to do with a move whose avowed purpose was to ensure the active cooperation of religious believers in promoting national morality, a concept they believed would be defined mainly by the state.[8]

■ ■ ■

IN THE CROWDED HOUSE that served as both home and office for the staffs of the national and Tokyo YWCAs, there was an addition to the household a few days after Caroline's return when the maid, wife of the cook, gave birth to a son. As the new parents were not Christians, Caroline 'gently enquired' and learned that they had decided not to follow the Shinto custom of taking the baby to the temple. 'Thinking it a very great pity not to have something for them,' she found on consultation that they would be pleased to have a service of thanksgiving at the house. On Caroline's invitation, the minister who was substituting for Dr. Uemura at Fujimichō church conducted a short service in the presence of 'our whole retinue,' as Caroline described the gathering of friends and relatives of the family, the nurse who had attended the birth, and a clutch of YWCA secretaries. After many photographs there was cake and tea for everyone.[9] Both religiously and socially it was a highly eclectic and egalitarian occasion of the kind that Caroline was adept at creating, always to her delight.

Thanks to her sojourn in the world beyond Japan, Macdonald was now looked on as an expert on several subjects. John R. Mott sent her a series of questions about Christian hostels for students, which she in turn circulated to several other people. The British SCM wanted to know about "'the working religion" of the Japanese educated woman of to-day. Pump some more people!!' At the same time David Cairns wrote asking for information about 'the disintegration of Japanese religions in face of western sciences!! So off I set again to pump another set of people on various aspects of the Cosmos.'[10]

Another survey began when the WSCF, through Mott, gave the YWCA $1,000 for a study of conditions among the growing number of Chinese women students in Japan. Very shortly, revolution broke out in China under the leadership of Sun Yat-sen. Most of the 10,000 Chinese males studying in Japan wanted to go home to join the struggle, but the beleaguered government that had sponsored most of them now had better things to do than help revolutionaries to come home. Caroline was caught up in the enthusiasm: 'Of course we are all revolutionaries here. Strength to their elbows. It's quite wonderful how the revolutionaries are holding things & gaining the confidence of everyone. Think of immemorial China – a republic!'[11] In a few months the new Republic of China was proclaimed and the long struggle to unite the country continued, a struggle of enormous import for Japan.

A majority of the some two hundred Chinese women students in Japan were under private sponsorship and wanted to stay to complete their studies, but the context of their lives was changing. With the WSCF money, the YWCA employed Jessie Ding, a young Chinese woman who had spent two years in the United States, to assess their needs, and she was soon in touch with more than forty Chinese women students, although it was believed that there were still many more in the city.[12]

Meanwhile, the work of the YWCA as a whole was gradually progressing. The Tokyo Association, under the presidency of Baroness Sannomiya Yaeno, held the largest gathering of women students Tokyo had ever seen, where several hundred young women heard addresses from Kawai Michi and a Japanese secretary of the YMCA. A more intensive program was conducted with sixty-five young women from Tokyo and Yokohama who attended an all-day training session on the principles and methods of the YWCA and went home full of enthusiasm.[13] Caroline was especially gratified by the appearance of progress in relations with the Japan Women's University. She had 'never got within 40 miles before, except to go through the sickening process about five times a year of visiting the school & seeing classes & drinking tea and smiling facetiously at all & sundry.' Now some graduates had invited her to speak to them at the university, and 'the President [Dr. Joseph Naruse] lent his presence to see probably if I spoke *heresy*, & then he invited us all to lunch.'[14] Whether this gesture meant that Naruse was relaxing his opposition to any presentation of religion in the university and would open the door for the YWCA remained to be seen.

Caroline was quickly falling back into the Jack-of-all-trades pattern of life she had vowed to abandon, and was as busy at as many different tasks as ever, including one day a week teaching English Bible at Tsuda College. To avoid excessive fatigue, she adhered firmly to a decision to sleep for half an hour every day at noon and took a few days' holiday among the temples and shrines and the autumn colours in Nikkō. She had not forgotten her resolve to study Japanese seriously and just before Christmas 1911 she seized on a chance to act.

That summer at the Nitobes' house in Karuizawa, she had met Matsumiya Yahei, until recently the proprietor of a newspaper in Maebashi, the capital of Gumma prefecture, about 110 kilometres inland north of Tokyo. Many missionaries testified to his brilliance as a teacher, and he was willing to take Caroline as a student. Further, Maebashi presented an opportunity for immersion in Japanese language and traditional living that her life in Tokyo could not offer.[15] Moreover, she now had a 'perfect jewel of a Japanese secretary' who could be trusted with many matters. Everyone could get along without her through Christmas and the extended New Year's holidays, and during the following two months she would return to Tokyo every two weeks to keep an eye on her office and make trips elsewhere as needed. In the face of opposition from every quarter, including the national executive committee of the YWCA and her colleagues on the staff, Caroline remained adamant. Her friendly critics continued to argue, as Tsuda Ume had done from the beginning, that if she would provide the 'steam' (ideas and inspiration) they would supply the language, but Caroline was convinced that 'in the end the steam would turn into hot air,' and that an investment of three months in concentrated language study promised greater returns than any other use of that time.[16]

Early in December Caroline made the four-hour train journey to Maebashi and took up residence in the Matsumiyas' large house, part of which had been turned into an inn. There she had two adjoining rooms, one nine-by-nine, the other twelve-by-twelve, space that was luxurious compared with her crowded living in Tokyo. For warmth there was a small firebox, and a maid brought her hot milk every night at bedtime. Sharp at 5:00 p.m. everyone else stood aside while the foreign lady had first use of the bath. She had experienced the traditional Japanese bath often before, but never on a daily basis, as it was too expensive for the residents of the Sanbanchō house to use that much hot water. Now, every day she screwed up her courage 'to leap into what is practically a cauldron of boiling water' and stay there as long as she could.[17]

Caroline found Maebashi, a town about the same size as Aberdeen (50,000), highly agreeable. Surrounded by mountains, the same as those seen from the other side in Karuizawa, with Mt. Asama beautifully visible, the air was clear and sharp, reminding her of autumn weather in southern Ontario. She walked regularly early in the morning and again in the late afternoon, and soon became familiar with the sights and sounds of the country town.[18]

The reputation of Matsumiya Yahei as a rigorous language teacher proved well founded. As he spoke no English, every class was entirely in Japanese. After a week Caroline believed she had made more progress than in any month since her arrival in Japan. Formal lessons from ten o'clock to noon every morning were preceded by at least an hour's preparation and followed by several hours more after lunch and her midday nap. Sometimes she felt that her progress was scarcely commensurate with the effort, but she was determined 'not to let it beat me. If I do, I *slump* for keeps. I have the idea that I have to sort of *save my soul*, & I'm going to do it with that in mind.'[19] The mastery of the Japanese language was a spiritual as well as an intellectual challenge.

Caroline's friends and colleagues, Japanese or foreign, continued to believe that her energy was misdirected; only Margaret Matthew encouraged her to persevere, although Caroline was sure the rest would praise her eventually.[20] 'They think I'm a B.A. (Born Ass) to be living in a Japanese hotel & grubbing at the lingo, and worst of all & what they can't understand – I don't even look like a martyr & I don't talk like one. They think I think it's fun!' Then with more than a hint that she must persuade herself, she added: 'So it is, *because* I think so! Is that Christian Science? Maybe it is. It's good doctrine anyway, if you practice it & I'm making an effort to!'[21]

By this time she was preparing short compositions or speeches on subjects as diverse as 'Leaves,' 'War,' 'Silk Worms,' and 'Women,' and had written explications of the parables of Jesus until she 'couldn't look a parable in the eye.' Amazingly, her teacher, who was not given to praise of anything short of perfection, actually said that her composition on the need for the East and the West to solve their problems together was good. Now there was practical satisfaction in being able to write 'thank you' notes and other short missives to Japanese friends in their own language. The 'winter's grind' was beginning to pay off.[22]

Caroline's formal language study was enhanced by her daily converse with members of the Matsumiya family, Yahei's wife, Shin, and three children, aged eight to thirteen. She found the children bright and delightful, tending to look upon her 'somewhat in the light of a pet monkey' for she often played 'house' or other games with them. Their nursemaid had learned good Japanese and the deportment of high society through her earlier employment in the local castle, and through the children Caroline profited as well. The younger members of the family remembered their erstwhile playmate as a very serious person who was never quite on their level, but had a lively sense of humour.[23]

On both sides of the family, the Matsumiyas were third-generation Christians and active in a local congregation established by American Congregational missionaries. Well accustomed to worshipping in Japanese, Caroline continued to do so by attending Sunday services with the Matsumiya family. Additional exposure to the Japanese language was provided at the midweek prayer meeting, followed by 'quite a jolly Bible class,' often led by Matsumiya.[24] Matsumiya Yahei held liberal social and political ideas and in many quarters was considered rather radical. He was a leader in the effort to keep licensed prostitution out of Gumma prefecture where it had been banned for twenty years, the only jurisdiction in Japan where prostitution was illegal.[25]

Caroline tried not to be absent from Maebashi and her language study any oftener than necessary, but there were some obligations to the national YWCA she could not avoid. She went north to Sendai to make five speeches in three days to missionaries and schoolgirls.[26] During a few days in Kyoto she tried to 'stir up strife and tumult' to expand work with women and students there, and in Kobe she was present at the birth of a new branch of the 'Y' for schoolgirls. In Osaka on YWCA business she stayed with Madam Hirooka Asa, a generous financial backer of Dr. Naruse's university for women, with whom Caroline had earlier discussed the interests of the YWCA. A daughter of the wealthy Mitsui family and famed as one of Japan's few women entrepreneurs, Madam Hirooka had single-handedly rescued her husband's failing banking interests from disaster. After separating from him she developed and managed large coal mines, a bank, an insurance company, and an agricultural enterprise in Korea. She also played the stock exchange to her advantage.[27]

Madam Hirooka lived, Caroline observed, attended by twenty-four servants, in 'a very grand foreign style house hideously furnished. If they'd only stick to Japanese simplicity,' she lamented, not for the first time reacting negatively to the western taste displayed by many wealthy Japanese. In contrast, the Nitobes' Tokyo house, 'an adaptation of Japanese beauty and European comfort,' showed what good taste could create with far less money than Madam Hirooka commanded.[28]

Just two months before Caroline's visit in her home, Madam Hirooka had created a public stir by being baptized on Christmas Day, at the age of sixty-four. After a lengthy study of the major religions, she had decided that only Christianity offered any hope to the women of Asia for liberation from the tyranny of tradition and law. Caroline found her 'an absolutely changed person,' vigorously engaged in preaching the gospel in the high places to which she had such ready access. Regaling her family with the tale of Madam Hirooka, Caroline reported that soon after her conversion she had summoned to her house 'all the most prominent sinners in town, bankers and other rich men & their wives' to hear Yamamuro Gumpei, head of the Salvation Army, on '"Sin and Salvation." They had to come when she invited them,' and Caroline was sure 'they squirmed for there were some arch sinners among them. The moral tone of the average rich man in Japan is *not* something that would grace the character of the Angel Gabriel. And Osaka is not the whitest place in Japan either!!'[29]

During her current visit with Madam Hirooka, Caroline was intrigued by a spirited discussion between her hostess and her daughter and a Japanese clergyman on 'tainted money.' All three asserted that 'most money in this country is tainted in the way it's been made ... and the only way to get it out of its abominations is to get hold of it' and direct it 'into decent channels ... for the advancement of mankind – and *womankind*.' As her companions talked, 'they consigned practically the whole Japanese nation to the bottomless pit for its iniquities. Then they took a whack at some missionaries who they say spend their spare time at dances in Kobe.' Caroline doubted that the situation was as totally dissolute as depicted, and she found it amusing that Madam Hirooka's daughter, who was not a Christian, should judge Christians 'by the standards of the strictest sect around.' As for dancing, she was unconvinced that it would do missionaries any harm, although she was not adept at it herself.[30]

These forays into the outside world broke the relative isolation of Maebashi and kept her from becoming 'imbecile with dullness,' a phrase borrowed from her favourite correspondent, David Cairns, but they did not advance her language study. As spring approached, she wanted to extend her stay in Maebashi until June, but the business of the national office forced her to return to Tokyo at the end of March.[31]

This decision did not create as big a hiatus in her language study as expected. Just then Matsumiya Yahei was beginning to listen to the view of his wife and friends that he ought to be doing something more worthy of his talents than innkeeping, which he did not enjoy, and should devote himself to full-time language teaching. Caroline quickly put her persuasive powers behind this proposal, enthusiastically supported by Galen Fisher, for they had often discussed the need for a first-class Japanese language school in Tokyo for missionaries and other foreigners. Thus Matsumiya Yahei and his family moved to Tokyo, taking up residence a two minutes' walk from Caroline's home. Henceforth, except during holidays, Caroline appeared at Matsumiya's house early every morning five days a week for a two-hour lesson in Japanese.[32]

After her return from Maebashi, Caroline began making some speeches in Japanese. Her first yielded two new members for the YWCA and she concluded that it was not a total failure.[33] An address to a gathering of 350 in Sendai presented a greater challenge when 'for once in [her] life' she gave 'a speech that wasn't long enough,' and she 'couldn't pad it out on the spur of the moment. It was 35 minutes long which would be long enough for most people *out of Japan!* Like a good sermon in Japan, a speech must be fifty minutes long, perhaps longer.'[34]

Of course the preparation of speeches in 'the vernacular' took a great deal more work than talks in English and were always carefully written out. Caroline despaired lest she be forever enslaved to her manuscript, but her teacher assured her that 'it was better to be enslaved than to be incorrect' and that she would eventually be able to speak freely. 'Patience and time and hard work were the price of liberty and Mr. Matsumiya exacted them without mercy.' She often had to persuade herself that the four hours a day she normally spent in language study – two hours of lessons and two of preparation – were not too much to achieve her 'pearl of great price,' fluency in Japanese.[35]

Less than a year after she began her study in Maebashi, Caroline and Kawai Michi 'passed a law of the Medes and Persians ... that Japanese only' was to be spoken at meetings of national YWCA committees, making Caroline's participation in those meetings more arduous, and she had 'to get a few impromptu speeches up [her] sleeve [*sic*]' on a variety of subjects.[36] Three months later she began to lead a Bible class in Japanese in one of the 'Y's student hostels, a task requiring a good deal of spontaneity, one that she carried out with increasing competence and satisfaction.[37]

■ ■ ■

ON HER RETURN TO TOKYO from Maebashi, Caroline rejoined the house-hunting that had been going on for three months, since the crowded conditions in the Sanbanchō office and residence of the YWCA staff could no longer be endured. It was decided that the national office and its personnel would move out, leaving the present house to the Tokyo association. Caroline's delight in finding a 'perfectly lovely place' was initially dashed when the owners refused to rent the house to foreigners. Only when Caroline secured recommendations from the greengrocer, her regular *jin-rikisha* men, and a former cook who wanted to go to the new house with Caroline was the deal concluded.[38]

The large Japanese house in Ushigome ward was well suited to the needs of the national YWCA and only ten minutes' walk from the Sanbanchō house. Ample space on three floors could be divided by movable walls into smaller rooms for offices and living accommodation, while leaving room for meetings of various sizes. Only Caroline and Ruth Ragan, one of the American secretaries, would live in the new 'Tamachi house,' as it was soon called from the name of its block. Both women would enjoy what by now seemed the luxury of having their own bedrooms.[39] 'To see the scenery from the third storey, you'd think we had a villa in the country,' Caroline exulted. In reality two tram lines ran past the house, which was just outside the moat around the grounds of the Imperial Palace, and thus well within the centre of the city.[40]

While the housing problem was being solved, Caroline and the executive committee of the YWCA were trying to persuade Kawai Michi to leave her full-time teaching position at Tsuda College to become national secretary and were busy raising money for her salary. Ever since Kawai's return from Bryn Mawr, Caroline had been hoping that Kawai's name would soon appear on the 'Y' letterhead above her own as the senior secretary. If Kawai refused the job, 'we'll only scrape the surface ... that's all,' but if she took it, 'you'll see things doing in Japan!!' Kawai was also a member of Fujimichō church, and Caroline was cheered by the knowledge that Dr. Uemura had advised Kawai to take the YWCA position, rather than become dean of a girls' school in Kobe.[41] When Kawai accepted, Caroline was jubilant: 'I have not lived in vain!' Not only was there to be a Japanese national secretary but she was the very best person imaginable.[42]

It had been hard to find the money for Kawai's salary, although she would not be employed full time, but Caroline was gratified that all of it was raised in Japan. From the outset, she 'was bound that the YWCA in Japan was not going to begin on starvation salaries. It's not necessary & we are going to start straight,' the more so because 'Kawai San has grubbed along long enough.' Caroline was proud that no Japanese woman in the country was paid more; the most obvious competitor, Tsuda Ume, drew no salary since the school was her own. To pay Kawai a respectable salary declared both the importance of her work and the opportunities for educated women in a changing Japan, and it might help to establish a standard of remuneration for others.[43]

The next pressing task was the organization of the summer conference for late July, especially the finding of a suitable site. Quite late in the day a hotel in the village of Ōtsu near Yokosuka on the seashore across Tokyo Bay, a three-hour train ride from Tokyo, was found. An unanticipated number of girls and teachers – 228 from 28 schools – registered for rooms that would accommodate only 120; thus many participants were lodged in farmers' houses nearby, while others lived in a large Buddhist temple in the neighbourhood. The main hall of the temple, just next to the temporary YWCA dormitory, was unusually busy as worshippers, accompanied by gongs and chants, attended services from dawn to dusk to pray for the emperor, who had suddenly become seriously ill.[44]

This was the most distinctively *Japanese* summer conference yet held. Led by Kawai Michi, all the leaders and speakers were Japanese, except for Caroline who conducted one of the daily Bible classes on 'Christ's Message of the Kingdom,' the only group in English. Madam Hirooka was present throughout the conference and gave the opening address on 'Christianity and the Woman Problem,' in which her views on the potential for female liberation in the Christian faith were forcefully expounded. Like so many women everywhere, before and after her, Hirooka was angered by the chauvinistic declarations of St. Paul, 'an old bachelor ... who didn't know much about women' as 'anyone can see.' However, St. Peter was worth heeding for 'he had a wife and understood women. One can see that from his epistle.' As for the gospels, 'Jesus made no distinction between the sexes' and thus 'we are all, women as well as men, children of God.'[45]

Out of respect for the ailing emperor, there was no 'stunt night' or skits with their accompanying hilarity at the conference. Early on the second last day of the conference the girls were called together and informed of the emperor's death and the cancellation of the rest of the gathering. They 'sat in dead silence with their heads bowed' and then went to prepare for their departure. After a brief farewell meeting when Yamamuro Gumpei of the Salvation Army spoke, appropriately, on 'Providence,' the girls left 'in quietness and order' with 'none of the usual hustle and bustle of leaving' and in a few hours everyone had gone.[46] Even the youngest had some inkling of the significance of the ending of the Meiji era and realized that the one coming to birth would be a new age in their country's history.

The New Era of Taishō and 'the Woman Question'

C AROLINE RETURNED to a Tokyo stunned by the death of the emperor who had reigned but not ruled over the nation for forty-five years, and had become for the populace the symbol of Japan's rise to greatness among the nations of the world. Thousands of people stood in mourning outside the Imperial Palace, millions read avidly the details in the press of the emperor's last days, and nearly everyone donned a black arm band in displays of grief and respect that brought together the whole nation in unprecedented unanimity of feeling. The outpouring of sentiment was a striking manifestation of the success of the architects of the Meiji Restoration in making the near-divine emperor the focus of national unity.[1] The significance of the emperor's death and Japan's prospects for the future were much discussed throughout the month of August among the missionaries and other foreigners in Karuizawa, where Caroline and her YWCA colleagues occupied the home of the Nitobes, lent to them while the owners were in America.[2]

The unity of national feeling was short-lived. On the night of 13 September, following a day of almost total silence in Tokyo, the emperor's funeral procession left the Imperial Palace as military salutes were fired and temple bells rang throughout the city. (According to Shinto custom the most sacred ceremonies were held at night.) Just as the cortege was leaving the palace, the hero of the Russo-Japanese war, General Nogi Maresuke, and his wife, Shizuko, clad in white robes, seated themselves in front of the emperor's portrait in their home not far from the parade ground across which the procession was moving. Then they solemnly went to join their emperor by committing ritual suicide, a custom officially outlawed 250 years earlier. After a period of initial disbelief, the people of Japan, especially intellectuals, were torn apart by debate over the meaning and the ethics of the Nogi suicides. The late emperor almost disappeared from public interest, and General Nogi was on the way to becoming the heroic example of service to the state. Was this act an admirable example of traditional samurai loyalty and selflessness that would elevate the moral character of the nation, or was it a piece of foolish theatre, unworthy of one of the leading countries of the modern world?[3] Many Japanese could reach no firm conclusion and agreed with an editorial in one of Tokyo's leading newspapers: 'Emotionally we express the greatest respect, rationally we regret we cannot approve ... We can appreciate the General's intention; we must not learn from his behavior.'[4]

Christians joined their fellow citizens in expressions of respect for the departed emperor, but like the rest of the population they were divided in their views of the Nogi suicides. Many, like Uemura Masahisa, admired Nogi, the national hero, but criticized the suicides as 'theatrical bushidō.'[5] Caroline entertained little ambivalence about Nogi and was distressed by the sentimental treatment accorded the affair in the foreign press. One example was the London *Times*' opinion that Nogi had shown that 'the spirit of Japan is not extinct.'[6] In Caroline's view, 'the Japanese nation does not need to be encouraged along those lines ... and the Japanese with their heads screwed on their shoulders don't respect foreigners who laud the suicide.'[7]

Nevertheless, Macdonald was intrigued and almost admiring of certain 'weird performances,' although not of the suicides of several men who decided to follow Nogi's example. In Sendai she met an army officer who had gone out at midnight when the cannon boomed out the hour of the emperor's funeral in Tokyo, and 'in order to purify himself to be worthy of worship stood on the stone curb of the well and poured cold water on him-self until he dropped unconscious. What a spirit,' she exclaimed, 'if only Christianized and turned in channels which will make for the betterment of the world.' In this case there seemed to be some hope that the spirit might be redirected, for the zealous officer had just attended a Salvation Army evangelistic meeting and afterwards had a long talk with Yamamuro Gumpei. Noting how 'the Emperor seems to have been forgotten,' Caroline's comment on Nogi revealed a good deal about the inclusiveness of her theology and about her view of the world to which Nogi had gone: 'Poor old General Nogi ... seeing as he must see now, he must be sorry for the awful mistake he made. He was altogether too good a man to be lost to Japan at this crisis ... I'm sure he understands now what he never did before, the true value of the life which God has given us as part of the larger life which is forever & ever.'[8]

With the proclamation of the reign of Taishō, the nation was filled with hope of new beginnings. Although nostalgia dominated the thinking of a few, there were insistent calls from politicians, intellectuals, and the press for an end to bureaucratic government by the oligarchy that had ruled on behalf of the emperor and the adoption instead of parliamentary govern-ment under political parties, a change that would bring greater public par-ticipation in the affairs of the state; how much participation was desirable was a subject of much debate. With bows to the past, advocates of a new type of politics almost always justified their views as being true expressions of the Meiji constitution of 1889, a 'Taishō restoration.'[9]

Caroline sensed the new atmosphere keenly: 'Things are humming in Japan politically and otherwise. *Public opinion* – a thing more honored in the breach than in the observance, is beginning to make itself heard ... There are great old discussions & excitements going on. The cork seems to have come out since the old Emperor's death & the dear only knows what we'll see in the next 10 years – *doings* at any rate!'[10]

What could be hoped for from the current ferment? Looking at Japanese society, Caroline could see 'nothing but problems. Humanly speaking there is no way out of it all. If this nation does not come to know God soon, I do not know what the end will be ... A nation without God is a spectacle which one shudders *really* to think on ... She [Japan] is civilized and educated, but she's *materialistic* to the core. But God can penetrate into life here and He *must*.'[11]

The controversy over General Nogi and the stirrings of the new Taishō era led Caroline 'to study anew Christ's conception of life,' and what it might mean in a Japanese context. 'When all shall have what X [Christ] calls life, then the Kingdom of God will be here on earth as it now is in heaven.' She believed the distinction between earth and heaven to be an artificial one: 'In my opinion, there's no difference in the thought of God & there will be none when we have *faith* to believe that there is none,'[12] a theological statement worthy of her mentor in Aberdeen.

This theme was pursued throughout the spring of 1913 in a Bible class Caroline led with young women who had studied abroad, all Christians, and a few young missionaries. As the basis of study she chose 'a truly wonderful book,' *Christ's Message of the Kingdom*, by A.G. Hogg, a missionary of the United Free Church of Scotland, who had served for the past decade as professor of theology in Madras Christian College in India. Caroline thought this 'the stiffest Bible study' she had ever tackled with a group, but it was 'good for our souls.'[13] Although Hogg had never been formally a student of David Cairns, he declared in the preface that the book's 'distinctive standpoint' owed more to Cairns than to anyone else, thanks to 'certain memorable conversations' the two had enjoyed. On the title page a quotation from Cairns indicated the primary theme of a work that was to be widely used in the several editions published in the next decade: 'For the first time in history there appeared on earth One [Jesus] who absolutely trusted the unseen, who had utter confidence that Love was at the heart of all things, utter confidence also in the Absolute Power of that Absolute Love and in the liberty of that Love to help Him.'[14]

Caroline often thought of David Cairns, but not always in a theological context. Since her departure from Aberdeen there had been several exchanges of letters with her '*beloved* Professor.' Cairns had given her an enthusiastic account of a large conference held by the British SCM in Liverpool at Christmas 1911, at which he had been one of the principal speakers, and had thanked her for the information she had forwarded to him on Japanese religions. 'Of course he wouldn't write for any other reason than to acknowledge my kindness,' she remarked wistfully to her mother.[15]

When Caroline learned that 'the Great Beast,' an expression of mingled awe and affection she often used when referring to eminent persons, was going to lecture at several centres in North America, she immediately arranged for Cairns to visit her family. Soon she rejoiced that Cairns 'came

& saw & conquered,' and that her mother thought she showed a good head in regarding him so highly.[16] Yet Caroline exhorted her family not to be too sure that she had lost her heart as well as her head: 'At any rate I've got a string attached to it, so I can haul it back any time without *too much* injury to life & limb.'[17]

Her sister Peg's report that the absent-minded professor had left behind his brush and comb set was hard to believe, for Caroline had never seen him 'when he looked as if he'd ever used one ... His hair always looked as if he'd been in a football game. It's a great relief to know that at any rate he carries one with him!! But that he ever *uses* it you'll never make me believe!'[18] Clearly Cairns's casual grooming was more amusing than alienating to his former student. 'Don't count your chickens before they are hatched, Peggie dear, that's all. They are a long way from being hatched yet.'[19]

Caroline regretted that her sister Nellie had been unable to meet Cairns: 'You might have looked him over & let me know if you thought he'd do. I'm much too scared of matrimony (ahem!) to trust my own judgment in such a case. But if you said so I am sure it would be all O.K. Of course, I suppose he would have to say so too. Aye there's the rub!!'[20] That autumn she often wore the blue suit she had bought in Aberdeen: 'It is nice to feel that my heart beats under something (albeit but a coat!) Aberdonian.'[21]

For some months after Caroline learned that 'the Great Beast of Aberdeen' was to be one of the theme speakers at the meeting of the WSCF at Lake Mohonk in upstate New York in June 1913, she was ambivalent about a suggestion from Ruth Rouse of the WSCF staff that she should attend, along with Kawai Michi who was expected to be the leader of the Japanese delegates. When Kawai decided firmly that she had too much work to do in Japan and implied that Caroline did too, she quickly abandoned any further consideration of the matter, except to set in motion the process of sending Tsuda Ume to the gathering. As with so many of her friends, Tsuda and Rouse made a side trip to London, Ontario, to visit the Macdonald family, to Caroline's great satisfaction.[22]

The work that kept Kawai and Caroline in Japan was increasingly diverse. Responding to frequent requests from foreign women travellers for a place to stay, the YWCA decided to open a *pension* or residential club in Tokyo. The venture owed much to the generosity of Annie Dalton, former vice-principal of Havergal Girls' School in Toronto and an active member of the Canadian YWCA, who advanced the money, organized the project, and agreed to run the house herself. In addition to providing a needed service for women travellers and a place for them to meet Japanese women, it was hoped that the residence would make a profit and perhaps interest some wealthy travellers in the YWCA.[23]

A development planned for the past two years came to fruition with the opening of club rooms in downtown Yokohama where young women workers in offices and commercial enterprises could meet for lunch and discussion. The enterprise was possible thanks to the success of a fundraising campaign in the port city and the availability of Ninomiya Tei, a recent graduate of Smith College, to take charge of the work.[24] Before the end of 1912 Caroline welcomed Molly Baker, a graduate of Stanford University whom Caroline had met and encouraged in California, for she believed Baker was well suited for work in Japan, except for her height of six feet. Two weeks later Emma Kaufman arrived, making good on her promise three years earlier that she would return to work for the association. Together Baker and Kaufman began their language study with an enthusiasm and perseverance that soon won Caroline's admiration. Later, when Ninomiya Tei left to be married, Baker became the first full-time YWCA secretary in Yokohama,[25] while Kaufman began a long career as an unpaid volunteer secretary with the Tokyo association.

Although, as a member of the national staff, Caroline had no direct responsibility for the activities of the Tokyo YWCA, she rejoiced when it began work with nurses in the city. The opportunity to expand into a sphere that was one of the most rapidly growing occupations for women came through a Japanese friend of Caroline who spent several months in hospital and felt that many nurses, spiritually ill equipped for their work, often treated their patients insensitively and with little kindness. When the sick woman became a Christian, she was instrumental in starting a Bible class for a dozen nurses in that hospital, but did not live to see whether exposure to Christianity changed the nurses' sense of vocation, for she died a year later.[26]

Caroline returned from Karuizawa on short notice to be with her dying friend for a few hours. None of the woman's family were Christians, but Caroline observed that 'they were tremendously moved by her strong faith and quietness in face of death.' Caroline had seen enough of death in Japan to believe that 'a Xtn [Christian] death takes on new meaning when one realizes the pandemonium that reigns at non-Christian services. A Christian funeral out here can never be wholly sad. That passage "I am the

Resurrection and the Life" thrills through one like a new message when the only thing a non-Christian can say in face of death is "It can't be helped"'[27]

Further contact with nurses came about when a hospital located just behind the Sanbanchō house of the Tokyo YWCA burned down. 'The calling back and forth after the fire which is the custom in Japan' began, Caroline observed, on the day of the disaster when the director of the hospital 'came over ... still begrimed and somewhat bloody to apologize for having caused them [the YWCA staff] the inconvenience of having a fire so near them!!' Although his daughter was a member of the YWCA and had recently become a Christian, the hospital director said he knew nothing of the Bible but believed that nurses needed something Christians could give them. Thanks to these discussions the rebuilt hospital included a 'Religion Room' where the YWCA was soon holding a Bible class for some thirty nurses.[28]

In Macdonald's view 'no class of young women needs to know the comfort of the Christian life more than nurses.' Working 'desperately long and strenuous hours ... in the midst of suffering all the time ... for low wages' and in the face of severe housing problems, they were often at the mercy of exploitive agencies devoted to finding employment and housing for nurses. Thus there was need for 'some Christian agency to help nurses, not only individually, but to provide facilities, social and physical, which will create an environment where spiritual truths will have a larger chance to take root and grow.' Caroline hoped that eventually the YWCA would play an important role in helping to raise standards of education and training that would give nursing recognition as a profession, rather than the 'trade' it was now perceived to be by both nurses and the public.[29]

Another departure from the earlier pattern of work was the Tokyo association's venture into Fuji Bōseki, a cotton spinning factory in Honjo ward employing about 1,800 young women. In response to an appeal from the matron of the company dormitory that housed the workers, and with the agreement of one manager who was a Christian, the YWCA and the Salvation Army organized a meeting that attracted more than 1,000 girls to a room provided by the factory administration.[30] A monthly meeting continued to draw about 800, while the factory management watched closely before issuing a formal invitation for the YWCA to continue its moral education among their employees. 'If things succeed in that factory, we can go anywhere,' Macdonald believed, noting that 50,000 women were currently employed in Tokyo factories.[31]

What was the measure of success? Four years earlier, when the leader of the Salvation Army, Yamamuro Gumpei, and Kawai Michi addressed women workers in a Tokyo cotton mill, they had stressed the holiness of all labour and the example of Jesus as a carpenter, a worker.[32] Since the proclamation of such a message seemed to imply acquiescence in the grim working conditions endured by the women, it may well have been considered 'successful' by the management of that factory. Macdonald's measure of success was somewhat different, one that other YWCA staff members shared. Kawai Michi, thanks to her exposure to the ideas of the international YWCA on industrial problems and perhaps to Caroline's influence, had modified her attitudes, for she now saw improvement of the conditions of women workers as a priority for the Japanese YWCA.[33]

For Macdonald the factory work was at least as important as a means of awakening the consciences of middle-class members of the YWCA to the social conditions around them as for any short-term impact it might have on working women themselves, although she hoped that would be considerable.[34] She continued to believe that educated and informed middle-class women could help to bring about amelioration more effective than the minimal factory laws passed by the Diet in 1911, some of which concerned women and children but were not to be operative for up to ten years.[35] After a year, the management of Fuji Bōseki decided it was risky to have the YWCA in its factory; however harmless Bible reading and hymn singing appeared, such innovations might encourage the girls, many of whom were in their early teens, to start thinking for themselves and an orderly workplace would be disrupted.[36] For the time being YWCA work in Tokyo factories was ended.

Macdonald undertook two special and related assignments that would give her a chance, she hoped, to strike a blow for Japanese women. In twenty-one countries or areas represented at the Edinburgh conference, a 'continuation committee' was established to promote the ecumenical missionary strategy developed by the conference. Plans were set afoot for a series of conferences sponsored by the several continuation committees in Asia, including one in Japan in April 1913 when John R. Mott, Ruth Rouse, and other Christian luminaries would be present. Macdonald, Tsuda Ume, and Annie B. West, an American Presbyterian missionary, were the only women members of the continuation committee for Japan. Caroline was gratified when the committee gave the three women all responsibility 'for informing Mr. Mott of our women's doings in Japan. They've signed a blank cheque ... We'll fill it in all right!!'[37] Nothing that had happened since Mott's visit to Japan in 1907, including his role at the Edinburgh conference, had changed Caroline's conviction that although Mott was 'a Great Beast' and an effective 'mover and shaker,' he had a limited appreciation of the needs of women in Japan, and in other countries as well. For months Caroline and her small committee gathered information Caroline hoped would 'startle Mr. Mott within an inch of his life.' She wanted him to understand that 'half of the population of Japan is women & that they are not all enjoying a fool's paradise to say nothing of any other kind.'[38]

At the same time, Macdonald served as secretary of a committee of Japanese and foreigners who were actively promoting the long-standing dream of establishing a Christian college for women in Japan, a position that forced her into a concentrated period of work to prepare a twenty-page pamphlet explaining the need for the college. In this she worked closely with the American Presbyterian missionary A.K. Reischauer and his wife, who were leading promoters of the plan. If Mott and other missionary leaders could be convinced of the necessity for the college and of the commitment of influential Japanese to the proposal, it was hoped that substantial resources would be forthcoming from overseas.[39]

The report emphasized the significance of work among women students and the 'supreme importance' of Christian hostels in large cities 'so that student life in government schools may be adequately touched in a spiritual way.' The creation of a Christian university for women, one that would have the best academic standards in the land, was given the highest priority. A significant section of the report called for a comprehensive study of the effect of changing commercial and industrial conditions on the lives of the increasing number of women who were working outside the home, and for the introduction of 'a greatly enlarged and ... entirely new type of social and evangelistic work' among working women.[40]

After a plea for greater emphasis on women's work in the total strategy for Christian expansion in Japan and for the appointment of more women missionaries 'qualified to deal with present social and industrial problems,' the statement stressed the need for 'the fullest co-ordination of men's and women's Christian work' and for 'the due representation of women in counsel and administration.'[41] Since no one had a larger hand in the preparation of the report and its recommendations than Macdonald herself, she was well satisfied with them. She was also fully aware that Mott and other leaders of the missionary world, as well as church leaders in Japan, would need constant prodding if there was to be any result of the conference's approval of the report.[42]

■ ■ ■

A MORE RADICAL AND PUBLIC DEBATE over the roles of women than any evident in the missionary movement was currently creating a considerable ferment in Japanese society. Beginning in the literary and theatrical world, it soon had major social and political ramifications. A new theatre movement reflecting the realism of western theatre rather than the stylized Kabuki tradition was beginning to deal with modern social conflicts and was introducing women actresses to the stage after an absence of 300 years. In the autumn of 1911, the popular press gave considerable attention to a university production of Ibsen's *A Doll's House*. The play's questioning of the absolute sanctity of marriage and of male dominance in the home had aroused controversy in many countries, nowhere more than in Japan. Early in 1912, the newly established literary magazine *Seitō* (Bluestocking), named for the feminist Bluestocking movement in England, featured an extended discussion of the play. Although the editor, Hiratsuka Raichō, and other middle-class women founded the periodical as a vehicle for the publication of their writing, they soon confronted social and political interests eager to suppress the expression of their talents.

As the group increasingly questioned the Japanese family system, *Seitō* published a translation of *Love and Marriage* by the Swedish feminist Ellen Key, including the introduction by Havelock Ellis, as well as their own sometimes iconoclastic articles on 'The New Woman.' On several occasions, issues of *Seitō* were censored, or leaders of the Bluestockings were summoned to the police station to answer for their views. Although the group included women of widely differing opinions, it appeared to authorities charged with the defence of government social and educational policies that the whole concept of 'good wives and wise mothers' was under attack. Some members of the group were demanding full social and political rights at a time when women were not even allowed to attend political meetings as observers, while a few put their theories on a free sexual morality into practice, bringing down upon their heads the wrath of government and public and creating dissension within their own ranks.[43] 'The woman question' was full of possibilities for social unrest and must be carefully watched.

Inevitably the YWCA and Tsuda College, especially the latter, felt the impact of the Bluestocking movement. Tsuda Ume rightly considered herself a 'new woman,' but she had little use for *Seitō* and its admirers. The upper-class parents of most Tsuda College students wanted their daughters to receive a modern education but neither they, nor Tsuda, wanted them to be totally westernized. The college stressed the validity of traditional Japanese virtues. Tsuda and her staff upheld Japanese manners and etiquette, not only as values in themselves but as the path to acceptance of the school and its graduates in Japanese society. It was assumed that virtually all women would marry and that their education would make them better wives and mothers in ways that did not altogether abandon tradition. Nevertheless, at a time when women's education emphasized 'domestic science,' Tsuda's endeavour to prepare women to become financially independent of men, capable of intellectual and spiritual cooperation with men, and active contributors to society, was radical.

A degree of affinity with the objectives of the Bluestockings did not prevent Tsuda and her colleagues from being highly critical of them. Although Tsuda frequently praised the desire for self-realization and the spirit of rebellion against 'unreasonable restraint of women's liberty,' she condemned the Bluestockings as an evil influence whose claims on behalf of women were 'lawless and immoral.' If hatred and rebellion were the result of 'self-realization and the awakening that education brings, must it end there?'[44] Kawai Michi shared Tsuda's views of the Bluestockings, prayed that God would 'save these poor girls from Satan,' and joined with other women to organize 'The Real New Women,' which undertook a campaign to 'uphold humanity' against a 'brutal liberation' of their sex. The campaign received little support and was soon abandoned.[45]

Tsuda and her fellow educators were forced to realize that they could not always protect their students from 'false' views of liberation. The ideas about the independence of women they themselves promoted might lead in many directions. The first editor of *Seitō*, Hiratsuka Raichō, disillusioned by the conservatism of Joseph Naruse and Japan Women's University, left to study at Tsuda College; she was disappointed there as well and did not stay very long. When the Bluestockings adopted an active feminist political stance, one Tsuda student, Kamichika Ichiko, became one of their most visible and forceful speakers. On an occasion when she returned to the college from a meeting of the Bluestockings, one of her teachers offered a prayer for her in the classroom. In the face of such pressure, Kamichika suddenly left the feminist group because of her fear that she would not be allowed to graduate if she persisted in the association.[46] Her contemporary at Tsuda, Yamakawa Kikue, adopted a socialist position that demanded the abolition of private property, which she saw as the basis of women's slavery.[47] Yamakawa felt that her teachers, Tsuda and Kawai, were 'pure idealists. They were ... naive and innocent, totally cut off from the real world. They were completely unaware of what the students were thinking about and what they were searching for.' Despite her feeling that 'the institution was as strict as a convent,' Yamakawa spent four years at Tsuda College and graduated to become a leader of the 'New Women.'[48] She remained an ardent feminist all her life, as were many Tsuda graduates. Her perception of the limitations of her education never destroyed Yamakawa's conviction that Tsuda Ume's rejection of 'the slave morality and spineless submissiveness' of other schools made her a true pioneer in the education of Japanese women.[49]

Through her teaching at Tsuda College, Macdonald was aware of the impact of the feminist debate on the students. For reasons not apparent, and avowing that she had not been a suffragist as recently as her sojourn in Aberdeen, she declared early in 1912 that she was one now.[50] That gave her some sympathy with some women in the current feminist movement, but on the whole she had little use for the Bluestockings. At the same time, despite the involvement of Kawai Michi, she thought 'the Real New Women' and their successors 'just as far removed from rational thinking.' Shortly after the formal demise of the *Seitō* group in 1916, she observed that 'many of the women are still writing arrant nonsense for the multifarious magazines that seem willing to publish any sort of trash.' As with Tsuda and Kawai, it was the freewheeling sexual morality of the more radical feminists that Caroline found most objectionable. She regretted that 'in more than one tragic and pathetic case these women have been logical enough to make attempts to live their theories, but most of them are willing to remain theorists and simply give advice which some of the weaker sisters follow in practice.'[51] Although Macdonald expressed herself in more moderate and less dramatic language than Tsuda and Kawai, she was, not surprisingly, in fundamental agreement with them, for they were her primary mentors in educational matters. While they advocated significant change in the status of women, Tsuda and Kawai and others like them also reflected the determination of Japanese leaders, male and female, to preserve a unique

Japanese culture. Macdonald had become increasingly sympathetic to their cautious, evolutionary philosophy.

While Christian women educators accepted and indeed argued for greater freedom for women in their choice of marriage partners, in their relationships with their husbands, and in their vocational choices, they also feared the consequences of the breakdown of old moralities. Caroline lamented that the education in the state schools was 'not making for a keener moral sense.' She sympathized with girls who 'are lectured about being good wives and wise mothers, until in sheer desperation they go off on the rebound into the wildest excesses; boys, who might do well to listen to a few lectures on the duty of being good husbands and wise fathers, are taught nothing which even remotely approaches the attitude men ought to take towards women, not even towards their mothers, sisters or wives ... It is not to be expected that the ordinary boy will grow up with any innate respect for women.'[52]

The need for women to be respected was at the core of Macdonald's rejection of any advocacy of sudden and radical change in their status. She was convinced that no real reformation could occur until women had self-respect and were respected by men. A different education for both women and men, not radical action that would destroy the whole social fabric, was the path toward establishing that respect. A little later, in 1918, she noted that there were twice as many geisha, licensed prostitutes and bar girls, as there were girls in high school, and that despite growing educational opportunities women were still too restricted to lowly occupations that required little education and did not command respect. The traditional education, with its emphasis on obedience to father, husband, and son, deprived women of self-respect and did nothing to foster new attitudes in men. Through a gradual process of education and expanding experience, women in this 'epoch of individuality' must be enabled to assume responsibility for their own words and deeds, not in a spirit of selfishness but out of respect for themselves and others.[53]

After the First World War, some former Bluestockings and other women began to organize 'The New Women's Association' to work for better education for women, the revision of laws that worked against women, and measures to protect mothers. High on their list of priorities was a campaign to make sure that the growing movement for 'universal suffrage' would not mean just male suffrage.[54]

Caroline had no difficulty in supporting these objectives and she wished the new organization well. Although she never lost interest in the education and advancement of women, by this time her life had taken a sudden and dramatic turn and she was well established in a new vocation.

Chapter 7

'God's Strange Leading'

O~N A FRIDAY EVENING~ in mid-October 1913, Caroline was relaxing with some of her YWCA colleagues around the table after dinner in the Tamachi house where they were celebrating her thirty-ninth birthday. At about ten o'clock the phone rang and Caroline answered. The others immediately sensed bad news, an impression confirmed by Caroline's face as she returned to the group. The call was from Annie West, an American Presbyterian missionary whose earlier work with prisoners of war had given her close ties to the Red Cross. West reported that a young man, Yamada Zen'ichi, an employee of the Red Cross and a member of Caroline's Sunday evening Bible class for the past two years, had come home that evening and murdered his wife and two small sons. He then went directly to the police station and gave himself up. Yamada had been baptized less than a year earlier, and his wife within the last month. Caroline was stunned by the news. What had happened to this devoted husband and father, 'one of the nicest Japanese young men' she had ever known?[1] She recalled that twice during the preceding month he had come to see her and she had not realized that he needed help. On one of these occasions she had been very busy and had exchanged only a few words with him. Was it possible that had she been more sensitive this tragedy could have been prevented? In the months and years to come she was never able to dismiss this question completely, although it did not oppress her.[2]

The next night Caroline joined Miss West and Yoshiyasu Nobutarō, the chief secretary of the Red Cross, and three of Yamada's young friends in an all-night vigil at Yamada's home. The two women and Yoshiyasu, a Christian, held an informal service, sang hymns, and talked with the shocked and grieving young men: Nishimura, Kobayashi, and Masuda, all in their twenties. At five in the morning they all started in procession to the Fujimichō church, walking beside the three coffins carried on poles by several men, for the funeral service at seven o'clock. This Sunday was to have been a day of rejoicing over the baptism of the Kanehoras, the couple who had been the servants in the Tamachi house for the past year. Now it was impossible for Caroline to prevent the murders from dominating her thoughts: 'Nothing matters anymore ... and one can only think of the awfulness of it for him when he comes to himself ... He couldn't have meant to do it. There must have come some awful snap in his brain. Such is the cost of friendship. Agony such as one cannot express, the actual bitterness of death – but nevertheless he is still a "brother beloved" & one can only pray – what one scarcely knows.'[3]

In six weeks' time, at the conclusion of the preliminary court examination, during which the public procurator established a case against Yamada, Macdonald was allowed to visit him in Ichigaya prison. Arriving early on a cold December morning, she was given the number 36 and prepared for a long, cold wait while each of the people ahead of her had the prescribed five-minute visit. Walking up and down to keep warm, her heart was 'away down where it shouldn't be. Of course I wanted to see him, but I could have screamed or run away or fainted. I had all feelings in turn.' Suddenly, just after number 12, number 36 was called, a privilege no doubt extended to her as a foreigner. Macdonald and Yamada spoke in the presence of a guard, as required. 'It was not easy for either of us.' Hard as it was to understand his frame of mind, she came away 'quite sure that he has found God's pardon and peace.'[4]

In the days that followed, Macdonald visited Yamada several times amid increasingly polite cooperation from prison officials who often admitted her before other visitors, sometimes prolonged her stay half an hour or more by neglecting to tell her time was up, or admitted her during periods when the regulations prohibited visiting.[5]

When the trial began on 23 December 1913, Macdonald and West were in the courtroom, honouring their promise to Yamada that they would be there to support him. They waited all morning in the company of Nishimura and Kobayashi, whose devotion to their friend over the past two months had moved Caroline deeply. She wondered 'what they would have done without us. They were nearly wild with excitement. They need to know God badly.' In the end the court postponed the trial for a month, thus giving Caroline time to develop the 'entirely new vocabulary in the vernacular' that she was learning from lawyers, prison officials, and policemen.[6]

Macdonald and West decided to seek the advice of one of the country's most distinguished lawyers, Miyaoka Tsunejirō, whom Caroline had met on board ship during her first trip home when he was counsellor to the Japanese Embassy in Washington. Miyaoka specialized in constitutional law and knew nothing about Yamada's case, but he was more than willing to help, and raised some disquieting questions about the competence of Yamada's lawyer, Tokumoto Kanzō, secured for him by the Red Cross.[7] Thereafter, thanks to the good offices of Miyaoka and Dr. Uemura, the most celebrated criminal lawyer in Japan, Uzawa Fusaaki, who was also an elder in Fujimichō church, agreed to join Tokumoto in defending Yamada. But first it was essential for Macdonald and West to engage in delicate negotiations with Tokumoto concerning Uzawa's role in the case. Despite their apprehensions that Tokumoto would be offended, he 'acted like a man all the way through' and earned a respect the two women never had reason to lose.[8]

As the new trial date drew near, Yamada told Caroline: 'I am trusting in God's grace, but the dark days come over me ... I can only keep trusting even then.' Macdonald and West tried to answer his questions about life after death. 'Poor boy. What we are asking him! To trust in face of that! But he must face it & conquer, before the day ... of the public trial & I am sure he *has*.'[9]

Yamada did not disappoint them. Although he later reported that he nearly lost consciousness two or three times while he was being questioned, he was very quiet, 'distinctly conscious of a voice beside him: "Do not be afraid. I am here with you," and he was given power again.' On the first day of the trial, Yamada found the courage to tell the truth in all its terrible detail, taking all the blame on himself. He confessed to having reacted jealously and violently to revelations of some actions of his wife two years earlier, and to having been enraged by her over-spending; now he attributed her actions to his own failure to set her a better example.[10]

Suddenly, on 16 February, the first anniversary of Yamada's baptism, when it was announced that the trial would be continued the next day, the eminent lawyer Uzawa was nowhere to be found. He had to appear in court to establish his participation in the case. Caroline and her associates were 'literally stricken to [their] knees in prayer that he might come if it were God's will.' At the same time Caroline was busy leaving messages with anyone who might conceivably see Uzawa.[11] The next morning Uzawa was in the courtroom. As agreed, Tokumoto requested a postponement to allow Uzawa to familiarize himself with the case. Macdonald was confident that now Uzawa would 'really get into touch with the truth in all its bearings.'[12]

Later, when the trial resumed, Uzawa made no attempt to minimize the gravity of Yamada's crime by pleading temporary insanity or any other extenuating circumstance. He rested his argument for clemency entirely on the ground that Yamada's total repentance and changed life had already brought the reformation of character that was the true object of punishment, and therefore a severe sentence was unnecessary. To Caroline's ears this was 'both good law and good religion,' as fine a Christian sermon as she had ever heard, and one to which the three judges listened attentively.[13] One of them, Judge Iyama, was visibly moved: 'He certainly saw visions as Uzawa-san testified to the grace of God in such a striking way ... The way he stared at the ceiling ... we thought his official head gear would topple off.'[14]

At the end of the trial, when Yamada was asked if he had anything to say, he 'stood and with a voice which was firm even when it broke said: "I did not tell any lies, & even if I receive capital punishment, I am content."' In Caroline's view 'perhaps nothing could impress the judges more than that perfectly simple statement.' The procurator, who usually got his way, as Caroline correctly understood, contended for life imprisonment. As she waited for the sentencing in a few days' time, she was confident that Yamada would not be given the ultimate penalty. She was profoundly thankful that she '*never* did believe in capital punishment, *for any* offence whatever. Of course nobody does except in theory.'[15]

In some measure Uzawa's plea for clemency was heeded. Yamada was sentenced to seventeen years in jail, but he might not have to serve that

long, for the law allowed a prison governor to release a prisoner for exceptionally good conduct after he had served a third of his sentence. Altogether
the sentence was a relief. Then within a few days came a bolt from the blue:
the procurator had appealed the sentence, arguing that it was too light.
Despite her awareness of the enormous power of procurators in the court
system, Caroline had not expected this turn of events. Why the procurator
should care was impossible for her to fathom. What was clear was that now
'our poor boy' would have to endure a second prolonged ordeal. It also
meant that her trip home in two months' time would probably have to be
postponed.[16]

She felt uncomfortable about 'what the girls [her YWCA colleagues]
would think if they knew [she] even contemplated' delaying the trip, for like
most foreigners they would not understand the depth of her involvement in
Yamada's fate.[17] Nor did she have any confidence that the officers of the
Canadian YWCA would understand the postponement when it would make
it impossible for her to attend the annual summer conference in Muskoka
or to fulfil other engagements for the association. All she could tell them was
that circumstances had arisen relating to 'a very special ministry.'[18]

This whole affair was revealing to her how much she was identified with
her Japanese friends. She had so often been asked, 'Can you ever get to
know the Japanese?' Recent events gave her a firm answer:

> Know the Japanese! I know some of them better than I know my own
> nationality. Witness this! In the church I go to ... everybody knows
> about this very great sorrow ... We are all one there. But I'd take a fit if
> it were announced at the foreign church. I'd hate to have people gossip
> about it! Some of my foreign friends do know, but I'd hate to have the
> foreign *populace* know, for among them are some ... who just wouldn't
> understand ... that my poor boy was a friend and not a case & I couldn't
> stand that.[19]

The trial before the Court of Appeal was scheduled for 1 June and in the
view of the lawyers would not be prolonged. Thus Caroline still had some
hope of going home that summer, although the prospect grew dimmer with
the illness of two of her YWCA colleagues and the demands of the summer
conference with a diminished staff. Her mother found it hard to accept the
idea that Caroline might not come home as planned and needed further
commentary on her daughter's situation:

Yes, mother dear ... crime is a serious and terrible thing ... No one who
has touched this thing minimizes the crime ... We all have had to shoul-
der our share ... but God has shown ... that his love extends deep enough
to cover it all ... 'Is God able to save to the uttermost?' is a serious question. It says so over and over again ... I will remember thy sins no more,
I have cast them into the depths of the sea ... It's a serious responsibility
... to tell a person who has done what my friend has done ... whether
these things are true ... If they are *not* true, then we make God untrue –
and if they are true, then God must honour His Word. And he has.[20]

It was 'not only the lad himself, but the others who are coming' that
kept her in Tokyo. In one of the most dramatic developments, the 'careless
young scamp,' Nishimura Saburō, Yamada's best friend, whom Caroline had
first met on the night of the murders, had 'turned serious,' a description she
often used of those who exhibited an enquiring spirit about religious and
moral questions. That stage reached, she was applying herself to the onerous
task of 'bringing [him] up by hand.' She had 'been with him at the prison, at
the courthouse, at the cemetery more than once, at the house on that night
before the funeral ... and in church.' She had visited his mother several
times and had had numerous discussions with him alone. Sometimes he
attended the Wednesday evening meetings Caroline had recently begun to
hold in her home for all who wished to discuss the Christian faith.[21]

Nishimura's devotion to Yamada was 'the most extraordinary thing'
Caroline had ever witnessed. She was sure it was the basis of his growing
understanding of 'God's love and patient endurance ... at his own wayward-
ness,' and was at the root of his decision to become a Christian. He was
under no illusion that this would be easy: 'He's gone too deep into experience of life & failure during the past few months ... There are lots of things
he doesn't know yet but what he's learned he hasn't learned in *books*.'
Although he didn't even know the Lord's Prayer yet, she had heard him
utter 'an extraordinary prayer for himself' that convinced her that he understood the meaning of Christ's death even if he knew little of His life.[22]
Moreover, another of Yamada's friends, Kobayashi, was attending the
Wednesday evening meetings and was 'on the point of tumbling over.'
Although he was still too 'bent on getting everything through his head ... his
soul is waking up ... and he will learn to know ... God's comfort, even in this
terrible thing.'[23]

Within Ichigaya prison, Yamada's 'marvellous sense of God's forgiveness' caused astonishment among many of the guards and some of the prisoners. One young guard had already declared "'*having seen the agony of our friend*, I have recognized my own sins, & am repentant and wish to follow Christ." That has been the strange part of it all,' Caroline observed. 'The agony of our friend has made us recognize *our own sins*.'[24]

As the trial before the Court of Appeal approached, Macdonald rejoiced over the four prison guards who had 'definitely begun to lead Xtian [Christian] lives.' Another forty, one third of the total number in Ichigaya prison, had given their names and home addresses to Macdonald or West so that they might receive Bibles and copies of a devotional guide, *Hibi No Kate* (Daily Food). Prison regulations forbade them to receive literature of any kind while on duty.[25] At a recent meeting near the prison, thirteen guards had shown up and others had expressed interest but were on duty. This expansion of 'the whole circle of God's wonderful working' brought 'vividness and reality' to Caroline's reading of Paul's letter to the Philippians: "'My bonds became manifest in Christ throughout the whole praetorian guard" & then "all the saints salute you, especially those that are of Caesar's household" ... The whole praetorian guard of this 20th century place are being mightily moved by the spirit of the Living God.' It was impossible to think of going home: 'I cannot leave the things which in this awful strange way God has thrust me into.'[26]

To Caroline's great surprise, Yamada's lawyer, Mr. Tokumoto, who had appeared to be entirely a-religious during eight months' connection with the case, was so overcome by the change in Yamada that he was asking questions. 'I don't understand this thing at all,' he told Macdonald. 'It's a strange case altogether. There's not the slightest need of that man being in prison any longer ... I'm ashamed to say that my ideas of God are very vague.' She was sure they would soon be clearer: 'He'll come in some day – & before long.'[27]

With so much change in her life, Caroline found the courage to determine that this year she would have a different kind of summer. She would not go to Karuizawa: 'I've always hated these summer places where you run the gamut of attending committee meetings, & refusing to go to tea parties, & being asked why you weren't at a certain tennis match or prayer meeting. You might as well be out of Japan altogether. Foreigners (that's our *color* of people) galore & I don't know a tenth of them & care for less than that number.' By staying in Tokyo she avoided a 'month of bad temper' and had the most satisfactory summer since she came to Japan. There was time for reading, visiting friends, a few days' quiet in the countryside, and, of first importance, her regular visits to Ichigaya prison. Her friends declared that she was 'the fittest looking of the whole YWCA bunch.' The others had gone to Karuizawa.[28]

By the end of the summer, the First World War had broken out in Europe. Macdonald was deeply thankful that she had been unable to go home. Had she gone, she 'might have been coralled [*sic*] in Canada & been obliged to stay. Gracious, I'd have been like a caged lion.' Although she hoped that Japan's involvement in the war would remain minimal, Caroline was glad that her adopted country had 'jumped in' on the right side. While observing that 'men are being slaughtered literally for no reason' in Europe, at the same time she had no doubt that Britain had entered the war on 'high principle' and 'democracy is bound to win.' It was 'the whole rotten system of militarism that's wrong and ... Germany is the most unfortunate country in existence even if she should win, which of course she won't, for God is not on the side of what Germany is standing for.' The defeat of Germany would be salutary for Japan, which had copied Germany in 'so many of her *material* things,' for defeat would demonstrate to 'this little nation ... that the race is *not* to the swift nor the battle to the strong in things material, and so it will all count in the advancement of God's Kingdom.'[29]

Among the few acts of war in East Asia was the Japanese capture in the autumn of 1914 of Tsingtao, the German concession on the coast of China, an event that had seemed inevitable from the outset. Caroline was thankful when 'that special phase' was over without much bloodshed. The fall of Tsingtao produced a sea of Union Jacks and Japanese flags in Tokyo: 'We are certainly "Allies" – may we be also in the things that make for the coming of the Prince of Peace.'[30]

■ ■ ■

THROUGH THAT LONG HOT SUMMER and into the autumn the trial before the Court of Appeal was postponed again and again. The respite provided opportunities to expand prison visitation and to invite guards to attend meetings of the great evangelistic campaign just begun by the Protestant churches throughout Japan. Macdonald and West now had contact with 80 of the 120 officials in Ichigaya prison, many of whom attended some of the evangelistic meetings. Increasingly, Macdonald admired the decency and kindness of prison guards: 'It's astonishing what serious men they are, poor fellows. They find their work mighty strenuous when it is only their daily work, & it's wonderful how changed it becomes when they think of it as a vocation "to bind up the broken hearted and to give release to the captives."'[31]

That autumn, two more guards and the wife of one were baptized, as was Yamada's friend Nishimura Saburō, with General Ōe, head of the army commissariat, and Macdonald as his sponsors. In the congregation of Fujimichō church at the baptism were fourteen people who had been brought together through their association with the prisoner Yamada. Several of them were soon to be baptized as well. For some time Nishimura had been conducting a Sunday school in his own neighbourhood where he spoke each Sunday to the more than sixty children 'in a wonderfully simple way.'[32] It was 'all quite beyond our believing but God is moving so palpably and so wonderfully that one can only give thanks.'[33]

At last, more than a year after the murders and five months after the first sentencing, the Appeal Court heard Yamada's case. Again the procurator pressed for a sentence of life imprisonment. To Caroline's astonishment, on the first day the defence lawyer, Tokumoto Kanzō, demonstrated how his own perceptions had expanded when he ended his presentation by saying that Dr. Uzawa 'would speak on the *religious* aspect of the case!!' The next day Dr. Uzawa was in fine form and again 'preached the gospel of God' which had so transformed the accused. Now Caroline could only pray that 'the judges may be willing to make a *great experiment*. She was certain that the case made for his transformation and exemplary conduct would save Yamada from life imprisonment. Like the lawyers, she believed the worst that could happen would be confirmation of the seventeen-year sentence.[34]

The Japanese judicial system was not ready for a 'great experiment': the sentence was life imprisonment. Yamada took the news as Caroline would have expected, 'without a turn of countenance. "Thou shalt keep him in *perfect peace* whose mind is stayed on thee." It was peace not merely self control ... no one saw any change of countenance on me either. I haven't faced judges and procurators 12 or 14 odd times and listened to what I have listened to without having grown to have complete charge of my own facial expression.'[35] In a Canadian court would the revelations of her countenance have been of such concern? Was it Christian faith or Japanese convention that required her apparent impassiveness?

The warden who came to lead Yamada from the courtroom was a 'big rough fellow' who had recently attended meetings in Caroline's home. He escorted Yamada in a friendly manner down the corridor, with a smile of reassurance to Macdonald and West. The next morning Macdonald went with Nishimura to see Yamada. A further appeal to the Supreme Court was open, but Yamada told his visitors: 'I submit to the judgment. I take it as my *vocation*.' The following day Macdonald and Dr. Uemura went to the prison, the last day before Yamada's transfer to Kosuge prison and a new way of life, where at best he would be allowed only monthly visits from Macdonald or West.[36]

Although she had prayed for a lighter sentence and was already consulting her lawyer friends about how to secure imperial clemency at the time of next year's coronation, Caroline saw the working of God in the heavier sentence: 'This will bring men to God when a light sentence might only have made them glad. God's power is shown here not by making the sentence light but by giving Himself to bear it – not because it can't be helped but as a *vocation*. You can't explain that apart from God! The light sentence might have been the sympathy of the judges!!'[37]

In Caroline's rather convoluted theology, the heavy sentence was already showing God's power. A twenty-five-year-old prison guard who had 'grown serious' several months earlier came to see her the morning after the sentencing. He had been on duty in Yamada's section of the prison for some months and had seen him on his return from court the day before. Macdonald asked after Yamada.

> The young man straightened himself up, looked at me and said, as if he were talking of an achievement of his own – 'He's perfectly quiet about it all ... And besides ... he doesn't want to appeal! He's perfectly content.' And then an awestruck look came over his countenance & he dropped his head for a moment and then looked at me & said, 'Christian power is a great thing isn't it?' ... My methods of evangelism are direct (a good deal directer than they used to be) and I made a personal application on the spot.[38]

Later that day, as she walked on the road to the prison, another guard waited and went through the gates with her into the prison garden where he engaged her in discussion. He was not surprised at Yamada's calm acceptance of his sentence and was sure that wherever he was sent now he would 'lighten dark places.' Macdonald replied: '"And think ... of those among yourselves who have already been *saved!* (That's a perfectly good Japanese word and it means exactly what it says!). Then I mentioned the names of two whom he knows & then ... And you!" And he replied quickly, "Yes, and I!"' This new declaration of faith confirmed her interpretation of the efficacy of the life sentence: 'How glad they all would have been if it had been light. But to think it was a *life* sentence and he took it as he did – and ... every man of them knew he would take it that way before they saw him.'[39]

As 1914 drew to a close Caroline looked back to its beginning: 'I don't believe I had begun to live until then but I am very much alive now ... both in body & in mind.' Nobody could have foreseen when she 'took the first step as a matter of course to stand by the boy' where it would all lead. 'Step by step it all came & woe unto Miss West & me had we refused it ... It wasn't my responsibility – it was God's & I knew I had the right to claim the means whereby to live & do it all.[40]

■ ■ ■

CAROLINE HAD REASON to look back even further, for it was ten years since she first set foot in Japan. To think herself 'back into pre-Japanese times' was impossible: 'Was there ever a time when I didn't know Kawai San & Mr. Uemura & Miss West, Miss Tsuda, & all the host who are dearer to me than my life. Was there ever a time when there was no YWCA in Japan? I suppose there was but I have forgotten. But I haven't forgotten one other spot on earth ... *my other home* in Canada.' Before long she would 'run home for a bit' to see her family, but for the present she must be faithful to the obligations of her life in Japan.[41]

Looking back over the past decade, nothing was more significant than the growth of her friendship with Annie West. Soon after her arrival in Japan, Macdonald met West, who had come to Japan at the age of twenty-one nearly thirty years earlier. A freelance American Presbyterian, West's work among prisoners of war in both the Sino-Japanese and Russo-Japanese wars had given her close connections with the army, the Red Cross, and the Imperial Court, which had decorated her for her services. Among foreigners in Tokyo few were better known than the tall, handsome woman with the generous head of light red hair. West recruited Macdonald to membership in the Red Cross and they had a shared interest in the YWCA. Later, when Yamada Zen'ichi worked for the Red Cross and joined Caroline's Bible class, they had another common interest, brought into sharp focus by the tragic murders. Neither of them then dreamed of how closely they would work together.

> And then when the day came that we knew we were one in heart. How could we have done it all together ... if God had not been preparing us during those years of seemingly ordinary providences that we might bear together the Cross he gave us & enter in together into the *fellowship of His suffering* ... In prisons, cemeteries, in houses over which the shadow of tragedy unretrievable from all human standpoint hangs ... where have we not been – together in body and spirit. May all the lessons we have learned & will learn be used that others may know Him. Oh God give us all what we need to be good friends, the kind of friend he was Himself to men & women & little children.[42]

At the end of 1914, when Yamada was transferred to Kosuge prison, an institution for prisoners awaiting execution or serving sentences of more than ten years, it seemed to Macdonald and West that their visits to Ichigaya would henceforth be rare, for Yamada had been the key to their admission to the prison. To Caroline 'it did not seem lack of faith to believe so,' it was just a recognition of reality. Before his departure Yamada had asked his friends to pray for thirty-one men awaiting execution. 'We did pray – for *nothing* definitely – but we did pray that somehow or other they might be comforted ... And then ... within two weeks – the names given us & permission to send things to them which would at least show these poor fellows that someone *cared* ... that they might really come to know that above all God did care.'[43]

Macdonald perceived other strange 'combinations of providences' at work. Early on the first Sunday morning in 1915, a woman with a baby on her back and another child by the hand came to thank her for the literature sent to her husband, Koizumi, one of those on death row in Ichigaya prison. Although the woman was only thirty-two, she looked fifty and 'as stupid as most women who'd been knocked about as she had been all her life, but she had had sense enough to come to us.' In a few minutes one of the recent converts among the prison guards, Kobayama, dropped in and the visitors recognized one another as old acquaintances. Kobayama prayed with the woman and promised to tell Koizumi that he had seen his wife. A few days later, Macdonald went with the 'weary and pathetic woman,' at her request, to visit her husband. 'These visits of the wives to their husbands,' exclaimed Caroline, 'what have they to say – what comfort can they give!' After a few minutes when the allotted visiting time had expired, the wife disappeared, as previously arranged, leaving Caroline alone with the 'quiet looking man of 40, crushed with it all,' and consumed with anxiety about his four young children.[44]

That was the beginning of Koizumi's transformation. Within six months he had become a Christian, Macdonald had arranged for the care of his children, his wife was a regular member of the Wednesday evening meetings, and his case had been appealed and the death sentence commuted to fifteen years' imprisonment. Macdonald could find no better explanation for all this than her own: 'It was because I was *saved.*' Then came the day of his transfer to Kosuge prison, when she and Koizumi's wife stood together and 'watched him depart through those gates which we had not thought to ever see him depart, those gates which to many already have become the gates of praise.'[45]

Now Macdonald had two friends in Kosuge prison, Yamada and Koizumi. She thought she would see them infrequently, for nobody but relatives were allowed to visit prisoners there, and neither she nor Miss West had any contact with officials of that prison. Within a few weeks, prospects changed dramatically when Arima Shirosuke was appointed governor of Kosuge.

Within a month of Arima's assumption of his duties at Kosuge, Macdonald met him and secured permission to visit Yamada and Koizumi, much to the surprise and delight of both men. At about the same time, the governor of Ichigaya prison made it clear that she and Annie West would continue to be welcome visitors to his prison. Contrary to their expectations, the doors to prison work were not closing but opening wider than ever.[46]

• • •

HER CONTACT WITH the wives and children of prisoners, as well as with prisoners, was adding to Macdonald's understanding of the lives of the poorer people of Tokyo. She had never been entirely unaware of them, thanks to her work with factory girls, and recently the YWCA had established a Travellers' Aid department and was developing a more active interest in 'neighbourhood work.' Modelled on similar services in North American railway stations and ocean ports, the Travellers' Aid program grew so rapidly that it was difficult to keep up with the demands for help from young women who were flocking into Tokyo from the countryside to look for work. Many of them had run away from poverty-stricken homes or had been turned out by their fathers or brothers without means of support. A young woman who had been a member of a night class Caroline had conducted among telephone workers shortly after her arrival in Japan gave her a tour of the world that absorbed many of these girls. After reading a book about the dark side of life in Tokyo, the young woman decided to conduct her own social survey. For five months she worked as a waitress in a large restaurant 'where other things went on besides feeding people.' Later she had opened a small shop in the 'Coney Island' of Tokyo, Asakusa, and now Caroline was going to 'nose about' with her for a day or two.[47]

On a spring morning in the company of their young guide, Macdonald and Ruth Ragan, an American member of the YWCA staff, set out on foot to view the slums of East Tokyo. First they passed through the notorious Yoshiwara district where thousands of licensed prostitutes conducted their business, the district Mrs. Nitobe had recently described to Caroline as 'HELL.' In the morning there was little activity in the spacious main street with the rows of cherry trees in bloom down the middle, and few signs of life in the windows of the houses displaying their colourful screens and rugs. However, it took little imagination for Caroline to visualize 'the horror of life' in Yoshiwara. 'Of course the whole section of the city – nay the whole country – is rotten because of it!' Then they moved on to their main destination, the slums of Asakusa where Caroline hoped the YWCA would eventually establish a settlement house. 'Wouldn't I like to get my fists on that section of the city and build a beautiful building in the midst of it for the little children & the young girls & boys & for the tired looking mothers we saw. I believe we could revolutionize life down there ... Yes, I want to see a settlement built on the edge of HELL.'[48] Already, with funds provided by Emma Kaufman's parents, who had recently visited their daughter in Tokyo, the YWCA had begun work with mothers and children in the vicinity of its two student hostels, while some members were beginning to think about creating a full-scale settlement house.[49]

Some weeks after her foray into the slums of East Tokyo, Macdonald and Annie West were keeping a midnight vigil with a stricken prison guard beside the body of his dead wife. They tried to bring comfort to him through 'the strange mingling ... of superstition and true religion' which possessed him. Eventually, when the man went to sleep, they began to discuss the future. There 'for the first time with any living soul' Caroline revealed the vision that had come to fill her imagination. It was not a tentative proposal, advanced for her friend's approval, for Caroline 'had faced it all not as a mere probability, but as a certainty in God's strange leading.'[50] She knew now that work with prisoners was no longer an avocation. It was her vocation, and it would form the basis for developing a settlement house that would revolutionize the life of East Tokyo.

The decision Caroline announced to Annie West was a more drastic turn in her life than perhaps even she realized at the time. Its radical nature was not fully evident in her own description of her action. Since the crisis precipitated by Yamada's murder of his family, Caroline had spoken a more conventionally evangelical language than she had used before, or would use in years to come. In her emphasis on 'sin,' 'forgiveness,' and 'saving,' she drew on terms long familiar to her and in common use among her missionary colleagues, most of whom saw their task as the salvation of individual souls. This vocabulary had always had meaning for her, not just in individual personal terms but in a social context as well. Briefly now, under the emotion aroused by recent events, the personal dimension seemed to be dominant. Her acute sense of her own sin and her preoccupation with forgiveness stemmed largely from her continuing anxiety about the degree of her responsibility for Yamada's crime.

That she felt as she did was a mark of her identification with her friends and was at least a partial rejection of the usual missionary role. Few missionaries would give up the summer retreat to Karuizawa, nor, as she observed, would they understand how any obligation in Japan could be compelling enough to dictate the abandonment of a furlough at home. Her new commitment was changing her whole focus. For the past decade she had worked mainly among educated middle- and upper-class women; now her major concern was with the most marginalized people in Japanese society, almost entirely males.

Nowhere was the highly developed Japanese sense of shame more evident than in social attitudes toward incarcerated criminals. A person sent to jail brought intense shame on his whole family, no less than on himself.[51] In her new vocation Caroline was among the lowliest of the low. In this position she viewed Japanese society from a different perspective than before, one that increasingly separated her from most of the foreign missionary community and involved her with Japanese reformers and activists.

C h a p t e r   8

Prisoners and Prisons

W<small>HEN</small> C<small>AROLINE</small> M<small>ACDONALD</small> became a prison worker, she was stepping into a well-established role for Christians in Japan. Her entry into prison work owed much to Annie West's long experience in Japanese prisons. Ever since the 1870s, both missionaries and Japanese Christians had been prison visitors and reformers. The brutality of the traditional penal system had been used to justify the imposition of the 'unequal treaties' of the 1850s, which exempted foreigners from the jurisdiction of Japanese courts. The early reformers received some encouragement from successive governments motivated less by humanitarian aspirations than by a desire to show the western world that Japanese prisons could be as good as those of other nations, and thus secure the abrogation of the treaties, an objective that was achieved in 1899.[1] The modern Japanese penal code, like the whole legal system instituted in the years following the Meiji Restoration, was based first on that of France and then greatly modified in accord with German models, which was clearly reflected in the Penal Code of 1907. The prison system was administered under laws adopted in 1908, which combined continental, English, and American methods and, like them, were declared to be educative rather than retributive in intent. Thus Japanese prisons were in theory similar to those of western countries. In the provision of training for prison officials, Japan probably led the world.[2]

In the formative years, Christians had been influential in shaping and administering the penal system, and now they were among the best-known theorists and practitioners of prison work in Japan. They included Hara Taneaki, who had studied American prisons and had just published a lengthy treatise on the protection of discharged prisoners based on his many years' experience as director of Tokyo Shutsugokunin Hogosho, a large centre for discharged prisoners. Tomeoka Kōsuke had toured the world to study prison and other social work agencies and was currently a senior official in the Ministry of Home Affairs with considerable responsibility for the administration of social work institutions.[3]

Macdonald's new friend, Governor Arima, recently appointed to Kosuge prison, was the disciple and colleague of Hara and Tomeoka. A native of Satsuma, famed for its formidable males, Arima became interested in Christianity while an official in the prisons on the northern island of Hokkaido. He was baptized by Tomeoka Kōsuke in Reinanzaka church (Congregational) in Tokyo where Tomeoka was minister when Arima was appointed to a position in the government's Bureau of Prisons.[4]

Subsequently, during successive governorships in several prisons, Arima's stature as a successful and humane governor grew rapidly. A considerable stir was created in Yokohama when the chief chaplain of the prison, a Buddhist priest, announced that thanks to Arima's example he had become a Christian.

Among Arima's innovations was his decision to allow prisoners to have brushes, ink, and paper for writing, thus setting a precedent that soon became the practice in all prisons. Under his direction, the Yokohama prison became the first in Japan to institute a special school for blind and deaf and dumb prisoners, and it also pioneered in separating juveniles from adult criminals. Arima organized a school and rehabilitation service as a private charity for youth discharged from prison. Later he established a reformatory for boys, an area in which Tomeoka had been the pioneer several years earlier, and subsequently he opened one for girls, the first of its kind in Japan. Arima and his mentor Tomeoka were instructors in the training program for prison guards and promoted their views among new recruits to the penal system.

In seventeen years as a prison governor, Arima Shirosuke had become well known as 'the Christian governor,' and famed as a humane administrator whose flexible attitude toward prison regulations sometimes got him into trouble. He was transferred from the governorship of Kobe prison to Kosuge in Tokyo so that his immediate superior, Tanita Saburō, director of the Bureau of Prisons, could keep an eye on him. The purpose of this surveillance was less to restrain Arima than to protect him from criticism. Tanita, who had studied in Germany, admired German penology, considered himself a reformer, and wanted to emphasize rehabilitation rather than punishment as the primary objective of the penal system. Although Arima's ideas on the treatment of prisoners were more radical than Tanita's and they often disagreed, Tanita saw Arima as the prison governor best able to provide practical demonstration of his reform program.[5]

Thus, thanks to his stature within the penal service, and his good works, Arima Shirosuke was famous long before Macdonald first met him early in 1914. He was soon playing an important part in her new career, and became her good friend.

■ ■ ■

WHILE HER VISITS to Yamada continued, Macdonald received a growing volume of letters from other prisoners in Kosuge prison requesting her to visit them. It was impossible to respond to all of them, but she sent Christian literature to everyone and selected for visits those whom she sensed she might be able to help. She was learning what a variety of background, experience, and aspirations lay beneath those red prison uniforms. As yet, her view of prisoners was highly personal and owed little to any theories about prison work.

Nothing impressed her more than the wives of prisoners: 'How they come day in and day out. Faithful women ...' Typical was one woman whose hope that her husband would soon be released had been dashed several times. Still she kept coming to see him every day for the few allotted minutes. 'Yes, dear woman,' Caroline observed, '"Love never faileth" & it will be thro' that that you will save him.'[6]

Some of the prisoners' wives seemed to visit their husbands from motives other than love: 'The pity of it is that some of them don't seem to care & it is said that ... [they] borrow fine clothes to impress their husbands.'

She was reminded of lines from a favourite poet, Coventry Patmore:

Ah wasteful woman she who may
In her own self set her own price.
How hath she cheapened paradise
How given for naught her priceless gift,
That spent with true respective thrift
Had made brutes men and men divine.[7]

Among the strangest prisoners she had yet encountered was one Okazaki, who had been in jail for seven years without coming to even a preliminary trial. A friendly guard explained that Okazaki was perfectly normal when in prison, but over and over again when he went to court he feigned madness and the case was postponed. Such a curious tale made it 'impossible not to have a psychological interest' in this prisoner, but that did not resolve Macdonald's uncertainty as to what she should say to him. As she registered, took her wooden number tag, and waited in the garden, she could find no answer. Taking her place in the usual 'cubby hole,' the screen went up and she was confronted by 'a tiny little man' who looked at her 'steadily but a little lamely.' After several minutes of rather repetitive talk from her and no sign of understanding from the prisoner, Caroline began to feel that she was just 'flailing in the air'; she persevered, all the while wondering how she could get behind 'that steady listening incomprehensive stare.'

Finally she asked the prisoner if he had any relatives. 'Quick as a flash his whole aspect changed ... he reeled for a moment, raised his arm and covered his face, & uttered a strange pathetic weird cry.' To her question whether he had a wife or mother he replied that he had a child, and taking his arm away from his face looked at Caroline 'out of two perfectly intelligent eyes.' Gradually she drew from him the information that his daughter had been a babe in arms when he entered prison. With his hands he measured out her length at about two feet, a memory which obviously moved him. Eventually he said, wonderingly, 'I suppose she's going to school now!' Macdonald made much of the fact that he remembered his child clearly, although he had not seen her for several years: 'Neither could God forget him.' Over and over she 'repeated about God's love,' so like his own for the babe in arms. Now 'his look was entirely different ... Poor soul. There isn't anyone without some access to the brain & heart.' When she beckoned to the guard, her friend Satamura, that she was finished, 'he came along in that big slow sympathetic way he has ... to within the range of [my] friend's vision – presto change – the strange silly look spread over his face.' The last sight she had was of a face 'suffused with that foolish smile.' It was hard to accept the fact that she could do little for him.[8]

This experience made her feel as she often did when she came out of 'the wee cubby hole. I want to cry, I want to bawl like a baby & sometimes I want to scream ... but I don't indulge in any of these safety valves for obvious reasons! It is the whole thing together that almost gets to be too much for me.' More and more she marvelled at the sensitivity of the vast majority of the prison guards: she heard them say 'over and over again of those within & whom the world calls wicked & abandoned, "No, he's not a *bad* man" ... Any fool can find the bad in us ... but it takes a deep hearted man & one who touches real life & at its worst if you will, to find the *good* – and it's there in us all, defaced as it may seem to be – the image of the God who made us.' If prison guards could maintain their faith that there was some good in everyone, who was she to despair?[9]

Macdonald had already declared, as she continued for years to insist, that her purpose was 'not to reform prisons, but to reform prisoners.'[10] Nevertheless, she became increasingly interested in prisons. She was convinced that she must learn more about prison work and services to ex-prisoners and their families elsewhere. Her reading and her contacts with Americans in Tokyo persuaded her that in the United States she would find the most advanced models of prison reform and other social services. Now the long-awaited trip to North America, while still a journey to visit her family, was becoming more and more a search for the instruments needed to further the Kingdom of God in Japan.

■ ■ ■

EARLY IN 1915 Macdonald wrote to the executive of the World's YWCA tendering her resignation from the YWCA of Japan, to take effect the following September, at the same time informing the Japanese and Canadian associations of her decision. She had completed ten years of service with the 'Y,' was now forty years old, and was convinced that the work needed someone younger. Under the direction of the capable Kawai Michi, the Japanese association was in the best of hands. If a foreigner were sent to take her place, Caroline thought she should be an appointee of the Foreign Department of the American YWCA, since it was the largest constituency for recruiting staff and raising funds. Fortunately, an appropriate American replacement was available; Margaret Matthew, who had been on furlough in the United States for almost two years, would be returning to the staff in Tokyo shortly. Given a few months overlap in their terms of office, the transition would be smooth. Among other developments, they would see the completion of the new building of the Tokyo 'Y.' In presenting her resignation, Caroline made no reference to her plans for the future.[11]

Although the Canadian YWCA joined the World's YWCA and the Japanese association in expressing regret at her departure, both the Foreign Committee in Toronto and Macdonald herself felt a degree of relief in the severing of their relationship. Over the years there had been frequent delays and misunderstandings over the payment of her salary and living allowance, due not only to slow communication across the Pacific but also to a certain laxness on her part in submitting accounts and reports. For the past year, when her time had been increasingly absorbed by the prison work, the 'Y' had scarcely received her undivided attention, and other irritations had been exacerbated. She thought some problems had arisen because, unlike the American Association, the Canadian 'Y' had failed to develop clear policies on foreign work and had no formal contracts with its secretaries.[12] She looked forward to a new life freer of institutional restraints, although as a freelancer she would have no regular financial support and would herself have to find the funds for her own maintenance and the expenses of her work.

The group gathered at Tokyo station on a hot July day to see Caroline off for Yokohama and the ship that would take her to North America was not as large as the one that bid her bon voyage in 1910, but it was decidedly more diverse. Yet it 'was no miscellaneous crowd ... Everyone stood out with an almost painful personality,' so vivid was 'the background upon [which] all these new relationships are painted.' There were ex-prisoners and prison guards, some with their wives, lawyers, people young and old from Fujimichō church, 'every one an outstanding testimony to the grace of God.' There, too, were Nishimura and Kobayashi and Yamada's other close friend, Masuda, and his family, who 'will come in soon.' Also on hand were Annie West, neighbours, members and staff of the YWCA, and the seven members of the Mitsukoshi boys' band, one of whom she had befriended after the death of his mother; now all the boys were her friends. Not least in her eyes were her servants, Kanehora and his wife: 'What should I have done could I not have trusted them?' With 'loyalty & love & sympathy' they had handled the constant telephone messages, the 'motley throngs' of visitors, the unexpected guests at meal times, all without a murmur. Altogether, these people, her friends, had defined the next stage of her life.[13]

The Canadian Pacific Empress boats had all been taken off the Yokohama-Vancouver route for the duration of the war, so an American ship bound for San Francisco was the alternative. Crossing the Pacific, Caroline thought deeply about the future: 'Has Japan got a heart or not? If she has & some of us no longer doubt it, how is it to be found. Who doubts the passionate devotion of Japan to its own ideals, the unquestioning loyalty to what it conceives to be the highest, be it political aggrandisement, commercial gain or what not ... Touch that cord for the Kingdom of God & what shall we have? But what does it mean to find the heart of even *one*, to say nothing of a nation.'[14]

After a brief stop in San Francisco she took the train to Chicago to sit at the feet of Jane Addams of Hull House, long the preeminent role model for women social workers in North America. Macdonald was especially interested in the Hull House work with ex-prisoners and in the juvenile court that Addams had helped to establish a decade and a half earlier, an institution as yet unknown in Japan.

Her next stop was in Detroit, where she talked with management and workers in the Ford Motor Company, whose experiment in industrial relations was creating widespread interest. She was greatly impressed by 'the common sense business methods and the human heart' she discerned, and especially by the company's profit sharing with its workers: 'They may be making motors – they are certainly making men and homes,' a theme that informed addresses on the Ford plan she gave later in Tokyo.[15]

From Detroit it was an easy train journey to London, Ontario, and six weeks' quiet visit with her family. Later, in Toronto, she renewed many old associations and observed the work of the University Settlement where her former YWCA colleague Sara Libby Carson had just been appointed as director, and whose board was chaired by her classmate and friend Frank Burton, professor of physics at the University of Toronto. At a meeting of the Foreign Committee of the YWCA, she gave a final report on her work in Japan, urging the committee to continue to support a Canadian secretary in Tokyo and to assist young Japanese women to study in Canada.[16]

In the end, there was no new Canadian appointee, since the most substantial supporters of Macdonald's work, notably Mary Ann Blackburn of

Ottawa, withdrew their contributions when their friend was no longer on the 'Y' staff. Under wartime conditions it proved impossible to find other funds.[17] At the end of the war, Onomi Hisa became the first of a succession of young Japanese women to study in Canada under either the sponsorship of the YWCA or Emma Kaufman, who remained a strong link between the Canadian and Japanese associations.

■ ■ ■

IN THE AUTUMN OF 1915 Macdonald was in New York. There, through the chairman of the National Committee on Prisons, Dr. E. Stagg Whitin, professor of criminology and social work at Columbia University, she was introduced to many American leaders in those fields and visited numerous institutions. Whitin was a leader in the movement that aimed to put the study of prisons and prisoners on a 'basis of scientific reality' by replacing 'speculation ... and academic moralizing' with listening to prisoners themselves and to doctors and psychiatrists who could help to interpret prisoners' experiences.[18] Whitin and his associates on the National Committee were also vigorous promoters of wages for industrial work in prisons. The idea that prisoners should help to pay the costs of their incarceration, while learning skills useful to them on their return to society, had already been put into practice in many prisons in both Japan and the United States. Less commonly accepted was the view of Whitin and the National Committee that prisoners' wages should also support their families outside.[19]

Macdonald's encounter with Whitin and the friendship she formed with Julia K. Jaffray, executive secretary of the National Committee, proved to be of enduring significance for her work. Jaffray was a Canadian from Galt, Ontario, and a Presbyterian; from the outset the two women found many acquaintances and interests in common, and their friendship developed quickly. Thanks to Whitin and Jaffray, Macdonald spent some time with Mary E. Richmond, director of the Charity Organization Department of the Russell Sage Foundation, who impressed on Macdonald her conviction about the value of keeping accurate and detailed records of individuals. This emphasis had made Richmond the prime advocate of the 'casework' approach to social problems and a central figure in the emergence of social work as a profession in the United States. Richmond was opposed to state relief of poverty, a position which brought her into conflict with the many American social activists who were advocating widows' and old age pensions.[20]

Richmond's insistence on the primary importance of rehabilitating the individual was fully in accord with Macdonald's current approach to prisoners.

In New York, Macdonald was also introduced to the debate surrounding the most controversial prison reformer of the day, Thomas Mott Osborne. A former mayor of Auburn, New York, Osborne became chairman of the New York Commission on Prison Reform in 1912. His conviction that self-government by prisoners would remedy most of the evils of the prison system, and provide a civic education that prepared men for life in society after their release, was tested when the 1,400 inmates of Auburn Penitentiary approved bylaws and elected representatives to the Mutual Welfare League, an instrument that gave them a considerable measure of self-government. This revolutionary experiment appeared to work well, notably in a substantially reduced rate of recidivism, and provoked a national debate on penal reform.[21]

Very shortly Osborne assumed the wardenship of Sing Sing prison in New York and immediately introduced the Mutual Welfare League to one of the largest and most chaotic prisons in the country. When Macdonald met Osborne he had been at Sing Sing less than a year, but the democratization of the institution was well under way. Spending a day within the walls of Sing Sing, she was deeply impressed by Osborne's attitudes toward the prisoners and by their loyalty to him. It seemed to her that Osborne was conducting 'a grand experiment in friendship' based on 'a divine enthusiasm for the individual ... What their system at Sing Sing is I know not. What kind of order and administration is not for me to say. I didn't see it. I only know you couldn't stick your nose in anywhere but there the gray coated or trousered men were working it seemed with a will – quietly and happily.'[22] To Macdonald it was scarcely too much to accept Osborne's presentation of the Mutual Welfare League as 'applied Christianity ... a practical effort to operate the prisons on the basis of the Golden Rule,' or to believe that the experiment was working.[23]

In New York Macdonald also observed the operations of a variety of other institutions and talked with their officials. At the Bellevue Hospital Clinic for Mental Defectives she found further applications of precise record keeping in casework, while the National Tuberculosis Association provided information about a disease that was a major health problem in the world, including Japan. The Society for the Prevention of Cruelty to Children, a juvenile court, and a children's court and its probation officers all impressed on Caroline the view that 'the cause of crime is the neglect of children.'

Here were lessons she might apply to helping the hundreds of small boys in their early teens, mostly motherless, who hung around the sake shops in Asakusa during the day and slept in any corner they could find at night.[24]

■ ■ ■

EARLY IN 1916 Macdonald was back in Tokyo. Among 'the perfect mob ... from all walks of life' who greeted her at the Tokyo station she was especially pleased to see 'among the nicest looking' two young ex-prisoners, 'who are more than making good and helping others also.'[25] They were an encouraging reminder of the major objective of her new life as a self-supporting, independent prison worker. Thanks to her resumption of part-time teaching at Tsuda College, where she was to instruct once more in Victorian literature and English Bible for nine hours a week, and to financial support from Emma Kaufman and Mary Borden, she would be able to cover her living expenses and purchase the literature needed to meet the growing demand from prisoners.

'It was so good to be back again' where her 'foot trod with a firm step in the place that was [hers] – for here it is – there is no doubt about that.' In her joy she indulged in a 'short weep' in the taxi on the way from the station to the Gobanchō home of Tsuda Ume and her friend and fellow teacher, Anna Hartshorne, where Caroline would live until she found a permanent residence. There to greet her was Annie West, soon followed by 'the lovable little laddie Ida-san,' the first member of the Mitsukoshi boys' band she had known, who had been baptized during her absence. Next came 'Nishimura-san, looking well & clear in the eye' despite his long hours as a clerk in the stock exchange, and then Kaneko Nobuji who was so impatient to see her that he had begged off work early and 'rushed to Gobanchō in his prison guard's uniform, to the consternation of Miss Hartshorne's maid.' He was eager to be the first to tell Macdonald that his wife had recently been baptized and to share his rejoicing in their new Christian home.[26]

Although it was late that night when Caroline got to bed, she was at the gate of Ichigaya prison before eight o'clock the next morning to see one of her friends, a prisoner named Hikida, whose terrible distress and recent attempt to commit suicide had been reported to her by Annie West. Caroline hoped it would help Hikida to know that she had not forgotten him and had come immediately to see him. Before she reached the prison gate she met 'the beloved Satamura-san,' the prison official who had treated her with such kindness and courtesy on 'that first awful day' when she had gone within the walls. Now they went in together, greeted warmly by a guard, Takahashi, whom she also counted among her friends. It was indeed good to be home.[27]

That night she went to dinner at the Tamachi house and stayed late, catching up on the local news. Her former YWCA colleagues, 'the blessed lambs,' seemed 'young ... oh so young.' Thanks to her recent experiences she felt considerably older. 'I wonder sometimes how many years older I have grown during the last two years,' she pondered in her journal. 'At any rate I have grown older in the knowledge of God's wonderful love & his absolute reality and in the knowledge of my own desprately [sic] poor life.' Was there here a note of continuing self-recrimination for failure to prevent Yamada's crime? If so, it was not dominating her life for 'He has given me work to do – & He will give the needed things – strength, purity, love – and His own abiding friendship.'[28]

Six weeks after her return Caroline rented a small Japanese-style house in Kojimachi near the Yasukuni Shrine and its surrounding park, and not far from her former Tamachi home. Apart from a small kitchen, the first floor was one large room where one sat on tatami mats on the floor; the two rooms on the second floor served as bedroom and study. Following Japanese custom, there was very little furniture in the house, except for a wardrobe in her bedroom and the desk in her study. Although she employed a cook, her only servant, this was not because she ate fancy meals. The fare at Caroline's table was always the plainest of Japanese food, and even for guests there was rarely any special dish. Many of her middle- and upper-class friends, while admiring the frugality of her lower-class standard of living, thought she must often be hungry. Except for some breakfasts she rarely ate a meal alone; all her guests, high and low, agreed that one thing that was never lacking in her house was good talk.[29]

Launching herself into her new life, Macdonald found that one of the most immediate challenges was the pile of 700 letters from prisoners that had accumulated during her six months' absence. Not wanting to seek assistance from people who wouldn't understand the 'pathetic wails' of her correspondents, she set one of her 'ex's, a lad of 23, & a fellow with heaps to him (he was by way of becoming a speculator when the law happily intervened & changed his career) ... to work on the letters, & you never saw a happier lad than he to be able to do something for me and to be entrusted with those letters.'[30]

1
Caroline Macdonald on graduation from the
University of Toronto, 1901

2

Caroline Macdonald before leaving for Japan, 1904

3

Leaders of the YWCA Summer Conference, 1912: *back row, second from left*, Kawai Michi, Caroline Macdonald, Matsu Tsuji, unknown, Hirooka Asako, Molly Baker, unknown, Ruth Ragan, unknown, Emma Kaufman

4
Hirooka Asako and Caroline Macdonald at the
YWCA Summer Conference, 1912

5
Caroline Macdonald, 1915, about the time
she left the YWCA

6

Entrance to the new YWCA building in Tokyo, 1915

7

Caroline Macdonald's colleagues and successors, the YWCA secretaries of Japan, 1915:
front row, left to right, Kawai Michi, Ruth Ragan, Katō Taka; *back row, second from left,*
Margaret Matthew; *fourth from left,* Molly Baker; *far right,* Mary Page

8

Kawai Michi and Emma Kaufman at the national conference of the Canadian YWCA, Elgin House, Muskoka, Ontario, 1916.

9
Arima Shirosuke shortly after his appointment
as governor of Kosuge prison, ca. 1915

10

Caroline Macdonald, Honorary Doctor of Laws
of the University of Toronto, 1925

11

Caroline Macdonald with Dr. Motoji Shinkuma, director of the
Japanese Bureau of Prisons, and his assistant Okabe Jō at the
garden party following the University of Toronto convocation, 1925

Once this backlog was cleared up she was able to deal with the correspondence herself, although this became increasingly demanding. She had early adopted a policy of acknowledging every communication and following up with a visit to the prisoner, if he was in one of the two Tokyo prisons to which she and Annie West had access. All the others were sent literature, either a Bible, a copy of a devotional guide, or some pamphlet prepared by the Christian Literature Society of Japan. To those who responded to these gifts, Macdonald wrote more personal letters, nearly always with the help of her language teacher Matsumiya Yahei, since her mastery of written Japanese fell short of her verbal command of the language. Matsumiya carried on this work over many years with utmost secrecy, because it concerned the private lives of prisoners. His interest in prison work was one more manifestation of his concern for social reform, which included his longtime activism in the anti-prostitution movement. Matsumiya was a socialist, although there was at present no political party that expressed his views. Now, as a disciple of the young Kagawa Toyohiko, who had just published his study of poverty in Japan, *Hinmin shinri no kenkyū* (A Study of the Psychology of the Poor), Matsumiya supported Kagawa's promotion of labour unions. Macdonald's frequent sessions with Matsumiya often included discussions of the current social scene, as well as the translation or correction of her letters to prisoners. All this was a valuable extension of her regular Japanese lessons with Matsumiya.[31]

Caroline found the ramifications of her prison work steadily expanding: 'A whole new world ... is springing up through meeting the various male and female relations of my *retired* friends.' The wife of one prisoner needed persuasion to enter hospital 'to get her fixed up in body and soul before her lord and master returns,' while another sought assistance in mending a quarrel with her daughter. Increasingly, men just released from prison, or wives anticipating their release, came to seek help on the basis of her new reputation as 'the mother of prisoners.' A prison official, Kashiwagi Kyūshichi, to whom she had never said more than good morning, came to tell her that he had been convicted of attempting to bribe one of his charges, a member of the Diet who was himself awaiting trial for bribery. She was touched by this man's belief that she would feel badly if she heard of his wrongdoing from someone else, and by his determination to admit his guilt to her before entering prison to serve his sentence. She 'braced him up and tried to help him see that there was a Power that could keep him braced, & that nothing else could.'[32]

The range of her contacts was illustrated, rather to her astonishment, when she attended the funeral of a prison warden. Among the more than 300 people who crowded a Buddhist temple, she and Annie West were the only non-Japanese, and apart from relatives, the only women. Before entering the temple they 'were greeted on all sides by ... chums low and high.' Where would this growing network of association and influence take her? 'The dear knows where these things I am touching will lead,' she wrote to Julia Jaffray. 'At any rate it is a personal touch I've got on people & that will grow.'[33]

Macdonald's interest in the prison as an institution was also growing, stimulated by her observations of prison life and by her continuing connection with American prison reformers. On the basis of her knowledge of prisons elsewhere she concluded that in Japan 'the prison system is good enough – but with the exception of that one place [Kosuge prison under Governor Arima] practically no effort is made to appeal to the bigger and better self. But it's coming!'[34]

Among welcome signs of change was the interest in juvenile courts, which Macdonald did her best to promote through speeches and articles on her impressions of American juvenile courts.[35] A hopeful sign for change was an event that had occurred at the time of the coronation of the emperor two years earlier, when a man who had spent twenty-three years in prison for theft and murder, and had later become a Christian and a respected social worker, had had his prison record erased from the official personal record required of all Japanese. Until this time anyone with a prison record carried it all his life and it was noted in his children's records, an 'iniquitous system' in Caroline's view. She hoped that the emperor's special clemency would become standard practice with the Ministry of Justice; in a society where family and group loyalty made the shame of being in prison so enormous, this would be a salutary step.[36]

Macdonald also joined those who were working for speedier administration of justice, a concern highlighted for her by the case of a man who had been sentenced to death and then endured seven years of misery and uncertainty in jail because the authorities failed to resolve their doubt about his guilt. During this time Macdonald and West visited him and he became a changed man. Subsequently, as an act of clemency, his sentence was commuted and he was transferred to Kosuge prison where they continued their visits, much to the prisoner's joy. For that man, as for many others condemned to long terms, Macdonald continued to hope for a broader application of the custom of clemency, which granted parole to prisoners for good behaviour, often after serving one-third of their terms.[37]

A further reason for hoping for change in the system was the appointment of an education officer to work with young men under twenty in one of the Tokyo prisons. The first holder of this position, a recent graduate of Tokyo Imperial University, confided to Macdonald that he brought few ideas to his new work and asked her for information about educational activities in American prisons, a request she endeavoured to meet despite her limited knowledge in this area.[38] Another positive development was Governor Arima's pioneering establishment of a monthly magazine, *Mado No Akari* (Light from the Window), for circulation within Kosuge prison. Written for prisoners, not by them, the magazine provided information about the outside world previously denied to inmates. Since newspapers were prohibited in prisons, Macdonald saw the new magazine as an important move toward ending the isolation from the world that was such a poor preparation for a return to normal life.[39]

Macdonald did not discourage the belief that she was something of an authority on American prisons. Her attempts to live up to that reputation, initially largely of her own creation, necessitated frequent requests to Julia Jaffray for a dozen or more copies of all the literature published by the National Committee on Prisons and related agencies, for the titles of new books Dr. Whitin was recommending, and generally for any information that would help her in promoting the ideas of her new American friends. In particular, she needed to be able to answer the questions of government and prison officials in Tokyo, who were following closely the fate of Thomas Mott Osborne and were impressed by the fact that Macdonald had met him in New York.[40]

Soon after her return to Japan several members of the prison bureaucracy queried her about the meaning of Osborne's sudden departure from the governorship of Sing Sing, reported in the Japanese newspapers as a 'resignation.' Governor Arima, who came to Caroline's home regularly for English lessons and usually stayed for dinner and discussion of 'the Cosmos,' was especially threatened by any discrediting of Osborne and his liberal humanitarian policies. Arima and his supporters in the Bureau of Prisons were relieved by Macdonald's assurances that the 'persecution' Osborne was undergoing at the hands of his enemies had led only to his 'temporary retirement,' that he was fighting back and would win, and that he remained the acknowledged leader of American prison reformers.[41]

In her efforts to sustain Osborne's prestige in Japan, Macdonald urged Julia Jaffray to draft a letter to her for Osborne's signature, denying that he had resigned and 'saying anything else you might like him to say' for the benefit of Japan. She made no apology for taking so bold an initiative, since Whitin had promised such a letter if she needed it. Moreover, Caroline believed that she was 'touching more prison people, officials and otherwise than anyone else. In fact no one else is touching the thing at all.' If the cause of prison reform was to be defended in Japan in the face of Osborne's apparent fall from grace, it was up to her.[42]

Although Macdonald was an enthusiast for Osborne's ideas, promoted the reading of his book *Within Prison Walls* among senior policymakers, and was instrumental in having it translated into Japanese by an official of the Bureau of Prisons, she entertained no illusion that self-government in prisons as practised by Osborne was applicable everywhere: 'Self government in Japan!! There isn't even self government outside of prisons in Japan! That ... must be relegated ... to pure fairy tale.' Nevertheless, Arima and like-minded reformers were moving in a humane direction and must be supported.[43]

When charges against Osborne were dropped, Macdonald and Arima and their friends rejoiced over his return to Sing Sing. Their satisfaction was short-lived, for within three months renewed political harassment forced his resignation. Even then, 'our Mr. Osborne' (Governor Arima) remained convinced of the value of Osborne's policies and continued to enquire about his current activities.[44] Legitimation of Osborne's views appeared to be conferred by his appointment as commandant of the Portsmouth Naval Prison in New Hampshire where he again introduced prisoner participation in the running of the institution. After three years, under pressure from senior military leaders and despite strong support from the assistant secretary of the navy, Franklin D. Roosevelt, Osborne was dismissed and his innovations abolished. The Mutual Welfare League lasted in Auburn Prison for another ten years and elements of it remained in Sing Sing for several decades. In the meantime, Osborne and his ideas continued to inspire prison reformers in Japan and throughout the world.

A potential path to influencing the system as well as individuals presented itself when the Ministry of Justice conducted a three-month training school for sixty prison officials from thirty different prisons all over the country. The men were housed in a dormitory near Kosuge prison, and

Macdonald passed them in the street as she went to the prison in the early morning and they to their school. Her prayer that 'God would let us touch them, if that were His will' was quickly answered. Within a week she met a young prison official from the far north of Japan who had been very impressed by a lecture given by Governor Arima and wanted to know more about Christianity. Before the school ended this young man became a Christian and went home to establish an 'enquirers' group' for thirty of his fellow workers. Some of the sixteen other officials, whose names he had given Macdonald, attended meetings at her home, and she continued to send literature to them after they were scattered to their homes. Thanks to these connections she was able to send Bibles and other books to numerous prison libraries outside Tokyo, a welcome expansion of her work.[45]

■ ■ ■

ALTOGETHER CAROLINE'S NEW LIFE was varied and demanding,

> making speeches in two languages on various & sundry topics, teaching English literature, holding audience with all and sundry in [my] own house, visiting friends (mostly gentlemen!) who find it inconvenient to come to see me, hunting up their wives & families & trying to straighten them up to be worthy of straightened up husbands, giving advice on everything under heaven from the management of a husband & the bringing up of children (being a specialist along these lines!) to the interpretation of 'The Hound of Heaven' to a group of college graduates, a lecture on prison reform to a group of rather elegant Japanese ladies who had probably until that moment thought it not quite proper to think there was such a thing as a prison.[46]

A growing number of people came to her house at all hours of the day and night. Often there were fifteen or sixteen visitors a day, many of whom simply sought the ear of a good listener, or wanted Caroline's advice on some problem. On a Sunday morning she never knew how many ex-prisoners, guards, or other friends might turn up to walk to church with her. On Saturday evenings 'the Mitsukoshi boys might drop in for English and music' and the whole house would vibrate with the sound of their brass instruments.[47]

Although she was an early riser, it was not unusual for a recently released prisoner or the distraught wife of a man newly arrested to be waiting for her long before breakfast. Sometimes the visitor was a man just out of jail who had lost all his friends and was fearful that with his prison record nobody would ever trust him. Now he was acting on the promise Macdonald had secured from him that immediately on his release he would come straight to her house where he could be certain to 'have *one* friend.'[48] Often she returned home at eleven o'clock at night to find a pair of Japanese shoes at the door, a certain sign that an unexpected visitor, frequently a total stranger, awaited her. Sometimes the caller was sent to the Salvation Army, but many times she bedded him down for the night and the discussion of his problem began over breakfast the next morning. Foreign guests were astonished and often alarmed to learn that Caroline never locked the doors of the house.[49]

Not all of Caroline's guests found it easy to accept her casual, democratic hospitality. Strong persuasion sometimes had to be applied, as in the case of an ex-prisoner who felt himself unworthy to sit down to supper with her. 'I finally told him that if it was true that God was our Father it followed naturally that we were brothers and sisters, and that it was not anything to be embarrassed at to sit down at his sister's table. You should have seen the light in his eye as he sat down. You have to talk just as if they were children.'[50]

Throughout this 'absolutely kaleidoscopic' life she was sustained by the faith that God would give her whatever emotional and physical resources she needed. Among all the gifts for which she was thankful was 'a perfectly astonishing' ability to go sound to sleep quickly and remain so until it was time to get up in the morning.[51] That was especially valuable in a time of world war when those whom God 'has not called ... into the strife in the way so many others have been called ... must be specially in season and out of season in the special things ... given us.' She was sure it was helpful that she had not lost her sense of humour. 'In these days we have to hold on to every bit of the self that God has given us ... I do not believe it is sacrilege to believe that a sense of humour is God given, do you?,' she asked David Cairns, who currently held a senior position in the chaplaincy service of the British army.[52]

Soon after its publication, Caroline had greatly enjoyed reading H.G. Wells's partly comic novel *Mr. Britling Sees It Through*. Wells's depiction of the impact of the first two years of the war on a comfortable Edwardian family in Essex mirrored Macdonald's condemnation of all militarism, especially as manifested by Germany, as well as her optimism that the 'war to end all wars' would lead to a new international order.[53]

More than work, faith, a sense of humour, and the idealism of wartime sustained Caroline. In her new life as a prison worker she enjoyed the love and support of old friends. No one gave her such unquestioning love and loyalty as her fellow-countrywoman Emma Kaufman. Unlike Kaufman, some of Caroline's former YWCA colleagues were doubtful about her present use of her education and talents, but they remained her close friends. Whatever their intellectual doubts about her course of action, they had to respect her 'calling' and they had no intention of depriving themselves of her good company. Caroline continued to attend dinner parties with her former associates at the Tamachi house, and when staff members needed to escape from the YWCA, especially Mary Page, an American secretary, and Kawai Michi, they came to spend a day or so with Caroline. Kawai was in New York at the YWCA staff training school when Caroline returned to Tokyo at the beginning of 1916; six months later Caroline was delighted to welcome her home. Happily, Caroline found 'Kawai San ... the same darling old sixpence, but oh how I wish she were quieter in her soul or her body or something, but oh she's great, she's great – and *good*. I'm so glad she's back and is going to stay with me for awhile.'[54] When Caroline needed a break from routine, which she rarely admitted, she took the short train ride to Kamakura, the ancient feudal capital of Japan, to spend a few days with Tsuda Ume and Anna Hartshorne at their seaside retreat. Across the road was the country home of the Nitobes where Caroline was also a welcome house guest. Despite the hospitality of her friends, Caroline took few holidays. Occasionally, when she was excessively fatigued, she would stay in bed until noon, but there were few such breaks in her steady pace.

Through all her new activities Caroline's 'eyes were being opened,' and she was trying to discern the future pattern of her work.[55] Increasingly the questions she sought to answer concerned the relationship between the salvation of the individual and the transformation of society. More and more she believed they were inseparable and that to attempt one without the other was futile.

This conviction was confirmed whenever she visited Asakusa ward, as she sometimes did in the company of ex-prisoners who lived there, or of visitors whom she sought to interest in her plans for the settlement. Conditions in the Yoshiwara, or 'Vanity Fair' as Macdonald called it, appeared to have improved slightly since her first visits to the district. The licensed prostitutes no longer sat openly in the windows, but their pictures were displayed for customers to make their choices. 'What a horror it is! It goes on, night after night, and in its train disease & misery & crime! Why is it allowed?' She had heard reports that the police had cut the number of unlicensed brothels in half in the past two years, but the streets seemed as alive and active as ever. In Asakusa, social evil and personal degradation were clearly inseparable.[56]

For the present, the rehabilitation of individuals consumed most of her energy and provided much gratification. The young Nishimura remained steady in his faith and in his devotion to his neighbourhood Sunday school, but she wished he could find some alternative to the long hours he worked in the Tokyo Stock Exchange, to the detriment of his health.[57] The prison guards who had been converted continued to be faithful members of the church. Kashiwagi Kyūshichi, now out of prison after paying the penalty for his failed bribery attempt, had 'really given himself to God,' had settled down with his formerly estranged wife, and they were happier than ever before. Despite the two-hour boat and tram ride, Caroline accepted an invitation to their home in a distant suburb. Supper, shared with some twenty neighbours, was followed by a lengthy discussion of the meaning of Kashiwagi's new life, and Macdonald left with the hope that a regular meeting or Sunday school would be established in the neighbourhood.[58]

Another new Christian was an ex-soldier in his late fifties who, from a sense of duty to his country, had established a day nursery and a kindergarten in a poor suburb. 'It was magnificent and pitiful to see what he was trying to do with no resources but his own.' Caroline had 'seen nothing more wonderful than the change that has come over him as he has come to see that there is a higher master than his country, whose infinite resources can be turned into the salvation of the nation he has already served so well.' She was deeply moved when Dr. Uemura baptized the old soldier as 'a new soldier of Jesus Christ.'[59]

There were other new converts. One of them was a young man who had shared a cell with her first prison friend, Yamada Zen'ichi, and through his example had begun to read the Bible. For the previous six years in prison he had been studying to become a Buddhist priest, although his piety had not prevented him from winning the hatred of the prison officials for his obstreperous behaviour. In Yamada, as Caroline saw it, 'he touched the thing called *sympathy*. [Yamada] ... tried to *comfort* him,' although Yamada was in the same plight himself. 'Nobody had ever tried to comfort him before ... The officials had no more trouble with him ... he had something to live for now.' On his release, 'his Buddhist friends proceeded to get him married within three days and to make a priest of him.' Two months later he appeared at Macdonald's door to announce that Buddhism was not for him and that he wanted to become a Christian. The next night he brought his wife with him, and Macdonald was pleased to observe that in the short time since their sudden marriage 'they seem to have fallen in love, so all's well that ends well.' When the couple went to church the next day for the first time, 'the poor man went up in smoke' with excitement over this new experience, so she 'took them by the hair of the head to fetch them over here & try to get the poor fellow back to some of the normal things of life again.'[60]

One of the normal things to which he was introduced was the month-old baby of the couple who had recently become her servants. 'It's an awful cunning kid & as good as gold,' she explained to Julia Jaffray. 'As it isn't exactly mine I can praise it with impunity. It will make an excellent "evangelistic agency" for me!! I didn't exactly get the baby produced with this ulterior motive in view, but as it is here I see ways of making use of the wee thing!' In this instance, when she deposited the baby in the young man's arms, the response suggested that he looked forward to parenthood and she rejoiced.[61]

One of the toughest criminals she had met was a fifty-year-old Buddhist priest, condemned to death for several murders. Macdonald sent him books but got no response for some months, until the day she received a letter 'as long as the moral law' giving his whole life history. The next morning when she went to the prison to see him, an official she knew well told her he could not run the risk of exposing her to so unruly and violent a man, even under prison safeguards. In the next three weeks her correspondence with the prisoner convinced her and the prison officials that he was truly a changed man. Still, while she waited to be admitted to see him, one of the guards told her: '"Miss Macdonald – you know *he's* hopeless. You can't do anything for him." Well did I know,' she wrote, that 'I couldn't do anything for him.' She had with her a copy of the picture 'The Lost Sheep,' with 'the Shepherd hanging from the side of a steep hill ... his arm stretched out between the lamb below him and the vulture which is waiting to pounce ... "Look at that," I said. The official understood, and said, "Yes, I was wrong!" He is not a Christian, but I beg him to beware – he's nearer than he knows!'[62]

Eventually, in the presence of seven prison guards instead of the customary one, Caroline stood face to face, separated by the usual wire netting, with the prisoner, 'a decent looking man ... awfully pleased to see me ... who at once began to talk about the past.' As she often did, Macdonald quickly suggested that there was no point in discussing the past and that they should talk about the present and the future. After half an hour 'the officials forgot what they were there for & craned their necks to listen to me, for I talked in a very low tone of voice.' In a few days prison officials told her 'in awestruck tones' that the execution had taken place and that 'he went *very very* quietly.' She was reminded of Paul's Epistle to the Romans, verses that had growing significance for her as she ministered to men facing death: "'For none of us liveth to himself, and no man dieth to himself. Whether we live, we live unto the Lord. *Whether we die* we die unto the Lord. Whether we live therefore or die, we are the Lord's." That poor man's life was worse than useless, but in his death & his manner of going he showed forth the power of the Grace of God.'[63] That the manner of his death was one more demonstration of Macdonald's usefulness to prison officials in their difficult task of maintaining order and calm may have crossed her mind, but that was related to her own objectives only to the extent that it facilitated her admission to prisons. Once there she had a different agenda – to bring 'comfort' to every man who would receive it.[64]

Despite the growing number of individuals whose lives revealed dramatic change, there were disappointments too. Thus, Koizumi's wife, on whom Caroline had expended so much time and energy over more than a year, and whose husband had become a Christian in prison and was looking forward to a new life with his family on his release, was in deep trouble, although she seemed not to realize it. She was six months' pregnant, a consequence of her living with a widower twice her age, from whom she received ten yen a month and her clothes. The woman, who had earlier lied to Macdonald about her living arrangements, now refused to give up the widower. Macdonald, who had doubted the woman's reliability from the start, decided to consult Governor Arima the next time he came for English conversation. The 'always practical & precise' governor, who felt responsible because Koizumi was an inmate under his charge, determined to talk with her and then hunt up the widower and tell him that he was a criminal. If that did not secure their separation, he and Caroline would consult again. Somehow the conditions for the re-establishment of Koizumi's family must be assured before his release.[65]

This experience led Caroline to comment on her growing ability to remain impassive in the face of startling or bizarre news. While hearing the wife's tale, she 'sat cool as a cucumber and listened ... Am I getting hardened or used to it all? No. I am not. I can't help if I get excited. I can't think & give sound advice if I'm on the verge of nervous prostration all the time. Too many people depend on my sanity for me to become insane. May God keep me steady & true for His own name's sake.'[66]

Although Macdonald was spending more and more time within prison walls, the problems of wives and children outside and the difficulties of ex-prisoners in re-establishing themselves were constantly prodding her to look at the world beyond the walls. What she saw was 'all just a dreadful mess ... hopeless unless you begin all over again from the bottom & so few of us are willing to do that. We do love to build up on ruins & sooner or later it all tumbles down.'[67] It was time to start all over again from the bottom by making concrete plans for the new settlement house.

Chapter 9

'A Gentleman in Prison'

AS THE YEAR 1918 BEGAN, Caroline was delighted to greet it with old friends who were to be her house guests for the next two months, the Reverend J.A. Macdonald, former editor of the Toronto *Globe*, his wife, Grace, and their twenty-three-year-old daughter, Jean. Macdonald had lost his job with the *Globe* two years earlier because of his addresses to American peace conferences, when he failed to make a great enough distinction between British and German militarism to satisfy the newspaper's directors. Since then he had been in ill health and now believed that a sojourn in Japan and a visit to Korea would be helpful while increasing his knowledge of a part of the world new to him. From a lifelong concern with foreign missions, which had made him a leader in the Laymen's Missionary Movement in North America, Macdonald had a lively interest in the church in Japan.[1]

Caroline felt immediately that the companionship of the Macdonalds, and especially his interest in international affairs, would give her 'a new lease on life.' She thought Jean 'a nice little kiddie' who had still to learn to express herself. 'She's got enough of her father in her to have a lot bottled up that's got to get out some way, but it won't ever get out except by the channel of sympathy,' which Caroline thought she and her circle might open.[2]

Caroline's encounter with the father of a Tsuda College student who wanted to be baptized was an experience she could share with the Macdonalds as an illustration of the stresses created for individuals faced with the personal and social change she herself was promoting.

Her discussion with her student's father helped Caroline to understand better than she ever had before the anxieties of older Japanese who wanted their sons and daughters to acquire new knowledge, but often retained the hope that this could happen without a change in the attitudes of the young toward traditional customs and beliefs. 'It is awful to see your child going in new ways, whether good, bad, indifferent, you know not. It is specially true when they go changing their religion,' even when, as in this case, the father was not deeply committed to any religion. The father held Tsuda College and its teachers in great respect and thus had come to consult Caroline about 'these new notions that the daughter seemed really to be in earnest about.' In the end, the father said 'he'd take my word for it & let her be baptized if I'd guarantee that Xty [Christianity] was not a bad religion.' She admired 'the old man as he talked & showed his genuine concern in the matter,' and the daughter 'for having got her father to the point he was at.' Soon the girl was baptized with Caroline as one of her sponsors.[3]

While being introduced to missionaries and their work, the Macdonalds also heard Caroline's strictures on many leaders of the missionary movement in Japan, such as the members of the continuation committee of the Edinburgh conference, whose fifty members included four women. Caroline had been critical of this group for some time. 'How a body of earnest men can ... take themselves so seriously & do nothing but pass resolutions that don't amount to fudge & haggle over the wording of them, etc. etc.' was more than she could fathom. They were simply 'ponderous with the sense of their own importance and deceived themselves into thinking they were doing something.' She had the impression that the Japanese members of the committee agreed. The Congregationalist Dr. Kozaki Hiromichi usually went to sleep, while Dr. Uemura wandered about 'like a lost soul & when he does happen to sit down by accident, he's buried deep in his book, but he's got an ear cocked & occasionally makes a dry remark.' Meetings of the Christian Literature Society were also 'a bit of a fraud, for we don't do anything but listen to a long detailed financial account & the rehearsal by Dr. W. that we haven't any money for anything,' especially to purchase a piece of property 'which no one but Dr. W. wants to buy.' Altogether the bureaucracy of Christian organizations was less than inspiring.[4]

One missionary enterprise upon which Macdonald had expended considerable energy over some years came to completion early in 1918 with the opening of the Tokyo Women's Christian College. In this she had worked closely with the respected American Presbyterian missionary and teacher, Dr. A.K. Reischauer, and Mrs. Reischauer. The women's missionary societies of the Canadian Methodist Church and of Presbyterian, Baptist, and Reformed churches in the United States cooperated to support the first institution offering a full university program for women, equal to those available at universities for men. While Dr. Nitobe Inazō served as its first president, the effective academic head of the institution was a woman, Dr. Yasui Tetsuko, who soon became president. For Caroline and other members of the local planning committee, the admission of the first class of eighty-four young women from all parts of Japan called for a celebration. Although it was the youngest of the seven interdenominational colleges, 'the seven lamps of Asia' founded by North American women's missionary societies for the higher education of women, it soon became the largest.[5]

Macdonald's reservations about many missionary policies and practices did not inhibit her from enjoying the friendship of missionaries of several denominations who were actually doing valuable work in local situations. Not least among these were members of the sizeable Canadian Methodist mission in Tokyo, especially the Reverend Percy Price and his wife, who were engaged in social work in East Tokyo. From the same base, Annie Allen, whom Caroline had known well in the student YWCA in Toronto, worked among factory girls. The theology and practice of Canadian Methodists were very similar to her own, and thus it was not only their Canadian origins that made them congenial company. Caroline was glad to introduce the Macdonalds to these fellow Canadians, as well as to some of her American friends such as Galen Fisher and J. Merle Davis of the YMCA and their wives. Thanks to a recent survey of social conditions he had conducted in Tokyo, Davis was an unrivalled source of information on the life of the city for any visitor, and Fisher was always a well-informed guide to Japan.

Caroline also had friends among missionaries of more disparate backgrounds than the liberal Protestants among whom she usually moved, one of whom was Deaconess Susan Knapp, an American attached to Trinity Episcopal Cathedral who was engaged in social work among the poor of Honjo ward. Although so much of her work was practical, Caroline still loved a good theological argument of the kind she could have with the high church Knapp. After a lengthy exchange with her on the nature of the church, Caroline noted that 'with all their high church and their theories about the *elect* they don't scorn pointers from the great unwashed,' such as herself. Caroline was unable to work up any anxiety about whether she was one of the elect and doubted that she could ever grasp 'a standpoint which shuts people out if not actually from the Kingdom of God at least out of "covenanted blessings", so-called, because one hasn't gone through some material ritual. The whole notion is inconceivable to my dull mind. However, I suppose we are all better than our theology. I am not sure that I know what my theology is! I hope I am better than it is, anyway!' Whatever it was, she and her high church friend agreed that they had had 'a very delightful time.'[6]

Caroline also greatly enjoyed her frequent visits with Mrs. Bickersteth, widow of Bishop Edward Bickersteth, the pioneering Anglican bishop who had arrived in Japan in 1886. After her husband's death she had chosen to remain in Japan as a teacher at St. Hilda's Girls' School. The author of two books about Japan, Mary Bickersteth was a lively companion on any subject from theology to Japanese folk customs. She and Caroline had a running debate on the relative merits of Presbyterian and Episcopal forms of church government. On her friend's invitation, Caroline attended a lecture on the sacraments given by a visiting Anglican clergyman and found the discourse 'the most extraordinary thing [she] ever heard,' but later 'dinner with Mrs. Bickersteth was a joy.'[7] Theologies from other traditions were also of interest to Caroline. When the Indian philosopher, poet, and winner of the Nobel prize for literature, Rabindranath Tagore, spoke at Tokyo University, she described the lecture as 'marvellous oratory and clap trap ... virtues very often combined!'[8] Tagore's mysticism, which found God immanent throughout creation and not directly relevant to moral issues, was not for her. Among religious poets, Robert Browning was still more to her liking, and she was an active participant in the Browning Society of Tokyo.

Naturally a major subject of interest to the visiting Macdonalds was Caroline's prison work. They learned of her growing admiration for the sincerity and humaneness of so many of the men connected with the judicial system, whatever the limitations of the system itself. One official whom she was coming to appreciate at this time was Judge Miyake Shōtarō, a sensitive man in his early thirties, 'overcome by his job' with its power over life and death. In one lengthy session with Caroline he explained that when sentencing men he told them that he was sending them to prison not 'to punish them, but to give them time to think & reflect so that they might repent.' Recently Miyake had visited the prison to which most of these men were consigned and was dismayed to learn that the 2,000 inmates had neither time nor opportunity to reflect or do anything constructive. Miyake was not a Christian, but he deplored the absence of Bibles in the prison, save for seventeen copies in a library which contained little else of any value. In Caroline's sympathy for Miyake's distress she observed that 'the work of a judge is too great for mortal man ... It's enough to bring a man to God, or drive him to despair. It is bringing Miyake-san to God.'[9]

■ ■ ■

FOR TWO YEARS Macdonald had been interested in one of the country's most hardened and notorious criminals. Ishii Tōkichi had already spent nearly twenty of his forty-seven years in prison and late in 1915 landed in jail once more for one of the lesser of the many crimes he had committed since his last incarceration. In Tokyo prison he heard that a man was soon to be hanged for the murder of the geisha Oharu in Suzugamori, a suburb of Tokyo. For some months this had been one of the most famous unsolved murder cases in recent history. The murderer was actually Ishii, but a man named Komori, who had been Oharu's lover, was convicted because he appeared to be the last person who had seen her before the murder. As Ishii contemplated the suffering of Komori, about to die for a crime he had not committed, and the agony of the doomed man's family, he decided that since he could only die once he would confess his guilt and save the innocent Komori. Further, he would also confess that two months after the Oharu murder he had killed a man and his wife in Yokohama when they resisted his attempt to rob them.[10]

Following his confession, Ishii was deeply troubled by questions that had never bothered him before: 'What would happen if I should die just as I am? Was there such a thing as a soul? I did not know, but if there were must mine not go to hell?'[11] Ishii was in this state of mind early on New Year's Day 1916, when instead of the usual prison fare he received an unexpected holiday meal of *mochi*, the specially prepared rice eaten by all Japanese at that season. He was told that the food had been sent by two women of whom he had never heard, Miss West and Miss Macdonald. Overcoming his initial inclination to reject a gift from strangers, thanks to the assurance of a prison guard that the Christian missionaries who sent it were motivated by kindness and sympathy, he accepted the food.

A few days later he received a New Testament and two other Christian books, which he placed on a shelf without looking at them. Then Miss West visited him several times, but he paid little attention to her words. One day, out of boredom, Ishii began to read the New Testament and became caught up in the story of Jesus, whom Ishii perceived as a man who was crucified because he had religious opinions different from those of others, a negligible offence in Ishii's catalogue of crimes. As he read this story his attention was drawn to Jesus' words, 'Father, forgive them for they know not what they do.' Ishii felt 'pierced to the heart as if stabbed by a five-inch nail. What did the verse reveal to me? ... I do not know what to call it. I only know that with an unspeakably grateful heart I believed. Through this simple sentence I was led into the whole of Christianity.'[12]

Macdonald began to visit Ishii just before his preliminary trial for the murder of the geisha Oharu. In a most unusual proceeding, Ishii's court-appointed lawyer tried desperately to defend him in the face of Ishii's insistence that he had repented before God, was confessing his guilt, and ought to be hanged. After a nine-day hearing the judge acquitted Ishii on the grounds that there was no evidence to corroborate his confession. Ishii was profoundly disturbed by his acquittal, partly because it cast doubt on his honesty, and also because he feared that Komori might still be required to pay the penalty. When the state procurator took the case to the Appeal Court, Ishii was given a new lawyer, Suzuki Fujiya, a member of the Diet, for whom Ishii soon came to feel great respect and even affection. Suzuki visited Ishii frequently in prison, often sent him food, and above all investigated his case thoroughly for over a year, not only, as Ishii saw it, to 'prevent an innocent man from being hanged, but also to save my soul through getting the facts revealed.'[13]

Such a strange case was widely discussed among lawyers and judges and in the press, and Macdonald's name was frequently mentioned as one who knew the unusual prisoner. At one point in his investigation, Suzuki, whom Macdonald had never met, sent her an indirect enquiry about whether Ishii should be believed, and she was quick to give an opinion: 'No man with a lie on his soul, and deliberately repeating a lie, could have entered into a life of quiet and peace and joy and fearlessness as that man has, and so I believe what he says. Ask the prison officials. They'll tell you the same thing.' The Appeal Court also believed him and sentenced him to death. When Caroline saw Ishii the next day his naturally coarse face was radiant.[14]

A few days later a prison official ushered a stranger into Ishii's cell and introduced him as Governor Arima of Kosuge prison. Arima had come to speak with Ishii about his new faith. The governor met a rough-looking man who might readily inspire fear, 'but his eyes told a different story. They shone with a quiet, beautiful light ... and his spirit was brimming over with gentleness.' Arima's 'heart went out to him with a great tenderness.' As he was departing, the governor spoke words of encouragement to Ishii and promised to meet him in the next world, at the same time taking off his glove and grasping Ishii's hand. The prisoner was overcome by the fact that a man of such high rank would give his hand to an 'utterly worthless and abandoned criminal like myself ... thereby showing his heart of compassion.'[15]

This was only one of Ishii's frequent expressions of wonder at the kindness and understanding he received from prison officials and chaplains, from lawyers, many of them curious about his conversion and model behaviour, from Miss West and Miss Macdonald, 'the parents of my new life,' and from judges who came to visit him. That he was not treated as the beast he had once been but was accepted as a new man was '*all* due to Christ's mercy' and he could 'only thank God over and over again for all his gifts.'[16]

Soon after he was sentenced to die, Ishii began to write an account of his life, for he wished to tell others how his 'heart was changed through the power of Jesus Christ.' Since he had received only two years of formal schooling, had scarcely put pen to paper since then, and could write only in the simplest style, this was not an easy task, but he was determined 'to set down simply and truthfully' the important events from his childhood until the present time.[17] Macdonald was aware of Ishii's literary endeavour, of his intention to leave the manuscript to her, and of his hope that if it were published it would help others.

The date of an execution was never announced in advance. Thus when Macdonald visited Ishii early in July neither of them knew whether this would be their last meeting. He had finished his writing and spoke of his death joyfully. Despite her experience with the condemned, it was not easy to know what to say to a man who might be hanged tomorrow. She read part of Psalm 116, 'words penned centuries ago,' but as she 'stood there in a tiny cubby-hole and talked to him across a passage-way and through a wire screen, it seemed impossible to believe that they were not written for the very thing we faced there in the prison house: "I was brought low and he saved me. Return unto thy rest, O my soul, for the Lord hath dealt bountifully with thee." What had God done to this man ... that he should think that God had dealt bountifully with him? The psalm itself answered: "He hath delivered my soul from death, mine eyes from tears, and my feet from falling".'[18]

She reminded Ishii of the passage in Romans they had often discussed: 'No man liveth to himself and no man dieth to himself, for whether we live we live unto the Lord, whether we die we die unto the Lord. Whether we live therefore or die we are the Lord's.' Ishii gave a confident promise that he would remember this until the end.[19]

The end came ten days later. Caroline was informed that day by the Buddhist prison chaplain, who thus honoured Ishii's request that she be told of his death immediately. The chaplain wrote that 'he faced death rejoicing greatly in the grace of God, and with steadfastness and quietness of heart.' Ishii's last words were a poem he had written for her and requested the priest to write down. She translated it:

My name is defiled
My body dies in prison
But my soul, purified
Today returns to the City of God

A few days later when she visited the prison to collect Ishii's few belongings, a prison official asked her to affix her name and thumbprint beside Ishii's on his will. He had left her all he possessed – one sen, a copper coin worth a penny.[20] For the rest of her life Caroline wore the coin on a chain around her neck.

Macdonald read Ishii's simple and moving account of his life and was convinced that it must be published. She believed that his story had a universal appeal and would show every reader that 'if you get deep enough life is all one and the heart is touched only by love.'[21] On 25 December 1918, less than six months after Ishii's death, *Seito to Nareru Akutō* (The Scoundrel Who Became a Saint) was published in Tokyo.[22] Within the next three weeks the literary sections of five of Tokyo's daily newspapers featured brief reviews of the confessions of the notorious murderer of Oharu in Suzugamori. While noting Ishii's poor Japanese, all agreed that his sincerity would move his readers. Apparently the book found an appreciative audience in Japan for a second edition was published within four months and a third appeared a year later.[23]

Not all readers reacted sympathetically. Three months after the appearance of Ishii's memoirs, one of the most popular writers of the day, Kikuchi Kan, published a short story obviously based on Ishii's story. 'Aru Kōgisho' (A Letter of Protest) was in the form of a letter to the minister of justice from a young man whose sister and her husband had been murdered by a man who had also committed seven other murders. The story presents the argument that execution was a grossly insufficient punishment for a man who had caused agony to his victims and untold loss and suffering to as many as forty or fifty members of their families. Those families and society as a whole were robbed of whatever satisfaction they might have had in the murderer's imprisonment and death by the publication of his confession, which showed that far from going to the gallows with the appropriate shame and fear, he had died with joy and hope amid the praise of prison officials, even a governor. Was there anything more unfair or unreasonable than a prison system that allowed missionaries to visit and comfort prisoners and permitted a murderer to preach to prosecutors and prison officials who would then praise him for his faith? Who could comfort the survivors? Although claiming that he had nothing against Christianity, the writer charged that its influence robbed the victims' families and the nation of the punishment they had the right to exact, and he blamed the Ministry of Justice for allowing the publication of a confession so offensive to the survivors.[24] Did Kikuchi express the feelings of many of his fellow citizens? Even readers who did not follow the intricacies of Kikuchi's ethical arguments could easily conclude that Ishii's tale was one more example of the baneful effect of Christianity on the social fabric of Japan.

■ ■ ■

MACDONALD'S ASSOCIATION WITH ISHII reinforced one strand in her developing thought about Japanese society. Ishii had suffered an emotionally and materially deprived childhood, as had a majority of the men she saw in jail. She was increasingly convinced that had their early experiences and opportunities been more favourable most of them would not have landed there. Observations and questions about social conditions in Japan derived partly from her own experience, and reports on social service endeavours in North America, contributed to a course on social problems that Macdonald gave at the request of Tsuda Ume for a group of recent graduates of Tsuda College. In the minds of both women the purpose of the course was practical rather than theoretical, and they hoped that it would provide an incentive for young women to become involved in social service.[25]

At the same time the regular Wednesday evening meeting in Caroline's home was changing somewhat in character as discussion of the bearing of Christian faith on social issues assumed more importance. Over the past two years, attendance had grown steadily, sometimes reaching as many as sixty. The participants were nearly all men, since few women were able to break out of the tradition that inhibited their attendance at mixed gatherings. The guest speaker, often a member of Fujimichō church, spoke about an aspect of Christian faith or a related topic of social interest. If the speaker were of a literary bent, a work such as Francis Thompson's *The Hound of Heaven* was expounded. The roster of speakers was an increasingly varied one, but there was a core group that included Dr. Uemura, Governor Arima, and Matsumiya Yahei. Caroline's young friend Nishimura Saburō spoke more than once about his conversion and his Sunday school work, and later about working conditions on the Tokyo Stock Exchange. Some of the theological students in Dr. Uemura's seminary were welcomed as speakers, as was Governor Arima's son, recently returned from studying in the United States.[26] In Caroline's view, Arima Jr. with 'his good head and big heart' was 'a chip off the old block.'[27] Most of the doctors, lawyers, businessmen, professors, and government officials who came to these gatherings had never before been in the company of ex-prisoners or heard anything of their lives, in or out of prison. The diversity of participants reflected the intellectual and social turmoil of a time when minds in search of meaning were open to a wide variety of faiths and ideologies. Possibly Macdonald's Wednesday night 'salon' was the most egalitarian gathering in Tokyo, composed as it was of 'all sorts and conditions, men who have been in prison, the relatives of men in prison now, people out on bail, lawyers, prison officials, and ordinary sinners like you and me,' she explained to David Cairns. 'I fairly hug myself with joy at the mere conglomeration of it all.'[28]

Although as yet she had no precise plan for the next phase of her work, she believed the group included a number of 'splendid Christian Japanese men' who would help her 'when they get educated on various aspects of the Social Cosmos.'[29]

• • •

ONE WHO LEAST NEEDED EDUCATING on social issues, and was soon to become more knowledgeable about prison life, was Tagawa Daikichirō, who had spoken at the Wednesday meeting several times. In Tagawa, Macdonald was introduced to a type of prisoner previously unfamiliar to her, the political prisoner. Until this time she had known Tagawa only slightly, as an elder in Fujimichō church. The son of a scholar of the Chinese classics who had no use for any religion, Tagawa became a Christian while studying law at Waseda University and like so many Waseda graduates became active in public life. After practising law for a time, working as a journalist, and serving as deputy mayor of Tokyo, Tagawa was parliamentary secretary to Minister of Justice Ozaki Yukio, the most influential liberal democrat in the Diet. Like Ozaki, Tagawa was a fervent advocate of British constitutional democracy and a leader of the movement for universal suffrage.

Now at the age of forty-eight, as a member of the House of Representatives for the Kenseikai (Constitutional Association), Tagawa had acquired a reputation as one of the Diet's most outspoken critics of authoritarian government and of Japanese policies toward China. Unlike most Japanese, including some liberals, Tagawa welcomed the growth of Chinese nationalism as appropriate for a great people and had publicly criticized the Twenty-One Demands of 1915 through which Japan attempted to establish control over China.[30] Within Japan a major hindrance to the growth of democratic government was the influence of the declining but still powerful Genrō (Elder Statesmen), unofficial advisors to the emperor, who had recently ensured the accession of General Terauchi Masatake to the office of prime minister. The ideal of the Genrō was 'transcendental government,' with a cabinet composed of men who were above politics and ultimately responsible only to the 'national interest' as embodied in the emperor.[31] When Tagawa was bold enough to publish an article criticizing the most powerful of the three remaining Genrō, Yamagata Aritomo, for usurping the powers of the elected house and betraying the true interests of the state, conservative elements among the politicians and in the press resorted to a frequently used weapon for silencing opposition: under the Press Law they had him charged with disloyalty to the emperor.[32]

Tagawa's article appeared in a journal published by a group of Christian intellectuals led by the editor, Kashiwai En, who was also charged with lèse-majesté.[33] The whole affair was useful to the state for it seemed to prove that Christians could not be loyal members of Japanese society. Tagawa was eager to have his article translated for the local English press, where it would come to the attention of his friends in England and the United States, and perhaps provide overseas pressure that might modify the attack of his enemies. He appealed to Dr. Uemura and Macdonald to translate 'the fatal article which is causing such a commotion in the circles of justice,' as Macdonald described it. Getting 'the meaning better into [her] pate' necessitated lengthy discussion of the article with Uemura, whose authority as a guide to 'the realm of treason' she fully appreciated.[34]

Currently the Shintoists had two civil cases and a criminal action pending against Uemura,[35] and he was well known for his public role in the most famous treason controversies of the Meiji era – his support of Uchimura Kanzō in rejecting the Imperial Rescript on Education in 1891, and his holding of a memorial service for Ōishi Seinosuke, the Christian involved in 'the Great Treason Case' of 1911.[36] Although Uemura believed that a Christian pastor should play no direct role in political and social movements, he supported lay Christians who were social activists, especially when their actions reflected his own convictions on the proper limitations of state power over the individual.

Neither his membership in the Diet, nor anything Uemura, his political friends, or his fellow elder in Fujimichō church, Uzawa Fusaaki, and the other outstanding lawyers defending him could save Tagawa from being sentenced to five months in prison. Altogether 'it was a terribly iniquitous affair,' in Macdonald's opinion, 'but far from spoiling his influence in the community, it will enhance it. What fools ... dream that that way of managing the affairs of state will do anything to advance the nation.'[37]

On the evening before Tagawa was to enter prison to serve his sentence, Caroline joined other members of Fujimichō church to bid him farewell, as if he were going on a journey. She felt that this event brought her close to the experience of the early Christians, with Tagawa in the role of Peter or Paul. Amid prayers and triumphal hymns, members of the congregation assured Tagawa of their support of him and his cause.[38]

Her ready access to Ichigaya prison ensured that Macdonald was

Tagawa's first visitor and she remained one of the most faithful. Just before he entered prison, Tagawa's wife died, a result, Macdonald thought, of the ordeal the family was enduring. Later, Tagawa, not untouched by the traditional view of the prison as a place of utmost shame, refused to allow any of his seven children to visit him. Caroline thus became the primary message bearer between the prisoner and his family and many of his political associates. That experience added to her understanding of the liberal democratic movement and made her Tagawa's cherished friend. Tagawa was required to serve only half his sentence, but he was a recruit to the cause of work with prisoners, despite his discovery that prison life was less miserable than he had anticipated.[39]

After his release from prison, Tagawa was a frequent visitor in Macdonald's home and often shared a meal with her. Sometimes their common interest was the current *daidendō* (evangelistic campaign) of the Protestant churches in Tokyo, conducted under Tagawa's chairmanship. Caroline knew that it was his experience in prison that had moved Tagawa to undertake this responsibility, and he proved to be one of the most effective speakers in the campaign.[40] Despite her reservations about the efficacy of this kind of evangelism, Macdonald was busy 'hunting up' people she thought would benefit from attendance and was gratified when several of them signed up as *kyūdōsha* (enquirers). Altogether the *daidendō* yielded 3,000 *kyūdōsha*. She knew 'we won't get ... even a fraction into the church without years of toil,' but she was thankful that the campaign had 'scattered the news of the Gospel of the grace of God.' Her immediate responsibility was to nurture new enquirers among the students of Tsuda College, and among people who came to the Wednesday evening meetings.[41]

In Tagawa's renewed zeal he also undertook to organize Protestant lay people in Tokyo and Yokohama to consider how they could better serve the church. On his invitation, Macdonald arrived at the inaugural meeting to find that there was one other woman present, a missionary, who proved to be the only participant to object to a proposal that women should be equally represented in the organization and that both women should serve on the executive. In Caroline's view, the attitude of the men showed 'there's more fairness among Xtn [Christian] Japanese men about women than among the majority of missionaries.'[42]

Among the consequences of Tagawa's prison experience, the most significant for Macdonald was the kindling of his interest in prison reform.

She arranged a consultation in her home between Tagawa and Governor Arima, who had not met before. 'To see these two men, each with his interest in prison reform from his own standpoint,' was of high interest to her. 'Mr. Tagawa as is his wont when he gets worked up walked up and down with his hands in his pockets and discanted on the cosmos,' explaining to Arima his plan to buy a newspaper, the *Miyako Shinbun*, in whose pages he would educate the public on social issues. Caroline felt that among all the assorted meetings held in her house over the years, none was so 'fraught with possibilities for the Kingdom of God ... All great movements have begun with the two or three.'[43] However, Tagawa was 'lost for some time' to local reform since he was off to the United States to continue his association with leaders of the American Federation of Labour and to study the implications of the founding of the International Labour Organization, which would hold its first meeting in Washington in a few months.[44]

■ ■ ■

EARLY IN 1919, Macdonald found herself playing the power broker in the affairs of Tsuda College. For nearly two years it had been evident to everyone except Tsuda Ume and her close friend and confidant, Anna C. Hartshorne, that the acute asthma from which Tsuda suffered increasingly prevented her from giving active leadership as principal of the school. How to secure her resignation and the appointment of a suitable successor was not evident, but it was becoming imperative, since the uncertainty was creating tension in the daily life of the school. By the end of the first week of school in January, Caroline found 'the atmosphere electric with nerves ... and the whole thing is like a chicken with its head cut off. It is cut off ... because Miss Tsuda has lost herself and Miss Hartshorne also. That's the tragedy. But I must not let it get on my nerves.'[45]

It did not get on her nerves, for with her usual practical political sense she was busy organizing a solution to the growing crisis. In mid-January there was to be a meeting of the Board of Trustees, and she was determined that the present policy of drift must end then. With Emma Kaufman, she went to visit Tsuda with the good news that Kaufman's father would give 10,000 yen to the school, and then led gently into a discussion of the necessity for Tsuda to resign. It was a manoeuvre just short of bribery. A few days later, after further lengthy discussions with Tsuda and Hartshorne, the letter of resignation was in Caroline's hands.[46]

Now steps had to be taken to ensure that the meeting of the Board of Trustees went as it should, for 'the school must be saved for the larger life it will ... come into.' Fortunately, as one of the representatives of the teaching staff on the board, Macdonald would be present at the meeting. It was vital to have an acceptable nominee as principal, and there was none. On the day before the meeting, Caroline convinced Tsuji Matsu, an English teacher at the college, who had studied at Wellesley College and at Oxford, that there was nobody else who could do the job. Tsuji had to be persuaded that she was not disqualified by the fact that she was married. The next morning Caroline 'got together an effusion for the Board' in which she 'waxed quite eloquent' regarding Tsuji.[47]

Tsuda's letter of resignation was presented at the beginning of the meeting, which was chaired by Princess Ōyama, Tsuda's oldest friend and also the chair of the Board of Trustees.[48] Then Princess Ōyama requested that a letter be read from Awa Matsunosuke, a member of the board who was an expert on educational administration. Caroline's heart sank, for she knew that Awa was supporting another Tsuda teacher, a woman Caroline and others thought inadequate for the position.

To Caroline's astonishment, Awa's letter proposed that Dr. Nitobe be named acting principal, in her view a most unsatisfactory and temporary solution. She expected Dr. Nitobe to say that as he was leaving for the United States very soon he could not accept, but neither he nor anyone else in the room revealed what was on their minds. 'It's up to ACM [i.e., herself] this time,' she thought, abandoning her prepared speech and deciding that she must 'act in a very Japanese way, agreeing with the proposal just made,' but leading up to the traditional *keredomo* (however) that would turn things around. She declared that if Dr. Nitobe could give all his time to the college, there could be no better principal; however, she was sure he could not do that. Moreover, she asserted, 'we need a woman ... who has been abroad ... who has had educational experience ... Everyone agreed. They couldn't very well do otherwise. But was there such a woman? She was sitting there in front of them but they didn't seem to think of her.' There was silence. Just as Caroline was beginning 'to get frantic again,' Dr. Nitobe walked out of the room and she went after him. To her assertion that 'Mrs. Tsuji is your woman,' Nitobe protested that she wouldn't take the position. Caroline replied that she knew an offer would be accepted. Since Nitobe didn't want the job himself, he agreed and went back into the meeting to propose Tsuji

'The thing was done and ... ACM finally came home ... feeling she hadn't lived in vain,' confident that the future of Tsuda College was assured.[49]

■ ■ ■

SOON A LARGER POLITICAL ARENA claimed Macdonald's attention. In mid-March 1919, the Reverend A.E. Armstrong, assistant secretary of the Board of Foreign Missions of the Presbyterian Church in Canada, arrived in Tokyo from Korea with stories about atrocities perpetrated there by the Japanese police in suppressing the recent 'March First Movement' for the independence of Korea. Nowhere in Asia had Protestant missionaries been more successful than in Korea, and from the beginning Presbyterians had been by far the largest group of converts. After Japan's formal annexation of Korea in 1910, official relations had been ostensibly friendly but the authorities were always suspicious of the Christians. By 1919, many Korean Christians were active supporters of the nationalist movement; in the current unrest, half of the thirty-three signatories of the Declaration of Independence, which was rallying such widespread support, were Christians. One of them was the first native-born Presbyterian minister, and before long he and many of his clerical colleagues and their leading parishioners were in jail, their churches closed, or their services overseen by the police.[50]

Although Caroline had no formal relationship to his mission board, Armstrong apparently went to her because she was a fellow Presbyterian and Canadian, and was reputed to have connections that might be helpful. Immediately Caroline sent him to Galen Fisher of the YMCA who was close to Korean students in Tokyo. A gathering of 600 Korean students in the YMCA Hall had done much to precipitate the nationalist outburst in Seoul. She also arranged for Armstrong to meet with Uemura Masahisa.[51]

Uemura was in a key position on the Korean question as it concerned Japanese Christians. For some years, with the active support of Fujimichō church, he had spent two or three months every summer in evangelistic tours of the Japanese empire in Formosa and Korea, and beyond in Manchuria and Singapore. Uemura believed that Japan was right to 'make Korea her territory in order to lead her into civilization, and as a contribution to the advancement of mankind.'[52] Nevertheless, in keeping with his views on the separation of church and state, he refused an invitation from the governor-general to take charge of Christian work among Koreans at government expense.[53] In the earlier 1912 nationalist movement, when over one hundred Koreans, most of them Christians, were arrested and charged with plotting to overthrow the government, Uemura took an unusual position in an article in his paper, *Fukuin Shinpō*. Although disapproving of the nationalists' objective, he applauded their spirit because 'men who have the backbone and the spirit to fight for their independence give promise of being turned into respectable Japanese subjects.'[54]

Uemura's missionary work was not welcomed unreservedly in Korea. Two cultural and religious imperialisms were contending: Japanese Christians backed by military and political power sought ascendancy or at least major influence over a Korean church that was largely the creation of English-speaking North American missionaries who, like most missionaries everywhere, were identified with the national aspirations of their converts. Uemura was critical of missionaries 'who feel that the souls of Koreans are their monopoly' and adhere to 'the idea that the evangelizing of Korea depends exclusively on one people and not on others.'[55] Too many Korean missionaries failed to recognize that 'waves of rationalism are already attacking the Korean Church' and that their naive methods of evangelism and training ministers were failing to bring the faith of Koreans to maturity. In Uemura's view, 'the co-operation of Japanese Christians is necessary if Christianity is to be firmly planted in Korea.'[56]

In 1919, in the face of a far more serious insurrection than that of 1912, Uemura was committed to helping individual Koreans while refraining from criticism of his government's overall policy in Korea. After Armstrong met Uemura as Macdonald had arranged, she was distressed to learn that the mission board secretary had 'poured cold water on every suggestion that Mr. Uemura made'; finally she took Armstrong 'aside & put some pep in him & told him to go to & not say that nothing could be done.' Through Takahashi Korekiyo, minister of finance in the Hara cabinet who had once been a Christian and still had some sympathy for Christianity, Macdonald quickly arranged for a group of Korean missionaries planning to come to Tokyo to have an opportunity to lay the facts before Prime Minister Hara.[57]

In a month's time, the Reverend J.G. Holdcroft, an American Presbyterian missionary in Korea for over a decade, arrived in Tokyo. From the outset Macdonald found Holdcroft an unlikely agent for securing change in Japanese policies in Korea. Nevertheless, when he 'took to running after' her with appeals for help she 'took him by the hair of the head & fetched him over to Mr. Uemura,' who emphasized that the best way to help Korea was to get the atrocities there publicized in the leading papers in the United States and Britain, although he thought something could be done in Japan, such as meeting with Mr. Hora of the *Miyako* newspaper, which Caroline duly arranged at her house. Again Uemura advocated a meeting with the prime minister and told Holdcroft 'to get his ammunition ready.' To Macdonald's disgust he never did: 'If he'd only buck up & not be scared, we could do something for him.'[58]

Soon Holdcroft received reinforcements from Korea in the persons of two more American Presbyterians, the Reverend N.C. Whittemore and the Reverend W.C. Erdman. When the three men came to lunch with Caroline she was not encouraged, for they were clearly afraid that any protest they might make to the Japanese government would have negative repercussions in Korea. Erdman, whom she found 'very high and mighty,' wanted to make it clear that he wasn't asking for a meeting with the prime minister, to which Caroline declared that if she 'had such a tale to tell as they professed to have' she 'would sit on the prime minister's doorstep' until she was heard, but if they didn't want to see the prime minister she would go to the telephone and call off the interview that had been arranged. That 'fetched them up some and Mr. Erdman came off his high horse. That man may have an air of piety but he's a frivolous foolish man,' she told her journal. She could respect Holdcroft for 'he's at least serious ... even if he does take cold feet.' She was still convinced that 'if they had had backbone & not been afraid of the fetish they call their work they might have accomplished something.'[59]

Perhaps they did accomplish something. Within a week Prime Minister Hara met with Korean missionaries, first with Bishop Herbert Welch of the American Methodist Episcopal Church and the next day with the three Presbyterians who had consulted Macdonald accompanied by Dr. Ibuka Kajinosuke, president of Meiji Gakuin University, as interpreter. Hara gave the missionaries assurances that he regretted recent incidents in Korea and intended to bring about major transformation in government there, so that Koreans would have the same rights as Japanese, although this could not be done overnight.[60]

At the same time Caroline was calling on the wife of the head of the gendarmes or special police in Korea, to whom she had been introduced by her friend and fellow member of Fujimichō church, General Hibiki Nobusuke. It was Hibiki's view that 'if we were going to have reforms in Korea we'd have to start with the gendarmes,' and as the wife of the chief of the gendarmes had once been a Christian, but no longer attended church because of her husband's opposition, it might be possible to influence the chief through her. Caroline received a very cordial reception and left hoping that her visit had done some good.[61]

The combination of pressure from the outside world, much of it generated by missionaries, and Japan's desire to avoid further disruptions in the Korean economy led to a liberalization of policies in Korea during the next two years. The gendarmes were replaced by civilian police and torture of prisoners almost ceased, more Korean officials were appointed, there was a reduction in surveillance of Christians and other suspected nationalists, and Christian institutions of higher education were granted complete freedom.[62] Although Macdonald shared in the general satisfaction over these modifications in Japanese policies, there was no way of knowing how much credit she and her friends could take for them. They had done what they could, but attribution of credit was not a question on which she ever expended much emotional energy.

A few weeks later in the summer of 1919, when Caroline attended the annual interdenominational missionary meetings at Karuizawa, she found no reason to change her mind about the limitations of some missionaries. The place was full of argument about the pros and cons of interracial marriage, thanks to the recent wedding of a prominent American missionary and a Japanese woman. William Merrill Vories, who had gone to Japan in 1905 with the YMCA, was one of the most innovative and influential missionaries, widely known as the head of the independent Ōmi Mission, which had transformed a large rural area on the shores of Lake Biwa. His bride, Maki, daughter of Viscount Hitotsuyanagi, head of an ancient noble family opposed to Christianity, had become a Christian while studying at Bryn Mawr College. Although marriage to foreigners was not common, it was occurring with increasing frequency, but this was the first time a member of the Japanese nobility had married a foreigner of no rank. As a friend of both the bride and the groom, Caroline was invited to the wedding and thoroughly enjoyed the beautiful and historic event. She failed to understand those, especially missionaries, who were scandalized by 'mixed' marriages: 'The only objection any of them seem to have is that the color of the skin is different. These pious people who think that God has set bounds in color ... have a very curious notion of the scheme of things.'[63]

In time, Macdonald's views on interracial marriages became even firmer. In 1925, when two prominent Canadian Presbyterian clergymen asked whether she thought such arrangements were the Lord's will, she replied: 'I can't be so sure always what the Lord's will is – but I think we too often give up our common sense & then blame things on the Lord.' Despite their look of pained surprise, she continued: 'It stands to reason that if we are ever going to get anywhere, different nationalities & races have got to get mixed up. At any rate, Lord's will or no Lord's will, we are getting mixed up & we'll have to look at the question in a Christian manner.' The eminent ministers made clear their distaste for pursuing the subject.[64]

Now, at Karuizawa the meetings of the social service committee of the Federated Missions confirmed her earlier impression that it was 'the most futile thing on record. Foreigners who won't confer with Japanese are such an anomaly that one can scarcely believe they exist. But they do.' They were the main targets of the forthright address she was about to deliver.[65]

The missionaries assembled in Karuizawa no doubt expected Macdonald to focus on her prison work. Although she began her speech with comment about prisons she quickly moved on to broader concerns. Too many people believed that the prison was the solution to 'the criminal problem,' which was 'not itself a problem at all ... but a symptom of disease in the body politic.'[66]

In her view, the disease in Japanese society was more widespread and deeply rooted than most missionaries understood and they were having less impact than they liked to believe. Christians derived satisfaction from their increasing numbers, but the increase was not even keeping pace with the growth of population. Children who started out as Christians in Sunday schools, high schools, and colleges often fell by the wayside, and there were losses through the marriage of Christian girls to non-Christians, who were sometimes 'decent moral men' but often much less than that. 'We sweat and labour over individual students, we convert them and baptize them and grad-uate them and turn them out.' Unfortunately, women's education was inad-equate for the real world: it failed to inform women of the legal protection that gave them freedom to live independently of parental control if they wished to do so, and it failed to give them the means of economic independence.

Similarly, young men were given 'a few pious teachings without much reference to the real circumstances of life, we tell them to be good children ... and then we dump them into Hell.' It was not hard to see why there were so many young men among the 50,000 people who crowded Asakusa Park every night where there were lights, music, and singing. The theatres, where the movies often glorified crime, the restaurants with their bar girls, and the geisha houses, were cheerful and attractive, 'and there isn't that much that is bright and attractive in a young lad's life in this country.' She knew only too well how often the lights of Asakusa had been the beginning of crime for a young man or husband and of misery for his family. Further, Asakusa was the centre of one of the most entrenched social evils in Japan, venereal disease, and almost nothing was being done by Christians or anyone else to combat it.[67]

A large proportion of the men she met in prison were there because of troubles involving women, troubles Macdonald believed owed much to a family life and an educational system that taught a man to believe that 'he is the lord of creation ... including his natural prey – the woman. *Men trained to own and control and dispose of women trained to serve and kowtow ...* What are we doing ... to teach men categorically that women are not slaves, not mere playthings and conveniences for men?'[68]

Implying that many members of her audience were doing very little, she asserted that mission boards and organizations themselves scarcely showed 'overwhelming respect for women. There are more women missionaries in Japan than men ... and I think we are doing at least as good work as our brethren and as much of it ... Where are our women ... on your executives, your committees, your conferences?' On the program of this very conference, she noted, she was the only woman among nine male speakers.[69]

Women were not mere passive victims but often played a direct role in the creation of Japan's woes. Too many women, indoctrinated with the belief in male supremacy, were weak and over-indulgent mothers, unable to give their sons any firm direction as they grew up. Macdonald saw this type of mother behind many of the young criminals she visited and more than once she had berated a mother for her failure to restrain and guide a son.[70]

Quite another type of woman shaped the commercial and political morality of Japan, the geisha, 'capable, worldly-wise, astute.' When statesmen and businessmen wanted advice or recreation, they went to these women, not to their wives, who were too rarely accepted as companions. Too many novels about Japan pictured the geisha as 'a frail, innocent child who falls sometimes through her own innocence,' a depiction which harmed 'the multitudes of decent women in Japan who know better than we do who the geisha are.' In Macdonald's perspective, one shared by many of her Japanese contemporaries, the geisha were at the heart of much of the corruption and crime in society. 'Why do men gamble and embezzle and steal? How do they use their ill-gotten gain?' Rivalry over a geisha all too often led to 'a quarrel, knives, and the gallows.' Far from being 'innocent little entertainers,' the geisha were 'sophisticated women of the world, trained from childhood for their nefarious trade.'[71]

What were Christians doing to create a different kind of female power and influence? 'Are we sending out from our schools as virile a type, but with other ideals? Or are we educating our young women still to be content with merely being a so called "good wife and wise mother," in its strict Japanese application?'[72]

Moving on to more general issues, Macdonald observed that in every area of society an overwhelming barrier to a better life was sheer overwork. Her friend Nishimura, whose work in the stock exchange kept him there from nine in the morning until midnight six days a week for months on end, was only one example. In the recent evangelistic campaign the churches held meetings from morning to night,

> but most people are working morning, noon and night, and even then can scarcely make ends meet. It is all very well to quote 'What does it profit a man if he gain the whole world and lose his own soul,' but these people are losing both the world and their own souls into the bargain, because industrial conditions and the stress of living are such that they have *actually and really no time to be saved* ... If you and I ... worked in a factory 16 hours a day or even 12 at the minimum, seven days in the week, practically 365 days in the year, year in and year out, till we fell at our task, and were then pushed aside for another unfortunate to take our place, how much backbone would be left in you and me? If you and I had been born with syphilis in our blood, with inherited tendencies to tuberculosis, and then lived under the triple influences of Asakusa Park, the Yoshiwara, and the superstitions and disease breeding surroundings of the temple, all within fifteen minutes walk of one another ... how much vim would there be remaining to us to stand up for principle?[73]

Given all the circumstances, Macdonald found it remarkable that anyone had the energy to protest against social conditions, and she applauded workers such as those who were currently on strike against all the Tokyo newspapers: 'It is high time they struck or did something if the nation is to save its soul.' She was not sure whether the few missionaries who had contact with factory workers, especially women workers, were 'helping them to be contented with their long hours and practical slavery' or awakening them 'to realize their own worth, to believe that they are not mere merchandise ... If we ... are making people contented with intolerable conditions ... then we are ... not promoting the Kingdom of God. The Christian message is not a palliative nor a sedative but a cure, and until we begin to work for a cure ... we are something less than Christian.' It was time for missionaries to stop appointing committees to investigate and conferences to congratulate themselves on the noble work they had done in the last 50 years and get to work to remove the underlying causes which rendered so much of their work ineffective.[74] She did not exclude herself: 'In the almost 15 years since I have been in Japan I have gathered more statistics, have written more stuff, and have done more talking than I ever hope to be forgiven for ... Until we ... missionaries or laymen, make up our minds to ... destroy utterly the entrenched evils of this land that are dragging down to death the flower and hope of the nation, we trifle with life and have got no business to be here.'[75]

These themes continued to be central to the Wednesday night meetings in her home, as they were of an article on 'The Individual in the Social Problem.' While Macdonald asserted that the rescue of individuals was worthwhile, she excoriated those who believed it mattered much if a few young girls were saved from being sold by their parents to become geisha or prostitutes, or a handful of the 100,000 juvenile delinquents who passed through the courts each year were reformed, or a marriage here and there was patched up when family life was so often destroyed by drunkenness, loose living, and venereal disease. What ideals of womanhood and family life were expressed by the fact that there were twice as many licensed prostitutes, geisha, and restaurant girls in Japan as there were girls in high school?[76]

Altogether, Macdonald's diagnosis of the ills of Japanese life called in question much of the very basis of society, especially the roles of women and the assumptions behind industrialization. It also cast doubt on the efficacy of much of the work done by missionaries and by the Japanese church. Increasingly, her vision of a settlement house in Asakusa seemed a radical and creative approach to the transformation of the individual and society.

C h a p t e r   1 0

Tackling 'the Social Cosmos'

B Y M I D - 1 9 1 9 Macdonald had decided that the 'splendid Christian men' she had been educating about 'the Social Cosmos' ought to be ready to back her plans for a settlement house. A long talk with Dr. Uemura assured her of his enthusiastic support, and together they reviewed the names of the men most likely to be helpful. Once again Caroline reflected that Uemura was 'an extraordinary man.'¹ To have his full support was enormously sustaining for her personally and there was no doubt about his influence with others. Over a period of a few weeks Macdonald visited each of the proposed committee members, several of whom were members of Fujimichō church, and was greatly encouraged by the willingness of each to join the committee, and by their unanimous conviction that this was the right time to build 'the Hull House of Tokyo.' Although overseas friends would be asked for substantial assistance, Uemura and Macdonald shared the conviction that the enterprise would only succeed if responsibility and control were placed firmly in Japanese hands.²

Dr. Uzawa Fusaaki, now a member of the executive committee of the Seiyūkai, the governing political party, agreed to serve as chairman. Other members were Judge Mitsui Hisatsuji, of the eminent business family, who served as secretary, while Funao Eitaro, an official of the Mitsui Company and superintendent of the Mitsui Charity Hospital, agreed to act as treasurer. Another was Tagawa Daikichirō, who since his sojourn in prison had once again been returned to the Diet when his constituents, refusing to accept his rejection of a nomination, had re-elected him in a landslide vote. Matsuyama Tsunejirō, another member of the Diet, well known among Christians as a hymn writer, also agreed to join the committee. Itō Kōjirō, manager of the Tokyo Steel Tube Company, and Konō Jūzō, a prominent oil merchant and University of Toronto graduate, were drawn from the business community. Governor Arima Shirosuke agreed to serve, as did General Hibiki Nobusuke, Fugenji Tetsukichi, a prominent lawyer, and Dr. Uemura's son-in-law Kawato Shūzō, a professor at Waseda University. In its middle- and upper-class composition, the board of Tokyo Neighbourhood House, or 'Shinrinkan' (The Home of the Friendless Stranger) as it was to be known in Japan, was very like those of the North American settlement houses on which Macdonald's enterprise was modelled.[3] Already she had named her home, the centre for her present work, Shinrinkan.

The total budget for the settlement house was set at $300,000, of which $75,000 was to be raised in Japan and the remainder in North America. The prospectus, prepared mainly by Dr. Uzawa and translated into English by Caroline for circulation in North America, emphasized the 'radically practical' nature of a social settlement that would 'go far to enable the people to live in security, decency, and happiness.' The success of the undertaking was assured, thanks to the combination of 'character, experience, and earnestness' present in Caroline Macdonald who was the heart of the enterprise.[4]

A more detailed outline of the activities of the new settlement house divided the program into five categories. The educational component would include a model kindergarten, after-school activities for boys and girls, lectures and movies, and aesthetic education. For health care there was to be neighbourhood nursing, a dispensary, and general medical advice. For recreation there would be a playground, calisthenics would be taught, and social gatherings arranged. Religious activities would include a Sunday school, a variety of meetings for study and discussion, and personal counselling. A 'miscellaneous' category listed endeavours covering areas to which

Macdonald had been giving increasing attention: an employment bureau, a domestic service exchange for women, legal counselling, and 'moral instruction of labourers.'⁵ This last expression was vague enough to encompass both the conservative attitudes of some members of the board and Macdonald's growing association with the labour movement. At the same time it would sound 'safe' to authorities ever vigilant to detect 'dangerous thought.' Macdonald was aware that there were already some fine examples of Christian settlement work in East Tokyo, including the chain of centres run by her Canadian Methodist friends. As well, there was the less extensive but expanding work of the Salvation Army and of the WCTU in Honjo ward, and a growing number of social welfare enterprises both private and public in several areas of the city. Taken altogether they fell far short of meeting the needs of the less fortunate citizens of the growing city, a fact recognized by politicians, bureaucrats, and philanthropists. The Shinrinkan of the future would provide social services on a large scale, but what would set it apart from other institutions would be the in-service training of social workers that would give it a unique role in developing the social service network for the whole city.

■ ■ ■

AT THE END OF AUGUST 1919, more than a hundred friends and colleagues, including three judges, two prison governors, several journalists, and members of the board of Shinrinkan, gathered at the Tokyo station to see Caroline off for Yokohama whence the CPR's *Monteagle* would take her to Vancouver. After some weeks of relaxation with her family in London, she was ready to embark on the fundraising that was the primary objective of her trip to North America.⁶

In Toronto the key people were her undergraduate classmate, the physicist Frank Burton, and an old family friend and active Presbyterian layman, J.K. Macdonald, whose numerous business involvements included the presidency of the Confederation Life Association. They agreed to be chairman and honorary chairman respectively of the Canadian committee to support her work in Tokyo. Margaret Wrong, lecturer in history at the University of Toronto, became secretary, and Allison Patterson, secretary to the president of the university, Sir Robert Falconer, was treasurer. Additional members included Lady Falconer, Frank Burton's wife as well as his brother, C.L. Burton, who was president of the Robert Simpson Company department store, and Caroline's old YWCA associates, Emma Kaufman and Dr. Clara Benson. Mrs. J.A. Macdonald, wife of the former editor of the *Globe*, who had recently seen so much of Caroline's work at first hand, was glad to help. The names of Chancellor R.P. Bowles of Victoria College and T.A. Russell, president of the Russell Motor Car Company, would help, it was hoped, to tap the resources of Toronto's prosperous Methodists. This committee undertook to raise $10,000 a year for the operating expenses of the settlement, mainly to cover staff salaries, including Macdonald's salary and expenses.[7]

Macdonald addressed several gatherings in Toronto, from a well-attended Sunday evening service in the university's Convocation Hall to a Kiwanis Club meeting. She prepared a substantial brochure, *The Prisons of Tokyo and a Social Service Opportunity*, outlining the development of her 'unique work,' giving the names of the Christian sponsors in Japan, describing the financial responsibility they had assumed, and citing the approval of non-Christian Japanese officials. Anticipating questioners who might wonder why the work was not to be conducted by the mission board of a church, the brochure explained that this was precluded by the necessity for close cooperation with the Japanese government, but assured prospective donors that 'Miss Macdonald would never curtail the essentially Christian nature of her efforts in order to obtain thereby financial support from non-Christian sources.'[8]

In an address to the Foreign Mission Board of the Presbyterian Church, Caroline trod on delicate ground, for many of its missionaries were critical of Japanese expansionism. Lamenting that Canadian Presbyterians had no mission in Japan proper, Caroline suggested that although their substantial work in the outposts of the Japanese Empire – Korea and Formosa – had made them aware of certain aspects of Japanese militarism, it had limited their understanding of the Protestant church in Japan itself. Her presentation of how Canadian Presbyterians 'could touch the Japanese Empire and Japanese Presbyterianism at its centre' fell on receptive ears. Thereafter the Presbyterian WMS voted to contribute $2,500 to the Canadian committee for Shinrinkan.[9]

In the spring of 1920 she was in New York where the American committee for 'The Tokyo Social Settlement' or 'Riverside House' was being organized with her friends E. Stagg Whitin and Julia Jaffray as chairman and secretary respectively. Much of the organizing was done by Jaffray in consultation with Macdonald's good friend Galen M. Fisher, who had just returned to the United States after twenty years as national secretary of the YMCA in Japan. An informed and perceptive observer of Japanese society, Fisher's close association with Caroline in many common endeavours made him eager to endorse her 'rare combination of grit and grace, of Scottish common sense and religious power,' as well as her knowledge of social conditions in Japan.[10] Others who joined the New York Committee included Bertha Conde, the senior secretary of the Student Division of the American YWCA, Harry Emerson Fosdick, minister of the wealthy First Presbyterian Church in New York, William Adams Brown of Union Theological Seminary, Robert A. Wood, director of Boston's famed settlement, South End House, G.A. Holliday of the Methodist Episcopal Church and a former teacher in Japan, and J. Merle Davis, honorary general secretary of the Tokyo YMCA, who had just returned to the United States from Tokyo. In contrast to the more general formulation of the Japanese Board of Trustees, the American committee's statement of the purpose of the Tokyo settlement house emphasized the pioneering role of the enterprise in the formal training of social workers as a model for other institutions of social improvement, and as a weapon for a direct attack on Tokyo's social problems. The committee also commended the settlement as a promoter of friendly relations between Japan and the United States and Canada. In its publicity the committee stated clearly that control of the institution would be vested in the Tokyo Board, and its finances administered according to the rules of its incorporation under Japanese law.[11]

The New York committee agreed to postpone any major campaign until after the distractions of the presidential election campaign in the autumn of 1920 were past, when potential contributors might be more open to an appeal for work in Japan.[12] Thus it seemed to Macdonald that everything was now in place for acquiring the material resources that would make her dream of a social laboratory and training centre in the heart of Tokyo come true. After an absence of nearly nine months it was time to return to Japan, where the next steps must be taken.

■ ■ ■

IN LATE MAY 1920, the *Empress of Russia* sailed from Vancouver bound for Yokohama with the usual mixed crowd of diplomats, missionaries, students, businessmen, and tourists. To a gathering of fellow passengers Caroline told the story of Ishii, a tale one of them thought had 'something of the glamour of *The Arabian Nights* and something of the naked hellishness of Poe's *Tales of Mystery*.'[13] The commentator was Dr. John Kelman, the Scottish-born scholarly minister of New York's wealthy Fifth Avenue Presbyterian Church. With his wife, Kelman was embarked on a three months' visit to Japan and China.

Kelman added his voice to those already urging Macdonald to publish Ishii's story in English. None had argued more eloquently for an English version than a senior prison official who believed that Ishii's tale showed how 'a man uneducated, steeped in crime, condemned to death for murder ... is touched by one of another nation, and a woman at that, with traditions and history and education as different from his as night is from day; but the universal message of the love of God flashes across the gulf of human differences and the man's soul responds.'[14] In the hope that Ishii's book would speak to the world as his life had never done, and supported by Kelman's promise to find a publisher in the United States, Macdonald agreed to prepare an English translation. The timing could scarcely have been more opportune and she had high hopes that the book would assist the American fundraising campaign.[15]

On her return to Tokyo, Caroline's first obligation was to her friends in prison and immediately she began a heavy schedule of prison visiting, seeing ten or fifteen prisoners a day for several weeks. For the moment there was little to be done with the Board of Trustees for the settlement, since the chairman, Dr. Uzawa, was fully occupied with a session of the Diet, and Dr. Uemura was off on a preaching mission in Manchuria. That was fortunate, for it left time for her first priority – the translation of the manuscript before the Kelmans' return to the United States.[16]

To escape the summer heat in Tokyo, Caroline retreated to Karuizawa for two weeks, where she worked as hard as she had ever done in her life and came back reasonably well pleased with the result. Ishii's simple Japanese was within her power to translate as a more sophisticated style of writing would not have been, but it was difficult to put it into language 'not ... too high falutin & yet ... well put together English.'[17] While not hesitating to depart from a literal translation occasionally, she believed that she had managed to reproduce the 'straitforward [sic] simplicity of the original' and had remained faithful to the spirit of Ishii's testament.[18] When Dr. Kelman went over it with her, he was elated and departed with the manuscript, confident that there would be no problem in finding a publisher.[19]

Within six months, Kelman reported that the Canadian-born, highly respected New York publisher George H. Doran would probably accept the manuscript not as 'a Sunday School story or a piece of missionary propaganda, but a piece of international politics and first rate psychology!' Macdonald was sure that Kelman was right in 'aiming higher than popular reading ... The thing seems so simple that it will take specialists in psychology and criminology to see its significance.' For English readers the book would also be a good introduction to another culture: 'Japanese characteristics bristle, not only in [Ishii] himself, but in the naive way he reveals prison officials, lawyers, Buddhist priests, etc.'[20] The universal significance of his pilgrimage scarcely needed comment: 'Poor fellow, he will not have lived or died in vain if people of other races are helped to see that human nature is *just* human nature ... that there is only one God who can reveal himself to such a soul.'[21] Given her conviction about the universality of its message and the purpose for which she would use the profits, it seemed right to dedicate the book 'To all in every land who have never had a chance.'

George Doran published the volume as *A Gentleman in Prison,* a title Caroline thought rather curious. Kelman agreed that it was not perfect, but it was the only title Doran would touch among the several he had submitted.[22] Kelman thought it acceptable because, as he wrote in his foreword to the book, 'Ishii was one of God's aristocrats. Even in his unregenerate days one notes the generous largeness of his nature, and the instinctive diligence of his spirit.' Kelman would not vouch entirely for Ishii's theology, which included a belief in 'immortality ... so absolute ... that we are startled to find him bent on cultivating his mind during the few days that are left to him, in order that he may be intellectually fitted to take up the new life in heaven when his hour shall come.' For both Macdonald and Kelman, the most touching aspect of Ishii's faith was his conviction that Christians never worried, were never afraid of death, and that in thought and conduct they always lived up to the highest principles and ideals of Christ. Kelman noted that until Ishii's conversion 'the only Christians he had ever known were the two women who told him of Jesus in his cell.'[23]

• • •

MACDONALD HAD NOT BEEN IDLE while awaiting news of the fate of the manuscript. One of the four prisons in Tokyo had thus far remained closed to her because of the governor's hostility to Christianity. Now a senior official whom she had known well in another prison had been appointed governor there, and the way was open for work in a large institution whose inmates were all recidivists, including some she had known elsewhere in their careers as criminals.

Further, the work with ex-prisoners and their families was even more demanding than previously, for in the economic slump of the postwar period it was increasingly difficult to find work for men released from jail or for wives who were trying to support themselves and their children while their men were in prison.[24]

At the same time there were all Caroline's other interests and responsibilities. While Kawai Michi was away from her work as general secretary of the YWCA on an extended visit to Korea, Caroline added to the volunteer work she had always done for the 'Y' since she ceased to be a member of the staff. This year at the annual conference of the YWCA she presented a strong argument for co-education, to begin with some joint activities between the YWCA and the YMCA and eventually to extend to Christian schools. If women were to be equal partners in Christian marriages and in the reformation of society, Caroline argued, they had to learn to study, work, and play with men when they were young. This was an idea whose time was far away and the proposal fell on Japanese ears unable to hear of such revolutionary change.[25]

Despite her vow that she would no longer teach, Tsuda College had been 'up a gum tree' for a 'tough' English teacher and had prevailed on her to come back for two hours a week, and that meant lessons to prepare and essays and examinations to mark once more. Thus one afternoon a week she rushed off to discuss Tennyson's 'The Higher Pantheism' or Browning's 'Andrea del Sarto' with the graduating class. She was tough enough, although reluctant, to 'decapitate' two students, 'poor lambs' who should never have been allowed to get that far because 'they didn't have the heads, that's all.' For some weeks she led a Saturday afternoon study session with recent Tsuda College graduates on a currently popular book among liberal Christians everywhere, T.R. Glover's *The Jesus of History*. She was anxious to keep in touch with these young women, some of whom she hoped to recruit to social work training in the new settlement house, while others could be expected to work as volunteers.[26]

Assignments that had to be conducted in Japanese required careful and time-consuming preparation, such as the weekly civics class that Macdonald gave at Tokyo Women's Christian College, probably the first of its kind to be given anywhere at the university level. She lectured at the summer school on social work arranged by the Tokyo city government for 400 policemen, city officials, and social workers on the causes of crime. She spoke on the same subject to 1,000 students at Keiō University, to small meetings of labourers at her house, and to 600 parents in the Tokyo Kindergarten Association. She shared an unusual evening with a Buddhist priest in his temple when they both addressed an audience of 500 on the social implications of their respective faiths and were invited for a return engagement.[27]

In addition to her increasing involvement with groups and public activities, there was still a constant stream of individuals coming in and out of Macdonald's home looking for moral support and help of every kind. Some of her visitors stayed for extended periods, such as the eight-year-old boy whose father had just gone to jail for the sixth time. Caroline undertook to cure the boy of the lying and stealing that threatened to lead him in the same path as his father. When verbal exhortation failed, she resorted to an old-fashioned spanking, observing that the treatment would have been easier on her if she had had her mother's old strap. The result was 'a sudden transference into an angel – without a lapse for three weeks.' He remained 'a noisy little Turk' but that did not bother her. 'It was correction of his morals not his manners' she was after. After three months, satisfied that 'he had quit his evil ways & was on the path of rectitude,' she sent the boy to a friend in the country who would look after him.[28]

Although Caroline frequently promised herself that she would reduce her activities, especially those involving committee meetings, she took up one new responsibility with alacrity. In the autumn of 1920, Dr. Uemura won his battle for equal status for women in the Presbyterian-Reformed Church in Japan when the General Assembly agreed that henceforth women were eligible for ordination as elders and ministers on the same basis as men. Foreigners (i.e., missionaries) would never have allowed this change had they still controlled the church, Macdonald noted, observing also that American Presbyterians had recently voted down such a proposal and that as far as she knew Canadian Presbyterians had never as much as considered the question. That the assembly of Japanese Presbyterians, composed entirely of males, had voted unanimously to act on the New Testament message that there should be 'neither male nor female' in the church was a source of great satisfaction to Caroline.[29]

When Fujimichō church implemented the new policy, it decided to elect eight new elders, all of whom would be women. Adopting a method of election that Caroline thought was 'total democracy,' there were no nominations. Each of the more than 1,500 church members could vote for any female member. Caroline was among the eight who received the most votes. That this was a signal honour for a foreigner did not escape her. Nothing could have indicated more clearly her acceptance by the congregation with which she had identified herself so fully and her eldership remained a source of pride to the end of her days.[30]

Whatever else commanded Caroline's attention she was always thinking about the plans for the settlement. Throughout the summer of 1921 the search was intensified for a suitable site at the right price, either with or without a usable building, a difficult task in an area as crowded as Asakusa. All the while, the increasing participation in the activities conducted in her house underlined its inadequacies as a centre for her work.

While the search for property continued, the news from New York was not entirely encouraging for the committee there had to admit that the fundraising campaign had got off to a slow start. That was only one reason she was glad to welcome Dr. Harry Emerson Fosdick and his wife to Tokyo, for it gave her an opportunity to show the need for the settlement to an influential member of the American committee. Earlier, her eager anticipation of the daily lectures the theologically liberal Fosdick gave to the missionaries assembled at Karuizawa had proven more than justified.[31] Some members of his audience were less satisfied, for as Fosdick soon learned, 'the missionary community was split wide open – on one side, some of the largest personalities and intelligent views one could meet anywhere; on the other, such narrowness and obscurantism as seemed downright incredible.' The main bones of contention were 'higher criticism' and the authority of the Bible, and the related questions of Christian attitudes to Japanese culture and contemporary social issues. Fosdick found it 'like walking a tight rope to address such audiences.' For the first time he saw 'in its full intensity ... [the] ... fundamentalism' that was shortly to drive him out of the Presbyterian church and into the pulpit of Riverside Church, New York, endowed by the liberal Baptist Rockefellers, where he would remain for three decades.[32] Macdonald had learned to deal with this familiar situation mainly by staying out of the way of the ultra-conservatives, an option not open to Fosdick. A further direct contact with the New York committee developed when Tagawa Daikichirō, again re-elected to the Diet and also to the Tokyo city council, went to New York to observe the proceedings of the conference on naval disarmament on behalf of his party, the Kenseikai. From the outset Tagawa had been a supporter of the League of Nations and was now one of the leading internationalists in Japan. Macdonald was pleased that so distinguished and personable a member of the Board of Trustees would 'rustle for the settlement' during his time in America and that he would also visit her family in London.[33]

While a decision about what one or two wealthy families in Japan would do to support the settlement hung in the balance, Caroline's friends on the New York committee cabled that they were appealing to the Laura Spelman Rockefeller Fund for $250,000 and anticipated a favourable response. Her hopes rose and she pursued the search for a good site with renewed vigour. In the meantime, the Canadian committee had provided a new typewriter and a mimeographing machine, and even more important, employed a private secretary for Caroline. Fortunately, the right person was available in Molly Baker, an American who had served as general secretary of the Yokohama YWCA during the war and was willing to return to Japan for a two-year period. Baker's knowledge of business methods and Japanese customs, and a fair command of the Japanese language meant that she would need very little 'breaking in.' Even before Baker's arrival, Caroline felt that 'a 1,000 years had been lifted from the top of [her] head.' Now she would be much more efficient with all her work, including the financial campaign for the settlement.[34]

Caroline had more than a suspicion that Emma Kaufman had contributed to the Canadian committee the money for Molly Baker's salary. In a more direct fashion, Kaufman, who had for some months made life easier for her friend by lending Caroline her automobile, now gave her a Ford sedan for which the upkeep would be provided by a well-wisher in Dr. Kelman's New York congregation. That included the wages of a chauffeur, who with the freedom customarily enjoyed by servants in Japan remarked that the car suited Macdonald well as it was 'so small and cunning.'[35] Kaufman's material support was also manifest in her generous use of her recently built house in the Sadowara district. Kaufman's parents had provided the money to build a well-heated, sunny, western-style house, hoping that their daughter's chronic bronchitis, which threatened to send Kaufman home to Canada for good, would be controlled. The large and comfortable house was well appointed with fine North American furniture, silver, and china, in sharp contrast to the austerity of Caroline's domestic style. Supported by a Japanese couple, the Nishimuras, who remained her servants for twenty-five years, Kaufman enjoyed entertaining and the ample dining room was often the scene of dinner parties in which Caroline was included. When Caroline needed an escape from all the activity in her own house, she was always welcome to retreat to Kaufman's home for a quiet dinner and a long night's sleep, and in the morning the two women would go to the hairdresser and the masseuse.[36]

By the end of the summer of 1921 Macdonald's most immediate concern, apart from the difficulty of finding a site for the settlement, was the tardiness of the Canadian committee in raising the balance of the promised funds for the expansion of the staff. The matter was urgent for she was eager to issue a firm invitation to E. St. John Catchpool, the vice-warden of the famous East London settlement, Toynbee Hall, and his wife, a medical doctor. At the end of 1918, when Catchpool, a Quaker, was on his way home from work with the Friends' relief service in Russia, he had spent some time in Tokyo where he was much impressed by Macdonald's achievements and her dreams for the future. More recently the Catchpools had declared their interest in coming to Tokyo to join the settlement. Caroline feared that if she delayed too long she would lose them. In the meantime, the Catchpools' intention to join the staff of the settlement was a major vote of confidence that should be useful to the American committee.[37]

By the spring of 1922 the financial prospects for the settlement were dim. Galen Fisher and other key members of the American committee had been forced to conclude that there was no hope of support from the Rockefeller interests, at least until very substantial funds had been raised from other sources, or until the Tokyo Neighbourhood House had established some organic relationship with an organization with which the Rockefellers were already acquainted. It appeared that the lack of such a connection was the main reason for the rejection of the committee's initial appeal. Now the committee was exploring other sources, mainly wealthy individuals, especially women.[38] In Japan things were not going well either, for the two big companies from whom most was expected had failed to come through: the Mitsui and Mitsubishi corporations had contributed not 50,000 yen each as had been hoped but only 10,000, although the former suggested that further gifts would be forthcoming once the settlement was in operation.[39]

Despite this discouragement Macdonald remained optimistic for the long run. For the short run she desperately needed money for current operating expenses and therefore sold the car, hoping this would not offend the donor of the vehicle. On the contrary, within a month Emma Kaufman repeated her generous gift when she acquired a new Ford and gave Caroline her older model.[40]

As she surveyed the prospects in Japan, Macdonald was cheered by the knowledge that she not only had an outstanding organizing committee but strong support within Fujimichō church and from Tsuda College and many of its graduates, who were likely to be married to men of substance. Further, her friend, Hani Motoko, long known as Japan's first woman journalist, had promised to launch an appeal to the 85,000 readers of the magazine she and her husband edited, *Fujin No Tomo* (Women's Friend), as soon as the settlement could be presented to the public in a more tangible form. That would bring the claims of Shinrinkan before the middle-class women whom Hani sought to educate on the reform of the home and of the external forces that affected home and family. Hani, a Christian, had just established a school for girls, Jijū Gakuen (Freedom School), whose progressive educational methods emphasized classroom discussion as a preparation for participation in public affairs and where Hani proposed to interest students in Shinrinkan. Caroline had worked with Hani on the curriculum for the new school and taught some classes in English and civics after it opened.[41]

There was also the prospect of government support, thanks to current changes in policy. Since the end of the war the Japanese authorities, their sense of urgency sharpened by growing social unrest, had taken a new interest in the rapidly growing private charities and social welfare activities. Since 1920 they had been regulating them through a Bureau of Social Affairs, which was under the auspices of a more powerful and centralized Home Ministry than had existed previously. The bureau also became responsible for labour affairs, previously the responsibility of several ministries.

During the past decade the government had shown some interest in research on social problems and on social work education but had allocated little money for implementing programs. Rather it had confined itself to administering the very limited provisions of the *Jukyū kisoku* (Poor Relief Regulation) of 1874, Japan's first Poor Law. Based on Japanese customs rooted in feudal times, it expressed a doctrine of 'mutual fellowship' that recognized, at least in principle, a minimal community responsibility for the most poverty-stricken members of society. Similarly, the new law emphasized the primary responsibility of family and relatives to look after their own. The same philosophy inspired the coordinating organization, the Central Charity Association, founded in 1908 and dominated by government officials, big industrialists, and pro-government academics. Its purpose was not to work with the poor or to improve the services available to them, for it was primarily a research and educational organization. However, the association's interest in western ideas of social amelioration indirectly fostered the growth of modern (i.e., American) social work in Japan.[42]

By 1920 the limitations of the existing Poor Law and of social services generally were becoming evident to many Japanese, including some influential bureaucrats. The government realized that it could not itself care for all the country's needy citizens, and it therefore encouraged the development of private charities while also expanding public services for the poor. One result was a substantial growth of private charity and social welfare agencies, including some under Christian auspices. Along with this expansion came increasing government regulation, mainly through the Bureau of Social Affairs.[43]

Nowhere were the inadequacies of the existing social services more evident than in Tokyo. With a population of two million in 1920, and another two million in prefectures outside the formal boundaries of the city, the human consequences of rapid industrialization and urbanization were highly visible. Thus toward the end of 1919, a bill to establish a social bureau for the city of Tokyo was passed unanimously by the City Assembly. Each ward of the city was divided into districts where well-to-do volunteers were recruited to establish the number and needs of the poor in the district and often to administer assistance provided by the bureau. The first chief of the Tokyo Social Bureau, Kubota Bunzō, was succeeded by a series of graduates of the Law Department of Tokyo Imperial University whose ideas on social policy were strongly influenced by the German social thought promoted by their academic mentors.[44] Bureaucrats and politicians were propelled by the conviction that if action were taken in time, the development of social and economic conditions that would lead to revolution could be prevented. In its first three years the Tokyo Social Bureau conducted studies on a wide range of social needs and on facilities needed to meet them.[45]

An indication of the growing involvement of government in social work was manifested in the interest and cooperation of several levels of the bureaucracy in the Bureau of Prisons of the Ministry of Justice, in the Home Ministry, and in the Tokyo city government. The last two promised financial support for Shinrinkan once it was under way, and the Home Ministry was prepared to make a low-interest loan to cover part of the purchase price of land.[46]

In Macdonald's mind it was essential to raise as much interest and money in Japan as possible and not to wait until large sums were contributed from abroad. Thus when the New York committee insisted that she come to the United States in the autumn of 1922 to address various fundraising events and to personally lobby wealthy women, she refused. Although she appreciated the hard work of the Tokyo committee members, they were all very busy men and she feared that without her to pull them together they would await her return before doing anything further, which could prove disastrous. Moreover, she could not afford the trip, since she had only recently repaid her debts for the last one, and the New York committee had made it clear that the bills for this one would have to be met out of the money she raised in the States.[47]

An even greater consideration was her advance into new work, especially her involvement in plans for a juvenile court in Tokyo and her growing association with the labour movement. All this was essential for the future work of the settlement and it would be irresponsible to leave it at this stage. Caroline concluded that 'if they cannot raise the money without me, then we'll have to do without the settlement, that's all ... They only want me for a show anyway. It was suggested that I wear Japanese costume when I speak! I wouldn't do that even for the sake of getting the money. I'm not quite such a fool as all that!'[48]

As an alternative to going to New York, Caroline made 'a brilliant suggestion,' one that would assist fundraising by answering a question that was sometimes raised by interested Americans: 'Who would carry on if Miss Macdonald disappeared?' The Catchpools were problematic. More likely was a young woman Caroline had known well at Tsuda College before she became interested in Christianity or in social problems, who was now in her senior year at Wellesley College and was planning to return to Japan to work at Shinrinkan. Takizawa Matsuyo, 'the cleverest girl they have turned out of Miss Tsuda's school for many a long day,' in Macdonald's view, was a student of the social sciences, spoke English exceptionally well, and was a fine actress.[49] To study industrial conditions she had spent a summer working in an American factory, and another summer had accompanied Jane Addams to the International Peace Conference in Vienna and elsewhere in Europe. Before coming back to Japan in 1924, she planned to live and work for a year in an American settlement house, possibly Hull House.[50] Caroline could scarcely imagine a more qualified successor, and for immediate purposes she was the ideal emissary 'for creating the Japanese interest' in New York – and she could legitimately wear a kimono.[51]

• • •

WHILE PLANS FOR THE SETTLEMENT inched ahead slowly, the work Macdonald conducted from her own home expanded steadily. She was working more and more with Judge Mitsui Hisatsuji, a Tokyo judge before whom most juvenile offenders under fourteen were tried, thanks to common consent among his fellow judges that he had a special understanding of children. The Diet's passage in 1922 of a bill to establish a court specifically for juveniles was the culmination of several years of persuasion by Judge Mitsui and others whose hands had been strengthened by information and support provided by Macdonald on the operation of American juvenile courts.

As anticipated, when the Tokyo juvenile court was opened at the beginning of 1923 Judge Mitsui was appointed chief judge, to Macdonald's great satisfaction. In her eyes Mitsui was a man whose 'whole soul is taken up in the effort to reclaim these delinquent children before they develop into thorough going criminals.' Mitsui's years as a Sunday school superintendent had made him a student of children, with whom he never lost the quiet, patient, fatherly manner that encouraged them to tell their stories in court. Later, when the children were out on suspended sentence or in a reformatory or juvenile prison, Judge Mitsui remembered their birthdays and sent them New Year's greetings. Such devotion to his juvenile delinquents, Macdonald observed, exceeded even that of the renowned Judge Ben B. Lindsey of the Denver juvenile court, the leading exponent of the reform of the American justice system in its treatment of juveniles.[52]

It was also a source of gratification to Macdonald that along with the establishment of the juvenile court the Tokyo Social Bureau had appointed twenty-six workers, including ten women, to develop social services for children. Some were truant officers who would begin to enforce the law requiring school attendance until age fourteen, while others assisted children before and after their time in reformatories and prisons. All this was a long step forward in the right direction, but a major problem was finding suitable people for this work. Both Macdonald and Judge Mitsui saw a large role for the expanded settlement in training personnel who would be able 'to do what no government can do, namely, supply incentive and spiritual force to the constructive social work which will be necessary to make the actual laws effective.'[53]

In her discussion of juvenile problems, Macdonald always recognized that court and prison work was largely ameliorative. The real war of prevention must be fought in the streets of Asakusa against a ready supply of dime novels, corrupting movies, the influence of the thieves in the park around the Kannon Temple who bragged of their exploits and often recruited children to their ranks, and against the examples of the geisha and the licensed prostitutes of nearby Yoshiwara.[54] Only when Caroline and a group of colleagues were living on the battlefield would they be able to make real advances against these enemies.

Beyond the particular problems of East Tokyo, Macdonald saw more general conditions arising from the growing gulf between the rich and the poor, sweated labour in the factories, the inadequate enforcement of the compulsory school law, and the severe overcrowding of primary schools that so diminished the prospects of the children of the poor. Such problems characterized all industrializing societies, but here they were accentuated because of the rapidity of Japan's evolution from a feudal past. Given the lack of any real public opinion, these conditions were bound to continue unless politicians and bureaucrats could be educated to change them.[55]

As the work of the juvenile court developed, an increasing number of young offenders released on probation were assigned to Macdonald's supervision. Often several boys at a time were housed overnight in her home when they came out of prison or reformatory, and there was the occasional escape to deal with in the middle of the night. She spent many hours counselling parents in the homes to which some of the boys returned, talking with boys who were going to a group home on the Bonin Islands or to new employment, or in visiting or writing letters to boys who were trying to make a new start in life. The work with juveniles could have consumed all of Macdonald's time and it soon became necessary to put some of this work under the direction of Matsui Harukichi, a man who had already worked with her for some time as a volunteer.[56]

Caroline could not allow plans for the future to absorb too much of her energy, for present opportunities were demanding, and her capacity to seize them always had implications for the character of Shinrinkan. Nowhere was this truer than in her growing involvement with labour activists.

Chapter 11

'Jesus Was a Labouring Man'

T HE SOCIAL AND POLITICAL UNREST that had grown remark-
ably during the last year of the First World War continued to cause ferment
at every level of society after the war. Liberal academics, such as Caroline's
friends Dr. Nitobe Inazō and Dr. Yoshino Sakuzō and their students, reforming journalists, and lawyers all discussed 'reconstruction' and shared the
hope that in Japan, as in Europe, autocracy and militarism would give way
to democracy. That there was also an awakening popular social movement
seemed evident in the 'Rice Riots' of August 1918.

The awareness of factory workers and farmers that far from profiting
from the great industrial expansion of the war years they had actually fallen
behind, was focused on the dramatic increase in the price of rice, amount-
ing to 60 per cent in eighteen months. The nationwide riots were spontaneous and unorganized, with very little leadership. For nearly two weeks
more than 700,000 protesters in cities, towns, and villages surged through
the streets, smashing the shops of rice merchants and looting the homes of

the wealthy, while strikes or revolts occurred in several mining areas. By the time the police and the army crushed the disturbances, 6,000 protesters had been arrested and were later fined or sentenced to jail terms from six months to life.[1]

The rice riots demonstrated for the first time in modern Japanese history that there was a basis for a mass movement that might in the long run have radical implications. In the short run they dramatized the Terauchi government's inability to deal with inflation, while its vigorous suppression of popular protest brought increasing conflict with the proponents of democratic, responsible government. In the face of this pressure, the Terauchi government resigned in September 1918, to be succeeded by the first truly party government in Japan, headed by Hara Takashi, leader of the majority party, the Seiyūkai, and the first commoner to hold the premiership. In the longer run, the riots contributed to changes in the production, distribution, and pricing of rice, to modest improvements in social welfare provisions in some prefectures, and perhaps to an increase in confidence within many groups that organized advocacy could improve their lot.[2]

To Macdonald, the government's response to social unrest seemed futile and underlined the need for an effective labour movement. Those who thought oppressive social conditions could be altered by 'some cheap rice thrown down to the people when riots occur,' or by 'capitalists discanting on the fatherly relation between capital and labor' were irrelevant or worse.[3]

■ ■ ■

THE ECONOMIC EXPANSION of the war years and the failure of wages to keep pace with the cost of living, as underlined by the rice riots, breathed new life into Japan's nascent labour movement, especially the major trade union, the Yūaikai, led by Suzuki Bunji. Macdonald apparently met Suzuki sometime in 1919, although he may have participated in the Wednesday evening meetings at Shinrinkan at an earlier date.

Ever since its founding in 1912, the Yūaikai (The Friendly Society) had correctly represented policies of social amelioration and cooperation between capital and labour similar to those of the friendly societies in Britain on which the union was modelled. Also like them, the Yūaikai endeavoured to increase the self-respect and confidence of workers through lectures, reading, and self-improvement programs.

Suzuki Bunji, son of a poor samurai family, and a Christian, had managed to secure a good education in the social sciences at Tokyo University. His pragmatic moderation was rooted in Christian humanism and in the German theories of social reform then popular in the university. He had actively discouraged members of the Yūaikai from joining the rice riots of 1918. Apart from his innate conservatism, Suzuki's caution was dictated by the fear that more aggressive policies would expose the Yūaikai to the police repression that always threatened it.[4]

During and after the war the number of industrial disputes mushroomed annually, and Suzuki was under growing pressure to offer more aggressive direction to industrial workers by expanding the leadership of the Yūaikai beyond himself and a small group of intellectuals in Tokyo, thereby making the union a national political force. Much of this pressure came from the Yūaikai's branches in western Japan, where the dominant influence was Kagawa Toyohiko, a Christian already well known for his social work in the slums of Kobe. Suzuki's study of the methods of the American Federation of Labor during two recent visits to the United States also conditioned him to adopt more vigorous tactics.

At its annual convention in August 1919, the Yūaikai became the Dai Nihon Rōdō Sōdōmei-Yūaikai (The Friendly Society Labour Federation of Greater Japan). Encouraged by its own restructuring and growth, and by the belief that the newly formed party cabinet of Prime Minister Hara would be more responsive than its predecessors to demands for democratic change, Sōdōmei adopted a platform that included the whole program of the new International Labour Organization (ILO). In major cities Sōdōmei organized rallies in support of universal suffrage, the granting of full legal status to trade unions, the establishment of a minimum wage and a workers' compensation system, democratization of education, and the right of workers to select their own representatives on Japan's delegation to the ILO. When the government and employers' delegates totally ignored the labour representative at the first meeting of the ILO in Washington in 1920, Suzuki was confirmed in his growing belief that in the world of government and business in Japan, there was still overwhelming apathy, if not hostility, toward labour. Soon Suzuki announced his conversion to socialism and declared that the Sōdōmei must become more democratic in its governance and more aggressive in presenting the claims of labour.[5]

Through her association with Suzuki and his friends, Macdonald began to learn more about the aspirations and problems of the labour movement and shared their disappointment when the Hara government continued to enforce Article 17 of the Public Peace Police Act, thus ensuring that arrest and imprisonment was still the fate of many strikers and labour organizers.[6]

At the beginning of the 1920s the organized labour movement in Japan was still but a decade old, and most local unions had been organized for only two or three years. Both government and employers made some concessions in this period of union growth, often in the form of promoting factory councils, bodies that fell short of possessing even the power of company unions. By providing workers' representatives with an opportunity to express their views, the councils acknowledged, however slightly, the persistent demand of workers for respect as human beings and for a sense of belonging to the enterprise and to society, but decision-making remained firmly in the hands of management.[7]

In close association with business, the government established the Kyōchōkai (Harmonization Society) to promote cooperation between labour and management. Substantially endowed by its sponsors, this attempt to subvert the union movement proved to be less inhibiting to the growth of unions than most of its earliest promoters intended. Consisting of prominent businessmen, senior government officials, and academic labour specialists, the Kyōchōkai confined itself in the end to research on problems of labour-capital relations and the provision of mechanisms for the arbitration of industrial disputes, although the latter were not often brought into play. Initially, Suzuki Bunji and many other labour leaders declined to cooperate with the Kyōchōkai because of its failure to support basic labour legislation, the repeal of Article 17, and universal suffrage.[8]

In the economic depression of the early twenties, organized labour was struggling to hold its few recent gains. In a time of rising unemployment and in the absence of any job protection for strikers, the number of strikes declined dramatically. Nevertheless, there were some significant disputes, one of them particularly important for the direction of Macdonald's work.

Early in 1921 during a strike in a small electrical factory in the outskirts of Tokyo, eleven men were arrested on charges of inciting their fellow workers to violence, charges that Macdonald later concluded were without foundation, although she did not know that at the time. A young man whom she knew in Fujimichō church, Shioji Tatsuo, brought her the names of the eleven and asked her to do what she could for them since she had access to the prison where they were held.[9]

Shioji had interested Macdonald from her first knowledge of him. Three years earlier when he was a newspaper reporter 'fast going to anarchism,' thanks to his association with the printers' union where anarchist ideas were strong, Shioji had met Dr. Uemura and had decided to study theology. Although Macdonald had noted no radical change in Shioji's 'notions about the rottenness of society,' his ideas about methods of reform had changed considerably and now, while studying, he also worked for Sōdōmei, and was seeking to interest young workers in Christianity, an effort that included his leadership of a Sunday evening Bible class held in Caroline's home.[10]

Macdonald wasted no time in sending books to the imprisoned strikers and then visiting them and their wives. Several strikers were frequent visitors to Shinrinkan while they were out on bail awaiting trial, and some attended Shioji's Bible class for a while. Eight of them were eventually freed, but the leader of the strike was sentenced to two years in jail. Caroline arranged for his wife to work in the home of one of her wealthy Japanese friends where she and her two small children could live reasonably well until her husband's release.[11]

In the summer of 1921, hundreds of workers in the Mitsubishi and Kawasaki shipyards in Kobe went on strike and were soon followed by workers in other Kobe factories. The Christian labour leader, Kagawa Toyohiko, one of the strike leaders, was among the many arrested. Before the six-week dispute ended, as many as 30,000 workers had marched in one procession through the streets of Kobe in support of the strike. At a crucial point, Suzuki Bunji and other Sōdōmei leaders from Tokyo were summoned to augment the local leadership in what had become the most significant strike in Japanese history until that time. Labour's limited resources and an excess of theorists over men who could agree on common action ensured that the strike would end in disaster. And yet this experience of a strike enhanced the militancy of even the most moderate workers, especially the more than 200 strikers who were arrested.[12]

Shortly, when Sōdōmei decided to open a night school for working men, Macdonald was asked to take charge of the English class and have it meet at Shinrinkan. Every Saturday night about twenty men arrived for lessons in elementary English with Macdonald and Molly Baker. Macdonald found them as serious as any students she had ever taught: 'For sheer earnestness commend me to these young laborers, who after a day's work as machinists and shoe makers and blacksmiths, come to a night school to improve their minds.'¹³

In accord with her usual policy, Macdonald refrained from initiating any discussion of religion with this labour school English class. She had found such restraint 'the most expeditious way to get people to study about Christ.' Inevitably, left to themselves, members of a group would ask whether they could 'talk about God' after the class. This class was no exception: 'We began to talk about God, and to sing hymns, and we learned a hymn in English, "Jesus, Lover of My Soul."' Later, at Caroline's annual Christmas entertainment, the men sang this hymn 'with more unction than tune.'¹⁴

At another Christmas party for their families and fellow workers, one member of the group volunteered to explain some pictures of the life of Christ. 'Let us not ever forget,' he kept reminding his audience, that 'Jesus was a labouring man.' In discussing a picture of the temptation of Christ in the desert, the speaker, who had never seen a Bible until two months earlier, declared that 'Jesus had to go away alone and fight out in agony the battle of his future, how he should work and in what way he should accomplish his purpose. And our problem is just the same.' Caroline was well satisfied with his explication for it was evident that 'Jesus was not to him a dim figure of theology or history, but a labourer like himself, a carpenter who had to look into the future as these labour men must also do, if their lives and sacrifice and blood and tears are not to be in vain.'¹⁵

At this same gathering, another speaker was Matsuoka Komakichi, general secretary of Sōdōmei, whom Macdonald had met recently. Since the transformation of the Yūaikai into the more aggressive Sōdōmei, Matsuoka had become more powerful than Suzuki Bunji, although Suzuki was to remain president of Sōdōmei for the next decade. Unlike Suzuki, Matsuoka was a worker and not an intellectual; he had first joined the Yūaikai when he was a skilled lathe worker at the Muroran Steel Works in Hokkaido. At the age of seventeen he had become a Christian, but by the time Macdonald first met him in his mid-thirties he was lapsed in his faith. In the early autumn of 1921, when Matsuoka visited Macdonald at his own request to discuss the welfare of imprisoned trade unionists,¹⁶ he was initiating a relationship in which mutual respect and friendship blossomed quickly.

Matsuoka became a regular visitor to Shinrinkan and there his interest in Christianity was rekindled. Within a few months of their meeting,

Matsuoka made 'a directly Xtn [Christian] speech' at Shinrinkan, one that interested Macdonald greatly as she observed 'that horizontal look in his eye' which she believed 'portends for the future deep things.'[17]

Through her friendship with Matsuoka, Macdonald was drawn further into the concerns of one section of the labour movement. In theory, Sōdōmei was a centralized national organization of regional federations in turn composed of local unions, and in principle, policy was made at the national headquarters. In practice, Sōdōmei was a looser structure than its bureaucratic form suggested. Reflecting a common feature of Japanese social organization, it was held together by informal cliques headed by *oyakata* (father figure or leader), each of whom had his *kokata* (child figure or follower) placed in strategic positions of power. Over some years, Matsuoka, himself an early Suzuki *kokata*, had been building a network based partly on this kind of personal loyalty, mainly among iron and steel workers in the Tokyo-Yokohama area. At the beginning of the 1920s, power in Sōdōmei was shared by three *oyakata*: Matsuoka; Nishio Suehiro, an ironworker whose base was primarily in the Osaka region; and Asō Hisashi, whose clique was composed largely of intellectuals who had been fellow members of Shinjinkai (The New Man Society), an organization character- ized by its eclectic views, including a disposition to espouse anarchism.[18]

Macdonald's association with Matsuoka placed her with the moderate or conservative wing of Sōdōmei. From both experience and social philoso- phy that is where she belonged. Increasingly, as Sōdōmei became more committed to political action, the various factions within it were being defined less by personal loyalties than by differing views on policy. Nothing was more powerful in forcing definitions than the current influence of anar- chists and their promotion of a class consciousness they hoped would ignite a revolution of industrial workers against the whole capitalist order. Most Sōdōmei leaders favoured gradual change through parliamentary means, the expansion of the suffrage, the legalization of trade unions and collective bargaining, and improvement of working conditions. As well, many were socialists in varying degrees of conviction and precision concerning the action needed to achieve their objectives.[19]

Matsuoka and Nishio, whose disagreements were minimized by their common antagonism toward Asō Hisashi and the radical intellectuals and mine union leaders whom he inspired, succeeded in thwarting the efforts of the anarchists to take control. Thus, in Sōdōmei's national convention in

1920 they secured a rejection of calls for a massive general strike to inaugurate the destruction of the social order. They were also able to sustain support for the principle of centralization especially in decisions on the calling and conduct of strikes. That the anarchists retained some capacity to stir up trouble was illustrated when they took the lead in expelling Kagawa Toyohiko from the leadership of the labour movement in the Kansai region. Nevertheless, their influence was declining, due partly to their inherent mistrust of organization and planning, and to workers' caution in espousing militancy during an economic recession. It was also due to the success of Matsuoka, Nishio, and other Sōdōmei leaders in convincing their followers that the building of labour unions and reform through parliamentary influence would better serve their interests. That success owed much to workers' fears that more militant action would bring down the heavy hand of the government and of the police.[20]

■ ■ ■

THERE WAS LITTLE DISAGREEMENT among Sōdōmei leaders over an episode that occurred in the spring of 1922, when Japanese authorities tried to prevent the pioneering leader of the American birth control movement, Margaret Sanger, from visiting Japan. In the end, the government yielded to appeals from Baroness Ishimoto Shizue, who had recently observed the work of Sanger's birth control clinic in New York, and a group of doctors, social workers, and labour leaders who were eager to have Sanger deliver her message on population control to the Japanese public. Their enthusiasm was not shared by the government, or by business and military interests for whom any threat to the existence of a pool of surplus labour and plentiful recruits for the army was 'dangerous thought.'[21]

Sanger was permitted to spend ten days in Japan on condition that she refrain from discussing birth control, although she was permitted to discuss 'population.' At a public meeting in Tokyo, she respected the prohibition, but her supporters organized 'private' gatherings, receptions, and interviews in their homes where, with Baroness Ishimoto standing at the door to identify police spies, the gospel of birth control was spread among hundreds of influential men and women. By invitation, Macdonald attended at least two of these meetings with Sanger, including a small breakfast party. Although Caroline 'didn't need any pointers personally' on birth control, she found Sanger 'a very interesting and nice woman' who had 'got the right end' of the population issue. Sanger spoke so well that Macdonald thought even 'the most finicky' would be unable to find fault with her.[22]

Thanks to the enormous publicity, much of it provoked by the government's hostility, Sanger's visit had a greater impact than it might otherwise have enjoyed as the country was deluged with newspaper and magazine articles on birth control. Soon the Japan Birth Control Institute was organized under the leadership of Professor Abe Isoo of Waseda University, a prominent Christian well known to Macdonald, and with the active support of Matsuoka Komakichi and other labour leaders.[23] As Macdonald clearly recognized, in the success of this movement lay long-term mitigation of some of Japan's social problems. However, it would be an uphill battle, for as she observed, 'the authorities think it better to born babies and then let them die. It gives them something to do to compile statistics!'[24]

Shortly, Macdonald was gratified to meet two other American visitors, the social scientists Charles and Mary Beard. Tokyo's reforming mayor, Gotō Shimpei, had invited Charles Beard to recommend improvements in city government. Macdonald was well placed to assist Mary Beard in pursuing her interest in labour and in Japanese women, and they met several times during the Beards' six months in Tokyo. On one occasion Macdonald took Mary Beard to a Sunday morning service in the Tokyo Labour Church where Macdonald delivered a sermon in Japanese on which she had worked for many hours. Held within the factory of the Mikimoto Company, producers of pearls, the service was attended by sixty of the firm's eighty employees.[25]

Although labour churches were to be found in some industrial cities in North America and Britain, this was the only one in Japan, and Macdonald had been interested in it ever since its founding in 1919 by Saitō Shinkichi, a member of the Mikimoto family.[26] Following extensive travel in the West, Saitō had introduced many technological advances in the Mikimoto factory, as well as an educational program intended to enhance the workers' sense of dignity.

Thereafter, Saitō's conversion to Christianity and his theological studies at Dōshisha University brought new motivation to his interest in the reform of industrial relations. When Saitō successfully arbitrated a bitter dispute in the Mikimoto factory, the workers chose him as the factory manager, a choice accepted by his brother, Mikimoto Kōkichi, president of the company. Henceforth, workers elected representatives to consult with management on the improvement of working conditions. Mikimoto's highly skilled workers, as well as office and maintenance staff, soon enjoyed shorter hours and better wages than before, as well as recreation programs and subsidized night school classes to further their general education. In contrast with most factories, where one or two Sundays a month might be holidays, every Sunday was a day free of work in the Mikimoto firm, one reason for the high level of worker participation in the Sunday services held in the factory. A few workers quit in the face of Saitō's prohibition of smoking and drinking, but for the sake of the advantages of employment at Mikimoto a majority accepted the strict rule, one their families applauded.[27]

On assuming the management of the factory, Saitō began the practice of calling the employees together to hear talks on Christianity, and this was the beginning of the Tokyo Labour Church. Within a few months, the leader among the older workers, Tateki Tatsugorō, and thirty others were baptized in the Hongō Congregational Church. Subsequently other employees became Christians, although some workers, older ones adhering to their traditional Buddhism, resented the 'Christianization' of their factory, while younger people were drawn to materialism and Marxism. Soon Saitō secured the assistance of Makino Toraji in conducting Sunday services and midweek Bible study in the factory. Makino had studied sociology and theology at Yale University and was currently a reforming bureaucrat, an employee of the Home Ministry working with the Tokyo Bureau of Social Affairs.[28]

When Macdonald took Mary Beard to the service in the Mikimoto factory, Makino had departed for a tour of Manchuria, leaving the direction of the church to Usa Toshihiko, who had been lecturing at the church for some months. After studying theology at Meiji Gakuin, Usa had engaged in social work in the slums of Tokyo until Kagawa Toyohiko invited him to start an employment bureau in Kobe. When the government implemented its Employment Exchange Act in 1921, Usa was appointed to the staff of the Central Employment Agency in Tokyo and later became its director.[29]

Apart from her connections with its leaders, the Mikimoto experiment in industrial relations was uniquely interesting to Macdonald. Unlike the labour churches of the time in Britain and North America, the Tokyo Labour Church was avowedly and traditionally Christian, devoted to religious conversion as well as to the reform of working conditions. Further, whereas western labour churches perceived themselves as an arm of the larger labour movement, the Christian workers of Mikimoto appear to have been unconnected with any faction of organized labour.[30] Although there was a high degree of 'familial paternalism'[31] in their style of management, the owner-managers of Mikimoto accepted a degree of worker participation and self-government greater than any conferred by the works councils or company unions that some employers of the day reluctantly tolerated.

It was easier to see the company as a family in a relatively small firm like Mikimoto than in large enterprises in textiles, electronics, and heavy industry. There is no evidence as to Caroline's view of the significance of the Mikimoto example. At least it accommodated her rejection of violence, but it was scarcely consistent with the western-inspired methods and objectives of her friends in Sōdōmei. Within a decade it would be evident that in its expression of Japanese values based on complex traditions of loyalty, obligation, and cooperation, the Mikimoto experiment was the more accurate forecast of the future shape of industrial relations in Japan.

■ ■ ■

A PARTICULARLY DIFFICULT QUESTION for Sōdōmei leaders arose in the wake of the Washington Disarmament Conference when Japan agreed to substantial limitation of her naval forces. In the Yokohama dockyards, where there had been several strikes since the end of the war, there were now renewed protests against further dismissal of workers without any compensation. 'The laborers are in favour of disarmament,' Macdonald observed, 'but naturally they are not in favour of starving for it, while their employers continue to flourish like a green bay tree.'[32]

During one of these disputes in Yokohama, Matsuoka and a lieutenant were arrested and held briefly. The next day Macdonald went to visit their wives but found they needed no morale boosting from her 'for they [were] trumps.' Shortly after leaving the Matsuoka house she was stopped by two policemen and asked to identify herself. Twice she enquired why they wanted her name and was told: 'You have just been at Matsuoka's house.' She agreed, but why did it matter? 'He's head of Sōdōmei,' the police declared, as if that made her misdemeanour obvious.[33] Although the incident ended there, it was an example of the pervasive suspicion of labour throughout Japanese officialdom and a reminder that activism carried risk, much less to Caroline than to her new friends.

In addition to Matsuoka, those friends included other Sōdōmei leaders such as Fukuoka Kinjirō,[34] an electronics worker who had become a Yūaikai organizer at an early age and had recently been fired from a Hitachi factory for recruiting workers who had lost their jobs elsewhere for union activism. The Hitachi management viewed this as a betrayal of the trust it had placed in Fukuoka as a labour recruiter. Now, nothing daunted, Fukuoka was employed at an electrical equipment factory, Okabe Denki, and was organizing a branch of the Kantō Iron Workers Union. At the same time, he and Matsuoka were attending weekly discussions with Macdonald on the Sermon on the Mount.[35] Whatever was made of 'blessed are the peacemakers' and the assurance that 'the meek shall inherit the earth,' the message was not 'harmonization' at any price nor a command to abjure strikes. More inspiration could be found in the sermon's blessing on those who 'hunger and thirst after righteousness' and suffer persecution for the sake of the Kingdom of God.

Matsuoka sometimes spoke at the Wednesday night meeting or participated in other discussions at Shinrinkan, as did several other Sōdōmei leaders. One was Uchida Tōshichi, a metal worker who was currently the president of a 500-member union of electrical workers and a man of growing influence in the labour movement in the Kantō area. Another was Koizumi Shichizō who had first known Matsuoka in the Muroran Iron Works in Hokkaido and had joined the Yūaikai there. More recently he had worked as a machine repairman at the Kikkōman Soya Company in Noda. Outraged at working conditions there, he had organized a 1,500-member branch of the Brewers' Union and brought it into affiliation with Sōdōmei. Very soon the company fired him for his efforts.

Labour sympathizers who were not directly connected with a union often came to Shinrinkan. Kimura Sakari, a Christian, who had worked for a time in shipbuilding and had recently graduated from Waseda University in economics, was now lecturing at Sōdōmei's labour school. Kinoshita Hanji, also a Christian and a student at Waseda, was editing a paper intended to raise class consciousness among the poor. Akiyama Kiyoshi, a journalist with anarchist sympathies whom Macdonald considered 'an arch labor agitator' and one who 'loved to hold the floor' in any discussion, had first come to her attention while he was imprisoned for his activities during a strike. In a few months he was so much at home at Shinrinkan that he wanted to have his wedding there. Although the bride was an hour and a half late for the ceremony, Macdonald and Akiyama's other friends rejoiced in the occasion.[36]

When the merits of anarchism were being debated, another active participant was Tsuruoka Sadayuki, a former Yūaikai organizer who had gradually come under the influence of anarchism and left the Yūaikai to form a more leftist union among steel casters in Tokyo and then led them in a strike. In 1922 he was reconsidering his political stance and was becoming more conservative but he remained anti-Sōdōmei. When Macdonald or her friends needed advice on legal questions, they had the services of the well-known lawyer Yamazaki Kesaya, who with his wife became Caroline's valued friends during this period. After his graduation from Meiji Law School, Yamazaki had studied in the United States where he became a socialist under the influence of other Japanese scholars. From the time when he had defended the Christian socialist Katayama Sen, imprisoned for his active support of the Tokyo tramway strike of 1911, Yamazaki had championed a succession of Tokyo's labour and socialist leaders in their encounters with repressive laws. An organizer of the Japan Socialist League and later of the Fabian Society of Japan, Yamazaki had also recently founded a national association of lawyers pledged to defend human rights. Another Christian lawyer active in Macdonald's circle was Katayama Tetsu, who had for some years conducted a legal aid service for the poor at the YMCA and in 1920 was appointed legal advisor to Sōdōmei.

A group with an active interest in labour issues were the bureaucrats in the Social Bureau of the Home Ministry and some of them participated in discussions at Shinrinkan. Especially willing were two Christians, Nambara Shigeru and Kawanishi Jitsuzō, both graduates of the First Higher School where they had come under the influence of its principal, Dr. Nitobe Inazō, and both former members of Bible study groups led by Uchimura Kanzō. Nambara and Kawanishi were the first officials of the Bureau of Social Affairs to endorse the legal recognition of trade unions, and in 1919 Nambara had drafted the Home Ministry's first labour union bill. Influenced by his study of English labour legislation, Nambara proposed to legalize trade unions and to repeal Article 17, but the government failed to bring the bill before the Diet.[37]

Kawai Eijirō was a former bureaucrat who spoke occasionally at Shinrinkan. His social views had been formed by his interest in Marxism, by his association with Dr. Nitobe and with Uchimura Kanzō (although he never formally became a Christian), and by his observation of labour and welfare legislation in the United States and western Europe. As a factory inspector he was charged with the enforcement of Japan's rudimentary Factory Law of 1911, brought into force in 1916, but he resigned in 1919 to become a professor of economics at Tokyo University when his arguments in favour of legal recognition of trade unions were totally rejected by the government. At the end of 1922, Kawai was temporarily removed from the ranks of active reformers in Japan when he left for three years' study in England. There he pursued the interest in English liberalism that later made him the foremost interpreter of the thought of Thomas Hill Green and the application of his democratic socialism in Japan.[38]

The discussion of social issues at Shinrinkan was a microcosm of the debate going on in the country as a whole, especially among academics and bureaucrats who had studied abroad, and businessmen who supported the Kenseikai, the largest opposition party in the Diet. Through a modest program of social insurance, legalization of trade unions, and the adoption of universal manhood suffrage, the Kenseikai hoped to create a more liberal society that would reflect the interest of the urban middle class in a stable social order. The model for many intellectuals and Kenseikai leaders was Britain's 'New Liberalism' of the decade before the First World War.[39] Despite the socialist professions of some of Macdonald's friends in Sōdōmei, they had no political arm, and socialist ideas seem to have played little part in discussions at Shinrinkan at this time.

It was in 1922 that Macdonald first met Uchimura Kanzō, perhaps through some of the reformist bureaucrats who had come under his influence. Given Uchimura's eminence as a Christian thinker and founder of the influential 'non-church movement,' and a friendship with Uemura Masahisa that overrode their opposing views on the necessity of the church, it is surprising that Macdonald did not meet Uchimura sooner. In any case, her reputation preceded her, for Uchimura recorded in his journal that he was glad 'to receive a visit from the Canadian Miss Macdonald who enjoys such success with long-term prisoners.' Having heard that her parents were 'straight-laced Scots,' Uchimura 'felt great pleasure in meeting someone from the same country as our Carlyle. Of course she is a Christian, but she should rather be called a friend of humanity than a missionary,' and he 'thanked God that [he] had been given such a fine new friend.'[40]

Most of the participants in the organized programs at Shinrinkan were still nearly all men, a fact Caroline regretted, while recognizing the force of social conventions that could not be changed quickly. She had little hope of developing work with women labourers until the new settlement was established in an area closer to their work, for women found it even more difficult than men to travel to her home in Kojimachi. Macdonald had a few contacts among women workers, notably a young factory worker whom one of the Sōdōmei leaders had introduced. The woman had become a Christian during the past year and now, as Macdonald explained, 'she wanted to touch young women laborers spiritually so that they will have a foundation for leadership upon which to work for the countless masses of exploited women laborers.'[41]

In the meantime, the wives of some of the men who were in jail for strike activities urged Macdonald to give them knitting lessons. Since Japan was not a wool-producing country and had only recently begun to import wool, knitting was a skill largely unknown. Ever since her arrival in Japan, Caroline had been teaching a few women to knit, but now her services were in such demand that she sometimes feared that her 'end was to be that of a knitting teacher.' Six months after she started the class it boasted some forty members, most of them the wives of working men or prisoners, while a few were themselves factory workers. An eager group, the women wanted to learn to make knitted articles for sale to help support themselves and their children when their husbands were incarcerated or otherwise unemployed. While that alone was a worthy objective, Caroline saw further value in a gathering that pulled women out of their homes into a group where they talked with one another, the more so when she was able to direct the discussion to the causes of strikes and the necessity for the women to stand behind their men.[42] Such an elementary yet fundamental form of education justified her role as a knitting teacher.

As the organized groups at Shinrinkan were winding up before a break for the summer of 1922, Caroline looked back at the past year, noting that average attendance at the night school English class had gone up from fifteen to twenty-five and at the meeting for religious discussion from thirty to thirty-seven. The increase was modest, but considering the long hours men worked, usually with only two days off a month, she marvelled that any of them came at all. At the same time the Wednesday evening meeting, increasingly diverse in composition, was averaging around fifty.[43]

Throughout these developments Macdonald adhered firmly to her views about 'Christian propaganda.' When a learned Japanese came to give a talk to the labour school ostensibly on the theory of evolution, about which she concluded he knew little, and instead tried to evangelize his audience, Macdonald was irate: 'I will not bring people to the house & then insist on them listening to Xtny [Christianity] willy nilly ... I want them to want to hear Xtny & not simply listen because they get English. I am not trading my wares in that way – & it isn't even a good way to *dendō* [evangelize] to my mind.'⁴⁴

What could Macdonald hope to accomplish by her involvement with labouring men and their families? She made no pretence to expertise in labour relations, although on several occasions when a reputedly informed professor gave a discourse on religion and labour she felt qualified to deplore the speaker's ignorance of both aspects of the matter. Neither was she, nor were Christians like Suzuki and Matsuoka, under the illusion that they could or should try to create a 'Christian' labour movement, or that union activity was a 'Christian witness' aimed at the conversion of workers. Rather, she and her friends held to a pragmatic belief that the building of labour unions was crucial in winning recognition of the dignity of working men and women and of their right to a better standard of living. As an outsider, both in Japanese society as a whole and in the workers' world, Macdonald could play no direct part in labour's struggles. However, at Shinrinkan she could promote education that reflected the intense debate that was going on among liberals and social democrats in Japan as they sought to adapt western ideas of democracy to Japanese circumstances: the aspirations and opportunities of organized labour formed a significant part of that debate. More important than any contribution Macdonald might make directly to the education of labour leaders and their sympathizers was her friendship and moral support.

None of them appreciated that more than one of the most regular visitors to Shinrinkan, Matsuoka Komakichi. In the year following the beginning of his friendship with Macdonald, he often attended the English class and the Wednesday night meeting, and sometimes more informal discussions as well, except when he was prevented by some urgent labour business. He made it clear that 'it wasn't just for the English that he came.' Matsuoka, who had been brought up by his father after his mother's death when he was three months old, received much more than that at Shinrinkan. 'He had,' he said, 'the same feeling as if he were coming to his mother's house.' During his years 'away from Christian help,' he told Caroline, 'I was so lonely,' but now he was 'a new man again, heartened and encouraged.'⁴⁵

At last Caroline thought she understood 'that horizontal look' she often observed in Matsuoka's eyes: he had a vision of what his future would bring.

'When that look comes,' she felt 'as if he saw the future, with suffering and tribulation, & with his mind at peace, a grim peace, but peace nevertheless, because he has already faced the issue and understands. And he feels for his wife, but she's made up her mind too. They have made it up together.' She was certain that Fukuoka Kinjirō would follow where Matsuoka led, 'for they are very closely knit together.'[46]

In the autumn of 1922, Sōdōmei prepared for its annual convention and Matsuoka briefed Macdonald on the issues. Sōdōmei faced numerous difficulties including a sharp decline in membership and revenue, due to the continuing recession, especially in heavy industry, and the caution of workers who could lose their jobs if they were too militant. While the anarchists still presented some challenge, there was now a new threat to the moderates from a small but growing number of Sōdōmei leaders who had secretly formed the Japan Communist party a few months earlier.[47]

Shortly before the meeting in Osaka, Macdonald sent Matsuoka a letter to tell him that on the morning the convention began, she and three of their mutual Japanese friends would meet together 'to pray that God's presence would be with him specially, as he really had the ultimate responsibility.' The friends did as promised. A few days later Matsuoka wrote to express his gratification at receiving her letter just before the procession marking the opening of the convention moved off into the streets of Osaka. In the park where the parade was being marshalled, he had slipped away into a grove of trees to pray for himself and his cause and then returned to lead the march of 40,000 workers.[48]

In recounting all this, but not for publication, to J.K. Macdonald in Toronto, Caroline wondered 'if God was ever more consciously invoked before on a labor procession by the one who led it through the streets. And all this touch on these lines came to me through sending Xtn [Christian] books to & visiting *strikers* in jail. The ways of God are strange.'[49] Was Macdonald trying to reassure her friend and benefactor in Toronto that her active interest in the labour movement was a religious endeavour and thus quite proper for a missionary?

The conservative Toronto financier might not have been reassured at all had Macdonald reported some of the resolutions adopted by the convention. In order to deal a decisive blow to the anarchists, the moderates cooperated with the Communists and thus approval was given to rhetoric and policies more radical than those of any previous Sōdōmei convention. These included a call for Japan's recognition of the new Soviet government in Russia, advocacy of a centralized organization to promote national industrial unionism, and a general rejection of any idea of cooperation between capital and labour. As was soon to become evident, the unity of the convention was more apparent than real, and labour's power was considerably weaker than its rhetoric and resolutions suggested.[50]

■ ■ ■

THE CHANGING CHARACTER of Macdonald's interests was well illustrated at her annual Christmas entertainment, where the members of her labour school class were much in evidence, a fact that impressed her new friends, the Reverend Walter Coates and his wife, Janet, Canadian Presbyterians who had been recently married in Tokyo and were studying Japanese for a year before proceeding to mission work in Formosa. Caroline enjoyed the well-educated, lively young couple who held the same ideals of social justice as her own, and she soon recruited them to teach at the labour school on Saturday evenings. They shared Caroline's gratification that the labour school students had taken so much responsibility for the organization of the Christmas program held in Caroline's house, substantially extended by the addition of a large tent on one side. A window dresser from a large department store spent hours arranging evergreens and ribbons, a metal worker created a brass star for the Christmas tree, and the programs were produced by a student who worked in a printer's shop.

The audience of more than 200, seated on the floor, included students from the labour school and their wives, many of them members of Caroline's knitting class, ex-prisoners and prison officials, some students, a few businessmen, some officials of the Tokyo Social Bureau, and diverse other guests. It was precisely the kind of 'strange crowd' that always delighted Caroline. After an hour of music featuring the *biwa* (Japanese lute), there were speeches, one by the vice-mayor of Tokyo that lauded Macdonald's social work, another by Anglican Bishop Samuel Heaslett that gave a message appropriate for the season. The climax of the evening was a tableau presented by members of the night school in which 'Eager Heart' found joy in meeting the wise men and hearing the message of the shepherds. At the end of the evening, as Caroline bade farewell to her visitors, she rejoiced in all that they represented of past labours and hope for the future.[51]

■ ■ ■

IN THE SPRING OF 1923, Macdonald was close to a major labour dispute for the first time. Matsuoka Komakichi and his friend Koizumi Sichizō, who had lost his job for organizing the brewery workers in the Kikkōman Soya Company in Noda just north of Tokyo, had interested her in the progress of the union there. A year after the formation of the Noda union, a former union official was bribed by unidentified parties to murder Koizumi, who was then placed under the care of special guards provided by the union. Subsequently, when the would-be assassin was killed on the street, Koizumi and eighteen others were arrested and accused of the murder in what appeared to be a 'frame-up' to discredit the whole union. Macdonald visited all of these men during the year and more of their imprisonment; then two men were found guilty of the attack and sentenced to five years' hard labour, while the others, including Koizumi, were released.[52]

When the brewers' union embarked on its first confrontation with the company to protest against Kikkōman's proposals for new schedules of wages and workloads, Macdonald was already well known to many of the local unionists. From the outset she thought relations between employer and employees at Kikkōman were very like those 'between the old feudal lord and his retainers.'[53] She was not exaggerating. In associating with members of the brewers' union she saw at close range the lives of workers of the lowest status, often referred to as *shōyuyamono* (soya sauce yokels). As the company paid wages too low to enable the workers to support a family, most of them lived in grossly crowded shelters and ate poor food (and too little of it), both provided by the company. Beginning work in the small hours of the morning on tasks that took them about five hours, most then went to other work, usually as farm labourers, to earn enough to ensure survival. It was a labour pattern typical of thousands of semi-agrarian workers who were paying a heavy price for Japan's 'modernization.'[54]

An initial failure to reach a settlement, and the company's suspension of workers in two factories, brought Matsuoka Komakichi and other Sōdōmei leaders into the dispute. Unable to secure more than minimal modification of the company's position, the union called a work boycott of the more than twenty Kikkōman factories in Noda, bringing most of the workers, 1,200 strong, out of the breweries.[55]

When the strike was a week old, Macdonald was invited by her union friends to go to Noda to address the strikers. From the roof of a one-storey building, the labour organizers' temporary platform, she spoke to several hundred strikers assembled below, all wearing the red head and armbands symbolic of protest, assuring them of their dignity as workers and of the justice of their cause.[56] It was probably coincidental that on the day after Macdonald's speech, the only incident of violence in the course of the strike occurred when a crowd on its way back from a pro-union rally in a park outside the town began to smash windows and knock over fences at one of the factories.[57] In retaliation the company fired 127 workers and the possibility of compromise became more remote. On the whole, Macdonald thought, 'The strike was carried on with the greatest decorum. The police ... left the preservation of peace in the hands of a committee of strikers who patroled [*sic*] the town day and night to see that nothing untoward happened,' and 'not even a petty larceny occurred.'[58]

After a month, when both sides faced increasing pressure from the townspeople and local politicians to settle the dispute, the company secured the intervention of the governor of the prefecture and imposed a 'negotiated compromise' with no benefit to the union except for the reinstatement of the discharged workers. While both sides professed satisfaction with the settlement, it was obvious, as Macdonald noted, that 'the whole affair was but an armed truce.' Now both company and union began to prepare the ground for a more fundamental test of strength, one that would draw Caroline even further into the struggles of her labouring friends.[59]

Chapter 12

'Turning Earth's Smoothness Rough'

O N THE MORNING of 1 September 1923, a brilliant summer day with a brisk wind blowing, Caroline went in her car to a northern sub-urb of Tokyo to visit an ex-prisoner. She was just completing her visit when suddenly at precisely twelve noon the earth began to shake violently. Like everyone else, Caroline ran out into the street to await whatever might come next; in the next half hour there were two additional major shocks; lesser ones would continue throughout the Kantō Plain for several days. Although the damage in this vicinity was less devastating than in Tokyo itself, there could be no doubt that an earthquake of enormous magnitude had occurred.

Roads were blocked and tram service and all other communication with central Tokyo was disrupted: the only way Caroline could relieve her anxiety about what had happened at home, especially to her household staff, the Matsuis, and their two young children, was to get there on foot. After a three-hour walk through scenes of increasing devastation, she arrived to find the whole neighbourhood, including the Matsui family, camped in the street. The roof of her house had collapsed, and when she entered to retrieve some papers from her desk the whole building rocked precariously. Very soon two members of her labour school class arrived, having walked miles from their collapsed or burning factories, determined to do what they could to help her. By five o'clock, fire was threatening her house, and the young men, joined by two ex-prisoners, moved all of Caroline's belongings out of the house to an open space not far away. By nine o'clock, when the fire was only a block away, she sent the Matsuis to Emma Kaufman's house, which was damaged only slightly. At eleven, believing that her own house would shortly go up in flames, she followed them. The next morning, much to everyone's astonishment, the house was still there: thanks to a three-storey restaurant that had not burned, the fire had been diverted from its apparent pathway and swept on down the street. Nevertheless the house was beyond repair and Caroline and Shinrinkan were homeless.[1]

In the days following the great Kantō earthquake, the full extent of the havoc was gradually revealed. Loss of life, due more to fire than to the earthquake, was eventually officially estimated at more than 100,000, and the number of injured at many more. Had the earthquake not occurred on the first day of school after the summer vacation when students went home early the number of casualties would have been even higher. The traditional wooden houses had a degree of flexibility in earthquakes but were simply tinder in a fire. Over 60 per cent of the buildings in Tokyo were destroyed, most of them by fire, and in many parts of the lower city such as Honjo ward the figure was as high as 90 per cent. In one slum area more than 30,000 people were cremated when a fire suddenly shifted direction and trapped them in the vacant lot to which they had fled for safety. Asakusa ward was wiped out, save for the great temple of Kannon, the Goddess of Mercy, which stood as it had for nearly 300 years. The Yoshiwara was burned out and 2,500 prostitutes, unable to escape from an enclosed area that had few exits, were incinerated. All told, of the fifteen wards within the city limits, seven had been virtually swept away, and all but one of the others were severely damaged. After one of the greatest natural cataclysms the human race had ever suffered, Tokyo would never be the same again, nor would the lives and work of Caroline and her friends.[2]

Three days after the initial shocks the fires were out or under control and amid endless tales of heroic deeds Caroline began to piece together reports of the destruction. Fujimichō church and Dr. Uemura's theological seminary were burned to the ground, although his own house survived. Within a week Uemura, using Caroline's car, was driving where he could to conduct Sunday services in the homes of members of the congregation.[3] The American built and supervised St. Luke's hospital, which served most foreigners in Tokyo, was gone. Caroline's Canadian Methodist friends had lost the Central Tabernacle and several smaller churches. The Tsuda College buildings were demolished, as was the Methodist institution Aoyama Gakuin and most of the Presbyterian Meiji Gakuin and its middle school, where Dr. Uzawa Fusaaki had recently become president. Another member of the Shinrinkan committee, Konō Jūzō, had lost his industrial plant and his beautiful home, while the Mitsui office building and the Mitsui bank were burned, with the result that Funao Eitarō had been transferred to the position of business manager of the Mitsui Charitable Hospital and would probably have less influence than when he first joined the committee.[4]

One member of the committee, Governor Arima, received a good deal of publicity in the aftermath of the catastrophe. When the earthquake brought down the walls of Kosuge prison, several inmates were killed and others injured. For the next three days and nights, 1,300 men, including 200 under life sentence, lived in the open without any special guard. While other prisons had handcuffed the prisoners, and in two of them a man was shot while trying to escape, Governor Arima refused to use force to restrain the Kosuge prisoners and there were no attempts at escape or trouble of any kind. For Macdonald 'it was a wonderful vindication of Mr. Arima's whole spirit. He treated them like men and they behaved like men.' Arima himself was surprised. As he wept he told Macdonald, 'I expected my men to behave well, but I did not think they would behave so well as they did.' She felt proud of them herself, for she counted more than 200 of them as friends.[5]

For many weeks after the earthquake, the Kosuge prisoners lived in tents and in partially destroyed sections of the buildings with only the usual guards and there were no attempts at escape. In other prisons, where security had been impaired by the earthquake, there was little disruption either, but the prisoners were under additional military guard. No doubt the behaviour of the Kosuge prisoners owed something to age-old traditions of loyalty to one's group and to the emperor, but clearly these were reinforced by the prisoners' respect and even affection for a unique prison governor. Later these events received considerable discussion in the literature on penology. Whether Christians or not, commentators were united in attributing

Arima's influence to the love and respect he had always shown toward his prisoners. For prison reformers in Japan and beyond, the theory and practice of Japan's reforming 'Mr. Osborne' was thus affirmed.[6]

A tragic example of group behaviour in the hours following the earthquake was the response of many Japanese to rumours that Koreans were setting fires, poisoning wells, and looting. Given the widespread willingness to believe the worst of Koreans, that was all that was necessary to precipitate a wild hunt for 'Korean bandits,' of whom as many as 6,000 were murdered by army reservists and civilian vigilantes. Two hundred Chinese suffered the same fate. The government of Count Yamamoto Gonbei, formed on the very day of the earthquake, made little effort to control these attacks and played down the number of deaths in the 'Korean incident' out of fear of negative publicity in the western press. These events were not conducive to the comfort of foreigners, but there were no attacks on westerners.[7]

■ ■ ■

ON THE DAY OF THE EARTHQUAKE Emma Kaufman was ready to leave Kitchener, Ontario, to return to Japan. Ignoring her family's attempt to persuade her to postpone her departure until more news of conditions in Tokyo was available, Kaufman argued that she must go to help her friends and colleagues and she set out as planned on the train to Vancouver. She was joined in Winnipeg by Margaret McNaughton, a McGill University graduate who was going to work with the YWCA in Japan. In Vancouver they purchased piles of blankets and basic clothing before embarking on the *Empress of Russia,* whose cargo consisted almost entirely of relief supplies sent to Japan by the Canadian government and the Red Cross. In two weeks they arrived in Kobe, the principal port in Japan since the total destruction of Yokohama. Finding it impossible to travel directly to Tokyo, Kaufman took the train to Karuizawa where she had a summer home and from there was able to reach Tokyo, three weeks after the earthquake and sooner than any of the absent Japanese staff members.

The YWCA had fared badly in the disaster: the national headquarters and those of both the Tokyo and Yokohama associations were gone, and two American staff members in Yokohama were dead. Emma Kaufman's home soon housed the offices of both the national and the Tokyo YWCA and numerous homeless persons in addition to Caroline and the Matsui family. Fortunately both the YWCA dormitories were intact and could be used to house staff members and others who had lost their homes. Many other homeless people were given shelter in a large tent erected amid the ruins of the Tokyo association's building, and from there the 'Y' conducted an extensive relief program in the neighbourhood.

Before leaving Canada, Kaufman had cabled Katō Taka, general secretary of the Tokyo YWCA who was studying in London, to advise her that she should complete her studies and try to raise funds in Britain for rebuilding the YWCA in Japan. Now, in Katō's absence, Kaufman took over the running of the Tokyo 'Y.' Cool and calm as always, the usually mild and gentle Kaufman revealed an unsuspected ability to make quick and harsh decisions. Thus she immediately fired most of the non-professional staff of the Tokyo association, on the grounds that their customary services were no longer needed. That was true, but Kaufman's action was distinctly 'un-Japanese' and caused some distress among her colleagues who felt that it was perhaps also 'un-Christian.'[8]

As a temporary resident in Kaufman's house, Caroline was inevitably drawn into the challenges facing her friends in the 'Y.' Naturally she was not indifferent to the misfortunes of an institution for which she had laboured over the years and which she believed was crucial for the future of Japanese women. However, the YWCA was not her direct responsibility. Rather, the question as to whether Shinrinkan was to have a future was the most pressing matter before her.

Was the earthquake not only the end of the old Shinrinkan but also the death of hope for a new one? Were all the doors that had been opened to Caroline, only some of which she had been able to enter, now to be closed forever? If they were she might as well go home for good. Although that possibility crossed her mind, she refused to consider it for long. Nor did she waste any time trying to answer people 'who kept wondering *why* the Lord sent an earthquake to Japan. I didn't know why any more than they did – but all I knew was that the Lord would give us spunk to face the earthquake & its consequences if we used the spunk he has already given us.' As always, 'foisting things off on the Lord when we have to think things out ourselves' was moral and spiritual bankruptcy.[9] While Caroline felt that 'one's own experiences seem ... small beside the general loss,' she believed that 'if our individual losses are not repaired, we cannot help with the general reparation.'[10]

Thus the need for an expanded social settlement was even greater than before the earthquake, although its short-term objective would be one not included in the original plans – the provision of immediate material relief. For the long run, in the years of rebuilding that faced the government and people of Tokyo, the educational and social objectives of Shinrinkan would be crucial. Now the earlier failure to secure a suitable site in Asakusa seemed nothing short of providential, for any enterprise there would almost certainly have been lost in the utter destruction of that area. Suddenly, two weeks after the earthquake a site was available, almost as if by a miracle.

The Anglican bishop of Tokyo, Samuel Heaslett, an admirer of Macdonald's work, wanted her to have a property under his control, St. Andrew's House in Shiba Ward, the only industrialized ward in the city that had not been destroyed. Many of Macdonald's labouring friends worked and lived there while others were in neighbouring areas to the west, the industrial centres of Mita, Omori, and Kawasaki. The location was excellent and the conditions of payment were attractive. The bishop was asking for only 10,000 yen now, the remaining 35,000 yen to be paid within a year without interest. The money already available from the Mitsui Company would cover the initial payment and the rest would have to be raised, as would the current and continuing operating costs. Macdonald, Dr. Uzawa, and other members of the committee were fully aware of the leap of faith they would be taking. It was hard to be hopeful about raising funds in Japan when so many individual enterprises and institutions both public and private had to be rebuilt. Neither could they be sure that their earlier requests for support from North America would not be lost in the generous outpouring of help with which the American and Canadian governments and voluntary agencies, especially in the United States, had responded to the Japanese catastrophe. Macdonald assured the committee that her friends in Canada and the United States would not fail her in this venture and it was agreed to go ahead.[11]

St. Andrew's House was well suited to the purposes of Shinrinkan. The property of over half an acre, formerly the home of a celibate Anglican order, the St. Andrew's Brotherhood, whose members had gradually died or left to get married, included a western-style residence with thirty rooms and a school with several classrooms. The buildings had been only slightly damaged by the earthquake and with a few repairs could be used immediately, leaving more extensive renovation until later. On 22 October, less than two months after the earthquake, a brief ceremony marked the official opening of the new Shinrinkan, attended by many old and new friends, and by a representative of the Home Ministry and the head of the Tokyo City Relief

Bureau, whose presence, Macdonald hoped, augured well for their future support. While recognizing the value of relief, both officials stressed the importance of the regular activities of the settlement in helping people get back to normal life, a message Shinrinkan was already acting upon.[12]

Once open, hundreds of people began to pass through the doors of the settlement. The largest group consisted of more than 400 unemployed women who were given several days' work at nominal pay, plus a mid-day meal, for making 1,000 quilts for the City Relief Bureau. Soon, some earlier activities were resumed, including the working men's English class, a Bible class, and the women's knitting class. During these days the steady stream of visitors included many pre-earthquake friends whose whereabouts had been unknown until now, and Macdonald rejoiced in their return. Many of her earlier friends she would never see again. Some were dead, others had fled to parental homes in the country, and some were too busy trying to make a new start.[13]

Most of the new visitors came from among the 6,000 homeless for whom the city had built barracks in nearby Shiba Park, as was done for thousands of others on sites throughout the city. Newly released prisoners continued to find their way to Shinrinkan, although the possibility of helping them to re-establish themselves was dim under current conditions. Now Judge Mitsui was more desperate than ever for places to send boys placed on probation, and there were usually several staying at Shinrinkan. Very shortly Caroline's assistant, Matsui Harukichi, was made a special probation officer of the juvenile court, an appointment that formally recognized work he had been doing for some time. In addition, Matsui and his wife continued to be responsible for the day-to-day running of the house, and their children were an important part of the household.[14]

From the day when it had been clear that Shinrinkan had a future, Caroline had given careful attention to recruiting a resident staff for the settlement and was happy with the small group she was able to bring together. The first to move in was Kimura Sakari, a Waseda graduate and secretary of Sōdōmei's Labour School, and his wife, Michiko, both of whom she had come to know well in the past three years. Another and more recent graduate of Waseda University who was currently studying theology came to help with secretarial work. Two other volunteers also became residents: Kubo Taka, a Tsuda College graduate, and Shidachi Yana, granddaughter of the great intellectual, Fukuzawa Yukichi, and daughter of Shidachi Tetsujirō, a prominent economist and financier and of his wife, Taki, president of the

Tokyo YWCA. Shidachi Yana, recently graduated from the University of London, where she had encountered left-wing ideas among students from various countries, was engaged to another worker in the settlement, Yuasa Kyōzō, a law student at Tokyo Imperial University, and like his fiancée, a Christian. The two labour school students, who had appeared at Macdonald's house to help her immediately after the earthquake, had continued to give service that she felt could never be repaid and they now became part of the resident household.[15]

The settlement also offered temporary employment and accommodation to five or six young people at a time, usually girls who had lost their employment when their factories burned down. They were typical of thousands of young workers whose prospects were bleak in the economic disruption wrought by the earthquake. On an average night the settlement accommodated fifteen people, resident staff, and visitors more or less temporary. During the day all available hands were put to work handling relief supplies, feeding the hungry, cleaning the house, or helping at rummage sales. Caroline's secretary and right-hand woman, Molly Baker, described the early months of the settlement:

> It seemed for a time as though all other work would give way to meeting people's physical needs. With but a handful of workers, but the power to enlist numbers in a special emergency, and a gift of finding the right person for the task needing to be done, Miss Macdonald started on the policy of refusing nothing which came to her to do if it seemed within the realm of possibility. One thousand quilts were sent to Tokyo from the women of Osaka: could we get any of them for our neighbors? Comfort bags came from abroad; someone was sent immediately to investigate. The city had bolts of factory cotton and the men in charge were said to be in a quandry [*sic*] as to what to do with them. Any woman could tell them that this was just the thing for quilt covers, curtains, aprons, etc. Bolts of flanellette [*sic*] were available in a relief store house: that would keep so many women busy for so many hours making undergarments. Nothing was refused. It might come in handy.[16]

Despite the pressing demands of each day, Macdonald did not abandon what she had learned about 'case work' and the systematic collection of social data. Kubo Taka and Shidachi Yana were set to work on a survey of the neighbourhood, especially of the needs of the families camped out in

Shiba Park. The chief priest of the great Zōjōji temple who had general supervision of these people welcomed help from the Shinrinkan workers since the priests of his sect were celibates and were not allowed to take an interest in the welfare of women and children.[17]

The survey quickly revealed that many people in the park and elsewhere in the neighbourhood were not getting essential supplies. The settlement's appeals for a share of public relief goods were met with generosity, and city trucks delivered quantities of rice, cooking utensils, blankets, and basic clothing to Shinrinkan for distribution.[18] Such cooperation was but one example of the increasing interaction of government with private social work agencies in the aftermath of the earthquake. Recognizing that these organizations were part of an already existing network whose services were invaluable in the emergency, the authorities in Tokyo prefecture channelled much of imperial, state, and foreign aid to particular agencies in needy areas of the city.[19]

One of the most dramatic responses to the social crisis precipitated by the earthquake was the speedy formation of the Federation of Women's Associations of Tokyo, an umbrella organization whose birth was a landmark in the history of Japanese women. Before any government started a relief program, a handful of leaders of Tokyo women's groups began to organize their members to keep basic services intact as far as possible, beginning with the distribution of milk. Mary Beard, who had just returned to Japan with her husband, gave advice gleaned from her experience with American women's organizations, while Macdonald and Emma Kaufman gave their fullest support. Dr. Yoshioka Yayoi, president of the Women's Medical College, and Kawai Michi, general secretary of the national YWCA, emerged as leaders, the latter chairing the new federation. When women banded together for the essentially conservative objective of restoring social order, they were providing leadership of a kind that Japanese society could accept and they thus acquired a credibility as citizens that was never entirely stripped from them with the return to more normal times.[20]

Macdonald believed that among all the current claims on the settlement, special attention should be given to the needs of unemployed women. Thus Shinrinkan established an industrial department under the direction of Kimura Michiko, an expert seamstress and instructor in knitting. Thousands of quilts and undergarments were made and sold at cost or given away on presentation of government vouchers available to those who demonstrated that they could not replace their losses. Hundreds of knitted sweaters were sold through the Japanese Co-operative society headed by Dr. Yoshino Sakuzō of Tokyo Imperial University to students there and at other universities and schools. The program gave work and wages to 200 women, but many more applicants had to be turned away.[21]

In the shortage of gathering places, many groups wanted to use Shinrinkan for their meetings, and this gave Macdonald and her staff new connections. Thus a group of Christians in the City Social Service Bureau and a similar group from the Electrical Services Bureau held their monthly meetings there, as did a labour union and the Women's Peace Society. Congregations trying to raise funds to restore their churches held bazaars and rummage sales, as well as Bible classes and other meetings. Every week the city Educational Department showed movies for the neighbourhood children who thus came to feel at home at Shinrinkan. That the settlement had quickly made a place for itself in the community was evident when more than 1,000 children and 500 adults turned out for the children's Christmas celebration and 600 for the adults' party. It was the biggest Christmas observance Caroline had ever presided over, and despite the generous space afforded by St. Andrew's House it was once again necessary to put up a tent to accommodate the crowd of friends old and new.[22]

Immediately after Christmas, Caroline had an enforced rest following a sudden operation for appendicitis. Since it could not be avoided, she was determined to enjoy her recuperation at the national YWCA staff house, formerly the home of the Nitobes, who were now in Geneva where Dr. Nitobe was under-secretary general of the League of Nations. This time away from the hectic life at Shinrinkan was an opportunity to recall with gratitude all the people who had kept the settlement going in the four months since the earthquake and whose support bade well for its future. There were donors large and small, many of them responding to Caroline's accounts of the settlement's work and needs, as printed and circulated by J.K. Macdonald, mainly to a Presbyterian church constituency in Canada. Macdonald himself professed eagerness to help with the new start for Shinrinkan, thinking that 'perhaps God had allowed him to live so long [eighty-six years] in order that he might do something like this.'[23] Caroline's sister Peg was vigorous in raising funds among her friends, and the women of Wingham Presbyterian Church had forwarded knitted sweaters for distribution. Money came from a benefit concert in an English village, from a pageant organized by a mother and daughter in a small town in southern Ontario, from a Chinese Presbyterian congregation in Mukden, and from a host of others around the world.[24]

From New York, Galen and Ella Fisher sent a gift of $2,000 from themselves and a few friends, and Fisher endeavoured to secure funds for Shinrinkan's relief work from the large sums forwarded from the United States to the Japanese government.[25] Making a strong case for the uniqueness of Macdonald's personal influence and abilities and the distinction of the Japanese sponsoring committee, Fisher proposed that the American Advisory Committee on Relief urge the Social Bureau of the Japanese government to make funds available from the Imperial Emergency Relief Committee for an institution that 'has at its command brains and personalities which are beyond price' and whose affairs were being 'conducted with such economy and wisdom that money granted would surely go further ... than an equal amount spent in the course of official routine.'[26] The American committee accepted this request and commended it to the Emergency Relief Bureau in Tokyo, which appeared to be unaware of the current relief work being done at Shinrinkan, and responded that as the bureau's sole concern was relief, it could not assist the settlement without making it impossible to refuse similar requests from an unlimited number of organizations. However, the door appeared to be left open by the suggestion that if the appeal were presented more fully to the authorities in Japan by someone as influential as Dr. Uzawa, it might be reconsidered.[27]

■ ■ ■

EARLY IN 1924 Caroline learned that the emperor wished to bestow on her the Sixth Order of Merit of the Order of the Sacred Treasure. To commemorate the marriage of the Prince Regent, the honour was to be given to twenty-four people active in educational and social work, including one other foreign woman, Hannah Riddell, an Anglican missionary in Kumomoto. The process that led to the decision to honour Caroline had begun before the earthquake and included a long and detailed statement from Governor Arima to officials of the Ministry of Justice outlining her services to prisoners and their families, and recently to juvenile delinquents.[28]

In the presence of a large assembly of judges, lawyers, prison officials, and representatives of the Ministry of Justice, each of those honoured was presented with two wooden boxes, the larger one square, the other oblong. Neither was to be opened until the recipients returned to their homes. In the large box Caroline found the expected gold cup, suitably inscribed, and in the other a beautifully written certificate bearing the imperial crest and the signature and seal of the minister of justice. The appreciation of her labours included a reference to 'spreading the Gospel of God.' Nobody could remember an occasion when such a distinctly Christian phrase had been used in an official document of this kind, and Caroline rejoiced in this public acknowledgment of the motivation of her work.[29]

She hoped fervently that official recognition would help with fundraising. While waiting for definitive news about money to complete the purchase of St. Andrew's House, she was able to meet operating expenses from the continuing gifts of friends in Japan and overseas, and from special events such as a three-day bazaar that attracted 1,500 buyers despite flooding of the barracks where it was held and a fairly severe earthquake.[30] At last her hope of having E. St. John Catchpool, assistant warden of Toynbee Hall, join the staff of Shinrinkan seemed close to realization when Japanese friends provided funds for his salary. Thus eight months after the earthquake, Catchpool spent two weeks at Shinrinkan contributing his work and advice and assessing the prospects of the settlement. Then Caroline waited for his decision, praying that it would be favourable, for Catchpool's experience would be a tremendous resource and she coveted the assistance of a man she believed was 'very much in possession of his own soul.'[31]

Meanwhile, some members of the board of Shinrinkan were pressing the settlement's claims for government funds and were so successful that the final payment to the Anglican church for the property was made three months before the deadline. Why Shinrinkan received a grant of 30,000 yen from the Home Ministry's earthquake fund remained forever a mystery to Caroline. According to the ministry's policy, funds were available only to institutions that had been burned out, 'so we were not really eligible and we were not yet a *zaidan*' (foundation), since all the documents connected with the application for incorporation had been lost in the earthquake. 'All the same they fixed us up in some way,' and she was not disposed to push anyone for the details.[32] While this was all very gratifying and the current financial statement looked well on paper, she could not forget that eventually 50,000 yen must be found to buy out the lease on the land on which the buildings sat, and additional funds would be needed for staff and programs. The best hope still seemed to rest with the continuing efforts of Galen Fisher and other friends to secure substantial grants in the United States.[33]

■ ■ ■

IN SHINRINKAN'S NEW LOCATION Macdonald's connections with the labour movement grew steadily. During the months immediately following the earthquake, both industrialists and unionists in Tokyo were preoccupied with the restoration of work places, and there was little scope for labour activism. Further, labour leaders had reason to feel apprehensive: immediately after the earthquake, the police, using the confusion as an excuse for following up the recent arrest of fifty members of the Communist party, had cast a much wider net to apprehend 1,300 Communists, socialists, anarchists, and labour activists. Some lost their lives, including the anarchist leader Ōsugi Sakae and his wife, Ito Noe, a leading women's rights advocate. Although only a handful of men connected with Sōdōmei were taken into custody, the general atmosphere was decidedly uncomfortable for reformers or dissidents. This persecution of left-wing leaders was the policy of the Home Ministry's Police Bureau but was not condemned by other agencies of that ministry or by the Ministry of Justice. A few days after the mass arrests there was evidence of the positive attitude developing within the Social Bureau toward the conservative or moderate labour movement when Count Gotō Shimpei, the reformist home minister in the new cabinet, called Suzuki Bunji to his office and invited Sōdōmei to play a significant role in several areas of the ministry's earthquake relief program. Suzuki and his colleagues, eager to prove that they were indeed the 'sober' and 'dependable' element in the labour movement, accepted with alacrity.[34]

Shortly, Prime Minister Yamamoto's declaration that the government was in principle committed to universal manhood suffrage encouraged Sōdōmei leaders to believe that their hope for the establishment of a parliamentary democracy would soon be realized. Further, within six months, in response to an ultimatum from the ILO, the government agreed to allow Sōdōmei to choose the workers' representatives to the international organization. This tacit recognition of unions signalled a new era in the government's attitude toward the moderate trade unions. Henceforth they were to be encouraged, in order to prevent the growth of more militant unions.[35] In this policy lies, perhaps, at least a partial answer to Macdonald's question as to why Shinrinkan had received a generous grant from the state: officials of the Bureau of Social Affairs believed that Macdonald and her colleagues were engaged in the 'right' kind of labour education.

Macdonald's labour connections seemed far from 'right' to some of her associates, and she welcomed opportunities to explain the basis of her social involvements. In a sermon at a service in Karuizawa, attended mainly by missionaries and their families holidaying there in the summer of 1924, she outlined what she was learning from 'stalwart young working men,' eager to study the Bible and 'to redeem society from its present intolerable conditions.' While these men 'listen breathlessly to Christ's teachings ... they listen critically. They are interested only secondarily in their own personal salvation. Any of them would gladly give himself any day for the Cause.' Although Macdonald was sure that her labour friends found inspiration in the New Testament, she very much doubted that the church was able to be 'the mediator of its own message that Christ came to save all of life and all of the world.' Outside of the church she knew many 'earnest souls who struggle bravely and believe sincerely in the brotherhood of man who do not know our common Father nor do they believe that there can be one. Religion they say is made use of to control and repress thought and progress and not to stimulate it.' The more conservative and dogmatic of her audience, whom she referred to obliquely as those who 'believe that the truth was once for all committed to the Saints – ourselves being the Saints,' could not have warmed to her assertion that people who rejected Christianity, including those who held a Marxist view of religion, might be serving the Kingdom of God. 'God is working ... in diversity of revelation ... to make the world really free.'[36]

Noting that 'Christ Himself spent most of his teaching time talking about the new society he came to found,' Macdonald outlined her view of the nature of that society: in it there would be 'no superior nations & inferior nations, *higher* classes and *lower* classes, working classes and leisure classes, – those terms do not belong within the precincts of the Kingdom of God.' Although she did not indicate how such an egalitarian society could be brought about, she was sure that it would bring a greater degree of individual freedom than the vast majority of Japanese had ever known.[37]

What was freedom in the new society? Macdonald liked the answer given by the English social psychologist, political philosopher, and Fabian socialist, Graham Wallas. His definition of freedom as 'the possibility of continuous initiative' appealed to her as an ideal not only for Japanese working people but for the whole human race.[38] At present only a small minority of humankind had the freedom to take initiative and make choices about their lives. How was that freedom to be achieved? Jesus had spoken often of the path to freedom: 'If ye abide in my word, ye shall know the truth, and the truth shall make you free.' Nobody would ever know the truth, Macdonald declared, who was constantly on guard against 'dangerous thoughts.' That was true not only for Japanese politicians and bureaucrats, but also for Christians, whom she exhorted to open their minds to new social and intellectual movements in the faith that all truth, whatever its source, belonged 'to the fullness of truth in God.'[39]

■ ■ ■

SOON AFTER HER RETURN from the rarefied atmosphere of the society of missionaries in Karuizawa, Macdonald was plunged into the real world of labour. In mid-August 1924, some one thousand employees of Nihon Denki (Japan Electric Company) in Tokyo went on strike. The strikers, whose union belonged to Sōdōmei, included a number of men who were members of Macdonald's English class in the Shinrinkan labour school. At the beginning of the strike one of them, a strike leader, asked Macdonald if the 200 women among the strikers could gather daily at Shinrinkan so that they would be safe and their solidarity strengthened. She agreed immediately without consulting any of the other Shinrinkan directors, although she was concerned that some might misunderstand the situation if the newspapers were to report, on the basis of appearances, that Shinrinkan had become the headquarters of the strikers. At the same time she met with leaders of the women's department of Sōdōmei to report that she would welcome the women as long as none of the strikers resorted to the use of force. Next she visited the district headquarters of the Metropolitan Police, to inform them of her plan to look after the women strikers, and announced that since she was 'neutral' she would not permit the distribution of propaganda leaflets from either side within Shinrinkan. When the police warned her not to instigate any action among the strikers, she asked them what they meant, whereupon the two parties apparently reached an agreement acceptable to both.[40]

During the fifty-three days of the strike, Caroline rarely left Shinrinkan, for she was not entirely sure what the ever-present police would do in her absence, but she was confident that she could 'manage them ... on the spot' and that there would be no violence. Several detectives appeared from time to time and received from her 'instructive discourses' on the causes and objectives of the strike and on the means of keeping the dispute peaceful. She had no worry about what the strikers would do, for she 'had them in the hollow of [her] hand from the beginning.'[41]

Most of the women strikers were in their late teens and had never before been involved in labour action of any kind. During the strike, Caroline employed many of them in knitting and paid out 2,000 yen in wages. She arranged a series of lectures on hygiene, and a member of the staff of St. Luke's hospital came to speak about nutrition, especially the dangers of *kakke* (beriberi) caused by a lack of vitamin B1, common among eaters of rice-based diets. The women listened to music and learned some hymns, but as usual there was no direct presentation of Christianity, nor, true to her declaration of 'neutrality,' did Macdonald initiate any discussion of labour issues.[42]

When the strike was about three weeks old, the police arrested ten of the leaders. Macdonald went to visit them in the police station and when they were transferred to jail she was given special permission to talk with them there. One of them, Mochizuki Akio, was a unionist already known to her; on her assurance that he was to be trusted and could guarantee that none of the ten men would engage in violence, all were released.[43]

Caroline's decision to make herself more or less a captive in her own house for the duration of the dispute did not mean that she gave all her attention to the strike, but it did make her even more than usually available to every caller who appeared at the door. A typical day included a variety of encounters:

> Before ... breakfast ... an official from the Prefectural office called to get information about the settlement. While he was here the first instalment of detectives arrived. The women strikers themselves were arriving all the time ... About eleven a graduate of Tsuda College turned up & asked me to read Rabbi Ben Ezra with her, which I did. Rabbi's "turning earth's smoothness rough" is very apropos of our present circumstances. One of the strike leaders dropped in to report progress (or rather lack of progress). Mr. Shidachi well known economist and financier, a member of the settlement committee, dropped in to see how the strike was progressing & also to talk over with me the educational work for the autumn. Before he had gone an official from the Dept. of Justice arrived ... to ask me to help him with a translation of American prison pamphlets ... Mr. Uchida, a former employee of the Japan Electric Co ... dropped in to commiserate with me on the length of time the strike is lasting ... & to beg my continued kind offices for the women. Hard on his heels came Ikematsu-san, a young scamp who got out of prison five months ago & ... has not mended his ways. Came to say that he has sold his sister into some disreputable place in

Shimonoseki & wished money to get her out! I suggested that he tele-graph his father from whom the girl had presumably run away and that if he didn't have money to send the telegram I'd do it for him. He did-n't take my offer. While he was still here Dr. Hora of Nagasaki Medical College came in ... He has made post mortem examinations of men who have undergone capital punishment ... He is ... visiting reformato-ries & juvenile prisons & testing the mentality of these young offend-ers. We have much in common as we are both keen on crime![44]

After nearly eight weeks the strike was settled with little benefit to the workers, a common outcome of strike action in this decade. Although exhausted, Caroline was well pleased with her role in the dispute; she believed that it was much easier for all concerned 'to be calm and rational because the women were being cared for here,' an opinion gratefully confirmed by the strike leaders. Moreover, her conduct during the strike had made the settlement 'very popular with the police.' Visiting the local police station two weeks after the end of the strike, she was greeted like an old friend and accepted a warm invitation to have tea with five policemen who had been at Shinrinkan regularly during the strike. 'We gossiped about the strike, and according to them, it was entirely due to my honorable shadow that the whole of society was not wrecked thereby! I am quite pleased that they should think so – I may have to do it again.'[45]

Despite her facetious comments, Macdonald was aware that she was not 'playing an easy game – my eyes are thoroughly open, but up to date I have all the lines in my hand. I labor under no delusions as to the seriousness of the tasks we are tackling, but I seem to have the confidence of people who might not themselves be willing to tackle the same things.' The interest and support of other members of the executive of the Tokyo Christian Social Workers' Association was gratifying: 'They were all rather struck dumb at our temerity in having the Nippon Denki strikers here, but realized that any Christian should have done the same thing,' but doubted whether they would have done it. All were agreed that they were 'sick of playing on the surface and Xians [Christians] ought to get down to some of the underlying causes.' Inspired by Macdonald and Yamamuro Gumpei, head of the Salvation Army, some members of the group determined 'to get together & think about *real* problems,' beginning with a session when Macdonald would tell them more about her ideas on how Christians could work with the labour movement.[46]

Not all Christians were convinced that any Christian should have acted as she did during this strike. Her concern about the attitudes of members of the board of Shinrinkan proved to be justified, for some of them questioned her judgment and registered their disapproval. Perhaps they were reassured by her assertion that she 'was not concerned with the merits of the strike, but with the morals and morale of the girls.' For Macdonald, the criticism demonstrated that there was ignorance about trade unions among the educated as well as among the uneducated, and gave her an opportunity to explain the objectives of sound, non-violent unions.[47] Her refusal to back away from support of the women workers won the admiration of Matsuoka and his friends. Later Matsuoka was to recall this episode as one that added to Macdonald's reputation. She was now not only 'the mother of prisoners' but also 'the mother of women laborers.'[48]

One of the most immediate and satisfying results of the recent strike was the request by some of the women strikers that Macdonald establish a women's labour night school where they could further their general education and understanding of the labour movement. Soon some sixty young women were attending the weekly meetings of the night school. Other new activities were added to the settlement's program in the autumn of 1924. Shōhi Kumiai (the Co-operative Society), modelled on similar consumer cooperatives in Britain, and the special enterprise of Shidachi Tetsujirō, met regularly there, as did a club of Christians working at Tokyo's city hall, the Tokyo Social Workers' Association, the city road workers' union, and several other unions. Members of all these groups and anyone else interested were invited to the fall series of lectures when Shidachi Tetsujirō spoke on economic problems, Miyake Shōtarō of the Department of Justice on law, and Tagawa Daikichirō on politics.[49]

On 18 October 1924, Shinrinkan was officially established as a *zaidan* (foundation). The foundation consisted of the settlement under the general supervision of the Home Ministry, but the work among prisoners remained Macdonald's private enterprise. Now 'St. Andrew's House, Tokyo Shinrinkan,' as the official letterhead identified the settlement, was closer to becoming the social laboratory of Caroline's dreams. There had been disappointments recently, notably the decision of the Catchpools not to join the staff, but there were other new resources in personnel. One of them was Yamada Zen'ichi, the man who had murdered his family, with such definitive consequences for Caroline's life. She had known that as was cus-

tomary on 11 February (*kigensetsu*), the anniversary of the legendary founding of the empire, there would be amnesty for selected prisoners, and she
had reason to believe that Yamada would be released for good behaviour, for
he had been a model prisoner and was one of the two most trusted inmates
of Kosuge prison. Early that morning a member of the prison staff phoned to
confirm her hopes. Then, as she reported to her family,

> the governor of the prison, my beloved Mr. Arima, Yamada San and I
> had lunch together. Yamada San ... was still in his prison clothes as his
> ordinary ones hadn't arrived. As this is the *great* public holiday of Japan
> the governor was in very grand regimentals, with his Imperial
> Decorations hanging around his neck ... I don't think the combination
> could have happened anywhere else on earth. Mr. Arima chatted away
> with Yamada San & asked me to let him go back to the prison tomor-
> row again to wind his work up as he has been doing a very important
> piece of work & it is difficult to find a successor![50]

Later in the day the Buddhist priest who was head chaplain of Kosuge
prison arrived at Shinrinkan, for he had promised that he would come on
the day 'a certain thing would happen' to express his joy at seeing Yamada
'at home.'[51] Before long Yamada was engaged in another important piece of
work as he gradually assumed responsibility for Shinrinkan's service to
released prisoners.

■ ■ ■

EARLY IN 1925 Caroline was preparing to leave Japan, her ultimate destination the International Prison Congress in London in August. A few weeks
before her departure she was saddened by the sudden death at the age of
sixty-nine of her much-loved minister, friend, and advisor, Uemura
Masahisa. Despite the shock, she could not entirely regret the manner of his
going for he had recently been in failing health, and a long illness would
have been terrible for a man accustomed to commanding so much intellectual and physical energy. At Uemura's funeral, she joined hundreds of
mourners who stood in the rough barracks that had since the earthquake
served as a church for the Fujimichō congregation to pay tribute to a leader
who had done as much as any other to shape Protestantism in Japan.[52] No
one had been more important in furthering Caroline's identification with
her adopted country. Without him, her life would never be the same again.

Chapter 13

'The Faith that Rebels'

ON HER ARRIVAL IN CANADA in April 1925 en route to England, Macdonald's first assignment was to go on a speaking tour with the American Methodist missionary to India, E. Stanley Jones, whose lectures were soon to appear as the most successful of his several books, *The Christ of the Indian Road*. Together they addressed large interdenominational audiences in several centres in southern Ontario on the missionary movement in India and Japan. In common with other liberal Protestants, Macdonald knew Jones from his books and had heard him speak on his work among educated Indians. Now, 'after travelling with him for a few days and orating with him [she felt] as if we were brothers. He's a darling ... I'm told he declined a *bishopric*. He showed a lot of sense. I've really got quite a crush on him. Don't be alarmed,' she told her family. 'It isn't the first crush I've had on a male man and it probably won't be *the last*.'[1]

The major topic of religious discussion in Canada in the spring of 1925 was the church union, which was to be officially consummated in June.

Methodists and Congregationalists had agreed relatively easily to enter the new United Church of Canada, but the Presbyterian church was torn apart over the union question. Nevertheless, a substantial majority of Presbyterians would become part of the new church. Macdonald encountered many Presbyterian families that were divided over the issue, although her own was solidly anti-unionist, as her father had been until his death a year earlier. She felt that the whole situation was 'a frightful tragedy,'[2] but the interdenominational character of her work in Japan and her absence from Canada during years of often acrimonious debate prevented her from investing much emotional energy in the controversy. She must also have been aware that to espouse one side or the other might alienate some of her financial supporters, to the detriment of her work in Japan. Thus on a spring Sunday in Toronto, 'being neither Union nor anti, there was no place to go to church.' She 'thought of going down to St. James Cathedral,' which was Anglican, but in the end stayed in her hotel 'to get a breath.'[3]

While in Toronto, Caroline wanted 'to get a ball or two rolling' with the Canadian committee for Shinrinkan, church boards, and other supporters. One of her most successful forays was a long luncheon with Frank Burton's brother whom she had known as 'Charlie' for many years. C.L. Burton, who had recently become president of the Robert Simpson Company, one of Canada's largest department stores, had earlier contributed through the Canadian committee. Now he announced his intention to buy a new car to facilitate Caroline's work in Tokyo, and to give her a good radio, for broadcasting had recently been introduced in Japan, as in Canada. She had not realized that she needed a radio, but rejected neither it nor Burton's declaration that she could have at cost anything she wanted from his department store to take back to Japan.[4]

Business completed, Caroline was glad to have three weeks for relaxation with her mother and her sister Peg before setting out for Chicago for a visit to Hull House, which had impressed her so much a decade earlier. Jane Addams and her associates welcomed her warmly, and for three days Caroline observed and discussed the work of America's most famous settlement. Thanks to Macdonald's request to Addams, Hull House also received Dr. Motoji Shinkuma, director of the Bureau of Prisons in Japan, and his deputy, Okabe Jō, who were visiting American prisons on their way to the International Prison Congress in London. Some of the younger Japanese bureaucrats considered Motoji conservative in his views on prisons and perhaps overly fond of academic planning. However, he appreciated Macdonald's prison work and the two were on good terms. She thought it would be helpful if he were to see Hull House's work in trying to prevent crime and could understand how its services augmented those of the juvenile court.[5]

On her return from Chicago, Caroline spent a few days in Brantford with her sister Nellie and her husband, C.L. Laing. Laing was manager of the Canadian Bank of Commerce and they owned a comfortable home on Dufferin Avenue, where many of the small industrial town's leading citizens lived. Soon it was time to go to Toronto for an event that had evoked in Caroline feelings of puzzlement and amusement, mixed with some pride.

Before leaving Japan she had received a letter from the registrar of the University of Toronto, her old friend James Brebner, announcing that the senate of the university wished to confer on her the honorary degree of Doctor of Laws at the spring convocation. On her arrival in Toronto, one of her first visits was to Brebner's office 'to find out what it all means.' She was 'rather knocked out about it,' feeling that she had 'never done anything for the Univ. of Toronto except get out of it as soon as possible, & keep away from it ever since.' She was to be the first woman to receive an LLD from the University of Toronto.[6] Two years earlier, Helen MacMurchy, the Toronto doctor who had pioneered in social welfare for women and children, had been given an honorary doctorate in medicine. But no woman had been proposed for the LLD since 1901, when the university senate had vetoed the nomination of the Duchess of York, now Queen Mary, on the grounds that to award the degree to any woman would set an undesirable precedent.[7] The LLD was to be reserved, the senate decreed, for distinguished public servants, academics, and university benefactors, none of whom, it appeared to assume, could be women.

When her former classmate, the physicist Frank Burton, took Caroline to Harcourts, makers of academic and ecclesiastical robes, to be measured for her doctoral gown, there was some uncertainty about its length, since the firm had never made one for a female. When Harcourts produced a photograph of Queen Mary wearing the robes of the Doctor of Civil Laws given her by Oxford, it was agreed amid some hilarity that this would do as a model.[8] Caroline was touched and gratified by the news that the gown ('awful crimson and pink') and the mortarboard with gold tassel were to be the gift of her classmates of 1901, while the university would 'cough up' the accompanying hood. However, she found it hard to take the coming event seriously: 'I pray the Lord that these things will not entirely damn my soul beyond redemption! There are to be 8 LLD's granted this year. One to the president of the CPR [Sir Edward Beatty], another to an R.C. Archbishop [Neil McNeill of the Diocese of Toronto], etc. – Holy Moses!'9 She could make sense of the honour only 'as a recognition of a piece of international fellowship work,' for as she explained to Jane Addams, 'I have done nothing either for my University or for anything else in my own country.'10

Her Toronto friends had less difficulty understanding the honour and they celebrated it with enthusiasm. Frank Burton hosted a dinner for friends and family at the King Edward Hotel. University Women's Club members held a garden party, well aware that in addition to honouring Caroline Macdonald they were marking an historic occasion for their sex and for the university. At the ceremony, the acting president of the university, Principal Maurice Hutton of University College, noting that he was presenting the LLD degree to the first woman to be so recognized, also implied that she might remain the only one for some time: 'If any follow her they will not win it in a field more honourable or more feminine. She has won the right to be here by her life work as a missionary.'11

Afterward, at a reception in the quadrangle of University College where she had so often walked and talked as an undergraduate, she joined the other degree recipients to receive congratulations, often from people she had not seen since those undergraduate days, and to introduce her Tokyo friends, Dr. Motoji and Mr. Okabe.

During the week of the honorary degree festivities at the university, the fifty-first General Assembly of the Presbyterian Church was meeting in the nearby College Street Church. It was an historic and emotional gathering, for in a few days a majority of its members were to become part of the new United Church of Canada. Concurrently, the Executive Council of the Presbyterian WMS was meeting, with Macdonald as the chief speaker. The women were happy to claim her as their own, marking the conferring of the honorary degree with a gift.12 It was a sad occasion too, for women who had worked together for many years would soon be divided; most of the members of the Presbyterian WMS would help to constitute the WMS of the United Church of Canada, taking with them proportionate responsibilities and financial resources.

A week later Macdonald addressed a gathering of members of the 'continuing Presbyterian' WMS, urging that educational work among women factory workers in Tokyo would be a fruitful avenue of service for Canadian Presbyterian women.[13] At the same time, the Reverend A.E. Armstrong, now secretary of the Board of Foreign Missions of the United Church, paid warm tribute to Macdonald's work, noting that she was 'probably the only Canadian woman who is an ordained elder,' and claimed her as 'one of our missionaries.' He appeared to assume that the annual contribution of $2,500 from the Presbyterian WMS would henceforth come from the United Church WMS.[14] For the time being it seemed that Macdonald might now enjoy the support of two churches, rather than just one, and that she would gain nothing from an effort to sort out the complexities of the situation.

In mid-June it was time to go to Montreal to embark for England on the CPR's SS *Melita*, leaving plenty of time for a good visit in London with her sister Leila and her family in their pleasant Chelsea home. Her sister Peg wondered whether Caroline would also visit Scotland, or to be more precise, would she go to see David Cairns, now the principal of his college in Aberdeen. Caroline declared that she would not, but she reported jokingly that a fortune-teller had told her that she would be married when she was fifty-three. 'Why wait for the 3. It seems hardly worthwhile to go to all the expense of going back ... to Japan.' Although she did not go to Scotland, Caroline did not hide her presence in Britain from Cairns. Consequently, she told her family, 'Scotland has come to me in the shape of my beloved Dr. Cairns (note the adjective!) & also his daughter Alison.' Later she learned that on his return to Aberdeen, Cairns, now sixty-three, had reported to his sister that Caroline was 'quite unchanged. Alas, I thought I'd changed for the better really!'[15] Nothing happened to interfere with her return to Japan.

The International Prison Congress of 1925 was the ninth since the congresses were initiated in 1872. Japan had been participating since 1895 and now a sizeable group led by Dr. Motoji was in attendance. In addition to the other official government representatives, Okabe Jō and Ōmori Kōta, the delegation included Yasutomi Seichū and Fujine Tokunin, Buddhist priests who were prison chaplains, as well as Kazahaya Yasoji, professor of law at Kyushu Imperial University, and Caroline's young friend the lawyer Yuasa Kyōzō. Yuasa's new wife, the former Shidachi Yana, was with him and the couple were shortly to take up residence in Toynbee Hall as volunteer workers in the settlement while he continued his legal studies. Mrs. Kazahaya

1
The Reverend Uemura Masahisa, 1922

2
Tagawa Daikichirō, president of Meiji Gakuin,
Tokyo, late 1920s

3
Mealtime in a Japanese prison, 1920s

4
Shinrinkan – 'The Home of the Friendless Stranger'
(St. Andrew's House) in Tokyo, 1926

5
Caroline Macdonald and a young friend, 1926

6
Actors in the Christmas play at Shinrinkan, 1922

7
Part of the audience at the Christmas party at Shinrinkan, 1922

8

The knitting class of the women's labour school singing
at the Christmas party at Shinrinkan, 1922

9

Graduation ceremony of the labour school at Shinrinkan, ca. 1926:
front row, second from left, Matsuoka Komakichi;
front row, seventh from left, Suzuki Bunji, Caroline Macdonald, Katayama Tetsu

10

Caroline Macdonald with staff and volunteers at Shinrinkan, summer 1926

11

Principal David S. Cairns, Aberdeen United Free College, 1928

12

Matsuoka Komakichi and Caroline Macdonald in Tokyo, preparing for the
International Labour Organization meeting in Geneva, 1929

13

Trade unionists bidding farewell to the labour delegation on their way to the
International Labour Organization meeting, Tokyo Station, 5 April 1929: *centre*,
Matsuoka Komakichi with his wife Katsuyo, their three sons, and Caroline Macdonald

14
At Osaka Station, 5 April 1929:
left to right, Matsuoka Komakichi, Caroline Macdonald, Matsuoka Katsuyo,
and youngest son; *far right*, Suzuki Bunji

and Macdonald completed the group, although none of the women had any official status. From the time of the first consideration of the agenda, Macdonald played an active role in the work of the delegation and was responsible for preparing the English version of Dr. Motoji's final statement to the congress.[16]

Throughout this gathering of penal experts from around the world, Macdonald was attending lectures and discussions. In retrospect she concluded that very little was accomplished by all the talk from criminologists, social workers, and prison officials. They were all knowledgeable, except about the experience of being a prisoner, 'although that defect ... did not in the least interfere with the positiveness with which we discussed the causes of crime and their remedy ... We were all there but the victim of our discussions.' She understood why the victims were not there: 'The criminal does not move in polite society as a rule unless he belongs to the aristocratic ... type usually known as the financier.'[17]

Macdonald found 'an astonishing lack of unanimity among the specialized scholars.' The professional criminologists seemed devoid of sympathy for their subject, while prison administrators, intent on making 'men into good prisoners, thought very little about ... creating new men.' Prison officials, with their daily experience of prisons, seemed more human. As for social workers, they 'were given a poor hearing when occasionally one of them dared to make himself heard above the din of erudition.' Altogether the congress confirmed her belief that 'if a man gets into a prison he will be a worse one when he comes out unless someone gets at that mysterious mechanism which is usually known by the name conscience.'[18] Nothing shook her conviction that there was no substitute for personal work with individual prisoners.

After the congress, delegates visited some English prisons. The one Caroline remembered most vividly was in Oxford. She was dismayed at what she saw 'a few streets away from ... England's most famous university, allegedly a beacon of "civilization."' The visitors were allowed to watch prisoners walking around in a small ring taking their exercise 'as if they were a circus.' Even she, 'who had seen so much of prisons and prisoners ... blushed for shame to think that an English prison for any purpose whatever would expose their victims in such a humiliating position to the public gaze of anyone.' Such an exhibition would not be allowed in Japan. Then she saw a group of prisoners sitting in a dark cellar picking oakum, an occupation entirely foreign to her. A special treat was provided for her and another visitor when an official led them to a room not usually shown to guests. Here the official proudly exhibited a long board upon which men were strapped and subjected to corporal punishment. When Macdonald asked what effect this had on the man administering the punishment, the official told her that he had used this equipment quite recently and had taken 'considerable satisfaction' in applying forty lashes to the perpetrator of some offensive crime. 'It seems scarcely worthwhile to concoct a system which brutalizes even the administrators,' she observed. Corporal punishment was banned in Japanese prisons. Not for the first time she concluded that whatever their limitations, Japanese prisons were by no means the worst in the world.[19]

■ ■ ■

WHEN THE *Empress of Australia* docked in Yokohama in mid-September 1925, the usual crowd of ex-prisoners and friends of all ages was on hand to greet Caroline. Within a few days she was welcoming the distinguished Canadian lawyer and former Liberal politician and Methodist N.W. Rowell, who had played a leading part in the formation of the United Church. Rowell was on a three-month trip to countries of the Pacific from Australia to Japan in the company of his daughter, Mary, who was soon to take up her duties as secretary of the Student Christian Movement at the University of Toronto. Mary was glad to tell Caroline how much she and other women in the Toronto class of 1925 had rejoiced at their graduation ceremony just four months earlier when Caroline had made history receiving the honorary doctorate. Both Rowells were familiar with Caroline's work and although their stay in Tokyo was brief, they were eager to see the life of Shinrinkan at first hand.[20]

As she took up her work again, 'everyone, *even* the police,' and including Dr. Uzawa, chairman of Shinrinkan's board of trustees, was telling her how well everything had gone during her six months' absence.[21] All agreed that Yamada Zen'ichi, to whom she had entrusted direction of the prison work, had done an admirable job. In a few days Caroline appeared at Kosuge prison wondering whom to visit first among the more than 150 prisoners she knew there. Most had requested a visit as soon as she returned. Governor Arima suggested a solution, and for the first time in her life she engaged in group visiting, talking with about twenty men together. Later she resumed her usual style of individual visits, beginning with those condemned to death, including one woman whose end came the day after Macdonald's visit.[22]

The context in which Macdonald's interest in labour would be expressed had changed somewhat during her absence from the country. The universal suffrage bill, which had reached the floor of the Diet early in 1925, had been passed, giving the vote to virtually all males twenty-five years of age and older, and almost quadrupling the electorate to nearly thirteen million. This reform had only been possible when the domination of the conservative Seiyūkai party in the Lower House of the Diet was broken by the creation of a Kenseikai government led by Katō Takaaki. A moderate reform coalition, the Kenseikai party enjoyed the support of several members of the board of Shinrinkan and many of Macdonald's friends in the legal profession.

Although most of the labour movement had never seen the franchise as a panacea, it had been central among Sōdōmei's policies for the past two years, and interest in forming a political party committed to workers' interests was high. There was more than one vision of the nature of that party. For some Sōdōmei leaders, including Matsuoka Komakichi and Suzuki Bunji, the choice was between the 'realism' of practical policies formulated in Japan by workers themselves to improve their conditions, and the 'utopianism' of Marxist rhetoric and ideology borrowed from the Comintern about the overthrow of capitalism.[23]

The wholesale arrest of Communists both before and after the earthquake had virtually eliminated the small Communist party and at the end of 1924 it had formally dissolved. Now, as Communists were being released from prison, where were they to go? In the continuing controversy about whether there was any place for them in Sōdōmei, Communists gained control of the important Kantō Iron Workers Union. After months of debate and negotiation among Sōdōmei's leaders, the anti-Communist wing, most vigorously led by Matsuoka Komakichi and Uchida Tōshichi, persuaded the central executive of Sōdōmei to expel twenty-five unions favourable to Communist leadership and policies. Those unions promptly formed the Nihon Rōdō Kumiai Hyōgikai (Japan Council of Labour Unions) and embarked on a struggle with Sōdōmei for control of the labour movement both on the factory floor and in the newly important polling booth.[24]

In the period leading up to this split, and afterwards, the two main factions of Japanese labour were united in condemning and resisting the Peace

Preservation Law of 1925. While honouring its promises to repeal the Peace Police Law of 1900, the government had at the same time passed the Peace Preservation Law, whose ambiguous phrases inhibited activities that might have encouraged the growth of genuine democracy. In a tussle between the Home Ministry, which wanted to narrow the scope of the law, and the Justice Ministry, the latter prevailed and the law remained vague, defining as a crime any action to alter the *kokutai* (national polity) or 'inciting' others to do so.[25]

Before the year was out, the government had used the new law to dissolve the Farmer-Labour Party on the day it was formed, on the grounds that the role played by the Hyōgikai and other radical groups in the new party proved it was a front for the Communists. Few tears were shed by the Sōdōmei leaders over the dissolution of the work of their radical rivals, nor by the bureaucrats in the Social Bureau of the Home Ministry who were promoting the idea of a 'sound' anti-Communist labour party.[26]

Less than a week after her return, Macdonald realized how little the daily realities of life had changed for her labour friends. Four Russian labour leaders were visiting Tokyo and she was amused to see 'the whole police force ... taking 40 fits.' On a night when the regular weekly meeting of a group of working men was in progress at Shinrinkan, 'the police ... thought they'd come here to see if the Russians were going to visit ... There were about 40 working men and about 50 police!' Caroline was careful not to give any hint that she would even consider asking the workers to disperse. After a while a senior police official turned up, a man whom Caroline knew well, for he had 'seen us through two strikes.' He sent the police home, declaring that 'he knew that the men who come to the settlement didn't make disturbances, etc. etc.'[27]

While this episode was more ridiculous than threatening, it demonstrated that although Macdonald and Shinrinkan enjoyed approval and even financial support from the Home Ministry, they were also subject to the attention of police forces controlled by a more conservative Ministry of Justice, a ministry that had resisted the postwar movement to 'democratize the police' and remained vigilant in the suppression of 'dangerous thought.' The ambiguities arising from conflicts between branches of the government and their respective bureaucracies, notably between the Home and Justice ministries, created interesting and complex challenges for all aspiring reformers in Taishō Japan.[28]

■ ■ ■

A SATISFYING EVENT on the labour front was the graduation of the first class of the night school for working girls. During Caroline's absence, the school had been recognized by the city's educational authorities, and the diplomas presented to the twelve graduates glistened with the scarlet wax of the official seals. The school was in session four evenings a week using the curriculum of the regular girls' high schools. The rather formal gathering was presided over by Dr. Uzawa, and addresses were given by a representative of Tokyo City Council and by Tsuji Matsu, the former principal of Tsuda College. The audience included 160 girls from factories in the neighbourhood and a sprinkling of young men, all 'looking very pleased with themselves over the achievements of their fellow women workers.' That only twelve students received diplomas for a full year's work when the average attendance had been about forty illustrated the difficulties facing working women who wished to advance their education; many had been forced to drop out from time to time because they were required to do overtime work in their factories, while others had suffered from ill health and could not keep up. Remarkably, three of the graduates were married women who had also carried home responsibilities. In the new class just begun, 130 students were registered and Caroline believed that the second graduating class would be considerably larger than the first.[29]

When Sōdōmei held its annual meeting in Tokyo in the autumn of 1925, several delegates from Osaka stayed at Shinrinkan and became interested in the settlement's educational programs among factory women. At their invitation, Macdonald visited Japan's largest industrial city to try to stimulate the education and organization of women workers there. Thus she found herself on a platform in Osaka addressing a labour rally attended by 500 men and 200 women and explaining the role of unions in the education of workers and the improvement of working conditions. Then, as the local unionists had requested, she directed her attention to the industrial suburb of Amagasaki just outside Osaka. It was agreed that for the time being nothing could be done in the largest cotton spinning mill there because of the active hostility of the owners, but in some smaller factories there was hope of expanding existing unions or starting them.[30]

Macdonald's experience in Amagasaki was gratifying on several counts, not least in confirming her hope that Tsuda College graduates would provide leadership in changing the lives of Japanese women. Before going to Osaka she had written to several of her former students living in the area, most of them high school teachers, and was delighted when seven turned up to meet with local labour leaders, two of whom were women. From the beginning the Tsuda women were astounded, first by the sight of men serving them tea and passing the cakes, and then by their genuine interest in the education of women and in 'the week of work' for women that was launched immediately. They were even more astonished to learn that three men, members of a local union, were cooking their own suppers so that their wives could attend the meetings. On successive evenings, with an average attendance of fifty, the Tsuda graduates taught knitting and encouraged general conversation among the factory women. The authorities scarcely blinked an eye at this development. Indeed, the mayor loaned a public room free of charge and not a single policeman appeared during the week. Obviously the chief of police thought women's meetings harmless, for 'he remarked facetiously that he was interested to see the labour unions taking to knitting.'[31]

Altogether Macdonald had contact with twenty-six Tsuda graduates in the Osaka area and hoped they would heed her admonitions about being worthy of the privileges they enjoyed as educated women. They could do that only if they endeavoured to understand the problems of society, which included understanding the trade union movement and continuing involvement with working women. As she told another group of Tsuda graduates a few weeks later, this might entail 'self sacrifice, persecution & misunderstanding, but in the end freedom of life for us all.' Even so, it would be a very long time 'before Japan's women as a whole are free to work together for the emancipation of the life of men & women & little children.'[32] Having fulfilled her function as an 'agitator' in Osaka, Caroline 'retired to the metropolis of Tokyo to stir up some more dust there.'[33]

The dust was already swirling in Tokyo around a strike against the Fuji Spinning Company, where some women workers had protested against conditions in the dormitories where they were compelled to live. When one of the leaders was fired, she came to live temporarily at Shinrinkan. Many of the company's male employees had gone out on strike in support of the women, and Macdonald accompanied Matsuoka to a meeting with them. While heartened by this male support for the women, she took her usual cautious line, declaring to the men that she had 'only one piece of advice ... to think out things with their heads and not with their fists.' As always, she was relieved when the strike was settled without violence, although with no advantage to the workers.[34]

Macdonald was under no illusion about the limited value of her behind-the-scenes support for women workers in the occasional strike. In the long run, the education of women was the only path to change, and she continued to pay great attention to the night school for factory girls. She was gratified that the second graduating class of twenty-nine was more than twice the size of the first one, while regular attendance in the current class had more than doubled. The school was attracting women from all parts of the city, including clothing workers, candy makers, and workers in electrical supply factories, breweries, and pharmaceutical firms.[35]

The settlement's knitting and cooking groups continued to be more popular than the more demanding high school classes. 'The desire to knit has taken such possession of feminine Japan that classes in the gentle art are regular institutions,' Caroline observed; one positive result was that 'a goodly number of women make a living as professional instructors.' Lessons in making 'simple, inexpensive Western dishes' added both 'variety and nutritious value to the ordinary Japanese food,' a form of basic education that accorded well with the work of Caroline's friend, the journalist Hani Motoko, through her magazine *Fujin No Tomo* (Women's Friend).[36]

There were continuing requests from women workers for classes in factories or labour union offices. One that flourished was in a government factory manufacturing railway workers' clothing. Since the management of the factory and the union were on amicable terms, the labour school was held in the factory itself in well-equipped rooms provided by the management. Shinrinkan met the girls' requests for instruction in knitting, embroidery, flower arrangement, planning the family budget, and cooking. Six months later, the general manager of the factory presented certificates from the settlement to 154 students before an audience of nearly 1,000 workers and relatives.[37]

Occasionally the police appeared at Shinrinkan to survey the scene. How could flower arranging or knitting threaten the public peace? Or how could it advance the labour movement? Sōdōmei's answer, and Macdonald's, was that this was the beginning of making women into citizens. To bring women together in the learning of any new skill not immediately related to their dull and monotonous daily work would enhance both their sense of individual dignity and their group solidarity, while contributing to their relaxation and general well being. Later there might be an opportunity for the Women's Bureau of Sōdōmei to organize discussions on issues such as housing and living conditions, and child care services.

Eventually, it was hoped, some of the women would be drawn into Sōdōmei's general educational program where they would be exposed to teaching about the principles of trade unionism in Japanese society. The road from flower arranging to social activism was usually a long one and women needed much encouragement. The road to political participation would be even longer. Since 1922, women had been allowed to attend and hold political meetings but not to join political parties. Women leaders who had hoped in vain that the suffrage bill of 1925 would be truly 'universal' knew they still faced a hard struggle.[38]

Nothing illustrated better the differences between Sōdōmei and its rival, the Hyōgikai, than their approaches to the political education of workers. Sōdōmei's numerous labour schools emphasized the development of individual skills and knowledge through a broad program of general education on the principles of trade unionism, democracy, parliamentary government, and good citizenship. The Hyōgikai organized cells devoted to study and action based largely on Marxist theory and made a determined effort to raise the class consciousness of workers. Successive governments allied with business and the military had no difficulty in deciding which branch of the labour movement deserved reluctant acceptance, while the more pro-labour bureaucrats in the Bureau of Social Affairs readily identified Sōdōmei as the representative of the moderate, 'sound' unionism they wished institutionalized in industrial relations. Sōdōmei leaders, not least Suzuki Bunji, were always eager to confirm their moderate image.[39]

Macdonald's interest in the education of women workers brought a new resident to Shinrinkan early in 1926. Akamatsu Tsuneko, the younger sister of Akamatsu Katsumaro, the leading exponent of the 'realist socialism' that increasingly characterized Sōdōmei's political direction, had worked with Kagawa Toyohiko in the slums of Kobe following the earthquake. Later in Tokyo she joined the labour movement and was put in charge of the cooperative store operated by the ironworkers union in the Okabe iron foundry. By the time she came to Shinrinkan, at the age of twenty-nine, she had organized a group of unionists' wives who shopped in the store, and had enlisted Matsuoka Katsuyo, Komakichi's wife, as instructor in kimono sewing and Shidachi Taki as the knitting teacher. Akamatsu soon established groups in other factories and was shortly appointed to the staff of the women's department of Sōdōmei. At Shinrinkan she taught calligraphy and Japanese in the girls' night school and was a valued addition to the settlement's resources.[40]

Akamatsu Tsuneko was not a Christian nor was her brother. Children of a Buddhist priest belonging to the Nishi Honganji sect, which had humanitarian interests, they were well disposed to the social teaching of liberal Protestants in Japan in their early years. Akamatsu Katsumaro, after a brief sojourn in the new Communist party, adopted a 'realist socialism' that owed something to the ideas of his Tokyo University professor (who was also his father-in-law), Yoshino Sakuzō. Akamatsu was a more sophisticated thinker than either Suzuki or Matsuoka, and his growing anti-communism provided the intellectual underpinning for their drive to disassociate Sōdōmei from Communists and build a cooperative relationship between labour unions and the state.[41]

During Akamatsu Tsuneko's three-year residence at Shinrinkan, she worked with women strikers and the wives of strikers in labour disputes all over Japan on behalf of the women's department of Sōdōmei.[42] Her work in organizing educational and mutual aid programs among cotton spinners in Numazu in Shizuoka prefecture helped to make the local union a model for factories where women were active in the membership and typified the practical pragmatism that represented Sōdōmei's ideal.[43]

Macdonald's association with Akamatsu increased her contacts with Japanese women actively involved in organizing female workers, as did the formation of the Women's Labour Committee for the ILO. When it was established in the spring of 1926, Katō Taka, general secretary of the Tokyo YWCA, was elected chairperson, while other members included Kubushiro Ochimi of the Women's Christian Temperance Union, Watanabe Matsuko, also of the YWCA, and Baroness Ishimoto Shizue. Macdonald was invited to serve as an advisory member of the committee, whose first major project was to send several of its members to make a survey of the appalling conditions of women labourers in coal mines in the Jōban district. The director of the women's committee, its only paid worker, was Ichikawa Fusae, on her way to becoming one of the most influential women in modern Japan. Formerly secretary of the women's department of the Yūaikai, and a leader of the now-dissolved New Women's Association, Ichikawa had recently spent more than two years in the United States where she had extensive contact with women leaders of trade unions and with the suffrage and peace movements. Shortly she resigned from her well-paid position with the ILO committee to devote her energies fully to the Women's Suffrage League and to adopt the austere style of life she was to follow for the next fifty years.[44]

• • •

WEDDINGS WERE OFTEN HELD at Shinrinkan, but none gave Caroline more pleasure than the one on the national holiday *kigensetsu* in 1927. The bride was Takizawa Matsuyo, the Wellesley graduate who had never given up the idea that she would return to help her former teacher. Now after eight years in the United States, armed with a doctorate in political economy from Columbia University, she was ready to work. The groom, Kimura Yonetarō, had spent twenty years in the United States, working at every kind of job to support and educate himself. Caroline, who had not known him until now, admired him for his achievement, yet found him still 'a quiet humble Xtn [Christian] man, even if he is B.A., M.A., B.D., Ph.D.' His doctorate was in philosophy and Christian ethics, and both he and his wife had been in close touch with American Federation of Labor activists in New York. The couple were to be in charge of the planning and implementation of Shinrinkan's whole program of education for working people, and Caroline rejoiced in a more coherent approach to this side of the settlement's work.[45]

Macdonald herself continued to play an active role in the work among women and girls both within the settlement house and outside in factories. Thus when Matsuoka asked her to engage in some 'soap box' oratory among female strikers at a cotton mill just outside Tokyo she did so several times, to what effect she was not sure, although the strike was settled with some small gains for the strikers. This experience impressed upon her yet again the long road Japanese women must walk to social and political awareness and influence. As she commented to Jane Addams: 'The men are more or less under a good deal of mental discipline but the girls are like sheep without a shepherd.' Nevertheless, she was confident that solid progress was being made in the education of working women and 'we shall I think, be able to carry it a good deal further during the coming year.'[46]

Despite her increasing interest in labouring people, Macdonald's other activities did not slacken. 'Prison visiting, letter writing, finding jobs for people, comforting the broken hearted, inspiring the despondent, and attending to various needs' filled most of her days. She rarely saw women prisoners, mainly because there were very few of them, but also because the women's prison for those serving terms of any duration was seventy-five miles away from Tokyo. Macdonald was deeply moved when she came down to breakfast one morning and found waiting for her a woman whom she had visited in a Tokyo prison after her conviction for shoplifting and robbery. She came to Macdonald's house soon after her release from the distant prison and there was 'a scene of joy and delight at meeting again, with a good many tears on her part, and considerable struggle' on Caroline's to keep her own tears back. In the woman's absence Caroline had been working to persuade her husband to forgive his wife for the shame she had brought on him and their teenage daughters; he had refused to visit her in prison and had forbidden his daughters to do so. Now Caroline was gratified to learn that the family was reunited and were beginning life together again. This story of 'the prodigal mother,' Macdonald explained, was 'no less classic' than the original story of the prodigal son, and 'just as much an illustration ... of the matchless love of God for those who go astray.'[47]

'The prodigal mother' and similar tales reminded Macdonald that most of her life concerned 'problems, not of high statesmanship or strategic situations, but of the daily lives of perplexities and agonies of the weary and heavy laden who come to us and expect to be comforted.' She and her colleagues needed 'increasingly and unceasingly a heart at leisure from itself to sooth and sympathize, that we can give unstintingly of all we have, as His work and His will are revealed to us.'[48] Nevertheless, despite the very personal nature of so much of her work, she never lost sight of large contexts and visions. As always, Macdonald was pleased to explain her work to visitors, who were calling on her in increasing numbers. Whether she recognized it or not, she was now one of the best-known foreigners in Tokyo and perhaps the most famous missionary in Japan, often called 'the white angel of Tokyo.'[49] Many visitors, especially those interested in prison work, had first heard of her through their reading of A Gentleman in Prison. Some of them were scarcely strangers, especially the Canadians who appeared frequently, eager to see the work of a famed fellow countrywoman.

One visitor was of unusual importance to her, and indeed she had more than a little to do with the invitation by the National Christian Council of Japan to David Cairns of Aberdeen to spend a month in Japan lecturing to university and college students. Later she had received a letter from Cairns asking her to cable a reply to a question, and she had done so. As she told Galen Fisher, who obviously knew of her feelings about Cairns, 'I said "yes."' She hated to add that she was only replying to a question about whether Cairns and his daughter, Alison, might stay with her in Tokyo during their forthcoming trip to the Orient. 'But you never can tell what these things will lead to. One "yes" requires another as time goes on,' she quipped to Fisher.[50]

In late June the two Cairnses arrived to stay at Shinrinkan for a week, before setting out for several other Japanese cities and then returning to Tokyo for a few days. Cairns was always exhilarated by travel, and his extraordinary intellectual curiosity was vigorously exercised whether he was trying to understand Japan's feudal history or grasp the speed of its recent modernization. His experience in Japan, and another two months lecturing to students in China, made him appreciate the growing force of foreign intellectual influences in Asia, notably Russian Marxism and secular humanism mainly in its American expressions. For several years Cairns had been focusing on questions concerning the relationship between Christian faith and science, and his lectures in this area to Japanese and Chinese students, many of them non-Christians, drew large and attentive audiences.[51]

Cairns had just sent to press the manuscript of what was to become his most influential book, *The Faith that Rebels: A Re-Examination of the Miracles of Jesus*. Cairns believed his attempt to show that a fuller understanding of the synoptic gospels would destroy the concept of a dual universe, material and spiritual, was sustained by recent developments in philosophy and psychology, and by a growing understanding of the limits of science. In Cairns's view, the miracles recorded in the New Testament were not exceptional events that proved the divinity of Christ, as much of Christian tradition affirmed, nor were they to be explained away as the mythology of a pre-scientific age, as contemporary 'modernists' did. Rather, the 'Gospel miracles were works of faith – the faith that rebels against evil.'[52] They were evidence that God sustains the whole created world, not just a domain designated as 'spiritual,' and that the world of nature is not a 'closed system.' Thus God could respond to faith with active intervention to overcome evils such as disease, hunger, war, and death itself. For Cairns this allowed unlimited scope for petitionary prayer, but it did not mean acquiescence before evil. Prayer and action must go together: 'We have no right to work for anything for which we cannot pray, and we have no right to pray for anything for which we may not work, if our work can do anything to secure its attainment. It may be that our prayers are not heard because God wishes us also to work. It may be that our mere work fails because God wishes us also to pray.'[53] It would have been hard to find a clearer statement of Caroline's own faith and practice.

Caroline had never lost her early interest in science and religion or in theology in general and she had much to discuss with her old mentor. She also greatly enjoyed showing the sights of Tokyo to this far from superficial sightseer and sharing her understanding of Japanese society and of the Japanese church. For Cairns the visit was an opportunity to see at first hand the life and work of one of his liveliest and most admired former students. How sad *was* Caroline when Cairns departed without asking a significant personal question that could be answered with a simple 'yes'?

■ ■ ■

HOWEVER MUCH visitors might be impressed by her reputation and her influence with governments and bureaucracies, Macdonald, along with other Christians in Japan, was far from taking the blessing of officialdom for granted. Early in 1927 the government introduced a 'Religions Bill' that would give the state, through the Ministry of Education, rigorous control over the three officially recognized religions – Buddhism, Shintoism, and Christianity. The bill came as a surprise, for it was only two years since the government had called, for the third time in fifteen years, a 'Conference of the Three Religions.' Although some critics feared that its purpose was to draw on the assumed conservatism of religion in the battle against 'dangerous thoughts,' no specific threat had arisen from the conference.[54] That could not be said of the proposed 'Religions Bill.'

Japanese Presbyterians, members of the Nihon Kirisuto Kyōkai (Church of Christ in Japan), issued one of the first of many strenuous protests against a measure that would give the state power to regulate religious ceremonies or teaching that were deemed to be 'prejudicial to peace and order.' It was a tribute to Macdonald's competence in Japanese, no less than to her awareness of what was at stake, that she was selected to work with a Japanese minister (whose earlier career as a judge made him knowledgeable in legal matters) in preparing an English translation of an extended summary of the lengthy bill.[55] Although there was much opposition from Buddhists, the fiercest resistance was from Christians, both resting their case mainly on grounds that Macdonald outlined for overseas friends: 'Religious liberty was granted by the Japanese Constitution in the early days of the new [Meiji] regime, forty years ago, and this bill ... challenges the very foundation of this liberty.' Thus the bill was potentially a serious threat and she believed that the current protest would 'undoubtedly be written into the history of the church.'[56]

It was well understood that for the present the proposed legislation was intended to curtail the current proliferation of strange new sects, usually

Shintoist, often under leaders claiming authority that came close to challenging that of the emperor. Nevertheless, although Christians believed that the days of overt discrimination against them were over, they could not ignore the broader implications of the bill. Thanks to the widespread condemnation of the measure, it was defeated in the Diet and was later dropped, but it was a warning that Japanese politicians and bureaucrats could not be relied upon to interpret the Meiji constitution in a liberal spirit, and that the state had a continuing interest in regulating religion,[57] however friendly an eye it might currently cast on institutions such as Shinrinkan.

C h a p t e r   1 4

From Noda to Geneva

AMID ALL HER OTHER INTERESTS in the mid-twenties, Macdonald kept an eye on the town of Noda north of Tokyo in the largely agrarian prefecture of Chiba, where her labour friends were expending a good deal of energy. Since the 1923 strike, the conviction had grown in both the Kikkōman company and the brewers' union that the settlement reached then was only a truce in preparation for the inevitable struggle to come. Then, as Macdonald observed, 'more fundamental problems would need to be discussed and settled. The working men realized they must consolidate their union and the Company was determined that it would be but a question of time until the Labour Union would be smashed to pieces.' As Caroline contemplated the coming confrontation, she thought it fortunate that the 'national leaders, [of Sōdōmei] belong to the branch of the Labour movement which ... [believes] ... in attaining their ends by constitutional and parliamentary methods.'[1]

Sōdōmei had established a labour school at Noda in 1925, which was soon one of the largest in the country, with about one hundred men pursuing the regular course of study each year. Hundreds more attended lectures by labour leaders and academics on the history of socialism, the labour movement, and on current issues in economics and politics. This program placed greater emphasis on political action than was often the case in Sōdōmei labour schools, for the federation's leaders, notably Suzuki and Matsuoka, were trying to make the Noda union a model of their approach to reform through parliamentary means.[2]

While pursuing its educational program, Sōdōmei was also vigorously recruiting members for the Noda branch of the brewers' union. Recruitment was often inhibited by the dual economic interests of the workers, many of whom also continued their traditional agricultural labour. Nonetheless, by 1927, with 1,500 members, the Noda union was one of the largest in Japan and accounted for nearly half the membership of the fourteen locals constituting the Kantō Brewers' Union. The union was building up its financial resources, including a special strike fund, said to be the biggest in the country.[3]

Macdonald took an active interest in the progress of the Noda union and believed it was 'transforming a town notorious for its drunkenness and gambling and its women.' She rejoiced that many men had given up 'drinking and other foolishness and occupied their time in education and discussion of the body politic,' while their wives were learning to knit and sew and sometimes to understand the reasons for union activities. The labour school was breaking down the isolation and ignorance of Noda's workers, who were realizing that 'the Company to which they and their ancestors had given themselves body and soul for the past hundred years ... [was] ... behind even the rest of Japan to say nothing of the world at large and that they themselves are behind in submitting to the conditions under which they work,' as well as to a feudal relationship between employer and employees.[4]

The Kikkōman Company, one of the largest enterprises in Japan, did not leave the battle for the workers' allegiance uncontested. The company instituted numerous reforms intended to convince its employees that 'co-operative industrialism' would be to their advantage. New rules defining the duties of managers and workers were promulgated, employees were assisted in completing their primary education, new dormitories for unmarried men were opened, a hospital for employees was built, and a health insurance program was made available at nominal cost.[5] Macdonald's scepticism about these developments was confirmed when 'both the hospital and the dormitories remained empty,' a situation confirming her view that the workers realized that 'no amount of so called social reform can take the place of a fair deal between employer and employee,' and showed that 'the men were educating themselves to discriminate between fundamental solutions to their problems and mere palliatives.'[6]

A strike was eventually precipitated when the company pushed aside the firm that for twenty-five years had been hauling soya products to the railroad dockings and to local markets, in favour of its own recently formed transportation company. It was no coincidence that the older company was unionized and its workers had declined to handle soya from the recently opened Factory 17 where the company refused to hire union members. This development brought on a brief conflict in 1925, but a second was the longest and perhaps the most crucial strike in Japan up to that time.[7]

In the spring of 1927 the employees presented the Kikkōman Company with six demands, the most important for a 10 per cent wage increase, and 20 per cent for the women who made up 7 per cent of the total work force of nearly 2,000. Other demands concerned apprenticeship training, promotion, and bonuses. The company countered with an offer for small improvements in the health insurance plan. After three weeks of negotiations, the workers suddenly withdrew their demands, an action Macdonald attributed to extreme caution in the national headquarters of Sōdōmei, which 'advised almost any compromise rather than strike, as the country was passing through a very serious financial crisis.'[8] The failure of the Bank of Taiwan, followed by the collapse of fifty smaller banks, adversely affected the whole economy and made a strike unpropitious in the eyes of Sōdōmei leaders. Suzuki and Matsuoka knew they must counter the charges of the more radical Hyōgikai that Sōdōmei's general aversion to strike action made it 'soft.' However, they could not afford to embark on a futile strike that would refute Sōdōmei claims to be the effective representative of labour. Those claims could be substantiated by its record during the previous year. Aggressive unionization by Sōdōmei and the Hyōgikai had almost doubled the membership of each and precipitated a marked increase in strikes, but the Sōdōmei unions achieved by far the greater number of victories, albeit modest ones.[9]

After weeks of discussions about whether the time was opportune, some of which took place at Shinrinkan, and despite increasing economic depression, the union took the plunge into strike action. That seemed the only answer to the company's announcement that in response to declining demand and a decrease in worker output it was lowering wages. In mid-September 1927, more than 1,300 workers, or 65 per cent of the work force, went on strike to secure better wages and benefits and recognition of collective bargaining through the union. The company soon started firing workers, beginning with those believed to be ringleaders in the strike. The local union called an emergency general assembly of workers and sent an SOS call to the headquarters of Sōdōmei, which brought Matsuoka and other members of the central executive to Noda.[10] On their invitation, Macdonald went with them and mounted the platform before the assembly to join in exhorting the workers and their families to stand firm in whatever happened next.[11] This was the first of several occasions during the dispute when Caroline gave inspirational talks to strikers and their families.[12]

Within three months, half the work force was discharged. By hiring new workers and running its most modern units at full capacity, the company managed to maintain production and in 1928 output soared to the highest level in history. The Kikkōman label continued to dominate the soya market, and the company needed only to outwait the strikers.[13] 'They could afford to wait,' Caroline observed, 'as they are among the most notoriously rich firms in all Japan.'[14]

Macdonald admired the conduct of the strikers: they 'were determined not to resort to force and the first act almost of the strike executive was to post notices that no drinking would be allowed among the strikers,' a rule she believed was 'rigidly obeyed.' Then the strikers set out 'to make every sort of peaceful demonstration possible to advertise themselves and their grievances in order to win public sympathy. They refused to pay local taxes. The children of the strikers refused to go to school and thereby brought the problem to the attention of the Education Department ... They marched on Tokyo in a body, the children included to interview the Home Minister, thereby calling the attention of the police to their troubles.'[15] At this point the police blocked mass marches but allowed morale-building meetings to continue.[16] The chief organizer of the more than 500 children who boycotted their schools was Akamatsu Tsuneko. Under her direction, the children worked as messengers, looked after younger children, and did housework. From Shinrinkan she brought films for the entertainment of the 'striking' boys and girls, much to their delight for many had never seen a movie before.[17]

When the strike was four months old, one desperate discharged employee, Horikoshi Umeo, staged a drama that captured the imagination of the whole country. The response to the sight of one man seeking redress directly from the emperor by trying to stop the imperial automobile in the streets of Tokyo to present his appeal, to no avail, illustrated traditional ideas of responsibility and loyalty, and increased public pressure for a settlement of the strike.[18] Macdonald was intrigued

> when newspapers sympathetic with the strikers from the beginning made this the occasion for further tirades on the company's bad behaviour and the exceeding patience of the strikers. Prominent businessmen came forward and offered mediations. The governor of the prefecture ... offered his resignation ... and the chief of police for the district followed suit with the same gesture of outraged loyalty. Even the president of the company felt it incumbent upon him to express his regret that His Majesty should have been subjected to any annoyance by a former employee of his and to bear a certain responsibility for the occurrence. For a few days everyone was apologizing to everyone else for the affair.[19]

The perpetrator of the crime against the emperor was arrested on the spot, as he expected. Appearing in court without a lawyer, he refused to defend himself and declared that the court should do with him as it deemed best. The maximum penalty was one year in prison, but he was given six months. Macdonald noted that 'fifty years ago he would have had his head cut off.' The episode reminded her of a classical Japanese tale about a peasant who, failing to secure redress from the overlord of a district where the farmers were desperately poor, had appealed directly to the shogun, and he and his whole family were executed for his audacity. That chronicle ended, Macdonald recalled, 'with the significant words: "The taxes of the oppressed farmers were afterwards remitted."'[20] It had been evident for many weeks that there could be no positive outcome for the oppressed in Noda. The union had earlier estimated that the strike would last no longer than six months at the most. After five months, Sōdōmei issued a statement over Matsuoka's signature admitting that the union had seriously miscalculated the situation and was prepared 'to accept any and all criticism.' Shortly, when Matsuoka announced that he was withdrawing all demands immediately, his bargaining position was virtually destroyed, although he held out for several weeks, vainly, for the reemployment of all discharged workers.[21]

With soya production continuing at an all-time high, the company was still in no hurry to settle the strike. Discussion with the union, scarcely worthy of description as 'negotiations,' thus proceeded at a leisurely pace over more than a month. The settlement gave the workers nothing, save the company's promise to rehire one third of the workers it had dismissed, and to give some financial compensation to the others. Macdonald was relieved by any settlement, for by this time that was the only important objective.[22]

Matsuoka had the disagreeable task of going before a crowd of angry workers assembled in the Noda theatre to tell them how little they had gained from the longest industrial dispute in Japanese history. In the face of some cries of 'Down with him!' Matsuoka stood his ground and argued earnestly that the terms of the settlement were not totally negative, an interpretation hard to swallow for the two-thirds of the employees who had lost their jobs. Eventually the audience grew quieter, and Matsuoka finished his report, which was accepted by a substantial majority. Observing that this was not a time to cheer, Matsuoka said that instead 'they would close the meeting ... by waiting together for a moment in silent prayer ... [Then] silence fell upon them which could be felt but not described and the change between the beginning and the end of the meeting was tremendous ... a wonderful spectacle,' Macdonald reported.[23] Then Matsuoka and other union leaders went off to sign the agreement and to spend the rest of the day and far into the night with representatives of the company and the mediation committee in the ritual eating, drinking, and mutual congratulation that marked such occasions.[24]

In the short run, the Noda strike destroyed the union and weakened Sōdōmei's position. However, it may be argued that later improvements in working conditions owed something to the company's fear of further collective action by workers, and that the disruption caused by the lengthy dispute made government and some employers more flexible in making concessions to labour.[25]

■ ■ ■

IT WAS NOT ONLY the economic interests of the brewery workers and the prestige of Sōdōmei that were at stake in the great Noda strike. There were also political interests at issue, for the newly formed Shakai Minshutō (Social Democratic Party) had officially backed the strikers. Macdonald was actively concerned with the fortunes of the new party, and she made Shinrinkan available for organizing meetings. Thanks to this hospitality, Caroline and the house were frequently under surveillance by police eager to uncover violations of the Peace Preservation Law.[26] The new party was closely allied with Sōdōmei, and many Sōdōmei leaders, including Suzuki Bunji, Nishio Suehiro, Akamatsu Katsumaro, and Matsuoka Komakichi were party officials. At local levels too there was the same informal overlapping of personnel between the Sōdōmei unions and the party. Taking as its model the Labour Party in Britain, the Shakai Minshutō tried from the beginning to appeal to a constituency beyond the ranks of the industrial working class.[27] Two non-unionists, both well known to Macdonald, held key positions: as chairman, Professor Abe Isoo provided continuity with the first Social Democratic Party, formed and dissolved on the same day in 1901. Another Christian, the lawyer Katayama Tetsu, an elder in Fujimichō church, served as secretary-general.

Unfortunately for its prospects, the Shakai Minshutō was not alone in appealing to left-of-centre voters. Soon after the promulgation of the new suffrage act, labour and agrarian leaders and intellectuals on the left tried to create a united socialist party, but within a year the proletarian movement had broken into four new parties and several local labour parties had been formed. Although the platforms of the parties were very similar in their apparent moderation, there was major division over the role of Communists in the parties and over the sincerity of the party leaders' commitment to parliamentary government. In successive divisions, the Shakai Minshutō, reflecting Sōdōmei's implacable hostility to communism, emerged as the most conservative of the left-wing parties.[28]

In the national election in the spring of 1928, the first under manhood suffrage, there were eighty-eight proletarian candidates backed by seven different parties. Their combined vote amounted to only 4.7 per cent of the total votes cast, the more radical Labour-Farmer party winning by far the largest share of the left-wing vote. However, thanks to the distribution of votes, the Shakai Minshutō claimed four of the eight candidates elected by the socialist parties, including Abe Isoo in a Tokyo district and Suzuki Bunji in Osaka. Matsuoka Komakichi had intended to be a candidate, but his involvement in the Noda strike prevented him from running. The Shakai Minshutō garnered 90 per cent of its votes from urban industrial workers with a smattering of support from intellectuals and other members of the urban middle class. Most of the voters supported one of the two major parties – the ruling conservative Seiyūkai and the Minseitō, somewhat more liberal but also supported by big business. Both parties mounted expensive and often corrupt election campaigns that the Shakai Minshutō could not begin to match. In the new Diet, the Seiyūkai, under Prime Minister Tanaka Giichi, had a majority of only one member over the Minseitō, leaving the balance of power with the proletarian parties.[29]

Before the deadlocked Diet ever met, the Tanaka government invoked the Peace Preservation Law to arrest more than 1,500 Communist party members and suspected sympathizers throughout the country. A month later, when the ban on news of the arrests was lifted, the government immediately dissolved the three leading parties of the left, including the Hyōgikai and the Japan Farmers' Union, thus striking a severe blow at the labour and agrarian movements. Although the Minseitō opposition had no objection in principle to the use of force against Communists, it expressed outrage that in excessive zeal to apprehend a few Communists, the government was suppressing legitimate political thought and activity. The Shakai Minshutō and Sōdōmei condemned the arrests, although only mildly, agreeing that the now-defunct parties had harboured those who were undermining 'sound unionism' and democratic reform. When the government went even further and introduced revisions to the Peace Preservation Law, including one that would impose the death penalty instead of the existing ten years' hard labour for those who sought to alter the *kokutai* (national polity), the social democrats were more vigorous in their opposition. When the opposition parties managed to defeat the revision of the Peace Preservation Law in the Lower House, the government secured approval of the measure from the Privy Council under a constitutional provision that allowed the council to issue imperial ordinances in emergencies when the Diet was not in session. While the next Diet approved the ordinance, as the constitution required, this was the beginning of a struggle that brought together the Minseitō, some Home Ministry bureaucrats, and the proletarian parties in resistance to the government's growing use of repression in dealing with social problems.[30] The continuing constitutional battle contributed to the fall of the Tanaka government and the succession of Hamaguchi Osachi of the Minseitō party as prime minister. Now the labour unions and social democrats looked forward to an era of liberal reform.[31]

■ ■ ■

ALTHOUGH SŌDŌMEI AND ITS POLITICAL WING, the Shakai Minshutō, as well as the work of the labour schools were of continuing interest to Macdonald, her prison work remained her primary occupation. Between 1926 and 1928, services provided to individuals increased by 1,500 to a total of nearly 5,000, despite the fact that Macdonald was out of the country for two extended periods totalling seven months. Always, and especially during her absence, Yamada Zen'ichi was increasingly valuable in the work with prisoners and ex-prisoners. Married again since his release from prison, his wife also helped with the work of Shinrinkan, mainly with the wives of prisoners.[32]

Emperor Taishō died at the end of 1926, and as the time of his funeral drew near in the spring of 1927, Macdonald and her co-workers awaited anxiously the announcement of the pardons and amnesties that were always granted to mark national mourning or rejoicing, hoping for good news of their 'special friends.' The clemency given was not nearly as wide in scope as the one three years earlier at the time of the wedding of the Prince Regent, now the Emperor Showa. Thus there were many prisoners and their families whose hopes had been raised and now needed to be comforted. At least Caroline was grateful that the death sentence given to a man she had been visiting for the past four years during a series of intricate trials had been commuted to life imprisonment. 'He had already entered into a life of peace and was prepared for death when the reprieve came,' she noted, and now 'he was as one who had come back from the dead.' She found here 'the very interpretation in the life of to-day ... that Browning tried to give us in his poem "Lazarus," when he came back to life after an experience of Heaven.'[33]

After knowing prisoners for nearly fifteen years, Macdonald was more convinced than ever that all too often prisons 'make men worse than they were.' In common with other countries, Japan spent millions every year

taking their finger prints, getting their life history and that of their forbears unto the third and fourth generation, finding out how they have escaped getting an education in a country where compulsory education obtains, taking physical tests and mental tests to ascertain whether they are normal or subnormal or abnormal, as if anyone knew just where such a fine line should be drawn when we are dealing with human beings, and then we shuck them all into one place and treat them all perfectly alike as if we had never discovered that they were different ... We deprive them of every vestige of self respect they may have had ... and we do all in our power to make them less able than they were formerly to perform their duties to society when we turn them out later into a world that has marched passed them while they were incarcerated without newspapers, without magazines, without ordinary human interest, in our efforts to punish and reform them. We have done neither. We ... have turned out a worse man into society than we turned into jail ... Why labour so to make men bad. We are all bad enough even at our best.[34]

The greatest reform Macdonald could recommend was the adoption of the principle that 'the first charge on the work of a prisoner should be for his dependents.' Nearly all prisoners in Japanese jails worked long hours for their own maintenance and the production of goods for sale. Thus the penal system was self-supporting, but the reformation of the incarcerated men would be more likely, she believed, if they had to assume responsibility for their dependents; often it was lack of such responsibility that had got them into prison. Once there, 'we have both the work and the power to compel [the prisoner] to work, not only for himself but for all his dependents ... Under conditions which I would stipulate he might have to live on one or two meals a day and do without an extra blanket in the winter time if he did not speed up to his obligations.'[35]

Macdonald believed that this idea would not be accepted until society got rid of the belief that retribution was the main objective of putting people in prison. 'Compensation is the only way that is effective, making men not less able but more able to do their duty by those they have wronged and to those for whom they are responsible until in the end the wronged and the wronger will forgive each other and by mutual compensation will bring a better world into being.' Macdonald made this argument frequently before a variety of audiences.[36]

Her fame continued to grow. This was thanks partly to the several English editions and the translations into other languages of *A Gentleman in Prison*, as well as to the award of a silver cup at the time of the Emperor Showa's enthronement, when 247 outstanding social workers, including eight foreigners, were honoured for their services. A few months later she was elected to the council of the Asiatic Society of Japan, the second woman to be so recognized by an organization devoted to the study of Japanese culture. For several decades after its inception in 1872, a majority of the members of the Asiatic Society had been Britons, but Americans were now just as active in its program of meetings devoted to the reading and discussion of papers on a broad range of topics. No other woman was elected until after the Second World War, and Japanese members were almost as notable by their absence.[37]

Many visitors from abroad who wished to meet Macdonald also wanted to see the inside of a prison; where she thought they could profit from the experience she took them to meet Dr. Motoji of the Ministry of Justice, from whom permission was needed to visit a prison. One such visitor was an Englishman interested in adult education in prisons, who was identified in Macdonald's diaries only as 'FLM.' He had gone to Japan believing that Japanese prisons were 'loathsome places,' a view confirmed by what he heard from Japanese themselves. Then he met Caroline Macdonald, 'a lady whose eyes sparkle and whose words can bite as well as charm ... who has ... founded an institution which may become a Japanese Toynbee Hall and who in the midst of her doing good has not forgotten how to buy a good pair of silk stockings.' One early May morning in 1927 Macdonald accompanied him on a visit to Kosuge prison, still under extensive reconstruction from the ravages of the great earthquake. The visitor was impressed that 'as much as possible the prison idea is being eliminated ... An endeavour, and ... it appears to be successful ... is being made to make the prison secure, easy to control, and reasonably escape proof, without imposing a lack of air, light, or ugliness and terror upon everybody inside.' Much more impressive than the buildings was Governor Arima:

> For years we have discussed the problem of personality and its making. Here in the East I have met an outstanding personality; one who has dared ... to put his belief into practice. But more, I have seen personalities being re-made. I do not know whether other Japanese prisons are as enlightened as this one ... but others like it are bound to follow. It is a more striking monument to the advancement and modernity of Japan than her railroads, power plants, army or navy, for it indicates that the spirit as well as the machinery of a new age has entered her womb.[38]

John Lewis Gillin, professor of sociology and criminology at the University of Wisconsin, was another informed visitor. After a tour of Kosuge prison Macdonald took him to Tokyo prison, where Arima had recently been transferred as governor. Talking with Arima and walking about with him as he conversed with his prisoners, Gillin concluded that Arima was 'one of the highest types of prison officials ... anywhere in the world.'[39] Such judgments from outsiders told Caroline nothing new, but it pleased her enormously to see the West learning from the East.

• • •

EARLY IN 1929 Sōdōmei elected Matsuoka Komakichi as its representative to the annual conference of the International Labour Organization in Geneva. Matsuoka had attended the same gathering in 1926, travelling afterwards in Germany, France, England, and the United States, but his limited command of English, or any other foreign language, had prevented him from getting the most out of the experience. Macdonald volunteered to accompany him this time as his interpreter wherever English was helpful. The expenses of the delegates – two representing the government, and one each from employers and labour – were paid by the government, but Macdonald had no official status and made the trip at her own expense.[40] What motives overcame that consideration and her usual reluctance to be away from her work? It was scarcely a desire to attend more committee meetings. Was it simply an act of friendship, done in the hope of contributing to a friend's enjoyment and education? Or did she want to see Matsuoka cut a bigger figure in Geneva than he otherwise might, to the advantage of the Japanese trade union movement, and Japanese prestige as a whole? Perhaps attendance at the ILO conference would increase her credibility as an interpreter of the aspirations of Sōdōmei and the Shakai Minshutō, especially within the Christian community in Japan?

In mid-April 1929, Macdonald and Matsuoka took a train to Osaka after a boisterous farewell from a crowd of Tokyo trade unionists. They were accompanied by Matsuoka's two advisors: Miyazaki Ryūsuke, a lawyer, a leader of the Federation of Japanese Farmers' Unions, and an activist in the Shakai Minshutō; and Watanabe Michitaro of the Japan Seamen's Union. In Osaka, as later at Kobe where they boarded ship, they were given a rousing send-off by hundreds of trade union members. Also on board were the two government representatives, Yoshisaka Shunzō and Yusawa Michio, officials of the Social Bureau in the Home Ministry. Macdonald knew all these men in varying degree and now made the acquaintance of Yoshisaka's wife who, like her husband, was fluent in both English and French. 'The busy capitalists,' as Matsuoka described the employers' delegate, industrialist

Iwasaki Seishichi and his advisors, were to leave later and travel to Europe through Siberia.[41]

The first port of call for the government and labour delegations was Shanghai. Matsuoka had been there three years earlier in pursuit of Sōdōmei's interest in forming a non-Communist organization of Asian workers. Now he was following up with further meetings, while Caroline was shown about the city by a Tsuda College graduate married to a resident Japanese businessman, met English and American missionary friends and one of her ex-prisoners, and visited a Japanese church and a social club. Then she and Matsuoka discussed China's future with a local warlord through a Japanese professor who spoke Chinese, and a whirlwind day ended when they attended a large student meeting at the YMCA where Matsuoka spoke about the common interests of Chinese and Japanese workers. During their twenty-eight hours in Shanghai, Matsuoka was constantly shadowed by a security officer acting for the Japanese consul-general in the city, and a detailed report was forwarded to the Ministry of Foreign Affairs in Tokyo. Macdonald's activities were also recorded, although in less detail.[42] A vigilant government must exercise surveillance even over those whom it considered more or less 'sound,' especially when they were in a country where Communists were more active than in Japan.

As the ship made its way from Shanghai to Hong Kong, Singapore, Colombo, through the Indian Ocean to the Suez Canal and Cairo, and across the Mediterranean to Marseilles, the government and labour delegates had ample time to discuss the questionnaires and draft conventions on the ILO conference agenda. Although the two groups often differed, that did not inhibit good social relations and they joined amicably in sightseeing in port and playing games on board ship. Since one of the subjects to be discussed in Geneva was the establishment of international safety standards and guarantees of proper care for sailors injured in foreign countries, Caroline prepared herself by learning the Japanese names for various parts of the ship. As she discovered in Geneva, Japan was in the vanguard among the nations in its care of injured foreign sailors.[43]

In Geneva, the delegates spent ten days in preparatory work before the official sessions began, a difficult period for Matsuoka and his labour colleagues, none of whom could function easily in either French or English, the two official languages of the conference. Consequently, Macdonald was kept very busy making sure they were well informed and able to participate fully.

Matsuoka's performance at the conference did nothing to diminish his country's stature, nor his own in Caroline's eyes, and she was proud of his 'open-minded and friendly' manner as he moved among the other delegates, and with 'his quiet dignity' as he presided over a dinner party for labour representatives from other countries. In plenary sessions of the conference, delegates spoke in their own tongues and speeches were translated by machine into several languages (not including Japanese). When it was Matsuoka's turn to address the assembly, he was heard with great attention and respect; although almost none of his audience understood him, no one left the huge hall. Then Macdonald translated his address into English, a task not unduly demanding for she was familiar with its content.[44]

After the Geneva conference, Macdonald and Matsuoka went to England, happy to be there just as Ramsay Macdonald was forming his second Labour government. With Caroline acting as interpreter, they met briefly with the prime minister and later at a garden party celebrating the new government they mingled with cabinet ministers and labour supporters. Subsequently, they had interviews with several labour leaders, including Walter Citrine, general secretary of the Trades Union Congress, and Ernest Bevin of the powerful Transport and General Workers' Union.[45]

One meeting gave Macdonald unusual satisfaction. She had always been astonished by Japanese women workers' curiosity about the progress of women in other countries, and had tried to foster this interest. The women in the Shinrinkan labour school found it hard to believe that in Britain women held many public offices, even seats in Parliament. Before her departure for Geneva, Macdonald had told a group of textile workers about Margaret Bondfield of the British Labour Party, who had begun as a draper's apprentice, later founded the National Federation of Women Workers, and became a member of Parliament. In recent years, Bondfield had led the fight in the ILO 'to have night work for women abolished from the face of the earth.' On 1 July 1929, night work for women in Japanese textile industries was to end, a reform Macdonald believed owed at least as much to international pressure as to domestic opinion. Thus the group of women workers at Shinrinkan sent a message to Bondfield thanking her for her part in the improvement of their lives. By the time Macdonald delivered it, the recipient had become the Right Honourable Margaret Bondfield, Minister of Labour in Ramsay Macdonald's cabinet, Britain's first woman cabinet minister. The new minister rejoiced with Macdonald and Matsuoka that

Japanese women textile workers would no longer be reporting for work at eleven o'clock at night.[46]

After two weeks in London, when Caroline spent a good deal of time with her sister Leila and her family, she and Matsuoka visited a number of industries in the Birmingham area observing factory life and meeting local unionists. In the Rhonda Valley in South Wales, where they met officials of the Coal Miners' Union, Caroline had her first experience of going underground in a mine to see working conditions at first hand. Altogether her contacts with the British labour movement were just as stimulating as the Geneva meetings and provided her with a good deal of information useful in her educational work at Shinrinkan.[47]

Once again she met David Cairns. Whether he made a special trip to London to see her or just happened to be there is unclear. Since they had last met in Tokyo, Cairns's study of the miracles of Jesus, *The Faith that Rebels*, had been published and was creating considerable stir in the theological world. After reading the book, Caroline had written to him seeking clarification of Cairns's conviction about the power of believers to 'reproduce' the healing miracles of Christ. Although she had friends who believed that prayer had cured their illnesses, Caroline tended to think that they underestimated the role of medical science.[48] Their discussion of science and religion, of the perennial question of 'the problem of evil,' Cairns's comments on his recent experience as moderator of the Church of Scotland, plus Caroline's account of the ILO conference and of Japanese affairs guaranteed that her meeting with Cairns, who still addressed her as 'Miss Macdonald,' was as intellectually stimulating as ever. As to whether it aroused old emotions from the past there is no hint.

In August 1929, Caroline was again in London, Ontario, intending to stay for two months before returning to Japan. Once there, she decided that Peg had looked after their mother, who now required someone with her constantly, for long enough and needed a break, and that she would take the primary responsibility for a few months. Although she was reluctant to be away from Tokyo for so long, there was some compensation in the opportunity to publicize Shinrinkan and its financial needs in Canada and she gave several talks mainly to church boards in Toronto. Regretfully, she had to tell N.W. Rowell, chairman of the Canadian Institute of International Affairs, that the delay in her return to Japan meant she could not after all be part of the Canadian delegation to the first meeting of the Institute of Pacific

Relations in Kyoto in October when the main subject was to be the growing tension between Japan and China.[49]

It was the beginning of March 1930 when Caroline began the journey back to Tokyo. Stopping for a few days in Vancouver, she spoke to gatherings of United Church and Presbyterian women about her work and was pleased to meet Mary Ellen Smith, the first woman to sit in the legislature of British Columbia and the first woman cabinet minister in the British Empire. Although Smith was no longer a member of the legislature, she continued to advocate measures beneficial to women and children, a model, in Macdonald's view, of what women could do in public service.[50]

When the ship docked in Honolulu, Caroline was met by old friends J. Merle Davis, formerly of the YMCA in Tokyo, and his wife. Davis was now the secretary of the recently established Institute of Pacific Relations and had been responsible for organizing the institute's Kyoto conference. Davis believed that the gathering had been a success, mainly because the Chinese and Japanese delegates had discussed painful questions, especially Japan's objectives in Manchuria. However, Caroline was not convinced that she had missed much by not being among the twenty-nine Canadian delegates, nor was she surprised by Davis's opinion that 'Mr. Rowell was the cleverest of the Canadian delegation.'[51]

In early April 1930 Caroline was back in Tokyo 'to find the cherry blossoms already turning pink and "hard times" in full bloom' as Japan, along with the rest of the world, was hit by 'the Great Depression.'[52] The labour scene drew her immediate attention. Tokyo streetcar and bus drivers were off work for the second time in a few months, and a strike was beginning against the Tōyō Muslin Company, employer of thousands of workers in cotton factories throughout the country. Tōyō Muslin had always opposed the formation of unions among its employees, most of whom were, as usual, girls between the ages of fourteen and eighteen, living in company dormitories. When the company announced a 30 per cent reduction in wages that were already among the lowest in industry, the workers began to walk out. Macdonald had no sympathy for a company that 'calls itself *very* enlightened. They used to pay a 70% dividend until night work for women was abolished and they had to enlarge their plants so as to get the work all done during the daytime.' Now the company was apologizing to the stockholders because it could pay only 36 per cent, still a more-than-handsome profit on investment in her view.[53]

Although organized workers tried to help the unorganized employees of Tōyō Muslin, it was extremely difficult for the strikers to continue their protest, especially after many of them were expelled from their dormitories and had to seek refuge wherever they could find it. Several were given accommodation at Shinrinkan. On the invitation of the Women's Committee of Sōdōmei, Macdonald agreed to speak at a strikers' rally near one of the company's Tokyo factories but was spared the trouble when the police banned the meeting.[54] The strike was settled 'to the disadvantage of the workers as usual,' Macdonald reported, 'but with the lesson written large in the skies that unless workers organize ... they have no hope of redress.'[55]

That was precisely the message workers were drawing from their situation in the current depression, much to the surprise and alarm of employers. Due to growing unemployment the total work force was shrinking, but union membership was increasing to an all-time high of 7.9 per cent of wage earners. Slightly less than 1 per cent of women workers were organized but the dispute with Tōyō, which broke out again in the autumn of 1930 in a strike that lasted two months, encouraged textile workers to take a more active interest in unionization. The problem of organizing women workers was the subject of many meetings at Shinrinkan.[56]

Unionizing women workers was, of course, the long-term objective of Shinrinkan's labour night school for women, and Caroline was gratified that the school had flourished in her absence. Shinrinkan's educational program among women in the government clothing factory was now in its sixth year and still growing, with classes in a wide range of subjects. These women enjoyed more favourable working conditions than their sisters in textile factories: their employer, the government, had accepted their union for fifteen years and their wages were better than in comparable private companies. Moreover, they lived in their own homes and thus had far more freedom than women housed in dormitories. They had never gone on strike, a fact Macdonald thought should be edifying to the many employers who contended that unions *caused* strikes.[57]

Just before Macdonald's return to Japan, the country held its second general election since the institution of manhood suffrage and the Shakai Minshutō (Social Democrats) had run a slate of thirty-three candidates. Despite the more liberal atmosphere under the Hamaguchi government, police surveillance of this election was tighter than ever. Policemen often sat on election platforms behind the candidates, the better to make notes on 'dangerous thought.' When Katayama Tetsu attempted in a speech to distinguish his party as socialist, not Communist, the police interrupted to warn him that he must not mention either.[58] This time Matsuoka Komakichi was a candidate, but was defeated despite the priority given to his campaign by his Sōdōmei colleagues. Although she regretted Matsuoka's defeat, Macdonald did not think it a great calamity for 'his real work' was with the union movement.[59] Only Nishio Suehiro in Osaka and Katayama Tetsu in Tokyo were elected from the Shakai Minshutō.

Since the parties of the left no longer held the balance of power, many progressive bureaucrats now threw themselves behind the majority Minseitō government, a move they hoped would enhance the relatively liberal character of the Minseitō under Prime Minister Hamaguchi, a principled believer in party government.[60]

Macdonald's participation in the ILO meeting in Geneva increased her prestige as an interpreter of the labour movement and she was in demand as a speaker on that subject. To a number of organizations she gave a basic course on the structure of the ILO and where it was needed, an outline of the development of the Japanese labour movement, and the election of Social Democratic representatives to the Diet. Often she stressed the opportunity given to labour leaders by the ILO to plead their cause before the whole world. While employers clung to the status quo and government representatives were cautious, the workers could be 'agitators for reform.'[61]

Wherever she spoke on the ILO, Macdonald emphasized the distinctive and positive role played by Matsuoka Komakichi in Geneva, a role worthy of the world's expectations of Japan as the leading power in Asia. Sōdōmei leaders and the progressive bureaucrats in the Home Ministry could not have had a more sympathetic interpreter of their view of the labour movement and of their country, and to the extent that the opinions of a foreigner mattered, Macdonald was helping to further their objectives.

When discussing labour matters publicly, Macdonald, in accord with her status as a 'guest' in the country, made no specific mention of the labour legislation currently promoted by the government. Soon after it came to office, amid much rhetoric about the inevitability of recognizing unions and the need to ensure that they were 'moderate and orderly,'[62] the Hamaguchi cabinet appointed a Commission on Social Policy and charged it with preparing a labour union bill. The decidedly reformist bent of the members appointed to the commission was reinforced by the pro-labour views of officials of the Social Bureau. The result, 'the Social Bureau draft,' was more favourable to labour than any measures previously proposed by any government or opposition party. It gave legal status to unions while exempting them from liability for damages resulting from strike action, and made incorporation voluntary. At the same time, the government was given power to dissolve any union that violated its own rules or the law.[63]

Labour leaders, especially those in Sōdōmei, were inclined, Macdonald knew, 'to accept the bill without much change not because they think it is perfect but because they think it is a start.' Like them, Macdonald was apprehensive lest the bitter opposition of employers would lead to a weakened bill before it ever reached the Diet.[64] Already the 'Social Bureau draft' had been watered down by the elimination of a provision making collective agreements legally binding, and by the failure to include any monetary penalty for managers who refused to hire union members; instead, the bill merely declared that employers 'must not' discriminate against unionists.[65]

Hamaguchi and most of his cabinet supported the 'Social Bureau draft' and tried to convince the business community of the benefits of the legislation, arguing that it should accept 'a moderate union law' now rather than face demands for a stiffer one later after the proletarian parties might gain more power. The government was gradually forced to retreat before mounting opposition from large business and industrial interests that propagated the view that unions were especially destructive in a time of worsening depression. A severely divided labour movement was ineffectual in countering the attack on it. After months of dissension within the governing Minseitō party, the labour union bill passed the Lower House of the Diet only to be defeated in the House of Peers, where the leaders of industry were powerfully represented.[66]

Another bill that interested Caroline was one introduced in the Lower House of the Diet. The bill proposed giving the municipal vote to women over the age of twenty-five, but it made little progress in the face of conservative opinion. This was not a great loss, for as Macdonald observed, 'the advanced women' also opposed it because it did not confer the parliamentary franchise granted to males three years earlier and thus fell far short of giving women political equality. She remained confident that it was only a matter of time before both bills, improved in scope, would become law.[67] Her belief that these reforms would come before very long proved to be unfounded. Not until after the Second World War was another labour bill introduced, nor did women become voters until then. The defeat of these bills and other social measures marked the end of the period of 'Taishō reform,' although this was yet to be made manifest.

There were other signs that an era was ending. In November 1930, in the central railway station in Tokyo, Prime Minister Hamaguchi was shot by a member of an extreme nationalist group angered by Hamaguchi's support of the London Naval Treaty, which extended the limitations on armaments in the Washington Treaty of 1921. Ratification of the treaty was being resisted by the Privy Council and the navy. Like most of the press and the public, Macdonald saw Hamaguchi's stand against the Privy Council and his government's conciliatory policy toward China as expressions of reason and the progress of democracy.[68] Although Hamaguchi did not die for some months, his liberal reform movement was in retreat well before he was replaced in the spring of 1931.

Despite these setbacks for her friends and for the causes in which they and Caroline believed, she remained optimistic, confident that 'ideas are greater than men and the world moves forward.' Nevertheless, it would only move forward with strenuous effort, and not through mere expressions of piety. In Japan, as elsewhere, 'the Kingdom of God will not come, while poverty, unemployment and homelessness stalk the land, no matter how many evangelistic meetings we may carry on.'[69]

As in her early years, 'the Kingdom of God' was still central to Macdonald's theology. Always an image of a divine order whose character was revealed in the life of Christ, the vision changed somewhat during the course of her life. While retaining her conviction about the importance of individual reformation, the balance had shifted toward social transformation and the realization of 'the abundant life.' Despite the influence of Uemura Masahisa and his 'high' view of the church as the primary embodiment of the Kingdom of God, and of David Cairns's insistence on working at theology, Caroline's concern with doctrine was somewhat in decline. That did not mean that she had become a secular reformer, but only that the declaration of St. James that 'faith without works is dead' was the core of her theology.

Chapter 15

'Whether We Live or Whether We Die'

SOON AFTER HER RETURN TO TOKYO, Macdonald began to reorganize her work to resolve problems that had become acute before her departure for Geneva. The rapid growth of the services offered at Shinrinkan had made St. Andrew's House in Shiba too crowded for effective work and she decided to establish a second centre. Almost before she began to look, she learned of the availability of a suitable Japanese-style house at No. 7 Takagichō in Aoyama ward, away from the centre of the city not far from the Meiji shrine, and soon the house was rented. On the ground floor several rooms could be thrown together to make a good-sized meeting space, and there were living quarters for the Yamadas. The two rooms upstairs would be her own living space, where she could escape from activities more easily than at St Andrew's House. The Aoyama house was to become the centre for the prison work, and she would continue her personal work among prisoners from there. Yamada would now devote his full time to prisoners and ex-prisoners. Since he had conducted that side of the work so admirably in her absence, Caroline was confident that he could assume increasing responsibility. The educational work would remain at the St Andrew's centre, where the classrooms and residence were excellent. That work was to be directed by Tsuda Masao, who had lived at St Andrew's for a year and a half and had supervised activities there while Caroline was away. A graduate of Kyoto Imperial University, Tsuda had experience as a journalist, had worked for the ILO in Geneva for two years, and was now with the Bureau of Social Affairs in the Home Ministry. Caroline was hopeful that Tsuda would 'gather up some likeminded with himself and they will all help to enlarge our borders.'[1]

Her move to Aoyama, 'one of the *very* nice parts of town,' troubled Caroline's conscience slightly and required some justification in her own mind. 'I have no intention,' she told Peg, 'of living in the slums & have no desire to live like some of my ex-prisoner friends – I'd rather pull them up than pull myself down.' In addition to being pleasant, Aoyama was well located for all her work and this would save her time and energy.[2]

Within a few weeks the wisdom of Caroline's move was clear. Without responsibility for the detailed running of the settlement, there was more time for prison work, for factory girls, and for general educational work. She was also freer to accept speaking engagements. Among many, she gave an address at a settlement house run by the Tokyo municipal government on social conditions in Britain, another to 125 theological students on prisons, and to a large group of working men she explained the functioning of the British parliament and the rise of the Labour party. That summer of 1930 she was once more a leader at the annual YWCA conference, where she conducted daily discussions of social problems in Japan. She also devoted many hours to helping Judge Miyake Shōtarō write a pamphlet in English on the Japanese judicial and prison systems, which the Foreign Office was to distribute through the foreign embassies in Tokyo. 'The Foreign Office people all know,' Caroline observed, 'that I had more than a finger in the pie.' She was well pleased with both the content and the appearance of the printed pamphlet and sent off copies to several friends, including her cousin Jim (James A.) Macdonald, chief justice of British Columbia, with whom she had often discussed legal matters on her sojourns in Vancouver. At the same time she was working with Matsuoka on an English translation of an article he had written on labour and agriculture.[3]

Her new freedom also allowed her to 'keep up [her] end in the social whirl' better than at the settlement house where she had to 'be on dress parade every night at 6 p.m.' when the classes of the labour school and other activities began. Now she was able to accept more invitations to embassy parties and other social events. She even gave the occasional dinner party such as one to celebrate the birth of a son to Judge Miyake and his wife, and another for the Matsuokas to meet members of the board of Shinrinkan, perhaps to show them that the head of Sōdōmei was not a raging radical.[4]

When the house was well used she rejoiced, reassured that it served objectives other than her own need for privacy and time to herself. As always, she was never happier than when some 'democratic' social situation developed, such as the evening when Judge Miyake came to mimeograph some university lectures he was to give. With Yamada running the machine, the two men were an odd-looking pair, since Yamada was nearly a foot shorter than the unusually tall, six-foot judge. They 'talked and laughed away like the two pals they are' until nearly midnight when Caroline sat down with them for tea and cake.[5]

The usual procession of ex-prisoners, wives of prisoners, students, and others soon found their way to the new Aoyama house. Students especially were feeling the government's application of the Peace Preservation Law as a response to popular discontent, and there were many arrests. The government, in Macdonald's opinion, was 'busy making young men into criminals by arresting them for what they call "dangerous thought."' Such was a young man whom she had never met before, who visited her after serving eight months in jail on a charge of lèse-majesté. His father, a juvenile court judge well known to Macdonald, had refused to have anything to do with his son after his release, and thus the student appealed to her to help him go to a friend in the country where he could find employment. At first she was doubtful about the truth of the young man's story about his father's attitude, but once convinced she gave him money to speed him on his way, thinking that if she 'were a father in this country I should feel quite distinguished to have a son with any kind of thoughts (instead of none) even if they were a bit dangerous. Most of the young people who are thinking at all have dangerous thoughts. Any thought at all is dangerous according to the present police regulations!'[6]

In addition to a change in residence, another move increased Caroline's efficiency when she acted on the offer of C.L. Burton of Simpsons in Toronto to buy a new car of her choosing. On the recommendation of friends in the British embassy who declared it to be the best small car on the market, despite its French origins, she chose a Citroën and was soon logging 1,600 kilometres a month mainly in moving from one prison to another.[7]

Caroline had a good reason for trying to make more time for herself. She wanted to write about her twenty-five years in Japan, 'not entirely for love or to edify the world ... but for *filthy lucre* ... to make a nest-egg for my old age,' she told Galen and Ella Fisher. She was uncertain that her observations would sell well, but she was disposed to accept the invitation of the SCM Press in Britain to write about the labour movement in Japan. Whatever she wrote, she thought it should appear first in magazines, but emphatically not in religious magazines. Ten years after the publication of *A Gentleman in Prison*, she felt that the book had been hidden away among religious and theological literature, and thus had not made the impact or the income she had anticipated. She agreed that the book was 'religious,' but for that very reason it was unfortunate that it had been labelled in a way that restricted its readership. Many times she had found 'religious people' saying blandly to her: 'I enjoyed your book very much.' The 'non-religious' said: 'Gosh! I didn't sleep a wink last night until I got that book finished!' Somehow any future writing must be rescued from being labelled 'religious' if she were to have influence and an income.[8]

■ ■ ■

A RECENT BUT MINOR CHANGE in the 'Cosmos' interested Macdonald greatly. During her absence, Canada had established diplomatic relations with Japan, making Canadians slightly more visible in Tokyo and less likely to be lumped together with Americans than before. Macdonald was pleased to add her name to those of the 150 or so Canadian residents in Japan, a majority of them missionaries, who had registered since Dominion Day, 1 July 1929, when the Red Ensign was first hoisted on the flagpole of the grounds of the temporary legation while a record of 'O Canada' was played.[9] The major concern of the first Canadian diplomatic post in Asia was trade, with matters relating to immigration of Japanese to Canada a secondary interest. As its first minister, the Canadian government appointed Herbert Marler, a wealthy Montreal notary and former Liberal cabinet minister, who proceeded to magnify the significance of his office and himself to the utmost. In this effort he was ably assisted by his wife, a member of the Allan family of Montreal shipping magnates. Beatrice Marler soon decided that

Macdonald was important enough to be invited to lunch, and later to other social events at the legation. This was not an especially select group, since the Marlers entertained more than 2,500 guests in their home during their first year in Tokyo.[10] Caroline reported to Peg that the Marlers were both 'quite fascinating' and 'she's tremendously handsome,' observing with some disapproval that the minister's open dislike of Japanese food limited his participation in Tokyo society.[11] The Marlers' pomposity, their lack of a sense of humour and proportion, Beatrice Marler's ignorance of the world around her, characteristics that alternately amused or offended members of the diplomatic community and the staff of the legation, were apparently not so evident to Caroline.[12]

When Canadians were invited to call on the minister and Mrs. Marler on 1 July 1930, Macdonald and Emma Kaufman were among the small group asked for dinner after the reception. With her old black evening dress renovated and her hair done by a hairdresser for the occasion, Caroline remarked sardonically that she supposed she would look as if she had 'stepped out of a Paris shop.'[13] After a few months of further observation, she reported that the 'indefatigable' Marlers were making 'everyone sit up and take notice. The Americans are quite in the shade & some of them don't fail to show it – "No need for the eagle to scream anymore since the Canadian legation came" they say. I always laugh & say "Oh well, I should think the eagle's throat would be a bit sore anyway so you ought to be thankful for a rest!!" They don't get any rise out of me.'[14] More than twenty-five years of association with the foreign community in Tokyo where Americans were by far the dominant element had done nothing to weaken her sense of being Canadian.[15]

For Caroline the most personal consequence of the opening of the Canadian legation was her easy friendship with the first secretary, Hugh Keenleyside and his wife, Katharine. Both graduates of the University of British Columbia, Katharine had done graduate work in dietetics and social work at Simmons College in Boston, while he had acquired a doctorate in history from Clark University and enjoyed a brief academic career before joining Canada's expanding Department of External Affairs in 1928. Caroline quickly developed a rapport with the young Keenleysides, who found her a stimulating guide to life in Japan. They were often visitors in one another's homes, where they enjoyed lively discussions of social and political issues, both local and international.[16] Hugh and Katharine Keenleyside were both cut from much the same Protestant social gospel 'cloth' as Caroline, and they were soon her strong admirers. In Hugh Keenleyside's eyes, Caroline was 'a truly astonishing woman,' one of the most remarkable people he had ever met.[17]

There were departures as well as arrivals that affected Caroline's circle of friends. Over several years she had seen a good deal of Hugh Byas, a Scot who was Tokyo correspondent for the *Times* of London and the *New York Times*, and his wife. Caroline valued their knowledge and understanding of Japan, and the intellectual capacity and enormous energy that had made Byas an authority on Far Eastern affairs, while they appreciated her sharp mind and her work. The announcement of their departure from Japan in the spring of 1930 was widely lamented, not least by Caroline, who attended several parties given by diplomats and journalists in their honour. Caroline was cheered by her conviction that the Byases would return before very long. Like herself, 'they could no more stay away from Japan than live on the moon.'[18]

■ ■ ■

CHANGE WAS THE ORDER OF THE DAY and Caroline was no longer a member of the Fujimichō church. After the death of Uemura Masahisa, the Fujimichō congregation was torn by controversy. A substantial group in the congregation, including Macdonald and Tagawa Daikichirō, wanted Takakura Tokutarō, Uemura's successor as principal of the Japan Theological Seminary, to be their minister.

Takakura was intellectually and spiritually the protégé of Uemura. While a student of law at Tokyo Imperial University, he had been baptized by Uemura in Fujimichō church and later studied theology in Uemura's seminary. After serving as a minister in several congregations and studying theology intermittently in Britain, he returned to Tokyo to teach in the seminary and founded a small congregation that met in his house in the Toyama district.

When the majority in the Fujimichō congregation behaved in what the minority perceived as a highly undemocratic manner by expressing their opposition to the calling of Takakura and insisting on the Reverend Miyoshi Tsutomu as their minister, some one hundred members, including Macdonald, left in 1927 to join Takakura in the Toyama church. This enlarged congregation, far too big for Takakura's house, continued to expand and to plan for a new church. Macdonald remained an elder in the dissident congregation and served as a member of the building committee for the new Shinanomachi church, which was dedicated in the spring of 1930.[19] As a gesture of friendship between Canada and Japan, and to honour a distinguished countrywoman, the only foreigner in the congregation, Ambassador Marler and Dr. Keenleyside presented the church with a silver communion service.[20]

That Caroline should join the Shinanomachi congregation was scarcely surprising. Her increasing emphasis on a gospel of social action did not mean that she thought theology unimportant, although she sometimes thought that theologians quibbled over nonessentials. As the most scholarly and systematic theologian to emerge from Japanese Protestantism, Takakura Tokutarō had a strong appeal to intellectuals. Widely read in European theology from Schleiermacher and other liberal German thinkers to the currently influential Emil Brunner and Karl Barth, he was primarily responsible for introducing the new 'dialectical theology' to Japan, but stopped short of adopting 'neo-orthodoxy.' Takakura's major mentors remained the Scottish theologians P.T. Forsyth and H.R. Mackintosh, contemporaries of David Cairns, and whose work was well known to Macdonald. Takakura rejected theological liberalism as represented in Japan by Ebina Danjō and his successors, but his biblical scholarship also set him apart from conservative evangelicals. Planted firmly in the mainstream of Protestant Christian thought, Takakura was to Macdonald and many others the logical successor to Uemura Masahisa.[21]

Caroline continued to carry on an intermittent correspondence with David Cairns on theological and other matters. In the summer of 1930, Cairns was preoccupied with preparation for the Baird Lectures he was to give at the University of Edinburgh. He had chosen 'a grandiose subject, the one great central problem in every human life, the problem of evil that all religions and philosophies ... attempt to grapple with.' He wanted to show 'that every one of the great truths of the Bible has been revealed (or discovered) relative to some phase of that problem.' Cairns was not sure his former star theological student would be enthusiastic about his project, for in their recent correspondence she had expressed an uncharacteristic impatience with the constant rethinking of Christian doctrine by theologians, and had argued that 'faith' and 'doctrine' must not be confused: many Christians who could not articulate any doctrine had faith, and expressed it in their lives. In response, Cairns contended for the practicality of theological formulations, asserting that he and Caroline were not disagreeing, since 'a doctrine is just a faith realized & made clear, & definitely related to some enduring need.'[22] He was 'troubled by the lack of *teaching* in Christian preaching to-day' when 'the scientific view is being taught everywhere as if it were a complete account of human life ... to say nothing of the Marxian & the Roman Catholic systems of dogma.' He kept working in the hope that 'we poor theorists,' lagging behind people like Macdonald who were engaged in practical tasks, 'could make the outlook a bit more coherent and up to date.'[23] Whether Cairns convinced Macdonald of the validity of his enterprise or not, he continued to appreciate her letters for their 'pleasant combativeness,' as well as for what North Americans called 'inspirational power, which seems to demand that one should immediately carry on the conversation!'[24]

■ ■ ■

MOST OF CAROLINE'S ENERGY continued to be expended in practical ways, especially in work with prisoners. The continuing depression made life more difficult than ever for ex-prisoners and their dependents. With increasing unemployment, 'the first person to be refused work or to lose his job is the man who has been in prison.'[25] While ex-prisoners and their families were still its first concern, during the winter of 1930-1 Shinrinkan provided temporary shelter for homeless men to the maximum of its capacity and gave work to nearly 2,000 by supplying them with small items they could peddle to earn their food while looking for a real job.[26]

Although the lot of some women was improved by the depression, since they were cheaper as factory workers and often kept their jobs when men were laid off, this was 'not a matter for congratulation but the reverse,' in Macdonald's view. Other women, including college graduates, were hit hard, since there were few teaching jobs now, and therefore enrolments in women's colleges were plummeting.[27]

In recent years Macdonald had interested members of the board of Shinrinkan in the possibility of establishing a farm for men just out of prison who had nowhere to go and no work, and all too often quickly fell into their old ways. In a country not very advanced in the rehabilitation of prisoners, she hoped the farm would become a model for other agencies. Her board shared her enthusiasm and wanted to proceed despite the difficulties of starting a new venture in such a difficult economic climate. During her recent sojourn in Canada, she had visited the prison farm run by the Ontario government at Guelph and had been favourably impressed. Now she was beginning to study the varieties of agriculture in Japan, including poultry and animal husbandry, to find an activity that would provide work and new skills to ex-prisoners and revenue for the running of the farm. She had already secured the interest of a senior official in the Department of Agriculture who promised to put her in touch with agricultural specialists who could advise on her project.[28]

The maintenance of the existing work, to say nothing of any new venture, required funds. Caroline was delighted when the Tokyo Amateur Dramatic Society, which regularly donated the proceeds from its productions to a charity, announced that this year it would support Shinrinkan. Two performances of Ernest Denny's comedy *Vanity*, in the auditorium of the Imperial Hotel, could be expected to raise about 1,500 yen. Caroline's confidence that 'everyone in the town will help, as I've never asked the community for anything,' proved to be justified. Mrs. Fleisher, wife of the owner of the *Japan Advertiser*, 'the most international figure in Tokyo,' agreed to chair the organizing committee. Before long, with the help of the Baroness de Bassompierre, wife of the Belgian ambassador, an impressive list of diplomats and their wives had agreed to lend their patronage to the event.[29]

The eighteen-page program for the performances was financed by advertisements from several Japanese companies and by Canadian firms doing business in Japan. A description of Macdonald's prison work noted that this was 'a field which other foreign charitable enterprises do not enter,' and concluded with an impressive statistical report covering the previous five years. This was also an opportunity to advertise *A Gentleman in Prison*, now in its third English edition, and available in six other languages.[30] In addition to giving Shinrinkan excellent publicity, the enterprise brought in over 3,800 yen, more than double the amount Caroline had hoped to make.[31]

■ ■ ■

WHILE PURSUING HER NEW PROJECT for the rehabilitation farm, Caroline reflected on her more than twenty-five years in Japan. In an address to new missionaries attending language school, she asked: 'Why do we leave our native lands and come to a perfectly unknown one to spend the best part of our lives ... among those for whom we have no special responsibility unless we ... assume it on our own?' To do that, many believed, was 'a most preposterous act [but] whatever may have been our reasons ... we have no reason to suppose that we have done anything specially worthy.' Although it required 'a certain spirit of adventure ... no special courage was needed to come to a country like Japan and live in the midst of another civilized people.' Altogether, Caroline declared: 'We may consider ourselves fortunate that a Committee at home could be found deluded enough to pay our fares and our salaries to give us a chance to live and work in a foreign land and in one of the world's great cities.'[32]

Macdonald had several pieces of advice to give the newcomers. The first was to realize that the cure for nostalgia and homesickness was 'to transfer our spiritual allegiance to the land in which we live' and to develop an 'international mind' that refused to make judgments on those different from themselves. 'We are here to improve and we begin to look for the flaws and the faults. We criticize and decry and deplore instead of understanding and appreciating. But for the mending of flaws we have no real responsibility. In our own country we are obliged to assume responsibility.' Long ago she had made up her mind that outside Japan she would 'never ... emphasize the differences between ourselves and the Japanese, but only our likenesses ... We who call ourselves Christians have no reason for talking about the differences among us. Any fool can see the differences. It takes a loving heart and a well balanced head to see that we are all one. The likenesses are fundamental, the differences are superficial.'[33]

She pleaded with the new missionaries not to be influenced by advisors who would find all sorts of reasons why they need not devote much energy to learning Japanese. 'We shall always be strangers in a strange land,' but there was no reason to remain even more of a stranger through failure to learn the language, even if it was the most difficult in the world. 'Don't give your Japanese friends a chance to think you are a fool because you cannot learn their language. They can learn yours.'[34]

Then she warned her listeners to beware of developing a 'statistical mind.' Although she had collected a good many statistics, they 'prove nothing except that they are the most unreliable authority extant.' As an example, she cited recent newspaper reports that Japan was suffering from a crime wave. In her view, these reports only showed that the 'police officers have had a wave of diligence' and that the size of the population was increasing. In actual fact, despite the depression, serious crime in Japan was decreasing significantly. This was but one instance where the received wisdom must be questioned. 'Don't take ready made opinions from your elders and presumably betters,' including those who were well established in their respective missions: 'You have come with new methods of education, with new ideas of life. Don't you let us old fogies entirely command the situation ... The Christ we teach is not the Christ of the first century but of the 20th.'[35]

Caroline's final exhortation to the recent arrivals was to 'cultivate, preserve, treasure and keep alive your God given sense of humour. If you are devoid of that virtue take the next boat out of Yokohama.' An infallible test for a sense of humour was 'Can you make a joke at your own expense, can you ridicule yourself in private as easily as you can ridicule others?'[36]

On the whole, Caroline Macdonald had lived by the precepts she taught. In their early encounters with Japan, westerners, including many missionaries, had emphasized the exotic and the unusual in the domain of the Mikado. By Macdonald's time there was more stress on the similarities, and even on aspects of the society that were 'superior.' Macdonald was not unique in her acceptance of much of Japanese culture, although she went far beyond most missionaries in stressing the 'superficiality' of differences. This attitude was, in part, related to her mastery of the Japanese language, which enabled her to 'think Japanese' to an extent unusual in a foreigner. The degree of her proficiency in spoken Japanese led some to say that 'if you closed your eyes, you wouldn't know the difference.'[37] Her determined effort to read and write the language with equal competence, while not realized, was further evidence of her identification with her adopted country.

■ ■ ■

EARLY IN 1931 Caroline began to suffer from frequent headaches and then from a persistent cough and wheezing, but she failed to heed the advice of her physician, Dr. Ikeda, to slow down. When her symptoms suddenly became worse, Emma Kaufman persuaded her to enter St. Luke's Hospital. After three weeks of observation and tests the diagnosis was a dismal one: she had a malignant growth on one of her lungs and it could not be treated. In the face of this news, her strongest desire was to see her family again and she decided to return to Canada. Fortunately, Emma Kaufman was to sail for Vancouver in a few days in the company of a Japanese member of the YWCA staff, who gave up her passage on the *Empress of Japan* so that Caroline could go home with Emma. Few of Caroline's Tokyo friends knew the seriousness of her illness, and there was little time for farewells. Yamada

Zen'ichi, whose crime had given shape to the last seventeen years of Caroline's life, came to the hospital tearfully, still seeing himself as the one lost sheep for whose salvation she had left the other ninety-nine. Tagawa Daikichirō was there to tell her that even among Japanese he never had so good a friend. A grief-stricken Matsuoka Komakichi and his wife, Katsuya, rushed to her bedside just before her departure, and Judge Miyake Shōtarō came to receive power of attorney in the affairs of Shinrinkan.[38]

Macdonald and Kaufman had each crossed the Pacific several times but never together until this sad journey. A few days in the Vancouver General Hospital confirmed the diagnosis of lung cancer. At the most, Caroline could expect to live for a year, suffering increasing and severe pain. 'She was wonderful in the way she took it,' Emma said, 'and her first thought was the burden she would be to her family, and to other people.'[39] Now the words she had so often repeated with men on death row had new meaning: 'Whether we live or whether we die, we are the Lord's.' At the end of their long train journey across Canada, Emma left Caroline with Peg and their mother in London, where Caroline was soon admitted to Victoria Hospital. In an unusual expression of appreciation by the Japanese government, an official from the Japanese embassy in Ottawa came to London bringing to her bedside a silver vase and a letter from the ministers of Foreign Affairs, Justice, and Home Affairs, thanking her for her contributions to their country.[40] Contrary to Caroline's fears, she was not a burden to anyone for long, since her condition grew worse rapidly. She died three months short of her fifty-seventh birthday, on 17 July, just seven weeks after leaving Tokyo. Her ninety-year-old mother, no longer quite in the world, could not grasp her daughter's death, but it was all too real for Peg and her sister Nell. The funeral service in the Wingham Presbyterian Church was 'officially Presbyterian,' conducted by several ministers of Maitland Presbytery. The Reverend A.E. Armstrong, representing the United Church of Canada, led some of the prayers. Caroline would have appreciated the humorous aspect of Armstrong's participation, with whom she had recently had a heated, even vitriolic, correspondence on her relationship to the United Church.[41] She might also have regretted that there was only one woman participant, Bessie MacMurchy, secretary of the Presbyterian WMS.[42] Caroline was buried beside her father in Wingham Cemetery, the only inscription, 'Caroline Macdonald of Japan 1874-1931.'

In Tokyo ten days later, nearly a thousand people overflowed

Shinanomachi church for a memorial service conducted by Macdonald's friend Tagawa Daikichirō, chairman of the board of Shinrinkan, a fellow elder, and president of Meiji Gakuin. Tagawa was assisted by two ministers of the Presbyterian church of Japan. The women spinners' section of Sōdōmei was represented by Funazuka Yoshiko, and many other trade union leaders were present. The mourners represented all classes from the Vice-Minister of Foreign Affairs, Nagai Matsuzō, to numerous ex-convicts. At the front of the church, in accord with Japanese custom, stood a large photograph of Macdonald in her Doctor of Laws gown, banked on either side with flowers, including two large wreaths from prisoners she had helped.[43] The governor of Kosuge prison, Yoshida Ritsu, placed before the photograph more than fifty letters written to Macdonald by inmates; then he addressed her spirit:

> You, a woman of culture and taste, left your faraway country to bring comfort and love to prisoners, the outcasts of society! You brought the word of God to these unfortunate ones, not as one performing a duty, but as a mother talking with her children ... At this moment, there are one hundred and thirty-two men in Kosuge who have been directly under your influence ... Only God and perhaps the Governor of Kosuge can know what expenditure of thought and vital force was needed for this stupendous labour of love ... You have been taken from us, but we are certain that the seed you have so patiently and lovingly planted in the hearts of the men of Kosuge, will grow and bear fruit, so be content with the labour you have performed so well.[44]

Dr. Motoji Shinkuma of the Department of Justice offered an appreciation of her work, as did representatives of other branches of the government. The Reverend D.R. McKenzie of the United Church of Canada, the senior Canadian missionary in Japan, spoke of her unusual capacities as a missionary, to intellectuals on the one hand and to the humblest of prisoners on the other. Tagawa Daikichirō emphasized her qualities as a friend and her role in converting many Christians to socialism; she was, he declared, a 'leader of Christian socialism' in Japan.[45]

Among the mourners at the memorial service were Hugh and Katharine Keenleyside. Since the Marlers were in Canada, Keenleyside represented the Canadian legation, but he was also there as a friend. Although they had known Caroline for only two years, the Keenleysides could recall no death that had touched them so deeply.[46] It was not just that Macdonald's work with prisoners was 'unparalleled in the social service records of Japan,' or that she was 'the most distinguished foreign woman in the country' and had 'done more than can be imagined to secure the goodwill of the Japanese people toward foreigners,' nor yet that she had added lustre to Canada's name. What impressed Hugh Keenleyside most was that while organizing and directing the work of others she had herself lived and worked 'among the very lowest classes of the community' and that 'there is not the faintest trace of self-advertisement in the whole of her career.'[47]

Later, other Canadians paid tribute to Macdonald when her graduating class of 1901 arranged a memorial service in the chapel of Knox College at the University of Toronto. Her friends enlisted the well-known oratorical talents of an admirer, N.W. Rowell, who delivered a eulogy based on an informed knowledge of her character and work, and on his own interest in foreign missions and international affairs. After describing her career and achievements, Rowell tried to discern the qualities that made her life so effective, finding first 'an unconquerable faith in God' and in 'the spark of goodness' in every human being. Added to her 'strong and vigorous intellect' and the courage to move in new directions was her genius for making and keeping friends, close to home and around the world. Not least among Macdonald's qualities, in Rowell's view, was her 'unfailing and saving sense of humour' which prevented her from being discouraged or despondent even in the face of the most sordid aspects of life.[48]

It was not only in Tokyo and Toronto that Macdonald's life was praised. The *Times* of London and the *New York Times* carried reports of her death, both emphasizing her remarkable influence among the lowliest members of Japanese society.[49] The religious press, her former YWCA and WSCF colleagues, and fellow missionaries joined in tributes, most of which stressed that the fruits of Macdonald's Christian faith had been made available to the world through a rare combination of intelligence, a gift for friendship, and an irrepressible sense of humour.[50] Caroline's old colleague in the YWCA, Ruth Rouse, who had observed missionaries in dozens of countries for over twenty-five years during the course of her travels on behalf of the WSCF, wrote to David Cairns that their friend 'was a really great missionary. Perhaps the greatest that you and I will ever know.'[51]

Soon after Caroline's death, her sister Peg had cabled the news to Cairns in Aberdeen. In reply Cairns wrote at length about his vivid memories of her in Aberdeen, Tokyo, and London and of his visit with her family. He still believed that Macdonald was 'the most distinguished student our college had during my time. That was only one of many reasons why she stood out as one of the finest and most remarkable women I have ever known,' one whose life was 'a great invitation to courage, hope, and faith.'[52] If he had ever been aware that her feeling for him had gone beyond admiration, he did not betray it now.

No one was better able to assess Macdonald's character and work from firsthand experience than the prison governor with whom she had worked most closely, Arima Shirosuke. Reflecting on her life, Arima asked questions that puzzled Macdonald's contemporaries and must engage anyone who contemplates her career.[53]

Arima found it easy to understand why a person would help relatives and close friends, although sympathy usually turned to anger if the relative or friend became a criminal. But why would a foreign woman who had no tie with criminals want to help men 'on whom their own countrymen had turned their backs, and whom most of us feared as if they were snakes, serpents, or savage beasts?' Yet Macdonald 'had *chosen* to be the friend of villains,' including those condemned to die. 'At first sight, her conduct seemed that of an insane person, but she had a plan which she executed resolutely and bravely with flaming passion.' Thus she had become the only woman ever allowed to visit regularly in the men's wards of Japanese prisons. Arima went so far as to assert that the service of this 'delicate woman' among the outcasts of a foreign country was 'unprecedented in world history.'

Arima found it almost impossible to explain the intensity of Macdonald's identification with the Japanese people. Why did she understand and love Japanese so much, to the extent that she became a 'Japanese patriot,' eager to increase Japan's reputation in the world? Arima believed that the inclusiveness of Macdonald's sympathies was rooted in her absolute conviction that every human being was a child of God. So sincerely did she hold this truth that it was the very essence of her being, enabling her to 'practice her faith effortlessly' in a manner that placed her 'beyond every prejudice' of religion, race, or class. Everyone she encountered responded to this openness by listening to what she had to say and continued to listen when it became apparent that there was no contradiction between her words and her actions. It was this congruence, evident every day, that 'amazed all of us who were near her.'

As a progressive prison official, although now retired, Arima was greatly interested in Macdonald's methods as a social worker, especially in the consequences of her belief that social reform began with the salvation of the individual. Arima knew social workers who abandoned clients they deemed a nuisance or threatening to the 'success' of their work. Macdonald's belief in the worth of every person and her conviction that 'to save one soul is a step toward saving the whole world' prevented her from sacrificing the individual for the sake of any enterprise or institution. Although Macdonald's primary objective was the conversion of individual souls, bringing them into 'eternal life,' Arima believed that she worked harder than other social workers to meet the material needs of those she served. No one would ever know how much she had spent from her own pocket to assist discharged prisoners and their families who needed food, clothing, shelter, or train fares, for she 'did good by stealth and left no record.'

For Arima, questions about Macdonald's motivation and methods were not simply academic or theoretical. Rather, to understand the spirit of 'our comrade and good companion' was a practical matter for social workers who wanted their labours to be effective. Arima believed that Macdonald's style of life flowed from 'a pure heart,' enabling her to live in a disinterested and unselfish manner. He found many New Testament phrases to describe his friend's spirit, the expression of 'the heart of Jesus,' a love that led her to spend her life for her friends. Her perseverance in good works was, he knew, sustained by the faith that God would give her the strength necessary to do His will, and therefore she did not worry. In the eyes of Arima Shirosuke, at least, Caroline Macdonald was 'a heart at leisure from itself.'

Epilogue

Two months after Caroline Macdonald's death, on 18 September 1931, the Japanese army invaded Manchuria and a new era in Japanese history began. There was little criticism of 'the Manchurian incident' among Japanese for the move was widely seen as simply a rationalization of a de facto authority exercised by Japan ever since the Sino-Japanese war of 1894. Most of the nation was caught up in a wave of patriotic euphoria. The outside world viewed matters differently. When the League of Nations condemned the aggression, Japan withdrew from the League, effectively isolating the nation from the international community into which it had been moving for the past two decades.

Among the several people with whom Macdonald had discussed international affairs from the time of her arrival in Japan, none was more prominent than Dr. Nitobe Inazō. Nitobe's experience as under-secretary of the League of Nations, his leadership of Japan's participation in the Institute of Pacific Relations, and his Quaker associations had made him Japan's best-known internationalist. At the same time, Nitobe was identified with Japanese colonialism. As a civil servant in Formosa (Taiwan) just after the turn of the century, he had used his training in agricultural science to develop the sugar industry there. More recently, as a professor at Tokyo Imperial University, he had specialized in colonial studies, emphasizing the economic and humanitarian benefits conferred by Japanese expansion. At the conference of the Institute of Pacific Relations in Shanghai in the spring of 1931 Nitobe defended his country's expansionist designs on China. A few months later he made no public condemnation of the movement of the Japanese military into Manchuria. Nitobe's commitment to the peaceful settlement of disputes came into sharp conflict with his patriotism, and with his wish to maintain his influence with those in power. During a trip to North America in 1933, undertaken to explain Japanese policies to increasingly unsympathetic audiences, he was rescued from his dilemma when he died in Victoria, British Columbia.[1] Many other Japanese in the circles in which Caroline had moved faced an intensification of their crises of loyalties.

Less than a year after the invasion of Manchuria, party government ended when Prime Minister Inukai Tsuyoshi was assassinated and the Bank of Japan was bombed by a group of army and navy officers. Japan's military leaders gradually assumed control of every aspect of the state. Elections were still fought by contending parties and the country was ostensibly ruled by cabinets headed by a prime minister, but parliament's power was steadily declining. Until the end of the war, Japan was ruled by a succession of 'national unity' cabinets headed by military men or their collaborators. Both the Seiyūkai and Minseitō parties adopted resolutions sharply rebuking the military, but their resistance was soon dissipated by internal dissension and the terrorist tactics of the military and its civilian sympathizers. A sign of the times was the suppression in 1935 of the works of Minobe Tatsukichi of Tokyo University and his expulsion from the House of Peers. Minobe, the leading theorist of parliamentary democracy, had long expounded the view that the emperor was an 'organ' of government rather than the divine source of all authority. Now he was charged with lèse majesté.[2]

These were increasingly difficult times for social democrats and for Christians, and for anyone who criticized government policy. Yanaihara Tadao, professor of colonial policy in Tokyo University and one of the most distinguished disciples of Uchimura Kanzō, was forced to resign from the faculty for his criticism of government policy toward China. Another

Christian, Yanaihara's academic senior, Nambara Shigeru, was forced out of the university because of his opposition to the government's promotion of nationalism as the only religion acceptable to the state.[3]

After the outbreak of full-scale war against China in the summer of 1937, the military quickly became the dominant element in government, industry, education, and religion. All Christians, whether prominent in public life or not, were under enormous pressures. Their claims to the universality of their faith, their international ties, and their long-standing public advocacy of peace, all made it more difficult than ever to achieve acceptance as patriotic Japanese. Gradually the vast majority did as most Christians in many times and places have done in similar circumstances: they acquiesced in government direction. They nourished the inner life of the churches and their families in a manner for which they had been well prepared by most of the missionaries, but as the war progressed and the whole nation became absorbed in it, the regular institutional life of the churches suffered. Many Christians were just too busy to give time to their churches, and Sundays often had to be devoted to patriotic activities. The National Council of Churches and the governing bodies of nearly all the denominations passed patriotic resolutions pledging full support to the Spiritual Mobilization Movement to promote national goals, and to the movement for Spiritual Awakening, devoted to the patriotic indoctrination of public school students. The powerful Indoctrination Bureau of the Ministry of Education gave detailed attention to the churches and their schools to ensure this resolve never faltered.[4]

Although most Christians supported the war, some did not. Among the 16,000 persons imprisoned during the conflict on suspicion of disloyalty many were Christians. They included 150 ministers of two branches of the Holiness Church, whose belief in the second coming of Christ involved a judgment on the emperor. Seventh Day Adventists had their property confiscated and their organization dissolved, and Jehovah's Witnesses also suffered. Eleven members of the Anglican-Episcopal Church were arrested and three bishops spent some months in jail, while Kagawa Toyohiko received much attention from police and was twice arrested for his peace sentiments, but released on suspended sentence.[5]

Under pressure from a government intent on controlling the churches efficiently, the Protestant denominations were forced to unite and the *Nihon Kirisuto Kyōdan* (United Church of Christ in Japan) was formally constituted in Fujimichō church in the early summer of 1941. The Anglican-Episcopal Church officially refused to enter the union, although about one-third of its members did join. Many Protestants had been working toward union for years, but they had little control over the structure of the new Kyōdan. While it enjoyed some flexibility in practice at local levels, the new Protestant church was in principle authoritarian, with all power given to a director accountable to the Ministry of Education.[6] Through the church, the army-directed Greater East Asia Ministry controlled Christian missions throughout the expanding empire. In this work, vigorous leadership was given by Caroline Macdonald's old friend in Fujimichō church, General Hibiki Nobusuke, who had directed Japanese missionary work in Manchuria during the decade since his retirement. In many parts of the empire, Kyōdan members and other Christians were agents of the 'pacification' efforts of their conquering nation.[7]

The churches were under increasing criticism for their connections with foreigners, and by 1940, on the advice of mission boards and embassies in Tokyo, an exodus of missionaries was well under way. When Japan attacked Pearl Harbour on 6 December 1941 and thus precipitated war with the United States, few remained. Most of those, Americans and the few remaining Canadians, were soon repatriated. For the first time in its history, Japanese Protestantism was led entirely by Japanese.[8]

■ ■ ■

WHEN CAROLINE MACDONALD and Emma Kaufman were together for the last time in the summer of 1931 in the hospital in London, Caroline had asked Kaufman to assure the leaders of the WMS of both the United and Presbyterian churches that the Tokyo prison work would continue after her death under the Shinrinkan board and Yamada Zen'ichi. She also stressed that support from Canada was still needed.[9] Kaufman assumed considerable responsibility for the future of Caroline's work and supported it herself, morally and financially, for the next decade. Following her return to Tokyo at the end of the summer of 1931, Kaufman enlisted the support of the Council of the Japan WMS, which, like Kaufman, was well impressed with the way Yamada had carried on the work since Macdonald's departure.[10] This, and the devotion of core members of the Shinrinkan board, notably Tagawa Daikichirō, Shidachi Tsunejirō, Judge Miyake Shōtarō, Miss Hoshino Ai, principal of Tsuda College, and Dr. Uzawa Fusaaki, gave the

WMS confidence that the enterprise could be maintained.[11] In retirement, Governor Arima Shirosuke gave what support he could to Shinrinkan until his death in 1934. His son, Shirō, of whom Caroline had such high hopes, then became superintendent of Yokohama Katei Gakuin, the reformatory founded by his father.

Everyone agreed it was impossible even to think of finding a successor to Macdonald, for as the WMS missionaries declared, 'hers was a unique personality and no one can do her work.' The settlement house work would have to be dropped. Yamada Zen'ichi would carry on the work with prisoners in his own way, including assistance to ex-prisoners in finding employment and rehabilitation. Regrettably, without Macdonald's vision and drive it would be impossible to find the resources for the rehabilitation farm she had hoped to establish, and that plan was abandoned.[12]

In 1932 the WMS of the United Church forwarded $1,500 for the support of Shinrinkan, but in subsequent years the amount was cut to $437.50. The reasons for this are unclear but may be connected with the impact of the depression on the WMS budget, or with declining expenses after 1935 when Shinrinkan moved from St. Andrew's House to a smaller property in the Shinjuku district of Tokyo. Yamada continued an active program, reporting in 1934-5 that more than 3,000 services had been provided to prisoners, plus over 1,000 more to ex-prisoners.[13] After the outbreak of war with China the reports of the prison work became briefer and less detailed, but the WMS continued an annual grant, estimated at $350 for 1941.[14] Subsequently, Shinrinkan apparently became a victim of war and closed its doors.

■ ■ ■

MACDONALD'S INFLUENCE on the penal system, or on settlement houses and social work, or on the labour movement in Japan is impossible to assess with any precision. Clearly, she was a source of support to reforming bureaucrats in the justice system and to practitioners of 'progressive' prison administration, especially to Governor Arima Shirosuke. She was instrumental in bringing American literature and ideas on prisons into Japanese thinking about the penal system, although she was by no means a unique source of information, since several leading penal reformers had studied in the United States. This flow of ideas was not a one-way stream, for Macdonald seized every opportunity to inform foreign visitors and participants in international conferences that Japan's treatment of criminals compared favourably with that of most of the civilized world, a fact that won appreciation from a bureaucracy and government concerned with its image overseas. More than any other activity, it was Macdonald's work with prisoners that made her famous in Japan, North America, and elsewhere. For many, 'the white angel of Tokyo' (a description she did not choose) was a model of Christian or humanitarian service to society.

Clearly, Macdonald had a direct impact on hundreds of the lowliest and most despised members of society through her work with individual prisoners, from the notorious Ishii, whom she made famous, and other murderers, to juvenile delinquents who were still 'young scamps' to be saved from a life of serious crime. Nowhere did Caroline's ability to give undivided attention to the person with her at the moment have a greater effect. Most prisoners had rarely, if ever, received attention of this quality. Some came to believe that such care flowed from their friend's Christian faith and was a manifestation of the love of God. Many more found it easy to see her as 'the mother of prisoners.' There are no statistics on how many men on death row gained the 'peace of mind' Caroline sought to bring them, nor is there any record of the number of released prisoners who made a new life for themselves and their families, at least partly because of her.

Macdonald was never under the illusion that reformed prisoners would themselves create a new social order. Through her contact with prisoners and with leaders of the labour movement, she understood better than most of her middle-class Christian friends what a price the masses of Japanese were paying for their country's 'modernization' and 'progress.' Despite her emphasis on the individual, Macdonald grasped the importance of social systems: she saw settlement houses, the labour movement, and women educators and voters as agents of change in the social structure. In retrospect it is easy to find this a rather naive view of what was required for any fundamental social change, but that was not so evident at the time. Macdonald was part of a sizeable company of reformers who were promoting in Japan the social reform ideas of American 'progressives,' and in some degree of British Fabians. That network included some missionaries and Japanese Christian leaders, as well as the many Japanese who had studied abroad, especially in the United States or Britain, and then became part of the government bureaucracy. While Macdonald's ideas and actions were part of this general context, she brought to her pursuits abilities and personal qualities that many around her considered unusual or perhaps unique.

■ ■ ■

In the decade following her death, Macdonald's friends faced dilemmas that she, as a foreigner, would not have experienced in quite the same way. Yet had she lived into this troubled era, her intense identification with Japan and her close friendships with many Japanese would have made their pain her own.

Kawai Michi, her closest Japanese friend in the YWCA, had left her job as national secretary of that organization in 1929 to fulfil her dream of establishing a Christian high school for girls, and later to open a junior college. With the help of former students at Tsuda College and some American and Japanese friends, Keisen Jogakuen (Fount of Blessing Girls' School) opened in 1929 in Kawai's house with nine pupils. The standard high school curriculum was taught, plus the Bible, horticulture, and international affairs, for one of Kawai's main objectives was to do peace education with young women. Within two years, the school moved to a western suburb of Tokyo and acquired a dormitory that soon housed students from as far away as Manchuria and California. The school also served as a community centre with programs including classes for women preparing to migrate to Manchuria, Korea, and California. Despite the difficult times, the school prospered and within a decade boasted 200 graduates. In the spring of 1941, Kawai was the only woman among a group of seven Japanese Christians, well known among Americans, who embarked on a peace mission to the United States aimed at reversing the deterioration of relations between the two countries.[15]

A few months after their principal's return, the girls of Keisen were engaged in war service, working in a felt factory or washing soldiers' clothes in a laundry, both set up in the school. In common with other students and with women who were performing all manner of tasks, they laboured under conditions of increasing physical hardship.[16] Struggling to protect the academic integrity of the school while meeting the extra demands of wartime, Kawai was also concerned about maintaining the life of the church, but found that in the face of the multitude of restrictions 'nothing at all' could be done in active proclamation of the Christian faith.[17] However, when the Ministry of Education asked her to delete from the school's charter any reference to the Christian basis of the institution, as many schools had been forced to do, she declared that she would close the school rather than comply. The school was not closed.[18]

Tagawa Daikichirō used his long-standing interest in constitutional matters in the controversy over the attendance of Christians at Shinto shrines.

Under pressure from military authorities, participation in shrine ceremonies was increasingly used as a test of loyalty. Christians argued that if shrine attendance was purely a patriotic act, then this should be made clear and they would have no difficulty. If it were a religious act, then attendance must be voluntary under the constitution. The distinction between 'respect' and 'worship,' proposed by the Anglican leader Dr. J.S. Motoda, enabled some Christians to attend shrines as a patriotic duty. In 1940, when the Home Ministry ordered the use of shrine tablets in every household, the rate of compliance among Christians was apparently low, and the National Council of Churches made known its continuing rejection of the demand. Fortunately, the government did not enforce the regulation.[19]

During the 1930s, Tagawa, long a critic of the traditional family system, was distressed by the state's use of the family to reinforce nationalism. Believing that the enfranchisement of women would bring major changes to the family, he continued, as he had done in the previous decade, to introduce women's suffrage bills in the Diet, despite the decreasing likelihood that they would be passed. Tagawa also stood against the tide on foreign policy. While most Japanese politicians and intellectuals were highly critical of western imperialism, Tagawa was among the few to declare that Japanese imperialism was no different and would have a distorting effect on democracy at home and throughout the Japanese empire. He told the National Christian Council of Japan in 1938 that God would put to flight the Japanese armies invading China.[20] In 1940 he was summoned before the Osaka police to answer charges that he had violated the criminal code by even suggesting the possibility of a negotiated settlement of the war with China. Although he was not long detained, this was a stern reminder of the consequences of dissent.[21] Like so many others of a liberal bent, both Christians and non-Christians, Tagawa then fell into silence.

Another politician who had been Macdonald's friend ever since the Yamada murder trial continued in a public role in the thirties. Dr. Uzawa Fusaaki, after serving six successive terms in the House of Representatives as a member of the conservative Seiyūkai Party, was elected to the House of Peers in 1928 and remained there until 1937. As an increasingly authoritarian state used the schools for the promotion of a militaristic patriotism, Uzawa served as a member of a succession of commissions charged with the revision and 'reform' of the educational system, a difficult task that constantly challenged his Christian faith.

The 1930s was a hard decade for Macdonald's friends in the labour movement. In 1936 Suzuki Bunji was elected to the Lower House under the banner of the Shakai Taishūtō (Social Masses' Party), which he had helped to form in a union of the Social Democratic Party with the Zenkoku Rōnō Taishūtō (National Labour-Farmer Masses' Party), believing that a 'popular front' would protect the socialist movement from increasing government pressure. Suzuki was re-elected in 1937 when his party won thirty-seven seats, an unprecedented number for any party of the left. In foreign policy, leaders of the Socialist Masses' Party moved from their earlier ambivalence about Japan's involvement in Manchuria to full support in 1937 for the 'holy war' in China.[22]

Katayama Tetsu, labour lawyer, organizer of the Social Democratic Party, and member of Fujimichō church, was another of the democratic socialists well known to Macdonald who joined the Socialist Masses' Party. Early in 1940 the Diet was stunned when a Minseitō member, Saitō Takao, attacked the government for its perseverance in a useless war in China. When the vote was taken on a motion to expel Saitō from the Diet for his 'treasonous' utterance, Katayama joined Suzuki Bunji, Abe Isoo, and Nishio Suehiro of the Shakai Taishūtō, and six others, in declaring their support for Saitō by walking out of the Diet.[23]

Macdonald's closest friend in the labour movement, Matsuoka Komakichi, had been the de facto head of Sōdōmei for some time before he officially succeeded Suzuki as president in 1932. He continued to move away from socialism and to advocate a 'sound unionism' that would pursue the economic and social well-being of workers. Supported by the reforming bureaucrats who were still influential in the Home Ministry, Matsuoka and other Sōdōmei leaders resisted attempts by industry to use demands for pro-ductivity at all costs to crush the unions. Between 1935 and 1938, labour made significant gains through legislation on workers' pension and compen-sation funds, working hours and safety, and an extension of the National Health Insurance Law that made it the most comprehensive social legisla-tion the nation had ever seen. However, the cooperative effort of the Social Bureau and Sōdōmei to secure improved methods of labour conciliation failed before the determined opposition of employers.

In politics Sōdōmei followed a pragmatic course. Thus, its alliance with the Socialist Masses' Party was a large factor in the party's impressive gains in the elections of 1936 and 1937. Yet Sōdōmei was extremely vulnerable to factionalism on both left and right, and, after 1938, to the government's Industrial Patriotic Movement (Sanpō), which aimed to create one massive labour front to ensure industrial peace and production for the war. With the rupture in the Social Masses' Party over the Saitō affair, Sōdōmei no longer had a political arm: Matsuoka, Abe Isoo, Suzuki Bunji, and others tried frantically to organize a new party, the Nationalist Labour Party, hoping to preserve a degree of labour autonomy. Five days before its inaugural meeting the government banned the party. Then there were mass defections from Sōdōmei unions to Sanpō and the Shakai Taishūtō announced its own dissolution, thus becoming the first political party to enter the government's 'New Order.' Within a matter of weeks, Matsuoka and Suzuki presided over the 'spontaneous dissolution' of Sōdōmei. Now the Industrial Patriotic Movement embraced all workers and employers, and political parties no longer existed.[24]

Until that time, Akamatsu Tsuneko, who had been so valuable in Shinrinkan's educational program for women workers, had done what she could to maintain the stability of the labour movement, especially as it affected women. In the early years of the war the lives of women changed little. In the interest of protecting women's functions as mothers, the government was reluctant to mobilize women for work in heavy industry, but in 1943 it began to employ large numbers of women on the railroads. When it conscripted women for armament factories, only single women and widows were called. Later, under revisions to the Factory Act, women could be employed in the most hazardous jobs, including pit mines, and thousands laboured there. Night work for women was revived in many industries and generally their working conditions and real wages declined.[25] The objectives of the trade union movement in the 1920s were now irrelevant. It was hard for Akamatsu Tsuneko and others like her to see the gains of decades lost in a few years, but the demands of patriotism and a heavy-handed government stilled the voice of protest.

During the 1930s Baroness Ishimoto Shizue continued her work of education about birth control. With Ishimoto as president, the Women's Birth Control League of Japan was organized in 1932, and two years later a clinic was opened in Tokyo. In the summer of 1937, Margaret Sanger returned to Japan to give lectures under the auspices of the League. Within a few months Baroness Ishimoto was arrested and imprisoned briefly for her 'dangerous thought' on birth control and her labour sympathies. Pressure from friends abroad contributed to her early release, but she was forced to close her birth control clinic.[26]

Governments that justified territorial expansion to accommodate Japan's overcrowded people at the same time urged women to produce more babies, future soldiers and industrial workers to create and maintain a far-flung empire, 'The Greater East Asian Co-Prosperity Sphere.' By 1941 the Ministry of Welfare had adopted a comprehensive policy aimed at increasing the quality and quantity of the population. Persons with hereditary diseases were to be sterilized and the healthy were prohibited from practising birth control. The ideal family would have at least five children and those with ten or more received monetary rewards for their contribution to the nation.[27] This recognition of women in their reproductive capacities was entirely opposed to the objectives of Baroness Ishimoto and the feminist movement over more than two decades. Far from defining women solely as mothers, they had always stressed the right of women to decide for themselves on the bearing of children. The penalties for advocating women's autonomy were now severe: for Ishimoto and her colleagues the only defence was silence.[28]

Whatever feminists thought about the state's regulation of human reproduction, or however much they regretted the decline in working conditions, most of them cooperated in the war effort. Typical of these was Ichikawa Fusae, whom Caroline Macdonald had known through the suffrage movement in the 1920s. To Ichikawa and others the state's emphasis on the central role of mothers in society seemed to be a step forward. Thus they greeted as a milestone in women's progress the Mother-Child Protection Law of 1937, the first maternal protection legislation in Japan, which provided medical care and welfare payments to poor single mothers of children under thirteen. Viewed in another way, it was one sign of the state's determination to regulate motherhood for its own purposes.[29]

Most feminists were willing to support the existing family system, essentially patriarchal and authoritarian, as long as the role of women was redefined and praised as central. 'When the state had recognized women's maternal contributions as comparable to soldiers' contributions, women willingly demonstrated their capabilities,' gratified that they were being accorded an official role outside the home.[30] In activities to which Ichikawa Fusae gave significant leadership, feminists helped to organize the home front to deal with food shortages, mobilization of women for factory work, war bond campaigns, and the provision of counselling services to families with problems arising from male absence from the home.[31] Japanese women demonstrated their capabilities and their utility to the state in much the same way as did women in other societies at war.

● ● ●

BY THE SUMMER OF 1945 Japan lay in ruin, humiliated and exhausted as few nations had ever been. More than two million soldiers had given their lives to create and defend an empire that was now lost. Another six million stationed throughout Asia would have to be brought home and integrated into a devastated society. As the Japanese people now learned, the atrocities committed by the imperial army would leave a legacy of hatred throughout Japan's former possessions. More than 600,000 civilians had lost their lives in Japan, while many others suffered from overwork and malnutrition. Much of Tokyo had been destroyed in successive fire bombings, while the cities of Hiroshima and Nagasaki were the first to know the destructive power of atomic bombs. Japan's manifest destiny in Asia had been proven to be an illusion and the emperor would shortly publicly renounce his divinity. A bewildered and confused population slowly took up the tasks of reconstruction under the supervision of the only conquerors Japan had ever known.

Under Allied occupation, which was in effect an American occupation headed by General Douglas MacArthur, the rebuilding of the nation began. Many of Caroline Macdonald's friends now took up their lives and public service where they had been forced to leave off before or during the war. Their views and their experience during the period of 'Taishō democracy' were highly relevant to the plans of the Supreme Commander for the Allied Powers (SCAP) to impose a democratic system of government on Japan. They were not among the 200,000 persons 'purged' by the occupation and banned from holding public office because of their active promotion of the extreme nationalism that had led Japan into war.

While continuing to serve as president of the Presbyterian college, Meiji Gakuin, which had survived the war with little damage, Tagawa Daikichirō became active again in the Social Democratic Party and was a peace activist through various organizations. Just before his death in 1947 he ran unsuccessfully for mayor of Tokyo. Uzawa Fusaaki, as counsel to the International Military Tribunal for the Far East established by the victorious Allies, played a part in the dismantling of the Japanese Empire. Miyake

Shōtarō, who had been chief justice of the appeal courts in several districts throughout the country, became a member of the Supreme Court of Japan, and continued to be well known as an essayist and drama critic.

Very quickly, Matsuoka Komakichi was busy building a reorganized Sōdōmei along lines approved by American labour experts, and in 1946 he again became its president. In the same year he was elected to the House of Representatives for the reconstituted Social Democratic Party and became Speaker of the House, a position to which he was re-elected four times. In that role, and as Japan's representative at numerous international labour gatherings, Caroline Macdonald would have been proud of her former protégé.

Katayama Tetsu led in the re-establishment of the Social Democratic Party, and in 1947, when it won the largest number of seats in the first election under the new Constitution, he became prime minister in a coalition of the non-Communist left, the first and only socialist, and the only Christian, ever to lead a Japanese government. Twenty-seven Christians were elected to the Diet and five were cabinet ministers. With the approval of the occupation authorities, the Katayama government brought in legislation that regulated the *zaibatsu* (financial combines) under a new anti-monopoly law, revised the criminal code, and created a new Ministry of Labour to administer labour legislation, which showed clearly the continuing influence of bureaucrats associated with the former Social Bureau, and of conservative unionists like Matsuoka Komakichi, who served on the committee to draft the new legislation.[32]

Faced by shortages of food and raw materials, massive unemployment, rapid inflation and widespread strikes, Katayama was subject to growing criticism from the left wing of the coalition, especially for his introduction of price and wage controls, and after only eight months in office his government was forced to resign. In a new administration led by Ashida Hitoshi of the Democratic party, the socialists, including Katayama, continued to play a prominent but no longer dominant role. That administration also lasted only eight months when it was succeeded early in 1949 by a government headed by Yoshida Shigeru, which gave the country a measure of stability until 1955.[33] Katayama lost his own seat in the Diet in the election of 1949 but continued to be active in the Social Democratic Party, endeavouring without success to prevent a serious split between left and right factions and eventually siding with the conservatives.[34]

After the war, one of the most dramatic political changes was the granting of the vote to women. Several women with whom Caroline Macdonald had worked lost no time in entering the political arena. Akamatsu Tsuneko, elected to the House of Councillors for the Social Democrats in the first postwar election, argued for the creation of a Women's and Minors' Bureau in the Katayama government's reorganized Ministry of Labour. The new bureau, modelled on the U.S. Women's Bureau and intended to improve working conditions for women and children, was headed by Yamakawa Kikue, the Tsuda College graduate who had been such a stormy petrel in the 1920s. Now she was the first woman to become a bureau chief in a government ministry. Akamatsu's work, and that of a host of other women, on an old battleground culminated in 1957 with the passage of an anti-prostitution law in the Diet. Later, Akamatsu was director of the women's section of Sōhyō (the General Council of Labour Unions), the largest labour organization in the country.[35]

Another prominent postwar Social Democratic politician was Baroness Ishimoto, now known as Katō Shizue, for during the war she had divorced the husband from whom she had been long separated and married Katō Kanju, former head of the miners' union and a leading socialist. Under an American occupation that encouraged discussion of population issues, Katō and her friends spread birth control information to enthusiastic audiences throughout the land. In the election of 1947, both Katōs were elected to the House of Representatives where Katō Shizue was the sponsor of the bill establishing the Women's and Minors' Bureau. Elected to the House of Councillors in 1950, she remained there until her defeat in 1974, sometimes taking positions rather independent of the socialist party to which she belonged. Throughout most of this time Katō headed the Family Planning Federation of Japan.[36]

One of the most successful politicians in postwar Japan was Ichikawa Fusae who pursued a highly independent course, maintaining her customary frugal lifestyle and refusing to join any major political party. She founded and served for some years as president of the League of Women Voters of Japan, one of the largest and most influential women's organizations in the country. On the basis of her campaigns against social inequality and government corruption, she was elected five times to the House of Councillors. In the last two elections, in 1975 and in 1980 (when she was 88), Ichikawa won her seat by the largest margins ever recorded.[37]

During the war years, the YWCA cooperated with other women's organizations in patriotic activities on the home front while its regular work was more and more curtailed. It suffered heavy property damage in several cities, nowhere more than in Tokyo where the national office, the secretaries' residence, and two student dormitories were totally destroyed. After the war ended, the Tokyo YWCA building, which had suffered some damage, was occupied by the Allied forces. The first passport issued to a Japanese after the war was given in 1946 to the daughter of Caroline Macdonald's pastor and friend, Uemura Masahisa. Uemura Tamaki, now Japan's first ordained woman minister and president of the YWCA of Japan, went to the United States at the invitation of the women of the Presbyterian Church USA for a year's observation of church life and women's activities.[38]

The first permits issued to civilian foreigners for work in postwar Japan were given to an American missionary who was to act as a contact person with SCAP in the return of missionaries to the country, and to G. Ernest Bott, Caroline Macdonald's friend of many years whose settlement work in East Tokyo for the United Church of Canada had been similar to her own. Thanks to Bott's connections in high places, especially with social welfare bureaucrats in the government, he and his wife, Edith, had been allowed to live freely in Tokyo during the first seven months of the war when other enemy aliens were being interned, and they were among the last foreigners to be repatriated. Now Bott was to be in charge of the coordination and distribution of the enormous quantities of relief that poured into Japan from churches and their agencies around the world, a task that made full use of his fine intelligence, his devotion to the Japanese people, and his impressive administrative skills. Many of his old friends in the government were still in place and this served his cause well. While the relief work of the churches was smaller than the aid given by governments, notably the American, it made a significant contribution to reconstruction. Administered without regard to religious faith, it made a deep impression on many Japanese and won the appreciation of SCAP and General MacArthur.[39]

From the beginning of the occupation, General MacArthur and his colleagues were well disposed toward Christianity. They encouraged missionaries and Japanese churches to make full use of the religious freedom guaranteed in the new constitution. Not surprisingly, given their American experience, they tended to see Christianity as the underpinning of the democracy they were endeavouring to implant in Japan and, before long, as a bulwark against communism. Coupled with the interest of a shocked, confused, and disillusioned populace in the religion of conquerors who had turned out to be far more benevolent than ever anticipated, many Japanese became interested in Christianity. Kagawa Toyohiko, grieving the destruction of all of the thirteen major social settlements he had established, and in failing health, traversed the country helping to restore these and similar agencies and preaching to thousands of people who were more open to the Christian gospel than ever before. On her return from the United States, the Reverend Uemura Tamaki was summoned to make weekly visits to the imperial palace for Bible teaching and hymn singing with Empress Nagako and her ladies-in-waiting; the empress was said to be taking notes on these sessions for the benefit of the emperor. When the occupation ended, the court quickly returned to its usual seclusion.[40] 'The Christian boom' anticipated by some was short-lived, and in the long run SCAP's official support was probably a disservice to Christianity.[41]

The Kyōdan (United Church of Christ) met once again in Fujimichō church in the early summer of 1946 in the new era of religious freedom. Already the work of rebuilding the one third of the churches, schools, and manses that had been destroyed in the war was under way. With government coercion removed, the Anglican-Episcopal and Lutheran churches, plus some Baptist and Presbyterian groups, and the Salvation Army, withdrew from the Kyōdan, but a majority of the churches decided to continue in the unity that had been forged during the war. Gradually, many of the earlier missionaries returned, along with some new colleagues, nearly always with the agreement of the Kyōdan or the other Japanese churches with which their denominations were affiliated. However, these missionaries were a declining proportion of the flood of those who entered Japan after the war. Most of the new missionaries were fundamentalists or conservative evangelicals representing independent missionary societies. Mainly Americans, they reflected the growth of this type of non-ecumenical Protestantism in the United States and, as at home, they were conservative in their economic and political views as well as in theology. As a rule they knew little of Japanese history or culture and had a limited interest in social issues except in their immediate bearing on adherence to a rigid personal morality.[42]

Their wartime experience had also made many of the leaders and members of the 'old-line' Japanese churches more conservative in theology and uncertain in their commitment to a social gospel. Before and during the war, many leading Protestant ministers were strongly influenced by their reading of the great Swiss theologian Karl Barth. While Barth's emphasis on the transcendence of the Kingdom of God and the absolute power of God may have helped the church to survive under an authoritarian government, it also reinforced the isolation of Christians. This disposition, coupled with the postwar need to rebuild churches, physically and spiritually, did little to encourage Christians to active engagement in social outreach or public life. Nevertheless, there were some church leaders who were developing a new social gospel that was firmly rooted in Japanese experience and in biblical insights about the human condition.[43]

After the war the YWCA quickly resumed its activities, mainly, as before, among urban, middle-class women. In common with other women's organizations, the YWCA participated enthusiastically in educating women in the exercise of their new political responsibilities and in promoting internationalism through association with their counterparts in other countries. The YWCA became and remained a centre of the peace movement among Japanese women, and many of its members were active in later manifestations of the women's movement.[44] Although Emma Kaufman, aged sixty-five in 1946, was no longer a staff member, she was back in Tokyo as soon as she could obtain permission to return. Her house in Sadowara had been totally destroyed in the war. Now she devoted energy and money to the restoration of the buildings and programs of the YWCA and to arrangements for young Japanese women to study in Canada and the United States. From her home in Toronto, Kaufman continued her interest in the Tokyo YWCA until well into the 1960s. In encouraging Emma Kaufman to join the staff of the Tokyo 'Y' fifty years earlier, Caroline Macdonald had made one of her most enduring contributions to Japanese women.

■ ■ ■

To DISCUSS THE WARTIME and postwar careers of women and men whose lives had earlier crossed Caroline Macdonald's path is not to suggest that her influence was definitive on any of them. No one recognized more clearly than she did herself that however identified she might be with the interests of her Japanese friends, as a foreigner she remained on the fringes of their society, forever an 'outsider.'

In the strict sense, the 'Taishō period' extends from 1912 to 1926, but it is often defined as the years from the Russo-Japanese war of 1904-5 to the

'Manchurian incident' of 1931, coinciding almost exactly with Macdonald's sojourn in Japan. In describing these years as 'the crucible of Japanese modernity,' Sharon Nolte suggests the spirit of experiment and possibility that permeated Japanese life in these years. It was a time that saw the rapid growth of an educated middle class whose members debated public issues, questioning the value of Japanese institutions, including the family, education, and the role of the state in the economy and the culture. Yet the possibilities for change were not as great as the more idealistic members of the new middle class often thought.

> The Meiji state created the setting for Taishō individualism by abolishing restrictions on occupation and residence and by encouraging the formation of a new urban professional and managerial class. Its policies however were aimed at national wealth and strength rather than at individual liberty or self-fulfillment; consequently, broadened social and political participation were coupled with indoctrination and censorship.[45]

Macdonald's middle-class friends were men and women intent on making the most of the liberalism and openness that was one side of this society. In Fujimichō church she was associated with leaders in business, the professions, and politics. For them, Protestant Christianity's emphasis on individual responsibility provided affirmation and confidence for their movement into a new society. In their support of Tsuda College, Tokyo Women's Christian College, and the YWCA, these same men, and their wives, were increasing the number of educated middle-class women who saw new civic and professional roles for themselves and their daughters, but without abandonment of responsibilities for home and family. Through the women to whose education she contributed and through the men and women with whom she worked on the board of Shinrinkan, in the labour movement, and the Social Democratic Party, Macdonald played a role in shaping 'Taishō democracy.' Although she was only one among many channels through which ideas about social equality and democracy were circulating, she was clearly important in the lives of those in her immediate circle.

Although 'Taishō reformers' have often been faulted for their impractical idealism and their failure to understand the political methods necessary to achieve their objectives, to a remarkable degree their issues proved to be the issues of postwar society when the United States imposed democracy on a defeated nation. By choosing to leave the Japanese administrative structure essentially intact and by failing to decentralize big business, the occupation effected less change than at first appeared. However, it provided a setting in which urban professionals, intellectuals, and managers could renew their efforts to realize the social and political objectives they had debated in the brief heyday of the Taishō era.[46] In this new age, Caroline's friends were able to work once again toward earlier goals.

■ ■ ■

A 'LIFE' DOES NOT CONSIST of influence on others or on response to events in the outside world. There is also a submerged internal life, not unaffected by or independent of the external one but far from synonymous with it. Given good enough sources, a biographer may describe the external life clearly, but to discern its inner structure and dynamics, and its meaning and satisfaction for the one who lived it, is infinitely more difficult.

For the vast majority of women of Caroline Macdonald's generation (and long after), the world's expectation, and their own, was that they would be 'unambiguously women.' That meant, as Carolyn Heilbrun writes, 'to put a man at the center of one's life and to allow to occur only what honours his prime position.'[47] Caroline Macdonald was not such a woman, for she did not put a man at the centre of her life. The paucity of information about Caroline's early life makes it impossible to say whether initially this was from necessity or choice. When she went to university she apparently had no definite career plans. At the age of thirty, when she decided to go to Japan, she had perhaps concluded that marriage and family were unlikely to be her lot. Yet her continuing and affectionate interest in David Cairns, an interest not solely intellectual and theological, suggests that she would have become an 'unambiguous woman' if he had asked her the right question. Or was she in some degree indulging in a romantic fantasy whose parameters were set by the conventions of her time? Convention required that 'romance' be part of a woman's life story. If Caroline was indeed entertaining a fantasy, her need to do so perhaps suggests how hard it was to be an 'ambiguous woman.'

As it was, Macdonald may be seen, again in Heilbrun's words, as an example of 'a woman's unconscious "fall" ... out of the marriage plot,' with its entirely conventional ending, 'into a condition where vocation is possible.'[48] Few women of her time had choices. When Caroline graduated from university, her two clearest choices were to become a physicist in the male world of science and the university, or to enter the female world of the YWCA and later the society of a foreign land. Choice took courage, and a sense of adventure, and was possible only because Caroline belonged to that minority of women who were 'educated enough to have had a choice, and brave enough to have made one.' Having made her choice, Caroline usually told her own story in male language, using male pronouns and adjectives, yet the reader never feels that she was 'trapped in a script she did not write.'[49]

While Macdonald's intelligence, education, and spirit of adventure all shaped her life, the definitive factor in her unusual career was her great capacity for friendship. This was rooted in her deep conviction that social and cultural differences were to be respected but were ultimately of little importance. For her the essential reality was that 'human nature is all one.' That meant that no one was beyond the touch of another human being or beyond some understanding of God's love. It was no accident that her favourite metaphor for God was 'Friend.' Friendship was crucial to Caroline's achievement in the world and it was also her personal nourishment, taking the place of immediate family. In Japan her closest friends initially were among the growing staff of the YWCA. More than most missionaries, Caroline also had close friends among Japanese, none closer than Tsuda Ume and Kawai Michi. In the YWCA she was part of a female culture that in considerable degree transcended national distinctions. Outside that culture, it was easier for Macdonald, a foreigner and a single woman, to enjoy the friendship of Japanese males than it was for a Japanese woman. Friends like Uemura Masahisa, Tagawa Daikichirō, Matsuoka Komakichi, Uzawa Fusaaki, Arima Shirosuke, and Miyake Shōtarō were part of her personal universe, as were men of a very different social class such as Yamada Zen'ichi, Ishii, and a host of lesser-known prisoners. Her middle-class male friends were also essential to her work, since only men had the influence and the money needed to implement her plans.

Macdonald often celebrated her good fortune in being paid for doing such interesting and rewarding work. Her experience accords with what we know about other women missionaries in Asia, and was no doubt true elsewhere in the world. Some women succumbed to the physical and emotional perils of overseas life, but most enjoyed long and satisfying careers, especially women who were university graduates. Although few were as 'free wheeling' as Caroline Macdonald, they were usually in positions where they enjoyed a high degree of personal freedom and independence. Especially in their work with women, they had the satisfaction of believing that they were contributing to social changes that would improve the lot of their Asian sisters.[50]

Some contemporary discussions of missionaries who practised a 'social gospel' suggest that these men and women ceased to be missionaries and became social workers, and therefore secularists. If one adopts a definition of 'secular' as being anything concerned with this world, then this view is valid. However, most social gospel missionaries made no such division between the 'religious' and the 'secular,' least of all Caroline Macdonald. The lively liberal evangelical Christian faith she took with her to Japan and never lost always had a strong social dimension. That faith freed her to be an 'ambiguous woman.' In the Empire of the Mikado she made her unique contribution to Japanese society and to the Kingdom of God.

Notes

Preface

1 Hugh L. Keenleyside, *Memoirs.* Vol. 1, *Hammer the Golden Day* (Toronto: McClelland and Stewart 1981), 215, 245n.
2 Carolyn G. Heilbrun, *Writing a Woman's Life* (New York: W.W. Norton 1988), 15.
3 Nancy F. Cott, 'What's in a Name? The Limits of Social Feminism; or, Expanding the Vocabulary of Women's History,' *Journal of American History* 76 (December 1989):809-29.

Chapter 1: Pioneering Canadian Roots

1 Interview with Peter Macdonald, *London Advertiser*, 12 August 1916; H.J. Morgan, *The Canadian Men and Women of the Time* (Toronto: William Briggs 1912), 683.
2 Except where otherwise indicated the following account of life in Wingham and the activities of the Macdonald family is based primarily on files from the *Wingham Times*, 1888-97; see also James Scott, *The Settlement of Huron County* (Toronto: Ryerson Press 1966), 271-5; *The Book of Turnberry, 1857-1957* (n.p., n.d.).
3 In its strongly Protestant character and in the growth of organizations for the promotion of Protestant social values, Wingham was typical of southern Ontario towns. See John W. Grant, *A Profusion of Spires: Religion in Nineteenth Century Ontario* (Toronto: University of Toronto Press 1988), chaps. 11 and 12.
4 Michael Gauvreau, *The Evangelical Century: College and Creed in English Canada from the Great Revival to the Great Depression* (Montreal and Kingston: McGill-Queen's University Press 1991), chap. 5; Brian J. Fraser, *The Social Uplifters: Presbyterian Progressives and the*

Social Gospel in Canada, 1875-1915 (Waterloo: Wilfrid Laurier University Press 1988), chap. 1.

5 Fraser, *Social Uplifters*, 13-17; A.C. Cheyne, *The Transforming of the Kirk: Victorian Scotland's Religious Revolution* (Edinburgh: Saint Andrew Press 1983), 55, 78-9.

6 Susan E. Houston and Alison Prentice, *Schooling and Scholars in Nineteenth Century Ontario* (Toronto: University of Toronto Press 1988), 339-44; J.G. Althouse, *The Ontario Teacher: A Historical Account of Progress 1800-1910* (Toronto: Ontario Teachers' Federation 1967), 59-87.

7 Annual Report of the Board of Education of the City of London, Ontario, 1897, Collegiate Institute, Report of the Principal, 5-7.

8 Jo LaPierre, 'The Academic Life of Canadian Coeds, 1880-1900,' *Historical Studies in Education* 2 (Fall 1990):225-45.

9 John McNab, *The White Angel of Tokyo: Miss Caroline Macdonald LL.D.* (Centenary Committee of the Canadian Churches, n.p., n.d.), 6-7.

10 Diana Pedersen, '"The Call to Service": The YWCA and the Canadian College Woman, 1886-1920,' in Paul Axelrod and John G. Reid, eds., *Youth, University, and Canadian Society: Essays in the Social History of Higher Education* (Kingston and Montreal: McGill-Queen's University Press 1989), 193.

11 Gauvreau, *Evangelical Century*, 201-15; Fraser, *Social Uplifters*, chap. 5.

12 *Toronto News*, 15 January 1916; *Toronto Star Weekly*, 10 August 1929. On the difficulties faced by Macdonald's contemporaries who endeavoured to have careers in science, see several essays in Marianne Gostonyi Ainley, ed., *Essays on Canadian Women in Science* (Montreal: Vehicule Press 1990), and Maralene F. and Geoffrey W. Rayner-Canham, *Harriet Brooks: Pioneer Nuclear Physicist* (Montreal and Kingston: McGill-Queen's University Press 1992). As recently as 1896, Elizabeth Laird, who led the graduating class in physics at the University of Toronto and later had a distinguished career in that field, had been denied admission to graduate study at Toronto. Nevertheless, after the turn of the century the department of physics proved to be somewhat more hospitable to women than most science departments, a development Macdonald could not have foreseen, although McLennan's encouragement suggests that some attitudes were changing. See Alison Prentice, 'Bluestockings, Feminists or Women Workers? A Preliminary Look at Women's Early Employment at the University of Toronto,' *Journal of the Canadian Historical Association*, new series 2 (1991):239-42, 249, 256.

13 Pedersen, '"The Call to Service,"' 196-203.

14 On the education and training of YWCA secretaries in the United States, see Nancy Boyd, *Emissaries: The Overseas Work of the American YWCA, 1895-1970* (New York: Woman's Press 1986), 18-26.

15 Ottawa YM-YW Archives (hereafter cited as Ottawa YWCA Papers), Sara Carson to Mrs. Blackburn, 16 August 1901.

16 Ottawa YWCA Papers, Minutes of Board of Management, 20 August 1901.

17 Diana Pedersen, '"Building Today for the Womanhood of Tomorrow": Boosters and the YWCA, 1890-1930,' *Urban History Review/Revue d'histoire urbaine* 25 (February 1987):228; on the Canadian YWCA as a whole, see Diana Pedersen, 'The Young Women's Christian Association in Canada, 1870-1920: "A Movement to Meet a Spiritual, Civic and National Need,"' Ph.D. thesis, Carleton University, 1987.

18 Ottawa YWCA Papers, Minutes of Board of Management, 10 September 1901.

19 Ibid., 24 September and 18 October 1901.

20 Fraser, *Social Uplifters*, chap. 3.

21 Ottawa YWCA Papers, Minutes of Board of Management, 18 October and 8 November 1901.

22 Ibid., 16 January 1902.

23 Ottawa YWCA Papers, Caroline Macdonald, Annual Report, 1901-2, 17-19.

24 Ottawa YWCA Papers, Minutes of Board of Management, 26 September 1902.

25 Ibid., 17 October 1902.

26 On missions as a significant interest among undergraduates, see A.B. McKillop, "'Marching as to War": Elements of Ontario Undergraduate Culture, 1880-1914,' in Axelrod and Reid, *Youth, University, and Canadian Society*, 77-8.

27 *World-Wide Evangelization: The Urgent Business of the Church*. Addresses delivered before the Fourth International Convention of the Student Volunteer Movement for Foreign Missions, Toronto, 26 February - 1 March 1902 (New York: Student Volunteer Movement 1902).

28 University of Toronto Archives, Annie Caroline Macdonald File A73-0026/259(90), CM to J.B. Brebner, 7 March 1902.

29 University of Toronto Archives, Caroline Macdonald, 'Impressions from the Convention,' written for *The Westminster* but not published, apparently because an earlier issue had covered the gathering extensively.

30 Sara Z. Burke, 'Science and Sentiment: Social Service and Gender at the University of Toronto, 1888-1910,' *Journal of the Canadian Historical Association*, new series 4 (1993):80-2.

31 Ottawa YWCA Papers, Annual Report, 1902-3, 9-15.

32 Anna V. Rice, A *History of the World's Young Women's Christian Association* (New York: Women's Press 1947), 64, 87-91.

33 Ottawa YWCA Papers, Annual Report, 1902-3, 11.

34 Rice, *History of the World's Young Women's Christian Association*, 90-1.

35 Archives of the YWCA of Japan (hereafter cited as Japan YWCA), 'Seventh Annual Report of the Executive Committee of the World's Young Women's Christian Association,' 1901, 8-11; Mary Q. Innis, *Unfold the Years: A History of the Young Women's Christian Association in Canada* (Toronto: McClelland & Stewart 1949), 66-7.

Chapter 2: Christ and the Empire of the Mikado

1 C.R. Boxer, *The Christian Century in Japan, 1509-1650* (Berkeley: University of California Press 1951); Richard H. Drummond, A *History of Christianity in Japan* (Grand Rapids, MI: William B. Eerdmans 1971), part 2.

2 Ibid., 139-45.

3 Ibid., 123-5; Charles W. Iglehart, A *Century of Protestant Christianity in Japan* (Tokyo: Charles E. Tuttle 1959), 26-31; Ernest E. Best, *Christian Faith and Cultural Crisis: The Japanese Case* (Leiden: E.J. Brill 1966), 20-7.

4 The foregoing account of early missionary activity is based on Drummond, *Christianity in Japan*, 145-62; Iglehart, *Protestant Christianity*, 33-44; Best, *Christian Faith*, 27-30.

5 On the symbolic significance of the Restoration, see Carol Gluck, *Japan's Modern Myths: Ideology in the Late Meiji Period* (Princeton, NJ: Princeton University Press 1985), 73-7.

6 Drummond, *Christianity in Japan*, 162-5; Iglehart, *Protestant Christianity*, 45-8; Best, *Christian Faith*, 39-41.

7 Iglehart, *Protestant Christianity*, 74.

8 Drummond, *Christianity in Japan*, 191.

9 Ronald P. Dore, *Education in Tokugawa Japan*, 2nd ed. (London: Athlone Press 1984), 301-16; Edwin O. Reischauer, *The Japanese* (Cambridge, MA: Harvard University Press 1981), 72-6.

10 The fullest study of the Christian samurai in English is Irwin Scheiner, *Christian Converts and Social Protest in Meiji Japan* (Berkeley: University of California Press 1970), chaps. 2-4; also Drummond, *Christianity in Japan*, 166-9; Best, *Christian Faith*, 95-9.

11 Iglehart, *Protestant Christianity*, 49-56; Drummond, *Christianity in Japan*, 166-73.

12 Drummond, *Christianity in Japan*, 166-73.

13 Ibid.

14 Gluck, *Japan's Modern Myths*, 42-9.

15 Best, *Christian Faith*, 99, 157-9; Scheiner, *Christian Converts*, chap. 5; Gluck, *Japan's Modern*

Myths, 42-9, 49-67, 169.
16 Gluck, *Japan's Modern Myths*, 146-56; for an account of the purpose and content of Japanese education by one closely associated with its administration, see Kikuchi Dairoku, *Japanese Education: Lectures Delivered in the University of London* (London: John Murray 1909).
17 Sharon H. Nolte and Sally Ann Hastings, 'The Meiji State's Policy toward Women, 1890-1910,' in Gail Lee Bernstein, ed., *Recreating Japanese Women, 1600-1945* (Berkeley: University of California Press 1991), 151-75.
18 Kikuchi, *Japanese Education*, chaps. 18 and 19 outline the curriculum in detail.
19 Nolte and Hastings, 'The Meiji State's Policy,' 172.
20 Ibid., 173.
21 Cited in Nolte and Hastings, 'The Meiji State's Policy,' 156. Nolte and Hastings go so far as to suggest that Meiji women were virtually 'civil servants,' 154.
22 Ibid., 134-5.
23 Gluck, *Japan's Modern Myths*, 49-58.
24 Iglehart, *Protestant Christianity*, 98-9.
25 On the origins and purposes of the rescript, see Gluck, *Japan's Modern Myths*, 102-11, 120-7.
26 Ibid., 133-5; Drummond, *Christianity in Japan*, 196-204; Iglehart, *Protestant Christianity*, 109-10. On Uchimura Kanzō and the non-church movement, see Carlo Caldarola, *Christianity: The Japanese Way* (Leiden: E.J. Brill 1979), chaps. 3-6; John F. Howes, 'Kanzō Uchimura: The Formative Years,' *Japan Christian Quarterly*, 20 (1954):194-208.
27 Otis Cary, *Japan and Its Regeneration* (New York: Fleming H. Revell 1904), 113; Iglehart, *Protestant Christianity*, 105-7; Scheiner, *Christian Converts*, 108-14; Sumiya Mikio, *Nihon no Shakaishisō: Kindaika to Kirisutokyō* (Social Thought and Christianity in Modern Japan) (Tokyo: Tokyo Daigaku Shuppankai 1968), 137-98; George O. Totten, *The Social Democratic Movement in Prewar Japan* (New Haven, CT: Yale University Press 1966), 21-7.
28 Iglehart, *Protestant Christianity*, 112-14.
29 Ibid., 119-20.
30 Representative views are discussed in Pat Barr, *The Deer Cry Pavilion: A Story of Westerners in Japan, 1868-1905* (London: Macmillan 1968), especially part 4; Jean-Pierre Lehmann, *The Image of Japan: From Feudal Isolation to World Power, 1850-1905* (London: George Allen & Unwin 1978), passim; Jane Elizabeth Tiers, 'Impressions of Meiji Japan by Five Victorian Women,' M.A. thesis, University of British Columbia, 1986. In volume and influence, missionary literature dominated the field, at least until the First World War. Although such writing promoted a cause, it was often fairly sophisticated in offering a social perspective on the Japanese and must have mitigated the provincialism of many readers. Much of what women in North America, especially the thousands who belonged to women's missionary societies, knew about the world beyond their own continent was derived from missionary literature. See Patricia R. Hill, *The World Their Household: The American Woman's Foreign Mission Movement and Cultural Transformation 1870-1920* (Ann Arbor: University of Michigan Press 1985), 140-52 and passim.
31 Rudyard Kipling, *From Sea to Sea*, vol. 1 (London: Macmillan 1900), 410, 415, cited in Lehmann, *The Image of Japan*, 34.
32 Basil Hall Chamberlain, *Things Japanese*, 4th ed. (New York: Charles Scribners & Sons 1904).
33 William Elliot Griffis, *The Mikado's Empire*, 10th ed., 2 vols. (New York: Harper 1903).
34 William E. Griffis, *Dux Christus: An Outline Study of Japan* (New York: Macmillan 1904).
35 Griffis, *The Mikado's Empire*, 559.
36 Griffis, *Dux Christus*, especially chap. 5. On the growth of the missionary movement among and to women, see Hill, *The World Their Household*, especially chaps. 2 and 3; Ruth C. Brouwer, *New Women for God: Canadian Presbyterian Women and India Missions, 1876-1914* (Toronto: University of Toronto Press 1990), 13-20 and passim.

37 Alice M. Bacon, *Japanese Girls and Women* (1891; reprint, Boston: Houghton Mifflin 1902). On Bacon, see Yasaka Takagi, 'Alice M. Bacon,' in Edward T. James et al., *Notable American Women, 1706-1950*, vol. 1 (Cambridge, MA: Harvard University Press 1971), 78-9.
38 Bacon, *Japanese Girls and Women*, 31.
39 Ibid.
40 Ibid.
41 Ibid., 203, 267-9, 319-25.
42 R.B. Peery, *The Gist of Japan* (New York: Fleming H. Revell 1897), 314-15.
43 Masao Maruyama, 'Japanese Thought,' *Journal of Social and Political Ideas in Japan* 2 (April 1964):41-8.
44 Ibid.
45 Sidney L. Gulick, *Evolution of the Japanese: A Study of Their Characteristics in Relation to the Principles of Social and Psychic Development* (New York: Fleming H. Revell 1903), passim, 414. See also Cary, *Japan and Its Regeneration*, 199; J.C. Calhoun Newton, *Japan: Country, Court, and People* (New York: Fleming H. Revell 1900).
46 John H. De Forest, *Sunrise in the Sunrise Kingdom* (New York: Fleming H. Revell 1904), 203.
47 Griffis, *Dux Christus*, 244-50.
48 Ibid., 268.
49 Ibid., 36.
50 Ibid., 247-8.
51 Ibid., 266-8.
52 Ibid., 276-7.

Chapter 3: 'Women's Work for Women'

1 National Archives of Canada, YWCA Papers (hereafter cited as NAC YWCA Papers), vol. 35, CM to Mrs. Robert Blackburn, 22 December 1904.
2 Ibid., CM to family, 9 January 1905.
3 Ibid.
4 Ibid.
5 Ibid., CM to Mrs. Robert Blackburn, 22 December 1904.
6 Ibid.
7 Ibid., CM to family, 9 January 1905.
8 Charles W. Iglehart, *A Century of Protestant Christianity in Japan* (Tokyo: Charles E. Tuttle 1959), 118-19.
9 Ibid., 115-9; Sumiya Mikio, *Nihon no shakaishisō: Kindaika to Kirisutokyō* (Social Thought and Christianity in Modern Japan) (Tokyo: Tokyo Daigaku Shuppankai 1968), 119-208; Nobuya Bamba and John F. Howes, *Pacifism in Japan: The Christian and Socialist Tradition* (Kyoto: Minerva Press 1978), passim; Sandra C. Taylor, 'The Ineffectual Voice: Japan Missionaries and American Foreign Policy, 1870-1941,' *Pacific Historical Review* 53 (February 1984):22-3.
10 Edward Seidensticker, *Low City, High City: Tokyo from Edo to the Earthquake* (Tokyo: Charles E. Tuttle 1984), 141-3; Carol Gluck, *Japan's Modern Myths: Ideology in the Late Meiji Period* (Princeton, NJ: Princeton University Press 1985), 89-90, 175.
11 Sharon H. Nolte and Sally A. Hastings, 'The Meiji State's Policy toward Women, 1890-1910,' in Gail Lee Bernstein, ed., *Recreating Japanese Women, 1600-1945* (Berkeley: University of California Press 1991), 157-61.
12 Ibid., 162.
13 Archives of the World's YWCA (hereafter cited as World's YWCA), Geneva, CM to Clarissa Spencer, 29 November 1905.
14 United Church of Canada Archives (UCCA), Caroline Macdonald Papers (hereafter cited as

CMP), Caroline Macdonald, Box 1, File 22 (hereafter cited in format CMP 1-22), 'Early Days of the YWCA in Japan,' [1925?].

15 World's YWCA, Geneva, CM to Clarissa Spencer, 29 November 1905.

16 Tsuda College Archives, Tokyo, Tsuda Ume to M. Carey Thomas, 9 August 1900.

17 Dorothy Robins-Mowry, *The Hidden Sun: Women of Modern Japan* (Boulder, CO: Westview Press 1983), 45-7; Shimada Noriko et al., 'Ume Tsuda and Motoko Hani: Echoes of American Cultural Feminism in Japan,' in Carol V.R. George, ed., *'Remember the Ladies': New Perspectives on Women in American History* (Syracuse, NY: Syracuse University Press 1975), 161-78.

18 World's YWCA, CM to Clarissa Spencer, 29 November 1905.

19 Ibid.

20 Ibid.

21 World's YWCA, *Report of the Third Conference, Paris*, 16-21 May 1906 (London: n.p. 1906), 66.

22 World's YWCA, CM to Clarissa Spencer, 29 November 1905.

23 Ibid.

24 NAC YWCA Papers, vol. 35, CM to Clara Benson, 9 February 1906.

25 Japan YWCA, Report of Miss Phillips on Hostels for Women Students, (n.d.).

26 Ibid.

27 Shiono Sachiko, 'Caroline Macdonald,' in Watanabe Matsuko, ed., *Emma Kaufman to Tokyo YWCA*, (Emma Kaufman and the Tokyo YWCA) (Tokyo YWCA 1963), 126-72.

28 CMP, Caroline Macdonald, 'Early Days of the YWCA in Japan,' [1925?]; NAC YWCA Papers, vol. 35, CM to Clara Benson, 9 February 1906.

29 Japan YWCA, 'The First YWCA Conference, Tokyo, July, 1906.' Unpublished report by Stella C. Fisher.

30 NAC YWCA Papers, vol. 35, CM to Clara Benson, 9 February 1906.

31 World's YWCA, *Report of the Third Conference*, 65-7.

32 NAC YWCA Papers, vol. 35, CM to friends, April 1907.

33 Sidney Checkland, 'John Campbell White,' *Dictionary of Scottish Business Biography*, vol. 1 (Aberdeen: University of Aberdeen Press 1986), 193-6.

34 NAC YWCA Papers, vol. 35., CM to friends, April 1907.

35 Ibid.

36 Japan YWCA, CM to friends, 30 November 1906, CM's summary of reporter's interview with chief of police.

37 NAC YWCA Papers, vol. 35, CM to friends, April 1907

38 Ibid., CM to Clara Benson, 15 June 1907.

39 Ibid., CM to friends, April 1907.

40 Ibid.

41 *Canada's Share in Foreign Association Work* (Toronto: Dominion Council of the YWCA 1910), 21.

42 NAC YWCA Papers, vol. 35, CM to friends, April 1907.

43 C. Howard Hopkins, *John R. Mott, 1865-1955* (Grand Rapids, MI: William B. Eerdmans 1979), 186-201, 255-7.

44 Ibid., 313.

45 Ibid., 315-16.

46 Ibid., 319.

47 Cited in ibid., 319-20.

48 Ibid., 314, 321, and passim.

49 It is evident in Macdonald's correspondence that she considered Mott given to excessive statement and that she thought him a pompous male chauvinist.

50 CMP, Caroline Macdonald, 'Early Days of the YWCA in Japan," [1925?]; Japan YWCA, CM

to Harriet Taylor, Secretary, Foreign Department of the American YWCA, February 1908.
51 Ibid.
52 Ibid.
53 *Five Years of Association Work in Japan* (Toronto: Dominion Council of the YWCA 1910), 16.
54 For a description of Karuizawa, see Bernard Leach, *Beyond East and West* (London: Faber & Faber 1978), chap. 5. On Canadians there, see A. Hamish Ion, *The Cross and the Rising Sun: The Canadian Protestant Missionary Movement in the Japanese Empire, 1872-1931* (Waterloo, ON: Wilfrid Laurier University Press 1990), 108-9.
55 NAC YWCA Papers, vol. 35, CM to Clara Benson, 1 September 1907. Macdonald was not unique among Canadians in finding the social life at Karuizawa oppressive; see Howard and Gwen R.P. Norman, *One Hundred Years in Japan, 1873-1973* (Toronto: Division of World Outreach, United Church of Canada 1981), 401.
56 NAC YWCA Papers, vol. 35, CM to Clara Benson, 1 September 1907.
57 Except where indicated otherwise, this account of Uemura is based on Aoyoshi Katsuhisa, *Dr. Masahisa Uemura: A Christian Leader* (Tokyo: Kyōbunkan 1941); Richard H. Drummond, *A History of Christianity in Japan* (Grand Rapids, MI: William B. Eerdmans 1971), 208-18; Galen M. Fisher, *Creative Forces in Japan* (New York: Missionary Education Movement of the United States and Canada 1923), 155-8; Iglehart, *Protestant Christianity*, 111-2; Charles H. Germany, *Protestant Theologies in Modern Japan: A History of Dominant Theological Currents from 1920-1960* (Tokyo: International Institute for the Study of Religions Press 1965), 19-27.
58 Takeda Kiyoko, *Ningenkan no Sōkohu: Kindai Nihon no shisō to Kirisutokyō* (The Struggle for Humanity: Modern Thought and Christianity in Japan) (Tokyo: Kōbundōshinsha 1959; rev. ed. 1967), 279-92; Robert Enns, '"Slander against Our People:" Tamura Naomi and the Japanese Bride Incident,' *Japanese Religions* 18 (January 1993):15-46.
59 Augusta Moore Stoehr, 'Mission Co-operation in Japan: The Meiji Gakuin Textbook Controversy,' *Journal of Presbyterian History* 54-3 (Fall 1976):336-54.
60 Aoyoshi, *Dr. Masahisa Uemura*, 45; Drummond, *Christianity in Japan*, 219-20; Takeda Kiyoko, 'Japan's First Christian Love Letters,' *Japan Christian Quarterly* 25-3 (1959), 212-18.
61 *Presbyterian*, 8 August and 12 September 1907.
62 NAC YWCA Papers, vol. 35, CM to J.A. Macdonald, 17 October 1907. The reference is to anti-Oriental rioting in Vancouver on 7 September 1907 following a large parade organized by the Asiatic Exclusion League. See W. Peter Ward, *White Canada Forever* (Montreal and Kingston: McGill-Queen's University Press 1978), 65-70.
63 NAC YWCA Papers, vol. 35, CM to J.A. Macdonald, 17 October 1907.
64 Ibid.
65 Ibid. At this time the *Presbyterian* carried almost weekly reports and editorial comment on Oriental immigration into Canada. The paper professed to present all sides of the question, while stressing the need to respect 'provincial rights' and noting that a majority of British Columbians, both employers and workers, were opposed to Oriental immigration. *Presbyterian*, 15, 29 August 1907; 12, 19 September 1907; 10 October 1907.
66 NAC YWCA Papers, vol. 35, CM to J.A. Macdonald, 17 October 1907.

Chapter 4: From Tokyo to Aberdeen: 'The Lady Student'
1 NAC YWCA Papers, vol. 35, CM to family, 16 January 1908.
2 Ibid.
3 *Canada's Share in Foreign Association Work* (Toronto: Dominion Council of the YWCA 1910), 34.
4 Ibid., 22-6, 34.
5 Ibid., 28.

6 NAC YWCA Papers, vol. 35, CM's report to Commission III, Edinburgh Conference 1910.
7 *Canada's Share*, 31; on Gaines, see Dorothy Robins-Mowry, 'Not a Foreigner, but a Sensei – a Teacher: Nannie B. Gaines of Hiroshima,' in Leslie A. Flemming, ed., *Women's Work for Women: Missionaries and Social Change in Asia* (Boulder, CO: Westview Press 1989), 87-115.
8 *Canada's Share*, 31.
9 Watanabe Matsuko, ed., *Emma Kaufman to Tokyo YWCA* (Emma Kaufman and the Tokyo YWCA) (Tokyo: YWCA 1963), 153.
10 *Canada's Share*, 33.
11 NAC YWCA Papers, vol. 35, CM to Mrs. G.S. [Mary] Phelps, 2 September 1910.
12 C. Howard Hopkins, *John R. Mott, 1865-1955* (Grand Rapids, MI: William B. Eerdmans 1979), 344.
13 NAC YWCA Papers, vol. 35, CM's report to Commission III. Macdonald's emphasis on the central place of education in missionary work put her in the mainstream of contemporary missionary thought and practice. By 1900, most Protestant missions placed more emphasis on education than on direct evangelism, a development accompanied by the increasing presence of women missionaries, who constituted more than half of missionary personnel in most fields, as they were even earlier in some areas. See William R. Hutchison, *Errand to the World: American Protestant Thought and Foreign Missions* (Chicago and London: University of Chicago Press 1987), 100-3; Patricia Hill, *The World Their Household: The American Woman's Foreign Mission Movement and Cultural Transformation 1870-1920* (Ann Arbor: University of Michigan Press 1985), 131-7; Flemming, *Women's Work*, intro., 3-5.
14 NAC YWCA Papers, vol. 35, CM's report to Commission III.
15 Ibid.
16 Ibid.
17 Ibid.
18 Ibid.
19 Ibid.
20 Ibid.
21 NAC YWCA Papers, vol. 35, CM to Mrs. G.S. [Mary] Phelps, 2 September 1910.
22 *Canada's Share*, 36.
23 NAC YWCA Papers, vol. 57, Foreign Committee Minutes, 1910-1913, Minutes of Meeting, 19 February 1910.
24 CMP, 3-37, Macdonald appointment book, 3 February 18, April 1910, and undated notes.
25 Ibid., 18 April - 9 May 1910.
26 Anna V. Rice, *A History of the World's Young Women's Christian Association* (New York: Women's Press 1947), 119.
27 Ibid., 124-9.
28 NAC YWCA Papers, vol. 35, CM to Mrs. G.S. [Mary] Phelps, 2 September 1910.
29 *World Missionary Conference, Edinburgh 1910, Official Handbook* (New York: Fleming H. Revell 1911); Hopkins, *John R. Mott, 1865-1955*, 342-61; W.R. Hogg, *Ecumenical Foundations: A History of the International Missionary Council* (New York: Harper 1952), chap. 3.
30 NAC YWCA Papers, vol. 35, CM to Mrs. G.S. [Mary] Phelps, 2 September 1910.
31 Ibid.
32 Ibid.
33 Ibid.
34 NAC YWCA Papers, vol. 57, Foreign Committee Minutes, 1910-1913, Minutes of Meeting, 4 October 1910.
35 NAC YWCA Papers, vol. 35, CM to sister Peg, 15 October 1910.
36 Ibid.
37 Ibid., CM to mother, 16 October 1910.

38 Ibid., CM to parents, 24 October 1910.
39 Ibid., CM to sister Peg, 15 October 1910.
40 NAC YWCA Papers, vol. 36, CM to Mrs. G.S. [Mary] Phelps, 3 January 1911.
41 Ibid., CM to sister Peg, 15 October 1910.
42 Ibid.
43 Ibid.
44 Ibid., CM to mother, 21 October 1910; CM to parents, 24 October 1910.
45 Ibid., CM to mother, 30 October 1910.
46 Ibid., CM to sister Peg, 15 October 1910.
47 CMP, 1-1, CM to family, 9 November 1910.
48 NAC YWCA Papers, vol. 35, CM to father, 13 November 1910.
49 CMP, 1-1, CM to family, 9 November 1910.
50 NAC YWCA Papers, vol. 35, CM to mother, 30 October 1910.
51 Ibid., CM to sister Peg, 15 October 1910.
52 Ibid.
53 Ibid.
54 Ibid.
55 Ibid., CM to mother, 21 October 1910; 30 October 1910; 21 October 1910
56 David S. Cairns, *An Autobiography, with a Memoir by D.M. Baillie* (London: SCM Press 1950), 10-15, 82-169, passim.
57 Ibid., 13-15, 117-18, 167-8.
58 J.R. Fleming, *A History of the Church in Scotland, 1875-1929* (Edinburgh: T & T Clark 1933), 234-7.
59 CMP, 1-19, Cairns to Margaret (Peg) Macdonald, 2 August 1931.
60 NAC YWCA Papers, vol. 35, CM to her mother, 30 October 191.
61 Cairns, *Autobiography*, 35, 104.
62 Ibid., 25, 212-15.
63 NAC YWCA Papers, vol. 35, CM to father, 13 November 1910; vol. 36., CM to Mrs. G.S. [Mary] Phelps, 3 January 1911.

Chapter 5: 'Grubbing at the Lingo'

1 NAC YWCA Papers, vol. 57, Foreign Committee Minutes, Minutes of Meeting, 10 December 1910 and 3 February 1911.
2 Ibid., 29 March 1911.
3 NAC YWCA Papers, vol. 35, CM to family, 30 August 1911.
4 Ibid., CM to family, 2 October 1911.
5 Ibid., CM to mother, 24 September 1911.
6 Ibid., CM to family, 18 November and 10 December 1910.
7 Richard H. Drummond, *A History of Christianity in Japan* (Grand Rapids, MI: William B. Eerdmans 1971), 211-12; Sheldon Garon, *The State and Labor in Modern Japan* (Berkeley: University of California Press 1987), 31-2.
8 Charles W. Iglehart, *A Century of Protestant Christianity in Japan* (Tokyo: Charles E. Tuttle 1959), 139-41; Kozaki Hiromichi, *Reminiscences of Seventy Years: The Autobiography of a Japanese Pastor* (Tokyo: Christian Literature Society of Japan 1933), 236-51; Carol Gluck, *Japan's Modern Myths: Ideology in the Late Meiji Period* (Princeton, NJ: Princeton University Press 1985), 93, 134-5.
9 NAC YWCA Papers, vol. 35, CM to sister Peg, 21 October 1911.
10 Ibid., 18 November 1911.
11 Ibid., CM to family, 18 November 1911.
12 NAC YWCA Papers, vol. 57, Report of CM, 10 June 1912; vol. 35., CM to family, 13 May 1912.

13 Ibid., vol. 35, CM to family, 18 November 1911.
14 Ibid., CM to sister Peg, 26 November 1911.
15 Ibid., CM to family, 10 December 1911.
16 Ibid.; CMP, 2-25, Caroline Macdonald, 'The Ability to Speak in the Japanese Language' [1923?].
17 NAC YWCA Papers, vol. 35, CM to family, 18 December 1911.
18 Ibid.
19 Ibid., 2 February 1912.
20 Ibid., 3 March 1912.
21 Ibid., 9 February 1912.
22 Ibid., 2 and 9 February 1912.
23 Ibid., 18 December 1911; Interview with Matsumiya's daughter, Morita Sakiko, in Kamakura, 3 December 1984.
24 NAC YWCA Papers, vol. 35, CM to family, 9 February 1912.
25 CMP, 1-4, CM to mother, 14 January 1912; Interview with Morita Sakiko in Kamakura, 3 December 1984.
26 NAC YWCA Papers, vol. 35, CM to mother, 14 March 1912.
27 Galen M. Fisher, *Creative Forces in Japan* (New York: Missionary Education Movement of the United States and Canada 1923), 135-7; Ernest W. Clement, *A Handbook of Modern Japan* (Chicago: A.C. McClurg 1904), 186-8.
28 NAC YWCA Papers, vol. 35, CM to family, 23 November 1912.
29 Ibid., 3 March 1912.
30 Ibid.
31 Ibid., 11 March 1912; 9 February and 26 March 1912.
32 Ibid.; Matsumiya Yahei, 'Makudonarudo joshi to watashi' (Miss Macdonald and I), *Joshi Seinen Kai* (December 1932).
33 NAC YWCA Papers, vol. 35, CM to family, 13 May 1912.
34 Ibid., CM to sister Peg, 30 November 1912.
35 CMP, 2-25, Caroline Macdonald, 'The Ability to Speak in the Japanese Language,' [1923?].
36 NAC YWCA Papers, vol. 35, CM to family, 7 October 1912.
37 Ibid., CM to Clara Benson, 25 January 1913.
38 Ibid., CM to family, 6 May 1912.
39 Ibid.; CM to Clara Benson, 10 June 1912.
40 Ibid., CM to family, 25 June 1912.
41 Ibid., 13 April 1912.
42 Ibid., CM to Clara Benson, 10 June 1912.
43 Ibid.
44 Ibid., vol. 35, Report of Summer Conference 1912, by Ruth Ragan
45 Tyler Dennett, *The Democratic Movement in Asia* (New York: Association Press 1918), 141, cited in Fisher, *Creative Forces*, 136-7.
46 NAC YWCA Papers, vol. 35, Report of Summer Conference 1912, by Ruth Ragan

Chapter 6: The New Era of Taishō and 'the Woman Question'

1 Edward Seidensticker, *Low City, High City: Tokyo from Edo to the Earthquake* (Tokyo: Charles E. Tuttle 1984), 252-4; Carol Gluck, *Japan's Modern Myths: Ideology in the Late Meiji Period* (Princeton, NJ: Princeton University Press 1985), 73-101, 215-21, 213-20; Edwin O. Reischauer, *The Japanese* (Cambridge, MA: Harvard University Press 1981), 244-7.
2 NAC YWCA Papers, vol. 35, CM to Clara Benson, 10 June 1912.
3 Gluck, *Japan's Modern Myths*, 221-7.
4 *Tokyo Asahi Shinbun*, 15 September 1912, cited in Gluck, *Japan's Modern Myths*, 222.

5 Ibid., 223-4; Charles W. Iglehart, *A Century of Protestant Christianity in Japan* (Tokyo: Charles E. Tuttle 1959), 136.
6 *Times*, 30 August 1912, cited in Gluck, *Japan's Modern Myths*, 222. Macdonald appears to have read the *Times* fairly regularly.
7 NAC YWCA Papers, vol. 35, CM to family, 7 October 1912.
8 Ibid., CM to sister Peg, 30 November 1912.
9 Gluck, *Japan's Modern Myths*, 227-37.
10 NAC YWCA Papers, vol. 35, CM to Clara Benson, 15 January 1913.
11 Ibid., CM to Una Saunders, 18 November 1912.
12 Ibid., CM to sister Peg, 30 November 1912.
13 NAC YWCA Papers, vol. 35, CM's report to Foreign Committee, Canadian YWCA, November 1913.
14 A.G. Hogg, *Christ's Message of the Kingdom: A Course of Daily Study for Private Students and for Bible Circles* (Edinburgh: T & T. Clark 1911; 9th ed., 1924).
15 NAC YWCA Papers, vol. 35, CM to mother, 2 February 1912.
16 Ibid., CM to sister Peg, 13 July 1912.
17 Ibid., CM to family, 13 May 1912.
18 Ibid., CM to sister Peg, 13 July 1912.
19 Ibid.
20 Ibid., CM to sister Nellie, 21 October 1912.
21 CMP, 1-3, CM to family, 11 November 1912.
22 NAC YWCA Papers, vol. 35, CM to family, 11 March and 18 November 1912; CM to Clara Benson, 15 January 1913.
23 Ibid., CM to family, 3 November 1912; CM to Clara Benson, 25 January 1913.
24 Ibid.
25 Ibid., CM to sister Peg, 30 November 1912.
26 Caroline Macdonald, 'The World of Japanese Women as It Appears to My Eyes,' *Meiji No Joshi* 9, no. 6 (1912):8-10; NAC YWCA Papers, vol. 35, CM to Una Saunders, 18 November 1912; CM to friends, November 1913.
27 NAC YWCA Papers, vol. 35, CM's report to Foreign Committee, Canadian YWCA, November 1913.
28 Ibid., CM to Clara Benson, 25 January 1913.
29 Caroline Macdonald, 'Does Japan Need the Social Message?' pamphlet, National Council of the YWCA, USA, 1913, 14-15.
30 NAC YWCA Papers, vol. 35, CM to family, 15 June 1912.
31 Ibid., CM to Clara Benson, 25 January 1913.
32 Yamakawa Kikue, *Onna nidai no ki* (Records of Two Generations of Women – Mother and Daughter (Tokyo: Heibonsha 1972), 140-1, cited in E. Patricia Tsurumi, *Factory Girls: Women in the Thread Mills of Meiji Japan* (Princeton, NJ: Princeton University Press 1990), 139-40.
33 *Three Years' Survey: Canada and Other Lands* (Toronto: Dominion Council of the YWCA 1914), 9-11.
34 NAC YWCA Papers, vol. 35, CM to Una Saunders, 18 November 1912.
35 Macdonald, 'Does Japan Need the Social Message?' 9-11.
36 *Mizu o kaze o hikari o nihon YWCA 80 nen 1905-1985* (Water, Wind, and Light: 80 Years of the Japanese YWCA 1905-1985) (Tokyo: Nihon YWCA 1987), 61-2.
37 NAC YWCA Papers, vol. 35, CM to family, 7 June 1912.
38 Ibid., CM to Clara Benson, 25 January 1913; CM to family, 11 March 1913.
39 Ibid., CM to Clara Benson, 25 January 1913; CM to friends, [1913].
40 *The Continuation Committee Conferences in Asia, 1912-1913* (New York: Missionary Education Movement of the United States and Canada 1913), 460-3.

41 Ibid.
42 NAC YWCA Papers, vol. 35, CM to friends, [1913].
43 Sharon Sievers, *Flowers in Salt: The Beginnings of Feminist Consciousness in Modern Japan* (Stanford, CA: Stanford University Press 1983), chap. 8; Dorothy Robins-Mowry, *The Hidden Sun: Women of Modern Japan* (Boulder, CO: Westview Press 1983), 58-61; Laura R. Rodd, 'Yosano Akiko and the Taishō Debate over the "New Woman,"' in Gail Lee Bernstein, ed., *Recreating Japanese Women, 1600-1945* (Berkeley: University of California Press 1991), 175-9.
44 Yoshikawa Riichi, *Tsuda Umeko Den* (A Biography of Tsuda Umeko) (Tokyo: Tsuda College Alumni Association 1961), 298. Chapter 6 is devoted to an extended speech by Tsuda on the history of women in modern Japan. A summary appeared later in the *Christian Science Monitor*, 13 October 1915.
45 Robins-Mowry, *The Hidden Sun*, 59.
46 Yamakawa, *Onna nidai no ki*, 155-9, cited in Sievers, *Flowers in Salt*, 172.
47 Rodd, 'Yosano Akiko and the Taishō Debate,' in Bernstein, ed., *Recreating Japanese Women*, 175-98, 176, 194.
48 Yamakawa, *Onna nidai no ki*, 160-1, cited in *Reflections on the Way to the Gallows: Rebel Women in Prewar Japan*, trans. and ed. with an introduction by Mikiso Hane (Berkeley: University of California Press 1988), 104.
49 Ibid., 165.
50 NAC YWCA Papers, vol. 35, CM to family, 26 March 1912.
51 Macdonald, 'The World of Japanese Women,' 8-10.
52 Ibid.
53 Caroline Macdonald, 'Are Japanese Women Respected?' *Joshi Seinen Kai* 15 (October 1918):12-13.
54 Robins-Mowry, *The Hidden Sun*, 65-7.

Chapter 7: 'God's Strange Leading'

1 CMP, 1-3, CM to family, 20 October 1913; Shiono Sachiko, 'Caroline Macdonald,' in Watanabe Matsuko, ed., *Emma Kaufman to Tokyo YWCA*, 22-3, 126-72.
2 CMP, 3-39, Macdonald diary, 24 June 1914. Yamada himself, at least in later life, believed that Macdonald's feeling that her failure was a cause of his sin was a source of her sense of responsibility for him. Yamada Zen'ichi, 'Makudonarudo joshi no omokage' (Memories of Miss Macdonald), *Jindō* (Humanity) nos. 311 and 312 (1932).
3 CMP, 1-3, CM to family, 20 October 1913.
4 Ibid., CM to family, 3 December 1913.
5 Ibid., CM to family, 3 and 30 December 1913.
6 Ibid. All trials were public except those in which the presence of an audience was deemed prejudicial to public order. John Gadsby, 'Some Notes on the History of the Japanese Code of Criminal Procedure,' *Law Quarterly Review* 30 (1914):448-63, 461-2.
7 CMP, 1-4, CM to family, 21 January 1914.
8 CMP, 3-43, Macdonald retrospective journal, 19 July 1915, 24.
9 CMP, 1-4, CM to family, 27 January 1914.
10 Ibid., CM to family, 3 and 9 February 1914.
11 CMP, 3-43, Macdonald retrospective journal, 19 July 1915, 11.
12 CMP, 3-38, Macdonald diary, 17 February 1914.
13 CMP, 1-4, CM to sister Peg, 13 March 1914.
14 CMP, 3-43, Macdonald retrospective journal, 19 July 1915, 12-13.
15 CMP 1-4, CM to sister Peg, 15 March 1914. Macdonald never abandoned her opposition to capital punishment and argued against it publicly. See her article 'Kangoku wa gakkō ni' (A Prison Should Be a School), *Chūō Horitsu Shinpō* (Journal of New Legislation) 1, no. 7 (1921): 25-6. On the powers of the procurator, see Nagashima Atsushi, 'The Accused and Society: The

Administration of Criminal Justice in Japan,' in Arthur T. Von Mehren, ed., *Law in Japan: The Legal Order in a Changing Society* (Cambridge, MA: Harvard University Press 1963), 298-302.
16 CMP, 1-4, CM to mother, 3 April 1914.
17 Ibid.
18 NAC YWCA Papers, vol. 35, CM to Clara Benson, 13 April 1914.
19 CMP, 1-4, CM to family, 25 April 1914. The foreign church is the Tokyo Union Church, where the services were in English and the ministers usually Americans.
20 Ibid., CM to mother, 22 May 1914.
21 Ibid., CM to family, 9 February 1914.
22 Ibid., CM to sister Peg, 15 March 1914.
23 Ibid., CM to family, 16 April 1914.
24 Ibid., CM to mother, 3 April 1914.
25 Ibid., CM to family, 22 May 1914.
26 Ibid., CM to family, 3 June 1914.
27 Ibid.
28 NAC YWCA Papers, vol. 35, CM to Clara Benson, 3 September 1914.
29 Ibid.
30 CMP, 1-4, CM to mother, 14 September 1914.
31 Ibid., CM to father, 19 November 1914.
32 Ibid., CM to family, 9 November 1914; CM to sister Peg, 29 November 1914; CMP, 3-40, Macdonald diary, 8 November 1914.
33 NAC YWCA Papers, vol. 35, CM to family, 24 October 1914.
34 CMP, 1-4, CM to sister Peg, 29 November 1914.
35 Ibid., CM to family, 13 December 1914.
36 Ibid., 9 December 1914.
37 Ibid.
38 Ibid.
39 Ibid.
40 Ibid.
41 Ibid.
42 CMP, 3-43, Macdonald retrospective journal, 20 July 1915, 22-6.
43 Ibid., 17-18.
44 Ibid., 18-19.
45 Ibid., 20-1.
46 CMP, 1-4, CM to family, 9 February 1914.
47 Ibid.
48 Ibid., 25 April 1914.
49 Ibid., CM to sister Peg, 15 March 1914; CM to family, 21 May 1914.
50 CMP, 3-43, Macdonald retrospective journal, 20 July 1915, 26.
51 John Gadsby, 'Some Notes on the History of the Japanese Code of Criminal Procedure,' *Law Quarterly Review* 30 (1914):448-63, 462.

Chapter 8: Prisoners and Prisons

1 Namae Takayuki, *Nihon Kirisutokyō shakaijigyōshi* (History of Christian Social Work in Japan) (Tokyo: Kyōbunkan 1931), chap. 6, part 2; Hara Taneaki, 'Prison Gate Work,' *Christian Movement in the Japanese Empire*, 1922, 191-7; Tomeoka Kōsuke, 'Prison System of Japan,' *Far East* 2 (August 1897):334-6; Nakazato Tatsuo, *Keimusagyō no honshitsu nitsuite no kenkyū* (The Principles of Penal Servitude), *Studies in Penal Policies* 44 (Tokyo: Hōmu Kenkyūjo 1958), 137.
2 CMP, 2-26, 'Outlines of Criminal Justice and Administration,' comp. by Dr. S. Motoji,

Ministry of Justice, n.d., trans. by Caroline Macdonald; Kenzo Takayanagi, 'A Century of Innovation: The Development of Japanese Law, 1869-1961,' in Arthur T. Von Mehren, ed., *Law in Japan: The Legal Order in a Changing Society* (Cambridge, MA: Harvard University Press 1963), 15-21; John L. Gillin, *Taming the Criminal: Adventures in Penology* (1931; reprint, Montclair, NJ: Patterson Smith 1969), chap. 1.

3 Namae Takayuki, *Nihon Kirisutokyō shakaijigyōshi* (History of Christian Social Work in Japan) (Tokyo: Kyōbunkan 1931), chap. 6, part 2.

4 On Arima's earlier life, see Miyoshi Akira, *Arima Shirosuke* (Tokyo: Yoshikawa Kyōbunkan 1967), 1-213; Ōkuma Miyoshi, *Meijijidai Runinshi* (Exiles of the Meiji Era) (Tokyo: Yūzankaku 1974), 200-5; Masaki Akira, *Shiganshū* (Volunteer Prisoner) (Tokyo: Nihon Keijiseisaku Kenkyūkai 1965), 11-12.

5 Miyoshi, *Arima Shirosuke*, 197-205.

6 CMP, 3-42, Macdonald diary, 25 May 1915.

7 Ibid. Macdonald's quotation from Patmore is not entirely accurate; she omitted two lines.

8 Ibid.

9 Ibid.

10 'Caroline Macdonald: An Appreciation,' *Missionary Monthly*, September 1931.

11 NAC YWCA Papers, vol. 35, CM to Executive Committee, World's YWCA, London, 16 January 1915.

12 CMP, 1-3, CM to family, 6 July 1914; CM to Clara Benson, 18 November 1914; NAC YWCA Papers, vol. 13, Minutes of the Foreign Committee, 1913-1917, passim.

13 CMP, 3-43, Macdonald retrospective journal, 19 July 1915, 9-10.

14 Ibid.

15 CMP, 3-48, Macdonald diary, 17 January 1916.

16 NAC YWCA Papers, vol. 13, Minutes of the Foreign Committee, 1913-1917, 27 September 1915.

17 Ibid., 29 March 1916.

18 E. Stagg Whitin, Introduction to Julia K. Jaffray, ed., *The Prison and the Prisoner: A Symposium* (Boston: Little, Brown 1917), vii-viii; see also E. Stagg Whitin, *Caged Man* (New York: Columbia University, Academy of Political Science 1913).

19 E. Stagg Whitin, 'Prison Labor Legislation in 1911,' in *The Treatment of the Offender*, Sixty-Seventh Annual Report of the Prison Association of New York, 1911 (Albany, NY: Prison Association 1912), 53.

20 CMP, 3-44, Notes on visits to New York institutions, 1915; CMP, 3-45, Macdonald diary, 7-25 October 1915. On Richmond, see Muriel W. Pumphrey, 'Mary Ellen Richmond, 1861-1928,' in Edward T. James et al., *Notable American Women*, vol. 3 (Cambridge, MA: Harvard University Press 1971), 152-4; Roy Lubove, *The Professional Altruist: The Emergence of Social Work as a Career, 1880-1930* (Cambridge, MA: Harvard University Press 1965), 45-9 and passim.

21 Blake McKelvey, *American Prisons: A History of Good Intentions* (Montclair, NJ: Patterson Smith 1977), 262-3; Charles Stastny and Gabrielle Tyrnauer, *Who Rules the Joint?: The Changing Political Culture of Maximum-Security Prisons in America* (Lexington, MA: Lexington Books 1982), 45-53, 64-5. See also Frank Tannenbaum, *Osborne of Sing Sing* (Chapel Hill, NC: University of North Carolina Press 1977); Rudolph W. Chamberlain, *There Is No Truce: A Life of Thomas Mott Osborne* (New York: Macmillan 1935).

22 CMP, 3-45, Macdonald diary, 25 October 1915.

23 Thomas Mott Osborne, *Society and Prisons: Some Suggestions for a New Penology* (New Haven: Yale University Press 1916), 233-5. See also statements by Osborne in Corrine Bacon, comp., *Prison Reform* (New York: H.W. Wilson 1917; reprint Montclair, NJ: Patterson Smith 1974), 129-37, 305-9.

24 CMP, 3-44, Macdonald diary, 7-14 October 1915; CMP, 3-48, Notes from speech to YWCA, Tokyo, 28 April 1916.

5 CMP, 1-5, CM to Julia K. Jaffray, 8 April 1916.
6 CMP, 3-46, Macdonald diary, 7 January 1916.
7 Ibid.
8 Ibid.
9 Shiono Sachiko, 'Caroline Macdonald,' in Watanabe Matsuko, ed., *Emma Kaufman to Tokyo YWCA* (Tokyo: YWCA 1963), 126-72.
0 CMP, 1-5, CM to Julia K. Jaffray, 8 April 1916.
1 Interview with Matsumiya's daughter, Morita Sachiko, in Kamakura, 3 December 1984; Shiono, 'Caroline Macdonald,' 162; CMP, 3-49, Macdonald diary, 9 September 1916.
2 Ibid., 29 April 1916.
3 Ibid.
4 CMP, 1-5, CM to Julia K. Jaffray, 8 April 1916.
5 Caroline Macdonald, 'The Juvenile Court in Chicago,' *Joshi Seinen Kai* 13, no. 7 (1916).
6 CMP, 1-5, CM to Julia K. Jaffray, 8 April 1916.
7 Ibid., CM to Jean Macdonald, 1 April 1916.
8 Ibid., CM to Julia K. Jaffray, 29 April 1916.
9 Ibid., CM to Julia K. Jaffray, 8 April 1916.
0 Ibid.
1 Ibid.; CM to Julia K. Jaffray, 29 April 1916. The extent of Macdonald's knowledge of the Osborne controversy is unclear. Much of what lay behind it was obscure to contemporary observers in the United States. A recent assessment suggests Osborne was the victim of public reaction to the speed and dramatic flamboyance with which he introduced his reforms, and to the resistance of prison guards and 'elite' middle-class inmates such as ex-bankers. These elements encouraged Republican politicians to bring Osborne, a Democrat, before a grand jury on charges ranging from perjury, failure to govern the prison, and illegal behaviour with inmates. Stastny and Tyranauer, *Who Rules the Joint?*, 50.
2 CMP, 1-6, CM to Julia K. Jaffray, 18 August 1917.
3 CMP, 1-5, CM to Julia K. Jaffray, 29 June 1916.
4 CMP, 1-6, CM to Julia K. Jaffray, 18 August 1917.
5 CMP, 1-5, CM to Mrs. Borden, 23 August 1916.
6 Ibid., CM to Julia K. Jaffray, 6 April 1916.
7 CMP, 3-46, Macdonald journal, 16 April 1916.
8 Ibid.
9 CMP, 1-6, CM to David Cairns, 21 January 1917.
0 Ibid.
1 Ibid., CM to Mrs. Borden, 25 February 1917.
2 Ibid. CM to David Cairns, 21 January 1917.
3 Ibid.
4 CMP, 3-49, Macdonald diary, 30 August 1916.
5 CMP, 1-6, CM to Mrs. Borden, 25 February 1917.
6 CMP, 3-52, Macdonald diary, 3 February 1917.
7 CMP, 3-49, Macdonald diary, 31 December 1916.
8 CMP, 1-6, CM to Mrs. Borden, 25 February 1917.
9 Ibid., CM to David Cairns, 21 January 1917.
0 CMP, 1-5, CM to Julia K. Jaffray, 5 August 1916.
1 Ibid.
2 Ibid., CM to Julia K. Jaffray, 29 June 1916.
3 Ibid.
4 In time, prison governors left Caroline in no doubt that her work made their lives easier. One told her: 'When they go quietly, as those do who are touched by your religion, we weep tears

of sympathy for them, but when they struggle & make a row it is terrible. We have to do our duty & we can't have sympathy.' CMP, 1-8, CM to family, 22 August 1919.
65 CMP, 3-52, Macdonald diary, 15 February 1917. Unfortunately, we do not know the end of this story.
66 Ibid., 14 February 1917.
67 Ibid.

Chapter 9: 'A Gentleman in Prison'

1 Brian J. Fraser, 'For the Uplift of the World: The Mission Thought of James A. Macdonald,' in John S. Moir and C.T. McIntire, eds., *Canadian Protestant and Catholic Missions, 1820s – 1960s: Historical Essays in Honour of John Webster Grant* (New York: Peter Lang 1988), 191-219.
2 CMP, 3-54, Macdonald diary, 1 and 3 January 1918.
3 Ibid., 3 February 1918.
4 CMP, 3-53, Macdonald diary, 8 and 10 October 1917. 'Dr. W.' refers to the Reverend Dr. S.H. Wainwright, an American Methodist who served for many years as secretary of the Christian Literature Society of Japan.
5 Kawai Michi and Kubushiro Ochimi, *Japanese Women Speak: A Message from the Christian Women of Japan to the Christian Women of America* (Boston: Central Committee on the United Study of Foreign Missions 1934), 88-91; Charles W. Iglehart, A *Century of Protestant Christianity in Japan* (Tokyo: Charles E. Tuttle 1959), 161.
6 CMP, 3-54, Macdonald diary, 15 January 1918.
7 CMP, 3-49, Macdonald diary, 9 and 21 November 1916.
8 Ibid., 11 June 1918.
9 Ibid., 19 February 1918.
10 A *Gentleman in Prison, with the Confessions of Tōkichi Ishii Written in Tokyo Prison*, prefaces by Caroline Macdonald, John Kelman, and Fujiya Suzuki, 2nd ed. (London: SCM Press 1927), 14-15.
11 A *Gentleman in Prison*, 71.
12 Ibid., 71-7 and passim.
13 Ibid., 103-4.
14 CMP, 1-7, CM to Julia K. Jaffray, 29 August 1918.
15 A *Gentleman in Prison*, 87-9.
16 Ibid., 155.
17 Ibid., 27.
18 A *Gentleman in Prison*, 156-7.
19 CMP, 3-55, Macdonald diary, 8 August 1918.
20 A *Gentleman in Prison*, 158-60; CMP, 3-55, Macdonald journal, 8 August 1918.
21 CMP, 1-7, CM to Julia K. Jaffray, 29 August 1918.
22 Published by Ishio Keibunkaku, the book was printed in the printing shop of Kosuge prison and contained prefaces by Tagawa Daikichirō, Governor Arima Shirosuke, Suzuki Fujiya (Ishii's lawyer), and Macdonald.
23 Reviews in: *Yomiuri Shinbun*, 11 January 1919; *Yorozu Chōhō*, 12 January 1919; *Tokyo Nichinichi Shinbum* (now *Mainichi Shinbun*), 16 January 1919; *Tokyo Ashi Shinbun*, 18 January 1919; *Jiji Shinpō*, 23 January 1919; statistics on the number published are unavailable. In 1933, as a tribute to Macdonald after her death, Tagawa Daikichirō was instrumental in arranging for the publication of a fourth Japanese edition by Kyōbunkan, Tokyo. It was published again in 1950 by one Hara of Shikoku Island. The author thanks Sasaki Shigenori, Librarian of the Archives of Prison Reform, Tokyo, for information on the publishing history of the book.
24 The story was first published in April 1919 in *Chūō Kōron*, a popular 'middle-brow' monthly, and republished several times, most recently in Kawamori Yoshizō, ed., *Mumei Sakka no Nikki* (Diary of a Writer Unknown to Fame) (Tokyo: Iwanami Bunko 1953; 7th ed., 1988).

5 CMP, 1-5, CM to Jean Macdonald, 1 April 1918.
6 CMP, 3-48, Macdonald diary, 1916-17.
7 CMP, 3-49, Macdonald diary, 27 December 1916.
8 CMP, 1-6, CM to David Cairns, 2 January 1917.
9 Ibid., CM to Julia K. Jaffray, 5 January 1917.
0 Sharon H. Nolte, *Liberalism in Modern Japan: Ishibashi Tanzan and His Teachers, 1905-1960* (Berkeley: University of California Press 1987), 148-50.
1 Peter Duus, *Party Rivalry and Political Change in Taishō Japan* (Cambridge, MA: Harvard University Press 1968), 83, 97.
2 Robert A. Scalapino, *Democracy and the Party Movement in Prewar Japan* (Cambridge, MA: Harvard University Press 1953), 303; Sugimoto Tamisaburō, 'Tagawa Daikichirō (1869-1947),' in *Nihon Kirusutokyō kyōikushi* (History of Christian Education in Japan), Kirisutokyō Gakkō Kyōiku Dōmei (Educational Federation of Christian Schools) (Tokyo: Shōbunsha 1977), 270-7; Winburn T. Thomas, 'Daikichirō Tagawa on Japanese Spirit and Christianity,' *Japan Christian Quarterly* 15 (July 1940):251-4.
3 'Hōhō o shiranutami' (People Who Don't Know the Way), *Bunmei Hyōron* 4 (January 1917).
4 CMP, 3-52, Macdonald journal, 14 February 1917.
5 None of the extensive records of Uemura's life refer to these charges, nor does his granddaughter, Kawato Machiko, recall hearing of them. Court records of the period have been destroyed. It seems probable that the charges were withdrawn.
6 Richard H. Drummond, *A History of Christianity in Japan* (Grand Rapids, MI: William B. Eerdmans 1971), 211-12; F.G. Notehelfer, *Kōtoku Shōsui: A Portrait of a Japanese Radical* (Cambridge, MA: Harvard University Press 1971), chap. 4.
7 CMP, 1-7, CM to Julia K. Jaffray, 29 August 1918.
8 William Axling, *Japan on the Upward Trail* (New York: Missionary Education Movement of the United States and Canada 1923), 98-103.
9 CMP, 1-7, CM to Julia K. Jaffray, 29 August 1919; Tagawa Daikichirō, 'Makudonarudo joshi o omou' (Remembering Miss Macdonald), *Shakai Jigyō* (Social Work) 16, no. 6 (1932).
0 CMP, 3-55, Macdonald diary, 9 and 10 February 1919.
1 Ibid., 10 February 1919.
2 Ibid., 22 February 1919.
3 Ibid., 7 March 1919.
4 Ibid., 12 and 17 March 1919.
5 Ibid., 13 and 10 January 1919.
6 Ibid., 7, 10, and 11 January 1919.
7 Ibid., 15 and 16 January 1919.
8 In 1872, as Yamakawa Sutematsu, Princess Ōyama was, like Tsuda Ume, one of the young girls who were the first sent abroad to study. Following her graduation from Vassar College, she married Lord Ōyama Iwao and was henceforth Princess Ōyama. Like Tsuda, she was always more competent in English than in Japanese.
9 CMP, 3-55, Macdonald diary, 16 January 1919. A biography of Princess Ōyama gives a different account of these events, never mentioning Macdonald and crediting Princess Ōyama with persuading Tsuji to accept the position. Macdonald's account is the more immediate and better documented. Two weeks after the inauguration of Tsuji as president of Tsuda College, Princess Ōyama died of Spanish influenza, which was an epidemic in Japan in 1918-19, as elsewhere in the world. Kuno Akiko, *Rokumeikan no Kifujin Ōyama Sutematsu: Nippon Hatsu no Joshi Ryūgakusei* (Lady in Rokumeikan: The First Woman Student Sent Abroad) (Tokyo: Chūōkōronsha 1988), 286-91.
0 CMP, 3-55, Macdonald diary, 20 March 1919; Wi Jo Kang, *Religion and Politics in Korea under Japanese Rule* (Lewiston, NY, and Queenston, ON: E. Mellen Press 1987), 14-26; Ki-baik Lee,

trans. by Edward W. Wagner, *A New History of Korea* (Cambridge, MA: Harvard University Press 1984), 338-45.
51 CMP, 3-55, Macdonald diary, 21 March 1919.
52 Aoyoshi Katsuhisa, *Dr. Masahisa Uemura: A Christian Leader* (Tokyo: Kyōbunkan 1941), 232. Another member of Caroline's circle who held expansionist views was Nitobe Inazō who had served as a colonial civil administrator in Formosa. See Miwa Kimitada, 'Nitobe Inazō, and the Development of Colonial Theories and Practices in Prewar Japan,' Research Papers, Series A-50, Institute of International Relations, Sophia University, 1987.
53 Aoyoshi, *Dr. Masahisa Uemura*, 233.
54 Ibid., 234.
55 Ibid., 249.
56 Ibid., 250-1.
57 CMP, 3-55, Macdonald diary, 21 March 1919.
58 Ibid., 27, 29 April 1919, 6 May 1919.
59 Ibid., 9 May 1919.
60 Hara Keiichirō, ed., *Hara Takashi Nikki* (Diary of Hara Takashi), vol. 8 (Tokyo, 1950), 216, cited in Kang, *Religion and Politics*, 26.
61 CMP, 3-55, Macdonald diary, 15 May 1919.
62 Kang, *Religion and Politics*, 26-32; Galen M. Fisher, *Creative Forces in Japan* (New York: Missionary Education Movement of the United States and Canada 1923), 54-5.
63 Ibid., 189-91; CMP, 2-55, Macdonald diary, 3 June 1919.
64 CMP, 1-13, CM to family, 19 June 1925. Macdonald's opinion on interracial marriage was a minority one among missionaries in the 1920s. See A. Jorgensen, 'Missionary Opinion on Race,' *Japan Christian Quarterly* 3, no. 3 (January 1928), cited in Carlo Caldarola, *Christianity: The Japanese Way* (Leiden: E.J. Brill 1979), 39.
65 CMP, 3-55, Macdonald diary, 3 and 5 August 1919.
66 Caroline Macdonald, 'The Environment of Our Work,' *Japan Evangelist*, August-September 1929, 310-15.
67 Ibid., 310.
68 Ibid., 312.
69 Ibid.
70 Ibid.
71 Ibid., 313. A recent study depicts a somewhat more complex social institution but generally accords well with Macdonald's view of the geisha. See Liza C. Dalby, *Geisha* (Berkeley: University of California Press 1983), 221-4 and passim; even under the best of circumstances, the geisha lived in 'rougher waters' than most women. Ibid., 312.
72 Macdonald, 'The Environment of Our Work,' 314.
73 Ibid., 313.
74 Ibid., 314.
75 Ibid., 313.
76 Caroline Macdonald, 'The Individual in the Social Problem,' *Christian Movement in the Japanese Empire 1919*, 4.

Chapter 10: Tackling 'the Social Cosmos'
1 CMP, 3-55, Macdonald diary, 20 May 1919.
2 Ibid., 20 May, 13 June, 15 July 1919.
3 CMP, 2-34, 'Prospectus of Tokyo Neighbourhood House,' [1919].
4 Ibid.
5 Ibid.
6 CMP, 3-55, Macdonald diary, 17 August 1919.
7 *The Prisons of Tokyo and a Social Service Opportunity* (n.p., [1920?]).

8 Ibid., 18
9 *Missionary Messenger,* 20 June 1920. Later Macdonald sent further reports of her work to this periodical; see issues of January, February, October 1921.
10 CMP, 1-11, Galen Fisher to D.H. Blake, 25 October 1923.
11 CMP, 2-34, 'Prospectus of Tokyo Neighbourhood House,' [1919].
12 CMP, 2-8, Minutes of the New York Committee of the Tokyo Social Settlement, 7 May 1920.
13 *A Gentleman in Prison, with the Confessions of Tokichi Ishii Written in Tokyo Prison,* prefaces by Caroline Macdonald, John Kelman, and Suzuki Fujiya, 2nd ed. (London: SCM Press 1927), Kelman's preface, 7-8.
14 Ibid., 13-14.
15 CMP, 1-8, CM to sister Peg, 1 August 1920.
16 Ibid., 13 August 1920.
17 Ibid.
18 Ibid.; *A Gentleman in Prison,* 16.
19 CMP, 1-8, CM to sister Peg, 17 August 1920.
20 CMP, 1-9, CM to family, 12 March 1921.
21 CMP, 1-8, CM to J.K. Macdonald, 1 August 1921.
22 Ibid. A year later, the book was published in London by an equally reputable publisher, Hodder & Stoughton.
23 *A Gentleman in Prison,* Kelman's preface, 8-12.
24 CMP, 1-9, CM to family, 21 September 1921.
25 Author's interview with Edith Bott, Toronto, 2 September 1984. Edith Bott and her husband, G. Ernest Bott, went to Japan in 1920 with the Canadian Methodist mission and quickly found a kindred spirit in Macdonald. Edith Bott remarked to the author that Macdonald was seen by many of her contemporaries as having '"a man's mind," which at the time was still considered a compliment!'
26 CMP, 1-10, CM to family, 17 March 1922.
27 Ibid.
28 CMP, 1-9, CM to family, 1 April 1921.
29 Ibid., CM to J.K. Macdonald, 21 August 1921; Canadian Presbyterians did not consider the question until the following year, when they decided that women could not be ordained as ministers or elders and thus had no place on the sessions of local congregations, in synods, or in the General Assembly. *Acts and Procedures of the Presbyterian Church in Canada,* 1922, 26, 279.
30 CMP, 1-9, CM to family, 12 March 1921.
31 Ibid., CM to father, 14 August 1921.
32 Harry Emerson Fosdick, *The Living of These Days: An Autobiography* (New York: Harper 1956), 135-6.
33 CMP, 1-9, CM to family, 4 September 1921.
34 Ibid., CM to mother, 29 September 1921; copy of the Rockefeller appeal in CMP, 1-10.
35 CMP, 1-9, CM to family, 20 June and 1 August 1921.
36 Watanabe Matsuko, ed., *Emma Kaufman to Tokyo YWCA* (Emma Kaufman and the Tokyo YWCA) (Tokyo: YWCA 1963), 8.
37 CMP, 1-9, CM to family, 20 June 1921.
38 CMP, 1-10, Galen M. Fisher to CM, 8 May 1922. It seems likely that the appeal suffered from changes that came with the appointment early in 1922 of Beardsley Ruml as director of the Laura Spelman Rockefeller Memorial. Ruml convinced the board of the foundation to phase out grants for general charitable purposes and social welfare projects in favour of large-scale support for university research in the social sciences. See Martin Bulmer, 'Support for Sociology in the 1920s: The Laura Spelman Rockefeller Memorial and the Beginnings of

Modern, Large-Scale Sociological Research in the University,' *American Sociologist* 17 (November 1982):185-92. Later, after the earthquake of 1923, the Laura Spelman Rockefeller Memorial and Mrs. Frank Vanderlip, sources from which the American Committee for Shinrinkan hoped to receive substantial support, devoted large sums to the rebuilding of Tsuda College. Without this competition for funds, Shinrinkan might have received more American support.

39 CMP, 1-10, CM to Galen M. Fisher, 24 August 1922.

40 Ibid., CM to family, 23 August 1922.

41 Ibid.; Noriko Shimada, Hiroko Takamura, Masako Ino, and Hisako Ito, 'Ume Tsuda and Motoko Hani: Echoes of American Cultural Feminism in Japan,' in Carol V.R. George, ed., *'Remember the Ladies': New Perspectives on Women in American History* (Syracuse, NY: Syracuse University Press 1975); Kawai Michi and Kubushiro Ochimi, *Japanese Women Speak: A Message from the Christian Women of Japan to the Christian Women of America* (Boston: Central Committee on the United Study of Foreign Missions 1934), 76-9, 123-4.

42 Tatara Toshio, '1400 Years of Japanese Social Work from Its Origins through the Allied Occupation, 552-1941,' Ph.D. thesis, Bryn Mawr, 1975, 73-128.

43 Sally Ann Hastings, 'The Government, the Citizen, and the Creation of a New Sense of Community: Social Welfare, Local Organizations, and Dissent in Tokyo, 1905-1937,' Ph.D. thesis, University of Chicago, 1980, 4, 11-12.

44 Ibid., 26-8.

45 Ibid., 28-31.

46 CMP, 1-10, CM to family, 23 August 1922.

47 Ibid., Galen M. Fisher to CM, 8 May 1922; CM to family, 23 August 1922.

48 Ibid., CM to family, 23 August 1922.

49 Ibid., CM to Julia K. Jaffray, 25 August 1922.

50 Ibid., Takizawa Matsuyo to CM, 4 July 1922.

51 Ibid., CM to Galen M. Fisher, 22 August 1922.

52 Caroline Macdonald, 'Juvenile Delinquency in Japan,' *The Christian Movement in the Japanese Empire* 1922, 8-9.

53 Ibid.

54 Ibid., 6-7; see also Caroline Macdonald, 'The Juvenile Court in Chicago,' *Joshi Seinen Kai* 13, no. 7 (1916):12-16.

55 Macdonald, 'Juvenile Delinquency,' 2-3.

56 CMP, 2-34, statement by Macdonald, 'Proposed Social Settlement House in Tokyo,' March 1923.

Chapter 11: 'Jesus Was a Labouring Man'

1 Peter Duus, *Party Rivalry and Political Change in Taishō Japan* (Cambridge, MA: Harvard University Press 1968), 111-12; Sheldon Garon, *The State and Labor in Modern Japan* (Berkeley: University of California Press, 1987), 40-1. Another account puts the figures much higher, with 10 million taking part in the uprisings and over 8,000 convicted of various offenses against the state. Jon Halliday, *A Political History of Japanese Capitalism* (New York: Pantheon 1975), 70-1.

2 Duus, *Party Rivalry*, 111-12; Robert A. Scalapino, *Democracy and the Party Movement in Prewar Japan* (Cambridge, MA: Harvard University Press 1953) 210-211; Michael Lewis, *Rioters and Citizens: Mass Protest in Imperial Japan* (Berkeley: University of California Press 1990), 242-53.

3 Caroline Macdonald, 'The Individual in the Social Problem,' *The Christian Movement in the Japanese Empire* 1919, 7-9.

4 Duus, *Party Rivalry*, 140-1.

5 Stephen S. Large, 'The Japanese Labor Movement, 1912-1919: Suzuki Bunji and the Yūaikai,' *Journal of Asian Studies* 39, no. 3 (1970):559-79.

6 Robert A. Scalapino, *The Early Japanese Labor Movement: Labor and Politics in a Developing*

Society (Berkeley: University of California Press 1983), 38-74; Stephen S. Large, *Organized Workers and Socialist Politics in Interwar Japan* (Cambridge: Cambridge University Press 1981), 21-7.

7 Andrew Gordon, *The Evolution of Labor Relations in Japan: Heavy Industry, 1853-1955* (Cambridge, MA: Harvard University Press 1985), 115-16; Garon, *State and Labor*, 54ff; Thomas C. Smith, 'The Right to Benevolence: Dignity and Japanese Workers, 1890-1920,' *Comparative Studies in Society and History* 26 (1984):587-613.

8 Garon, *State and Labor*, 51-3; Large, 'The Japanese Labor Movement, 1912-1919,' 576.

9 CMP, 2-23, 'A Bit of Ramification,' report from Macdonald to friends overseas, 22 March 1922.

10 Ibid.

11 Ibid.

12 Scalapino, *Early Japanese Labor Movement*, 106-8; Large, *Organized Workers*, 44-5.

13 CMP, 2-23, 'A Bit of Ramification,' 22 March 1922.

14 Ibid.

15 Ibid.

16 CMP, 1-9, CM to mother, 29 September 1921; CMP, 1-10, CM to J.K. Macdonald, 12 October 1922.

17 CMP, 3-47, Macdonald diary, 14 January 1922.

18 Large, *Organized Workers*, 33-5; Scalapino, *Early Japanese Labor Movement*, 102; Henry D. Smith II, *Japan's First Student Radicals* (Cambridge, MA: Harvard University Press 1972), passim.

19 Large, *Organized Workers*, 31-5.

20 Ibid., 42-5.

21 Ishimoto Shizue, *Facing Two Ways: The Story of My Life* (New York: Farrar & Rinehart 1935; reprint Stanford, CA: Stanford University Press 1984), 225-30; Margaret Sanger, *My Fight for Birth Control* (New York: Farrar & Rinehart 1931), 238-54.

22 CMP, 1-10, CM to family, 17 March 1922.

23 Ishimoto, *Facing Two Ways*, 253.

24 CMP, 3-47, Macdonald diary, 29 October 1922.

25 CMP, 1-10, CM to family, 17 March 1922. Mary Beard had recently published a short popular history of the labour movement in the United States, had begun her long collaboration with her husband in the writing of American history, and was already pursuing the research that led to her pioneering work, *Woman as Force in History* (1946). A recent study suggests that it was in a speech in Tokyo that Beard first formulated in a comprehensive way her views on the roles of women in the founding of civilization, and exhorted women throughout the world to use an understanding of their 'long past' as a source of strength in playing their part in the continued building of civilization. She attacked H.G. Wells's currently popular *Outline of History* (1920) for ignoring women. There is no direct evidence that Caroline Macdonald heard this address, but given her association with Beard it seems probable. Her sojourn in Japan initiated Beard's interest in the history of Japanese women from the mythical Sun Goddess to the present. Later, with encouragement and help from Katō (Ishimoto) Shizue, she published *The Force of Women in Japanese History* (1953). See Nancy F. Cott, *A Woman Making History: Mary Ritter Beard through her Letters* (New Haven and London: Yale University Press 1991), 25-8, 286-7.

26 Shinkichi, the fifth son of the Mikimoto family, was adopted as a baby by the Saitō family and therefore bore that name. The oldest son, Ryūzō, after graduating from Tokyo Imperial University, went to England and became the preeminent Japanese student of John Ruskin. He was of great assistance to the labour church in its early days.

27 Miyoshi Akira, *Kirisuto ni yoru Rōdōsha: Rōdō kyōkai no ayumi* (Labourers Who Rely on Christ: The History of the Labour Church) (Tokyo: Kirisuto Shimbunsha 1965), part 1, passim.

28 Ibid., part 2, passim. Makino Toraji later became president of Dōshisha University (1938-1947).

29 Ibid.

30 On labour churches see Richard Allen, *The Social Passion: Religion and Social Reform in*

Canada, 1914-28 (Toronto: University of Toronto Press 1971), passim; K.S. Inglis, *Churches and Working Classes in Victorian England* (London: Routledge & K. Paul 1963), chap. 6.

31 The phrase is used by numerous writers, including George O. Totten, 'Japanese Industrial Relations at the Crossroads: The Great Noda Strike of 1927-1928,' in Bernard Silberman and Harry Harootunian, eds., *Japan in Crisis: Essays on Taishō Democracy* (Princeton, NJ: Princeton University Press 1974), 399-401.

32 CMP, 1-10, CM to family, 17 March 1922.

33 Ibid., Macdonald diary, 8 March 1922, 347.

34 The labour activists mentioned below are all referred to in Macdonald's journal for 1922. Except where otherwise indicated, biographical data concerning them is drawn from Shiota Shōhei et al., eds. *Nihon shakaiundō jinmei jiten* (Biographical Dictionary of Social Movements in Japan) (Tokyo: Aoki Shoten 1979).

35 CMP, 3-47, Macdonald diary, 3 May 1922.

36 Ibid., 28 April and 7 May 1922.

37 Garon, *State and Labor,* 87-8; on Nambara, see Andrew E. Barshay, *State and Intellectual in Imperial Japan: The Public Man in Crisis* (Berkeley: University of California Press 1988), 35-122.

38 Hirai Atsuko, *Individualism and Socialism: The Life and Thought of Kawai Eijiro* (Cambridge, MA: Harvard University Press 1986).

39 Garon, *State and Labor,* 55-68.

40 Yamamoto Taijirō, ed., *Uchimura Kanzō Shokan Zenshū* (Collected Works and Correspondence of Uchimura Kanzō), vol. 2 (Tokyo: 1964-5), diary entry, 6 October 1922, 230. I am grateful to John F. Howes for locating and translating this entry.

41 CMP, 1-10, CM to J.K. Macdonald, 12 October 1922.

42 CMP, 3-47, Macdonald diary, 10 May, 28 October, and 11 November 1922.

43 CMP, 1-10, CM to family, 6 July, 23 August 1922.

44 CMP, 3-47, Macdonald diary, 11 November 1922.

45 CMP, 1-10, CM to J.K. Macdonald, 12 October 1922.

46 CMP, 3-47, Macdonald diary, 10 May 1922.

47 Scalapino, *Early Japanese Labor Movement,* 124; Large, *Organized Workers,* 45-8.

48 CMP, 1-10, CM to J.K. Macdonald, 12 October 1922.

49 Ibid.

50 Scalapino, *Early Japanese Labor Movement,* 124; Large, *Organized Workers,* 45-50.

51 This account of the Christmas entertainment is based on 'My Life: The Autobiography of Janet Cunningham Coates,' part I, 27-30. I am grateful to Dr. Donald Coates of Surrey, BC, for lending me a copy of this unpublished document by his mother. There is also a copy in the United Church of Canada Archives (UCCA), Victoria University, Toronto.

52 CMP, 2-25, Macdonald's unpublished ms., 'My Connection with Noda,' [Spring 1928?].

53 Ibid.

54 Totten, 'Japanese Industrial Relations at the Crossroads: The Great Noda Strike of 1927-1928,' 398-9.

55 W. Mark Fruin, *Kikkōman: Company, Clan and Community* (Cambridge, MA: Harvard University Press 1983), 183-9.

56 CMP, 2-25, Macdonald, 'My Connection with Noda.'

57 Fruin, *Kikkōman,* 188-9.

58 CMP, 2-25, Macdonald, 'My Connection with Noda.'

59 Ibid.; Fruin, 'Kikkōman,' 189-94.

Chapter 12: 'Turning Earth's Smoothness Rough'

1 CMP, 2-28, CM to J.K. Macdonald, [1?] September 1923.

2 Edward Seidensticker, *Low City, High City: Tokyo from Edo to the Earthquake* (Tokyo:

Charles E. Tuttle 1984), 3-8; A. Morgan Young, *Japan in Recent Times, 1912-1926* (New York: W. Morrow & Co. 1929; reprint Westport, CT: Greenwood Press, 1973), 295-306; Kawai Michi, *My Lantern* (Tokyo: privately printed 1939), 154-67.

3 CMP, 2-28, CM to J.K. Macdonald, 17 September 1923. Printed in Toronto *Globe*, 17 October 1923.

4 Report of the Reconstruction Survey Commission of the Japan National Christian Council, *Japan Advertiser*, 1 May 1924.

5 CMP, 1-11, CM to the Rev. A.E. Armstrong, [?] October 1923.

6 Miyoshi Akira, *Arima Shirosuke* (Tokyo: Yoshikawa Kyōbunkan 1967), 223-38; Masaki Akira, *Shiganshū* (Volunteer Prisoner) (Tokyo: Nihon Keijiseisaku Kenkyūkai 1965), 27-30; Nakao Bunsaku, 'Arima Shirosuke,' *Kesei* 72, no. 11 (1961):29-45; John Lewis Gillin, *Taming the Criminal: Adventures in Penology* (New York: Macmillan 1931; 2nd ed., Montclair, NJ: Patterson Smith 1969), 12-14.

7 Seidensticker, *Low City, High City*, 7; Richard H. Mitchell, *The Korean Minority in Japan* (Berkeley: University of California Press 1967), 38-41; Michael Weiner, *The Origins of the Korean Community in Japan, 1910-1923* (Atlantic Highland, NJ: Humanities Press International 1989), chap. 6. Macdonald's friend Yamazaki Kesaya and other members of the Civil Liberties Legal Association, which Yamazaki had founded, conducted an investigation of the Korean murders.

8 Watanabe Matsuko, ed., *Emma Kaufman to Tokyo YWCA* (Emma Kaufman and the Tokyo YWCA) (Tokyo: YWCA 1963), 45-71.

9 CMP, 1-13, CM to family, 19 June 1925.

10 CMP, 2-28, CM to J.K. Macdonald, [?] September 1923.

11 Ibid.

12 Ibid.

13 CMP, 1-11, form letter from CM to friends, 1 November 1923.

14 Ibid.

15 Ibid.

16 CMP, 2-24, Molly Baker, 'One Year of Tokyo Neighbourhood House,' 1 September 1924.

17 CMP, 1-11, form letter from CM to friends, 1 November 1923.

18 Ibid.

19 Sally Ann Hastings, 'The Government, the Citizen, and the Creation of a New Sense of Community: Social Welfare, Local Organizations, and Dissent in Tokyo, 1905-1937,' Ph.D. thesis, University of Chicago, 1980, 71-4, 81-4.

20 Kawai Michi, *My Lantern*, 161; Ishimoto Shizue, *Facing Two Ways: The Story of My Life* (New York: Farrar & Rinehart 1935; reprint, Stanford, CA: Stanford University Press 1984), 244-54; Dorothy Robins-Mowry, *Hidden Sun: Women of Modern Japan* (Boulder, CO: Westview Press 1983), 70-2.

21 CMP, 1-11, form letter from CM to friends, 1 November 1923.

22 CMP, 2-24, Molly Baker, 'One Year of Tokyo Neighbourhood House,' 1 September 1924; CMP, 1-11, CM to sister Peg, 31 December 1923.

23 CMP, 1-11, Rev. A.E. Armstrong to CM, 9 November 1923. The size of J.K. Macdonald's personal contribution cannot be ascertained. In the following year he forwarded nearly $5,000, but this appears to be money raised by the Canadian Committee. UCCA, United Church WMS, Dominion Board, Overseas Missions, Japan. See CMP, 1-2, Report of Caroline Macdonald to Presbyterian WMS Board, 1 July - 31 December 1924.

24 CMP, 1-11, CM to sister Peg, 31 December 1924.

25 Ibid.

26 Ibid., copy Galen Fisher to D.E. Blake, 15 October 1923. Blake was a New York lawyer who had lived in Japan and was a member of the American Advisory Committee on Japanese Relief.

27 Ibid., extract from letter of Ambassador Hanihara Masanao to D.E. Blake, 11 December 1923.

28 Archives of the Bureau of Prisons, Tokyo. Memorandum from Governor Arima to Miyagi Chōgorō, Director of the Protection Bureau, Ministry of Justice, 30 August 1923.
29 CMP, 2-31, Emma H. Fisher to J.K. Macdonald, 22 April 1924, as printed and circulated by Macdonald, 14 May 1924; *Toronto Star*, 22 July 1924; London *Free Press*, 26 July 1924.
30 CMP, 1-12, CM to Rev. A.E. Armstrong and Julia K. Jaffray, 25 October 1924.
31 Ibid., CM to J.K. Macdonald, [?] April 1924.
32 Ibid., CM to Rev. A.E. Armstrong and Julia K. Jaffray, 25 October 1924.
33 Ibid., Galen Fisher to Raymond B. Fosdick, 2 April 1924.
34 Sheldon Garon, *The State and Labor in Modern Japan* (Berkeley: University of California Press, 1987), 103-4; Stephen S. Large, *Organized Workers and Socialist Politics in Interwar Japan* (Cambridge: Cambridge University Press 1981), 52-6; George O. Totten, *The Social Democratic Movement in Prewar Japan* (New Haven, CT: Yale University Press 1966), 45-6.
35 Garon, *State and Labor*, 106-10.
36 CMP, 2-24, Caroline Macdonald unpublished ms. 'Karuizawa Vespers,' 27 July 1924.
37 Ibid.
38 Ibid. I am grateful to George Feaver for identifying the source of this expression. In an article entitled 'English Teachers' Organizations,' Wallas wrote of 'that continuous possibility of personal initiative which we vaguely mean by "freedom,"' *New Statesman* 5 (25 September 1915):586-7. It is not clear where Macdonald found the idea, which appears elsewhere in Wallas's writing, including *Our Social Heritage* (New Haven, CT: Yale University Press 1921), 250.
39 CMP, 2-24, 'Karuizawa Vespers,' 27 July 1924.
40 Tomeoka Kōsuke, 'Nihon no rōdōsha nitsuki' (About Japanese Labourers [based on Tomeoka's discussion with Macdonald regarding the Nihon Denki strike]), in *Tomeoka Kōsuke nikki* (Diary of Tomeoka Kōsuke), vol. 5 (Tokyo: Zaidanhojin Kyosei Kyokai 1979), 659-61. Also Yamada Zen'ichi, 'Makudonarudo joshi no omokage' (Memories of Miss Macdonald), *Jindō* (Humanity) nos. 311 and 312 (1932).
41 Ibid.; CMP, 1-12, CM to Rev. A.E. Armstrong and Julia K. Jaffray, 25 October 1924.
42 Tomeoka Kōsuke, *Tomeoka Kōsuke nikki*, 659-61.
43 Ibid. Mochizuki became Macdonald's good friend, took up residence in the settlement, began to study Christianity, was later baptised, and continued to help with the work of Shinrinkan.
44 CMP, 2-26, Ms. in CM's hand, re a day during the Nihon Denki strike. September 1924 [part of a letter to her family?].
45 CMP, 1-12, CM to Rev. A.E. Armstrong and Julia K. Jaffray, 25 October 1924.
46 Ibid.
47 Ibid.
48 CMP, 2-33, Matsuoka Komakichi, 'The Late Miss Macdonald, Mother of Women Labourers,' possibly the ms. for an unpublished speech, 1 August 1932.
49 CMP, 1-12, CM to Rev. A.E. Armstrong and Julia K. Jaffray, 25 October 1924. Despite his prominence in the business world, Shidachi Tsunejirō was under police surveillance at this time for his 'dangerous thought,' as Shidachi and his family were well aware. Interview by Toriumi Yuriko with Yuasa Yana, 11 April 1986.
50 CMP, CM to sister Peg, 11 February 1925.
51 Ibid.
52 Ibid.

Chapter 13: 'The Faith that Rebels'
1 CMP, 1-13, CM to family, 23 April 1925.
2 Ibid., CM to family, 9 September 1925.
3 Ibid., CM to family, 26 April 1925.
4 Ibid.

5 Jane Addams Memorial Collection, University of Illinois at Chicago (hereafter cited as JAMC), CM to Jane Addams, 27 May 1925.
6 CMP, 1-13, CM to family, 23 April 1926.
7 Ibid.; Toronto *Telegram*, 2 June 1925.
8 CMP, 1-13, CM to family, 23 April 1925.
9 Ibid.
10 JAMC, CM to Jane Addams, 27 May 1925.
11 Toronto *Globe*, 6 June 1925.
12 Ibid., 3 and 4 June 1925.
13 Ibid., 12 June 1925.
14 A.E. Armstrong, 'The Foreign Mission Task of the United Church,' *New Outlook* 1. no. 1 (10 June 1925):33.
15 CMP, 1-13, CM to family, 31 July 1925.
16 Kyōsei Library, Tokyo. Official Record of the 9th International Prison Congress, courtesy of Sasaki Shigenori.
17 CMP, 2-25, Caroline Macdonald, unpublished ms. 'The Five Men in a Row,' [1926?].
18 Ibid.
19 Ibid. Oakum was the loose fibre produced by picking old rope apart, and used for caulking. Convicts and paupers were commonly assigned to this task in earlier times, but it was rare by the twentieth century.
20 CMP, 1-13, CM to family, 23 September 1925.
21 Ibid.
22 CMP, 2-24, CM's 'Notes of 1925.'
23 Robert A. Scalapino, *The Early Japanese Labor Movement: Labor and Politics in a Developing Society* (Berkeley: University of California Press 1983), 173-5; Stephen S. Large, *Organized Workers and Socialist Politics in Interwar Japan* (Cambridge: Cambridge University Press 1981), 57-62. According to a major study in English, the Communist party experienced great difficulty in developing concrete policies appropriate to Japanese circumstances, but was united in the belief that parliamentary government would be of no benefit to workers. George Beckman and Okubo Genji, *The Japanese Communist Party, 1922-1945* (Stanford, CA: Stanford University Press 1969), 30-104, passim.
24 Large, *Organized Workers*, 62-9; Sheldon Garon, *The State and Labor in Modern Japan* (Berkeley: University of California Press, 1987), 114-15.
25 Richard H. Mitchell, *Thought Control in Prewar Japan* (Ithaca, NY: Cornell University Press 1976), chap. 2; Garon, *State and Labor*, 130-6.
26 Ibid., 117-18.
27 CMP, 1-13, CM to family, 23 September 1925.
28 Mitchell, *Thought Control*, 33-4.
29 CMP, 2-24, Caroline Macdonald, unpublished ms. 'I came back to find the working girls,' [1925].
30 Ibid., Macdonald's address to Tsuda College Alumnae, 17 December 1925.
31 Ibid.
32 Ibid.
33 CMP, 2-26; CMP, 2-24, CM's 'Notes of 1925.'
34 CMP, 2-26, Macdonald's address to Tsuda College Alumnae, 17 December 1925.
35 CMP, 1-15, CM's circular letter to friends, 8 February 1927.
36 Ibid. An example of a woman who obtained a measure of financial independence through knitting is the Baroness Ishimoto Shizue. Early in the 1920s, after separating from her husband, she established a wool shop with a knitting school attached, and employed women to knit at home the fashionable sweaters she then sold. Her book on knitting quickly sold 13,000

copies and she travelled as far as Hokkaido to teach knitting, at the same time spreading information about birth control. Ishimoto Shizue, *Facing Two Ways: The Story of My Life* (New York: Farrar & Rinehart 1935; reprint, Stanford, CA: Stanford University Press 1984), 208-11.

37 CMP, 1-15, CM's circular letter to friends, 8 February 1927.
38 Large, *Organized Workers*, 87-8.
39 Ibid., 88-9; Garon, *State and Labor*, 109-16.
40 *Michi Taezu, Akamatsu Tsuneko, sono hito Ashiato* (The Way Will Never Be Lost: The Person and Her Heritage), Zensen Dōmei Kyōsen Series no. 7 (Tokyo: Zensen Dōmei 1964), 27-30.
41 Large, *Organized Workers*, 57-62; George O. Totten, *Social Democratic Movement in Prewar Japan* (New Haven, CT: Yale University Press 1966), 70-1. Through several swings of view Akamatsu Katsumaro moved steadily to the right, strongly supported Japan's invasion of Manchuria, and promoted a Japanese version of national socialism in the 1930s.
42 *Michi Taezu, Akamatsu Tsuneko*, 30; Matsuko Watanabe, ed., *Emma Kaufman to Tokyo YWCA* (Emma Kaufman and the Tokyo YWCA) (Tokyo: YWCA 1963), 17.
43 Large, *Organized Workers*, 87-8.
44 Ichikawa Fusae, *Ichikawa Fusae no jiden: senzenhen* (The Autobiography of Ichikawa Fusae: The Prewar Period) (Tokyo: Shinjuku Shobo 1974), 130-1; Patricia Murray, 'Ichikawa Fusae and the Lonely Red Carpet,' *Japan Interpreter* 10, no. 2 (Autumn 1975):171-89; Dorothy Robins-Mowry, *The Hidden Sun: Women of Modern Japan* (Boulder, CO: Westview Press 1983), 77-8.
45 CMP, 1-15, CM to Galen Fisher, 15 February 1927.
46 JAMC, CM to Jane Addams, 25 July 1927.
47 CMP, 1-14, CM's circular to friends, 28 August 1926.
48 Ibid.
49 M.S. Murao and W.H. Murray Walton, *Japan and Christ: A Study in Religious Issues* (London: Church Missionary Society 1928), 57; John McNab, *The White Angel of Tokyo: Miss Caroline Macdonald LL.D.* (Centenary Committee of the Canadian Churches n.p., n.d).
50 CMP, 1-15, CM to Galen Fisher, 15 February 1927.
51 David S. Cairns, *An Autobiography, with a Memoir by D.M. Baillie* (London: SCM Press 1950), 27-31, 194.
52 David S. Cairns, *The Faith that Rebels: A Re-Examination of the Miracles of Jesus* (London: SCM Press 1928), chap. 1, 246.
53 Ibid., 180.
54 Charles W. Iglehart, *A Century of Protestant Christianity in Japan* (Tokyo: Charles E. Tuttle 1959), 185-6.
55 *Japan Advertiser*, 20 February 1927.
56 CMP, 1-15, CM to friends, 11 March 1927.
57 Iglehart, *Protestant Christianity*, 186-7.

Chapter 14: From Noda to Geneva
1 CMP, 2-25, Macdonald's unpublished ms., 'My Connection with Noda,' [Spring 1928?].
2 Ibid.
3 W. Mark Fruin, *Kikkōman: Company, Clan and Community* (Cambridge, MA: Harvard University Press 1983), 196-7; George O. Totten, 'Japanese Industrial Relations at the Crossroads: The Great Noda Strike of 1927-1928,' in Bernard Silberman and Harry Harootunian, eds., *Japan in Crisis: Essays on Taishō Democracy* (Princeton, NJ: Princeton University Press 1974), 411.
4 CMP, 2-25, Macdonald, 'My Connection with Noda.' Macdonald's assessment of the impact of the union on Noda was shared by other contemporary observers and confirmed by later scholars. See Totten, 'The Great Noda Strike,' 418.
5 Fruin, *Kikkōman*, 195-6.
6 CMP, 2-25, Macdonald, 'My Connection with Noda.'

7 Fruin, *Kikkōman*, 198-200.
8 Ibid., 201-2; Macdonald, 'My Connection with Noda.'
9 Fruin, *Kikkōman*, 194, 197; Sheldon Garon, *The State and Labor in Modern Japan* (Berkeley: University of California Press 1987), 115-16.
10 Fruin, *Kikkōman*, 202-3.
11 Diet Library, Tokyo, Records of the Ministry of Home Affairs, Annual Report of the Labor Movement in Shōwa 4 [1929], 'Labor Dispute of Noda Shōyu Kabushiki Kaisha,' 429.
12 CMP, 2-33, Matsuoka Komakichi, 'The Late Miss Macdonald, Mother of Women Labourers,' possibly the ms. for an unpublished speech, 1 August 1932.
13 Fruin, *Kikkōman*, 203.
14 CMP, 2-25, Macdonald, 'My Connection with Noda.'
15 Ibid.
16 Fruin, *Kikkōman*, 203
17 Diet Library, Records of the Home Ministry, Report of Nihon Shakai Mondai Kenkyūjo (Japan Research Institute on Social Problems), 24 June, Shōwa 3 [1928], 425, 'The Bloody Battle of Noda;' CMP, 2-25, Macdonald, 'My Connection with Noda.'
18 Totten, 'The Great Noda Strike,' 426-8.
19 CMP, 2-25, Macdonald, 'My Connection with Noda.'
20 Ibid.
21 Fruin, *Kikkōman*, 203-5.
22 Ibid., 205-6; CMP, 2-25, Macdonald, 'My Connection with Noda.'
23 Ibid.; also Namiki Shigetarō, ed., *Noda sōgi no keika nichiroku* (Daily Record of the Noda Dispute) (Noda: n.p. 1928; Chiba: Noda Shōyu Kabushikikaisha 1973), 160-1; *Asahi Shinbun*, 21 April 1928.
24 Fruin, *Kikkōman*, 206.
25 Totten, 'The Great Noda Strike,' 428-32; Stephen S. Large, *Organized Workers and Socialist Politics in Interwar Japan* (Cambridge: Cambridge University Press 1981), 119-20.
26 Shiono Sachiko, 'Caroline Macdonald,' in Watanabe Matsuko, ed., *Emma Kaufman to Tokyo YWCA* (Emma Kaufman and the Tokyo YWCA) (Tokyo: YWCA 1963), 17.
27 Large, *Organized Workers*, 120-1.
28 Kenneth Colegrove, 'Labor Parties in Japan,' *American Political Science Review* 23, no. 2 (1929):329-63; Large, *Organized Workers*, 102-18; George O. Totten, *The Social Democratic Movement in Prewar Japan* (New Haven, CT: Yale University Press 1966), 54-63.
29 Colegrove, 'Labor Parties in Japan,' 336; Totten, *Social Democratic Movement*, 298-302; Garon, *State and Labor*, 141-3.
30 Garon, *State and Labor*, 150-4; Richard H. Mitchell, *Thought Control in Prewar Japan* (Ithaca, NY: Cornell University Press 1976), 87-91.
31 Totten, *Social Democratic Movement*, 200-3; Garon, *State and Labor*, 156.
32 CMP, 2-36, 'Statistical Report of Prison Work from 1926 to 1930.'
33 CMP, 1-15, CM to friends, 1 March 1927.
34 CMP, 1-25, CM's typescript, 'What is the Matter with a Prison?' [1928?].
35 Ibid.
36 Ibid.
37 Shortly, Macdonald received another recognition with her election to the Council of the Asiatic Society of Japan. Douglas Moore Kenrick, *A Century of Western Studies in Japan: The First Hundred Years of the Asiatic Society of Japan 1872-1972*, Transactions of the Asiatic Society of Japan, 3rd series, vol. 14 (Tokyo: Asiatic Society 1978), 205, and passim.
38 CMP, 2-33, Report of 'FLM,' 1 June 1927.
39 John Lewis Gillin, *Taming the Criminal: Adventures in Penology* (New York: Macmillan 1931; 2nd ed., Montclair, NJ: Patterson Smith 1969), 1-6.

40 Matsuoka Komakichi, 'Kokusai rōdōkaigi no omoide' (Recollections of ILO conferences) *Minron* 15 (October 1948):23-9.
41 Ibid.
42 Ibid.; CMP, 2-26, CM's notes for speech on the ILO at Waseda University [1930]; Diplomatic Record Office, Tokyo, Letter #429, Shigemitsu Mamoru, Consul-General at Shanghai to Tanaka Giichi, Minister of Foreign Affairs, 18 April 1929.
43 Ibid., 2-26, CM's notes for speech on the ILO at Waseda University, [1930]; speech to Tokyo Women's Club, *Japan Advertiser*, 15 May 1930.
44 Ibid.
45 Matsuoka, 'Kokusai rōdōkaigi no omoide.'
46 CMP, 2-25, CM's untitled and unpublished ms. [Spring 1930]. A recent study assigns some importance to international pressure, but stresses the argument that in Japan night work was seen, as in other industrial nations, as detrimental to the health of young girls and thus to the exercise of their future responsibilities as wives and mothers. Janet Hunter, 'Factory Legislation and Employer Resistance; The Abolition of Night Work in the Cotton Spinning Industry,' in Tsunehiko Yui and Keiichirō Nakagawa, eds., *Japanese Management in Historical Perspective* (Tokyo: University of Tokyo Press 1989), 243-72.
47 Matsuoka, 'Kokusai rōdōkaigi no omoide'; CMP, 1-18, CM to Galen and Ella Fisher, 10 April 1930.
48 CMP, 1-17, David Cairns to CM, 8 February 1929.
49 CMP, 1-18, CM to Galen Fisher, 30 August 1929.
50 Ibid., CM to sister Peg, 8 April 1930.
51 Ibid., CM to sister Peg, 22 March 1930.
52 CMP, 2-25, CM's report to friends, [Spring 1930].
53 CMP, 1-18, CM to sister Peg, 11 April 1930.
54 Ibid.
55 CMP, 2-25, CM's report to friends, [Spring 1930].
56 Garon, *State and Labor*, 168; CMP, 1-18, CM to sister Peg, 11 April 1930.
57 CMP, 2-15, CM's report to friends, [Spring 1930].
58 Large, *Organized Workers*, 144.
59 CMP, 1-18, CM to Miss Varley, [Birmingham] 10 July 1930.
60 Garon, *State and Labor*, 157-62; Totten, *Social Democratic Movement*, 303-4.
61 *Japan Advertiser*, 24 April 1930; CMP, 2-26, CM's notes for speech on the ILO at Waseda University [1930]; CMP, 1-18, CM to sister Peg, 27 June 1930.
62 Large, *Organized Workers*, 146.
63 Garon, *State and Labor*, 162-3.
64 CMP, 1-18, CM to Miss Varley, [Birmingham] 10 June 1930.
65 Garon, *State and Labor*, 163.
66 Ibid., 165-86.
67 Caroline Macdonald, 'Problems in Japan and Their Solution,' *Glad Tidings*, October 1931, 339.
68 CMP, 1-18, CM to sister Peg, 7, 15, and 30 September 1930.
69 Macdonald, 'Problems in Japan,' 338.

Chapter 15: 'Whether We Live or Whether We Die'
1 CMP, 1-18, CM to sister Peg, 26 April 1930.
2 Ibid., 27 June 1930.
3 Ibid., CM to sister Peg, 7 September 1930; CM to Jim Macdonald, 15 September 1930.
4 Ibid., CM to sister Peg, 1 June 1930.
5 Ibid., 27 June 1930.

6 Ibid.
7 Ibid., CM to sister Peg, 21 April and 27 June 1930.
8 Ibid., CM to Galen and Ella Fisher, 10 April 1930.
9 Hugh L. Keenleyside, *Memoirs*, Vol. 1, *Hammer the Golden Day*, (Toronto: McClelland and Stewart 1981), 277.
10 Eber H. Rice, 'Sir Herbert Marler and the Canadian Legation in Tokyo,' in John Schultz and Miwa Kimitada, *Canada and Japan in the Twentieth Century* (Toronto: Oxford University Press 1991), 80.
11 CMP, 1-18, CM to sister Peg, 11 April 1930; CM to Galen and Ella Fisher, 10 April 1930.
12 Keenleyside, *Memoirs*, 286-90.
13 CMP, 1-18, CM to sister Peg, 27 June 1930.
14 CMP, 1-19, CM to sister Peg, 14 January 1931.
15 The strength of national feeling among Canadian missionaries in the face of American dominance in the larger missionary movement remained vivid in the memory of Edith Bott, who spent the interwar years in Japan and returned after 1945. Interview with author, Toronto, 21 September 1984. On a Canadian identity among missionaries in Japan, see Cyril H. Powles, 'The Development of Japanese-Canadian Relations in the Age of Missionary Activity, 1873-1930,' *Kanada Kenkyū Nenpō* (Annual Review of Canadian Studies [Tokyo]) 2 (1980):146-65.
16 CMP, 1-19, CM to sister Peg, 2 April 1931.
17 Keenleyside, *Memoirs*, 326-7.
18 CMP, 1-18, CM to sister Peg, 11 April 1930; CM to Galen and Ella Fisher, 10 April 1930. Hugh Byas returned to Tokyo as a foreign correspondent in 1932 and remained until 1938.
19 Oshio Tsutomu, *Takakura Tokutarō Den* (Tokyo: Shinkyō shuppansha 1954), 200-36. Apparently the disagreement was primarily over procedures and personalities rather than over theology.
20 Minutes of the Session, Shinanomachi church, 11 March 1928; interview with Rev. Ikeda Akira of Shinanomachi church, 28 November 1984. In 1984, Macdonald was still the only foreigner to have been a member of this congregation.
21 Richard H. Drummond, *A History of Christianity in Japan* (Grand Rapids, MI: William B. Eerdmans 1971), 295-6; Charles H. Germany, *Protestant Theologies in Modern Japan: A History of Dominant Theological Currents from 1920-1960* (Tokyo: International Institute for the Study of Religions Press 1965), 92-5. CM's papers reveal that she had read works by Forsythe and Mackintosh.
22 CMP, 1-18, Cairns to CM, 23 August 1930.
23 CMP, 1-19, Cairns to CM, 4 January 1931.
24 Ibid., Cairns to CM, 16 May 1931. CM probably did not read this letter, since it would have arrived in Japan after her departure and, if forwarded, would probably not have reached Canada before her death.
25 Caroline Macdonald, 'Problems in Japan and Their Solution,' *Glad Tidings*, October 1931, 337.
26 Ibid.
27 Ibid., 337-8
28 CMP, 1-19, CM to Dr. Frank Schofield, 15 April 1931.
29 Ibid., CM to sister Peg, 14 January 1931
30 Copy of program of Tokyo Amateur Dramatic Society in UCCA, WMS Dominion Board, Overseas Missions, Japan, box 1, file 2, Work among Prisoners – Correspondence with Dr. Caroline Macdonald 1926-1931.
31 CMP, 1-19, CM to sister Peg, 14 April 1931.
32 CMP, 2-24, Ms. of address by Macdonald to Language School, 20 February 1931.
33 Ibid.

34 Ibid.
35 Ibid.
36 Ibid.
37 Author's interview with Morita Sachiko, November 1984.
38 Yamada Zen'ichi, 'Makudonarudo joshi no omokage' (Memories of Miss Macdonald), *Jindō* (Humanity) nos. 311 and 312 (1932); Shiono Sachiko, 'Caroline Macdonald,' in Watanabe Matsuko, ed., *Emma Kaufman to Tokyo YWCA* (Emma Kaufman and the Tokyo YWCA) (Tokyo: YWCA 1963); CMP, 2-33, Matsuoka Komakichi, 'The Late Miss Macdonald, Mother of Women Labourers,' possibly the ms. for an unpublished speech, 1 August 1932.
39 UCCA, United Church of Canada, WMS, Overseas Missions, Japan, box 1, file 21, Emma Kaufman to Miss Bennett, 13 June 1931.
40 CMP, 1-19, Tagawa Daichikirō to Margaret (Peg) Macdonald, 20 July 1931.
41 CMP, 1-18, 1-19, contains CM's correspondence with Armstrong. Armstrong professed to believe that Macdonald was unfriendly to representatives of the United Church in Tokyo, an accusation she vehemently denied.
42 *Wingham Advance-Times*, 23 July 1931.
43 *Japan Advertiser*, 30 July 1930; Yamada, 'Makudonarudo joshi no omokage.'
44 Cited in N.W. Rowell, 'The Late Caroline Macdonald,' *University of Toronto Monthly* 32, no. 1 (October 1931), supplement, 29-30.
45 *Japan Advertiser*, 30 July 1931.
46 Keenleyside, *Memoirs*, 327.
47 CMP, 1-19, H.L. Keenleyside to O.D. Skelton, 10 July 1931. Keenleyside urged Skelton, under-secretary of state for external affairs, to seek recognition from the Canadian government for Macdonald's achievements.
48 Rowell, 'The Late Caroline Macdonald,' 19-30 passim.
49 *Times*, 19 July 1931; *New York Times*, 18 July 1931. These very similar reports were probably writ-ten by Hugh Byas.
50 Excerpts from a range of tributes were printed in *Glad Tidings*, October 1931, 330-6; also *Missionary Monthly*, September 1931, 397-8.
51 CMP, 1-19, David Cairns to Margaret (Peg) Macdonald, 2 August 1931.
52 Ibid.
53 The rest of this chapter is based on Arima Shirosuke, 'Ko-Makudonarudo joshi o omou' (Remembering the Late Miss Macdonald), *Hogojihō* (Protection Review) 6, nos. 5, 6, 7 (1932).

Epilogue
1 Miwa Kimitada, 'Nitobe Inazō and the Development of Colonial Theories and Practices in Prewar Japan,' Research Papers, Series A-50, 1987, Institute of International Relations, Sophia University, Tokyo; Thomas W. Burkman, 'Nitobe Inazō: From World Order to Regional Order,' in J. Thomas Rimer, *Culture and Identity: Japanese Intellectuals During the Interwar Years* (Princeton, NJ: Princeton University Press 1990), 197-212.
2 Edwin O. Reischauer, *The Japanese* (Cambridge, MA: Harvard University Press 1981), 98-100; George O. Totten, *The Social Democratic Movement in Prewar Japan* (New Haven, CT: Yale University Press 1966), 69-98, 105-8.
3 Wakao Fujita, 'Yanaihara Tadao,' in Nobuya Bamba and John Howes, *Pacifism in Japan: The Christian and Socialist Tradition* (Kyoto: Minerva Press 1978), 200-19.
4 Charles W. Iglehart, *A Century of Protestant Christianity in Japan* (Tokyo: Charles E. Tuttle 1959), 221-6; Gwen R.P. and Howard Norman, *One Hundred Years in Japan, 1873-1973* (Toronto: Division of World Outreach, United Church of Canada 1981), part 2, 415-18.
5 Ibid., 416-18; Iglehart, *Protestant Christianity*, 253-9.
6 Ibid., 229-35; Richard H. Drummond, *A History of Christianity in Japan* (Grand Rapids, MI:

William B. Eerdmans 1971), 256-62.

7 Norman, *One Hundred Years*, 415-16; Iglehart, *Protestant Christianity*, 244

8 Ibid., 243; Drummond, *Christianity in Japan*, 262.

9 UCCA, WMS Dominion Board, Overseas Missions, Japan, box 1, file 2. Correspondence with Dr. Caroline Macdonald 1926-1931. Note by Miss E.A. Preston of meeting with Emma Kaufman, 12 July 1931.

10 Ibid., box 5, file 71. Minutes of executive and council of the Japan WMS, Kamakura, 12-14 February 1932.

11 Ibid., box 1, file 4. Correspondence of executive secretary, 1932, Alice O. Strothard to Miss E.A. Preston, 24 February 1932.

12 Ibid. The extent to which the work of Shinrinkan depended on Macdonald may be viewed as a weakness; if it had been connected with a mission board or some other permanent institution, would it have survived longer? Dependence on 'charismatic' leadership was characteristic of many American settlements. See Mina Carson, *Settlement Folk: Social Thought and the American Settlement Movement, 1885-1930* (Chicago: University of Chicago Press 1990), 87-8. Regrettably, no evidence has been found concerning the community life of the resident workers in Shinrinkan.

13 *Tenth Annual Report of the Woman's Missionary Society of the United Church of Canada, 1934-35* (Toronto: Ryerson Press 1936), 86, 262.

14 *Fifteenth Annual Report of the Woman's Missionary Society of the United Church of Canada, 1939-40* (Toronto: Ryerson Press 1941), 378.

15 Kawai Michi, *My Lantern* (Tokyo: privately printed 1939), 178-204; Iglehart, *Protestant Christianity*, 168-85.

16 Kawai Michi, *Sliding Doors* (Tokyo: Keisen Jogakuen 1950), 50-1.

17 Richard T. Baker, *Darkness of the Sun: The Story of Christianity in the Japanese Empire* (New York: Abingdon Cokesbury Press 1947), 18-19.

18 Ibid., 109-10.

19 Drummond, *Christianity in Japan*, 253-4; Iglehart, *Protestant Christianity*, 219-20.

20 Charles W. Iglehart, *Cross and Crisis in Japan* (New York: Friendship Press 1957), 135.

21 Sharon H. Nolte, *Liberalism in Modern Japan: Ishibashi Tanzan and His Teachers, 1905-1960* (Berkeley: University of California Press 1987), 11-12, 336-7.

22 Stephen S. Large, *Organized Workers and Socialist Politics in Interwar Japan* (Cambridge: Cambridge University Press 1981), 156-8, 219-20.

23 Totten, *Social Democratic Movement*, 69-79, 89-105, 259-67.

24 Ibid., 259-69, 329-34; Sheldon Garon, *The State and Labor in Modern Japan* (Berkeley: University of California Press, 1987), 198-218; Large, *Organized Workers*, 196-230.

25 Miyake Yoshiko, 'Doubling Expectations: Motherhood and Women's Factory Work under State Management in Japan in the 1930s and 1940s,' in Gail Lee Bernstein, ed., *Recreating Japanese Women, 1600-1945* (Berkeley: University of California Press 1991), 284-7.

26 Dorothy Robins-Mowry, *The Hidden Sun: Women of Modern Japan* (Boulder, CO: Westview Press 1983), 75-6.

27 Miyake, 'Doubling Expectations,' 277-81.

28 Interview with Katō (Ishimoto) Shizue, 8 September 1972, cited in Robins-Mowry, *Hidden Sun*, 76.

29 Miyake, 'Doubling Expectations,' 272-4.

30 Ibid., 277.

31 Ibid., 273-5.

32 Charles H. Germany, *Protestant Theologies in Modern Japan: A History of Dominant Theological Currents from 1920-1960* (Tokyo: International Institute for the Study of Religions Press 1965), 183; Garon, *State and Labor*, 235-7; Allan B. Cole, George O. Totten, and Cecil

H. Uyehara, *Socialist Parties in Postwar Japan* (New Haven, CT: Yale University Press 1966), 21-2, 152-3. In retrospect, Katayama expressed great disappointment in the political sense of Japanese Christian leaders. Joseph Mitsuo Kitagawa, *The Christian Tradition beyond Its European Captivity* (Philadelphia: Trinity Press International 1992), 287-8, n. 33.

33 Cole et al., *Socialist Parties*, 15-20.

34 Ibid., 25-30.

35 Robins-Mowry, *Hidden Sun*, 107-8.

36 Ibid., 107, 124, 281-2.

37 Ibid., 88-9, 228-9, 230-2.

38 Watanabe Matsuko, ed., *Emma Kaufman to Tokyo YWCA* (Emma Kaufman and the Tokyo YWCA) (Tokyo: YWCA 1963); Robins-Mowry, *Hidden Sun*, 104-6, 110-111; Iglehart, *Protestant Christianity*, 203-4.

39 Iglehart, *Protestant Christianity*, 282-4; Norman, *One Hundred Years*, part 2, 406-8, 428-40.

40 Iglehart, *Cross and Crisis*, 57-8.

41 Iglehart, *Protestant Christianity*, 269-70, 290-1; Kitagawa, *Christian Tradition*, 72-4.

42 Ibid., 74; Drummond, *Christianity in Japan*, 280-3.

43 Ibid., 284-8; Kitagawa, *Christian Tradition*, 70-1, 77-9.

44 Watanabe, *Emma Kaufman*; Robins-Mowry, *Hidden Sun*, 104-6, 237, 268.

45 Sharon H. Nolte, 'Individualism in Taishō Japan,' *Journal of Asian Studies* 43, no. 4 (1984):668.

46 Nolte, *Liberalism in Modern Japan*, 333-42.

47 Carolyn G. Heilbrun, *Writing a Woman's Life* (New York: W.W. Norton 1988), 20-1.

48 Ibid., 51.

49 Ibid., 59, 42.

50 Ruth C. Brouwer, *New Women for God: Canadian Presbyterian Women and India Missions, 1876-1914* (Toronto: University of Toronto Press 1990), 169-70, 172-3, 175-9; Rosemary R. Gagan, *A Sensitive Independence: Canadian Methodist Women Missionaries in Canada and the Orient, 1881-1925* (Montreal and Kingston: McGill-Queen's University Press 1992), 110-14.

Select
Bibliography

Archival Sources

Archives of the YWCA of Japan, Tokyo
Various materials, 1901-15

National Archives of Canada
Young Women's Christian Association of Canada Papers, MG28 I198, vols. 9, 13, 35, 36, 57

Ottawa YM-YW Archives
Ottawa YWCA Papers, 1901-3

United Church of Canada Archives, Victoria University, Toronto
Caroline Macdonald Papers
Emma Kaufman Papers
United Church of Canada, Woman's Missionary Society, Dominion Board, Overseas Missions, Japan, 1926-32

University of Toronto Archives
Alumni Records, Annie Caroline Macdonald

Newspapers and Periodicals
Joshi Seinen Kai (The World of Young Women), 1912-22
Meiji No Joshi (Women of the Meiji Era), 1904-12
Wingham Times, 1888-97

Books, Articles, Pamphlets, and Theses

Akamatsu Tsuneko. *Zassō no yōni takumashiku* (Strong as Wild Grass). Tokyo: n.d.

Althaus, Mary E., Yoshiko Furuki, and Akiko Ueda, eds. *The Writings of Umeko Tsuda.* N.p.: 1980; 2nd ed. 1984

Aoyoshi Katsuhisa. *Dr. Masahisa Uemura: A Christian Leader.* Tokyo: Kyōbunkan 1941

Arima Shirosuke. 'Ko-Makudonarudo joshi o omou' (Remembering the Late Miss Macdonald). *Hogojihō* (Protection Review) 6, nos. 5-7 (1932)

Axelrod, Paul, and John G. Reid, eds. *Youth, University, and Canadian Society: Essays in the Social History of Higher Education.* Kingston and Montreal: McGill-Queen's University Press 1989

Bacon, Alice Mabel. *Japanese Girls and Women.* Boston: Houghton Mifflin 1891; 2nd ed. 1902

Bamba Nobuya, and John F. Howes, *Pacifism in Japan: The Christian and Socialist Tradition.* Kyoto: Minerva Press 1978

Baker, Richard Terrill. *Darkness of the Sun: The Story of Christianity in the Japanese Empire.* New York: Abingdon Cokesbury Press 1947

Barr, Pat. *The Deer Cry Pavilion: A Story of Westerners in Japan, 1868-1905.* London: Macmillan 1968

Beckman, George, and Okubo Genji. *The Japanese Communist Party, 1922-1945.* Stanford, CA: Stanford University Press 1969

Bernstein, Gail Lee, ed. *Recreating Japanese Women, 1600-1945.* Berkeley: University of California Press 1991

Best, Ernest E. *Christian Faith and Cultural Crisis: The Japanese Case.* Leiden: E.J. Brill 1966

Boyd, Nancy. *Emissaries: The Overseas Work of the American YWCA, 1895-1970.* New York: Woman's Press 1986

Bowie, Fiona, Deborah Kirkwood, and Shirley Ardener, eds. *Women and Missions Past and Present: Anthropological and Historical Perceptions.* Providence, RI, and Oxford: Berg Publishers 1993

Brouwer, Ruth Compton. *New Women for God: Canadian Presbyterian Women and India Missions, 1876-1914.* Toronto: University of Toronto Press 1990

Bureau of Social Affairs. *Social Work in Japan.* Tokyo: Home Office 1928

Burke, Sara Z. 'Science and Sentiment: Social Service and Gender at the University of Toronto, 1888-1910.' *Journal of the Canadian Historical Association,* new series 4 (1993):75-93

Burridge, Kenelm. *In the Way: A Study of Christian Missionary Endeavours.* Vancouver: UBC Press 1991

Cairns, David S. *Christianity in the Modern World.* London: Hodder & Stoughton 1906

———. *The Reasonableness of the Christian Faith.* London: Hodder & Stoughton 1918

———. *The Faith that Rebels: A Re-Examination of the Miracles of Jesus.* London: SCM Press 1928

———. *An Autobiography, with a Memoir by D.M. Baillie.* London: SCM Press 1950

Caldarola, Carlo. *Christianity: The Japanese Way.* Leiden: E.J. Brill 1979

Canada's Share in Foreign Association Work. Toronto: Dominion Council of the YWCA 1910

Carson, Mina. *Settlement Folk: Social Thought and the American Settlement Movement, 1885-1930.* Chicago: University of Chicago Press 1990

Cheyne, A.C. *The Transforming of the Kirk: Victorian Scotland's Religious Revolution.* Edinburgh: Saint Andrew Press 1983

The Christian Movement in the Japanese Empire. Tokyo: Conference of Federated Missions. Yearbook, annually, 1902-30

Cole, Allan B., George O. Totten, and Cecil H. Uyehara. *Socialist Parties in Postwar Japan.* New Haven, CT: Yale University Press 1966

Colegrove, Kenneth. 'Labor Parties in Japan.' *American Political Science Review* 23, no. 2 (1929):329-63

Cott, Nancy F. 'What's in a Name? The Limits of Social Feminism; or, Expanding the Vocabulary of Women's History.' *Journal of American History* 76 (December 1989):809-29
——. *A Woman Making History: Mary Ritter Beard through her Letters.* New Haven, CT, and London: Yale University Press 1991
Dalby, Liza Chrihfield. *Geisha.* Berkeley: University of California Press 1983
Davis, Allen F. *Spearheads for Reform: The Social Settlements and the Progressive Movement, 1890-1914.* New York: Oxford University Press 1967
Dohi Akio. 'Christianity and Politics in the Taishō Period of Democracy.' *Japanese Religions* 5, no. 4 (1969):24-40; 7, no. 3 (1972):42-68
Doi Takeo. *The Anatomy of Dependence.* Trans. by John Bester. Tokyo: Kodansha 1973
Drummond, Richard Henry. *A History of Christianity in Japan.* Grand Rapids, MI: William B. Eerdmans 1971
Duus, Peter. *Party Rivalry and Political Change in Taishō Japan.* Cambridge, MA: Harvard University Press 1968
Fairbank, John King. *The Missionary Enterprise in China and America.* Cambridge, MA: Harvard University Press 1974
Fisher, Galen M. *Creative Forces in Japan.* New York: Missionary Education Movement of the United States and Canada 1923
Five Years of Association Work in Japan. Toronto: Dominion Council of the YWCA 1910
Fleming, J.R. *A History of the Church in Scotland, 1875-1929.* Edinburgh: T & T Clark 1933
Flemming, Leslie A., ed. *Women's Work for Women: Missionaries and Social Change in Asia.* Boulder, CO: Westview Press 1989
Fraser, Brian J. *The Social Uplifters: Presbyterian Progressives and the Social Gospel in Canada, 1875-1915.* Waterloo: Wilfrid Laurier University Press 1988
Fruin, W. Mark. *Kikkōman: Company, Clan and Community.* Cambridge, MA: Harvard University Press 1983
Gadsby, John. 'Some Notes on the History of the Japanese Code of Criminal Procedure.' *Law Quarterly Review* 30 (1914):448-63
Gagan, Rosemary R. *A Sensitive Independence: Canadian Methodist Women Missionaries in Canada and the Orient, 1881-1925.* Montreal and Kingston: McGill-Queen's University Press 1992
Garon, Sheldon. *The State and Labor in Modern Japan.* Berkeley: University of California Press 1987
Gauvreau, Michael. *The Evangelical Century: College and Creed in English Canada from the Great Revival to the Great Depression.* Montreal and Kingston: McGill-Queen's University Press 1991
A Gentleman in Prison, with the Confessions of Tōkichi Ishii Written in Tokyo Prison. Prefaces by Caroline Macdonald, John Kelman, and Fujiya Suzuki, 2nd ed. London: SCM Press, 2nd ed. 1927
Germany, Charles H. *Protestant Theologies in Modern Japan: A History of Dominant Theological Currents from 1920-1960.* Tokyo: International Institute for the Study of Religions Press 1965
Gillin, John Lewis. *Taming the Criminal: Adventures in Penology.* New York: Macmillan 1931; 2nd ed., Montclair, NJ: Patterson Smith 1969
Gluck, Carol. *Japan's Modern Myths: Ideology in the Late Meiji Period.* Princeton, NJ: Princeton University Press 1985
Gordon, Andrew. *The Evolution of Labor Relations in Japan: Heavy Industry, 1853-1955.* Cambridge, MA: Harvard University Press 1985
——. 'Business and the Corporate State: The Business Lobby and Bureaucrats on Labor, 1911-1941.' In William D. Wray, ed., *Managing Industrial Enterprise: Cases from Japan's*

Prewar Experience, 53-85. Cambridge, MA: Harvard University Press 1989

Grant, John Webster. *A Profusion of Spires: Religion in Nineteenth Century Ontario.* Toronto: University of Toronto Press 1988

Griffis, William Elliot. *Dux Christus: An Outline Study of Japan.* New York: Macmillan 1904

Halliday, Jon. *A Political History of Japanese Capitalism.* New York: Pantheon 1975

Hane Mikiso. *Peasants, Rebels, and Outcasts: The Underside of Modern Japan.* New York: Pantheon 1982

Hastings, Sally Ann. 'The Government, the Citizen, and the Creation of a New Sense of Community: Social Welfare, Local Organizations, and Dissent in Tokyo, 1905-1937.' Ph.D. thesis, University of Chicago 1980

Heilbrun, Carolyn G. *Writing a Woman's Life.* New York: W.W. Norton 1988

Hill, Patricia R. *The World Their Household: The American Woman's Foreign Mission Movement and Cultural Transformation 1870-1920.* Ann Arbor: University of Michigan Press 1985

Hiyane Antei. *Nihon kinsei Kirisutokyō jinbutsushi* (History of Christian Personalities in Modern Japan). Tokyo: Kirisutokyō Hakkōsha 1935

Honig, Emily. *Sisters and Strangers: Women in the Shanghai Cotton Mills, 1919-1949.* Stanford, CA: Stanford University Press 1986

Hopkins, C. Howard. *John R. Mott, 1865-1955.* Grand Rapids, MI: William B. Eerdmans 1979

Hunter, Jane. *The Gospel of Gentility: American Women Missionaries in Turn-of-the-Century China.* New Haven, CT, and London: Yale University Press 1984

Hunter, Janet. 'Factory Legislation and Employer Resistance: The Abolition of Night Work in the Cotton-Spinning Industry.' In Yui Tsunehiko and Nakagawa Keiichirō, eds., *Japanese Management in Historical Perspective,* 243-72. Tokyo: University of Tokyo Press 1989

Hutchison, William R. *Errand to the World: American Protestant Thought and Foreign Missions.* Chicago and London: University of Chicago Press 1987

Iglehart, Charles W. *Cross and Crisis in Japan.* New York: Friendship Press 1957

——. *A Century of Protestant Christianity in Japan.* Tokyo: Charles E. Tuttle 1959

Innis, Mary Quayle. *Unfold the Years: A History of the Young Women's Christian Association in Canada.* Toronto: McClelland & Stewart 1949

Ion, A. Hamish. *The Cross and the Rising Sun: The Canadian Protestant Missionary Movement in the Japanese Empire, 1872-1931.* Waterloo, ON: Wilfrid Laurier University Press 1990

——. *The Cross and the Rising Sun.* Vol. 2, *The British Protestant Missionary Movement in Japan, Korea, and Taiwan, 1865-1945.* Waterloo, ON: Wilfrid Laurier University Press 1993

Irakawa Daikichi. *The Culture of the Meiji Period* (Meiji no bunka, 1970). Trans. and ed. by Marius B. Jansen. Princeton, NJ: Princeton University Press 1985

Ishimoto Shizue. *Facing Two Ways: The Story of My Life.* New York: Farrar & Rinehart 1935; reprint, Stanford, CA: Stanford University Press 1984

Itō Takashi. *Taishō ki 'kakushin' ha no seiritsu* (The Formation of the 'Reformers' of the Taishō Era). Tokyo: Haniwa Shobo 1978

Kang, Wi Jo. *Religion and Politics in Korea under Japanese Rule.* Lewiston, NY, and Queenston, ON: E. Mellen Press 1987

Kanō Masanao. *Taishō demokurashii no teiryū* (The Undercurrents of Taishō Democracy). Tokyo: NHK, Japan Broadcasting Corporation Press 1976

Kawai Michi. *My Lantern.* Tokyo: privately printed 1939

——. *Sliding Doors.* Tokyo: Keisen Jogakuen 1950

Kawai Michi and Kubushiro Ochimi. *Japanese Women Speak: A Message from the Christian Women of Japan to the Christian Women of America.* Boston: Central Committee on the United Study of Foreign Missions 1934

Keenleyside, Hugh L. *Memoirs.* Vol. 1, *Hammer the Golden Day.* Toronto: McClelland and Stewart 1981

Kikuchi Dairoku. *Japanese Education: Lectures delivered in the University of London.* London: John Murray 1909

Kitagawa, Joseph Mitsuo. *The Christian Tradition beyond Its European Captivity.* Philadelphia: Trinity Press International 1992

Koven, Seth, and Sonya Michel, eds. *Mothers of a New World: Maternalist Politics and the Origins of Welfare States.* New York and London: Routledge 1993

Kozaki Hiromichi. *Reminiscences of Seventy Years: The Autobiography of a Japanese Pastor.* Tokyo: Christian Literature Society of Japan 1933

Kuyama Yasushi, ed. *Kindai Nihon to Kirisutokyō* (Modern Japan and Christianity), vol. 2. Tokyo: Kirisutokyō Gakuto Kyōdaidan 1956

Lande, Aasulv. *Meiji Protestantism in History and Historiography.* Uppsala University 1988

Large, Stephen S. 'The Japanese Labor Movement, 1912-19: Suzuki Bunji and the Yūaikai.' *Journal of Asian Studies* 39, no. 3 (1970):559-79

——. *The Yūaikai 1912-1919: The Rise of Labor in Japan.* Tokyo: Sophia University Press 1972

——. *Organized Workers and Socialist Politics in Interwar Japan.* Cambridge: Cambridge University Press 1981

Lee, Chong-Sik. *The Politics of Korean Nationalism.* Berkeley: University of California Press 1963

Lehmann, Jean-Pierre. *The Image of Japan: From Feudal Isolation to World Power, 1850-1905.* London: George Allen & Unwin 1978

Lubove, Roy. *The Professional Altruist: The Emergence of Social Work as a Career, 1880-1930.* Cambridge, MA: Harvard University Press 1965

Macdonald, Caroline. 'The World of Japanese Women as It Appears to My Eyes.' *Meiji No Joshi* 9, no. 6 (1912):8-10

——. 'Does Japan Need the Social Message?' National Council of the YWCA, USA, 1913, 1-17

——. 'The Juvenile Court in Chicago.' *Joshi Seinen Kai* 13, no. 7 (1916)

——. 'The Woman Movement in Japan.' *The Christian Movement in the Japanese Empire,* 1917. Tokyo, 1917, 268-78

——. 'Are Japanese Women Respected?' *Joshi Seinen Kai* 15 (October 1918):12-13

——. 'The Individual in the Social Problem.' *The Christian Movement in the Japanese Empire,* 1919. Tokyo, 1919, 1-10

——. 'Kangoku wa gakkō ni' (A Prison Should Be a School). *Chūō Horitsu Shinpō* (Journal of New Legislation) 1, no. 7 (1921):25-6

——. 'Juvenile Delinquency in Japan.' *The Christian Movement in the Japanese Empire,* 1922. Tokyo, 1922, 279-90

——. 'The Environment of Our Work.' *Japan Evangelist* (August-September 1929):310-15

——. 'Problems in Japan and Their Solution.' *Glad Tidings,* October 1931, 336-8

McKelvey, Blake. *American Prisons: A History of Good Intentions.* Montclair, NJ: Patterson Smith 1977

McNab, John. *The White Angel of Tokyo: Miss Caroline Macdonald LL.D.* Centenary Committee of the Canadian Churches n.p., n.d.

Masaki Akira. *Shiganshū* (Volunteer Prisoner). Tokyo: Nihon Keijiseisaku Kenkyūkai 1965

Matsuoka Komakichi. 'The Late Miss Macdonald, Mother of Women Labourers.' 1 August 1932. Ms. of unpublished speech? (CMP 2-33)

——. 'Kokusai rōdōkaigi no omoide' (Recollections of ILO conferences). *Minron* 15 (October 1948): 23-9

Matsumiya Yahei. 'Makudonarudo joshi to watashi' (Miss Macdonald and I). *Joshi Seinen Kai,* December 1932

Michi Taezu, Akamatsu Tsuneko, sono hito Ashiato (The Way Will Never Be Lost: The Person and Her Heritage). Zensen Dōmei Kyōsen Series no. 7. Tokyo: Zensen Dōmei 1964

Mitchell, Richard H. *Thought Control in Prewar Japan.* Ithaca: Cornell University Press 1976

Miyoshi Akira. *Kirisuto ni yoru Rōdōsha: Rōdō kyōkai no ayumi* (Labourers Who Rely on Christ: The History of the Labour Church). Tokyo: Kirisuto Shimbunsha 1965

——. *Arima Shirosuke.* Tokyo: Yoshikawa Kyōbunkan 1967

Mizu o Kaze Hikari o nihon YWCA 80 nen 1905-1985 (Water, Wind, and Light: 80 Years of the Japanese YWCA 1905-1985). Tokyo: Nihon YWCA 1987

Murao, M.S., and W.H. Murray Walton. *Japan and Christ: A Study in Religious Issues.* London: Church Missionary Society 1928

Najita Tetsuo and J. Victor Koschmann. *Conflict in Modern Japanese History.* Princeton, NJ: Princeton University Press 1982

Nakamura Kikuo. *Matsuoka Komakichi den* (Biography of Matsuoka Komakichi). Tokyo: Keizai Ōraisha 1964

Nakane Chie. *Japanese Society.* Berkeley: University of California Press 1970

Nakazato Tatsuo. *Keimusagyō no honshitsu nitsuite no kenkyū* (The Principles of Penal Servitude). *Studies in Penal Policies,* vol. 44. Tokyo: Hōmu Kenkyūjo 1958

Namae Takayuki. *Nihon Kirisutokyō shakaijigyōshi* (History of Christian Social Work in Japan). Tokyo: Kyōbunkan 1931

Nihon Kirisutokyō kyōikushi (History of Christian Education in Japan). Kirisutokyō Gakkō Kyōiku Dōmei (Educational Federation of Christian Schools). Tokyo: Shōbunsha 1977

Nishiuchi Kiyoshi. *Nihon settsurumento kenkyū josetsu* (History of Settlement Work in Japan). Tokyo: Munetaka Shobo 1959

Nolte, Sharon H. 'Individualism in Taishō Japan.' *Journal of Asian Studies* 43, no. 4 (1984):667-83

——. *Liberalism in Modern Japan: Ishibashi Tanzan and His Teachers, 1905-1960.* Berkeley: University of California Press 1987

Nolte, Sharon H., and Sally Ann Hastings. 'The Meiji State's Policy toward Women, 1890-1910.' In Bernstein, ed., *Recreating Japanese Women,* 151-74

Norman, Gwen R.P., and Howard Norman. *One Hundred Years in Japan, 1873-1973.* Toronto: Division of World Outreach, United Church of Canada 1981

Ōkuma Miyoshi. *Meijijidai Runinshi* (Exiles of the Meiji Era). Tokyo: Yūzankaku 1974

Powles, Cyril H. 'The Development of Japanese-Canadian Relations in the Age of Missionary Activity, 1873-1930.' *Kanada Kenkyū Nenpō* (Annual Review of Canadian Studies [Tokyo]) 2 (1980):146-65

——. *Victorian Missionaries in Meiji Japan: The Shiba Sect, 1873-1900.* Toronto: University of Toronto-York University Joint Centre on Modern East Asia 1987

The Prisons of Tokyo and a Social Service Opportunity (private circulation, n.p., n.d. [1922?])

Reflections on the Way to the Gallows: Rebel Women in Prewar Japan. Trans. and ed. with an introduction by Mikiso Hane. Berkeley: University of California Press 1988

Reischauer, Edwin O. *The Japanese.* Cambridge, MA: Harvard University Press 1981

Rice, Anna V. *A History of the World's Young Women's Christian Association.* New York: Women's Press 1947

Rimer, J. Thomas, ed. *Culture and Identity: Japanese Intellectuals During the Interwar Years.* Princeton, NJ: Princeton University Press 1990

Robins-Mowry, Dorothy. *The Hidden Sun: Women of Modern Japan.* Boulder, CO: Westview Press 1983

Rodd, Laura Rasplica. 'Yosano Akiko and the Taishō Debate over the "New Woman."' In Bernstein, ed., *Recreating Japanese Women,* 175-98

Rowell, N.W. 'The Late Caroline Macdonald.' *University of Toronto Monthly* 32, no. 1 (October 1931), supplement, 19-30

Scalapino, Robert A. *Democracy and the Party Movement in Prewar Japan.* Cambridge, MA: Harvard University Press 1953

——. *The Early Japanese Labor Movement: Labor and Politics in a Developing Society.* Berkeley: University of California Press 1983

Scheiner, Irwin. *Christian Converts and Social Protest in Meiji Japan.* Berkeley: University of California Press 1970

Schultz, John, and Miwa Kimitada. *Canada and Japan in the Twentieth Century.* Toronto: Oxford University Press 1991

Seidensticker, Edward. *Low City, High City: Tokyo from Edo to the Earthquake.* Tokyo: Charles E. Tuttle 1984

Shiono Sachiko. 'Caroline Macdonald.' In Watanabe Matsuko, ed., *Emma Kaufman to Tokyo YWCA*, 126-72

Shiota Shōhei et. al., eds. *Nihon shakaiundō jinmei jiten* (Biographical Dictionary of Social Movements in Japan). Tokyo: Aoki Shoten 1979

Shimada Noriko, Hiroko Takamura, Masako Ino, and Hisako Ito. 'Ume Tsuda and Motoko Hani: Echoes of American Cultural Feminism in Japan.' In Carol V.R. George, ed., *'Remember the Ladies': New Perspectives on Women in American History.* Syracuse, NY: Syracuse University Press 1975

Sievers, Sharon. *Flowers in Salt: The Beginnings of Feminist Consciousness in Modern Japan.* Stanford, CA: Stanford University Press 1983

Silberman, Bernard, and Harry Harootunian, eds. *Japan in Crisis: Essays on Taishō Democracy.* Princeton, NJ: Princeton University Press 1974

Smith, Henry DeWitt II. *Japan's First Student Radicals.* Cambridge, MA: Harvard University Press 1972

Smith, Robert J. *Japanese Society: Tradition, Self, and the Social Order.* Cambridge: Cambridge University Press 1983

Smith, Thomas C. 'The Right to Benevolence: Dignity and Japanese Workers, 1890-1920.' *Comparative Studies in Society and History* 26 (1984):587-613

Stastny, Charles, and Gabrielle Tyrnauer. *Who Rules the Joint?: The Changing Political Culture of Maximum-Security Prisons in America.* Lexington, MA: Lexington Books 1982

Sumiya Mikio. *Kindai Nihon no keisei to Kirisutokyō* (Christianity and the Formation of Modern Japan). Tokyo: Shinkyo Shuppansha 1961

——. *Nihon rōdō undō shi* (A History of the Japanese Labor Movement). Tokyo: Yūshindo 1966

——. *Nihon no shakaishisō: Kindaika to Kirisutokyō* (Social Thought and Christianity in Modern Japan). Tokyo: Tokyo Daigaku Shuppankai 1968

Tagawa Daikichirō. 'Makudonarudo joshi o omou' (Remembering Miss Macdonald). *Shakai Jigyō* (Social Work) 16, no. 6 (1932)

——. 'Church and State in Modern Japan.' *Japan Christian Quarterly* 14, no. 2 (1939):173-87

Takeda Kiyoko. *Ningenkan no Sōkohu: Kindai Nihon no shisō to Kirisutokyō* (The Struggle for Humanity: Modern Thought and Christianity in Japan). Tokyo: Kōbundōshinsha 1959; rev. ed. 1967

——. 'Japanese Christianity: Between Orthodoxy and Heterodoxy.' In J. Victor Koschmann, ed., *Authority and the Individual in Japan: Citizen Protest in Historical Perspective*, 82-107. Tokyo: Tokyo University Press 1987

Tatara Toshio. '1400 Years of Japanese Social Work from Its Origins through the Allied Occupation, 552-1941.' Ph.D. thesis, Bryn Mawr 1975

Three Years' Survey: Canada and Other Lands. Toronto: Dominion Council of the YWCA 1914

Tiers, Jane Elizabeth. 'Impressions of Meiji Japan by Five Victorian Women.' M.A. thesis, University of British Columbia 1986

Totten, George O. *The Social Democratic Movement in Prewar Japan.* New Haven, CT: Yale University Press 1966

——. 'Japanese Industrial Relations at the Crossroads: The Great Noda Strike of 1927-1928.' In Silberman and Harootunian, eds., *Japan in Crisis*, 398-436

Tsurumi, E. Patricia. 'Female Textile Workers and the Failure of Early Trade Unionism in Japan.' *History Workshop* 18 (Autumn 1984): 3-27

——. *Factory Girls: Women in the Thread Mills of Meiji Japan*. Princeton, NJ: Princeton University Press 1990

Von Meren, Arthur Taylor, ed. *Law in Japan: The Legal Order in a Changing Society*. Cambridge, MA: Harvard University Press 1963

Watanabe Matsuko, ed. *Emma Kaufman to Tokyo YWCA* (Emma Kaufman and the Tokyo YWCA). Tokyo: YWCA 1963

World's Young Women's Christian Association. *Report of the Third Conference, Paris, 16-21 May 1906*. London 1906

Yamada Zen'ichi. 'Makudonarudo joshi no omokage' (Memories of Miss Macdonald). *Jindō* (Humanity), 311 and 312 (1932)

Yanagimoto Masaharu. 'Some Features of the Japanese Prison System.' *British Journal of Criminology* 10 (1970):209-24

Yoshikawa Riichi. *Tsuda Umeko Den* (A Biography of Tsuda Umeko). Tokyo: Tsuda College Alumni Association 1961

Young, A. Morgan. *Japan in Recent Times, 1912-1926*. New York: W. Morrow & Co. 1929; reprint, Westport, CT: Greenwood Press 1973

Index

Set in Electra

Printed and bound in Canada by Friesens

Copy-editor: Carolyn Bateman

Proofreader: Randy Schmidt

Indexer: Margalo Whyte

Designer: George Vaitkunas